REFRAMING PUBLIC POLICY

Reframing Public Policy

Discursive Politics and Deliberative Practices

FRANK FISCHER

OXFORD
UNIVERSITY PRESS

OXFORD
UNIVERSITY PRESS

Great Clarendon Street, Oxford OX2 6DP

Oxford University Press is a department of the University of Oxford.
It furthers the University's objective of excellence in research, scholarship,
and education by publishing worldwide in

Oxford New York

Auckland Cape Town Dar es Salaam Hong Kong Karachi Kuala Lumpur
Madrid Melbourne Mexico City Nairobi New Delhi Shanghai Taipei Toronto

With offices in

Argentina Austria Brazil Chile Czech Republic France Greece
Guatemala Hungary Italy Japan South Korea Poland Portugal
Singapore Switzerland Thailand Turkey Ukraine Vietnam

Oxford is a registered trade mark of Oxford University Press
in the UK and in certain other countries

Published in the United States
by Oxford University Press Inc., New York

© Frank Fischer 2003

The moral rights of the author have been asserted

Database right Oxford University Press (maker)

First published 2003

British Library Cataloguing in Publication Data

Data available

Library of Congress Cataloging in Publication Data

Data available

ISBN 0-19-924263-1
ISBN 0-19-924264-X (pbk.)

5 7 9 10 8 6 4

Typeset by Newgen Imaging Systems (P) ltd., Chennai, India
Printed in Great Britain
on acid-free paper by
Biddles Ltd., King's Lynn, Norfolk

To Sabine Braun

Preface

Reframing Public Policy brings together and examines the perspectives on public policy discourse, discursive policy analysis, and deliberative policymaking practices that have emerged in recent years to challenge the dominant technocratic, empiricist approach in public policy studies. The discussion offers a new perspective on an old but still troubling problem, namely, that the fields of political and policy studies have generally been guided by an overly empirical orientation that is largely insensitive to politics. The dominant neopositivist/empiricist approach has given rise to a methodological orientation—some say 'methodological fetish'—that brings ever more rigorous quantitative analysis to bear on topics of narrower and narrower import. In the process, the contemporary social sciences have neglected the basic value issues and social meanings inherent to their subject matter, and, largely as a consequence, turned more and more away from the big social and political questions that gave rise to them in the first place. As value issues and social meanings are among the essential driving forces of politics and policymaking, it is difficult to understand these processes detached from their normative realities. The consequences of this neglect have, moreover, long undercut or hobbled efforts to promote more democratic and socially just forms of policy analysis and policymaking.

The critique of empiricist policy inquiry (empiricism understood here not as the empirical per se but as an *orientation* to the empirical) is scarcely new. It extends back to the outset of the disciplinary effort. But the political theorists and others who have criticized neopositivism and its empiricist methods have mainly been relegated to the margins of the discipline or written off as troublesome characters, itself a story in discourse politics. Empirical research practices, despite their widely recognized limitations, have thus proven quite resistant to change. In recent years, however, the challenge has again been renewed through developments in critical, postempiricist, and postmodern theories in the humanities and social sciences. These perspectives have brought with them a more sophisticated emphasis on social meaning and values, this time through a deeper understanding of language and discourse. It is to an explication of these approaches that this work is devoted. The chapters that follow apply these perspectives to the study of public policy and policy analysis.

It is not that mainstream political and policy studies have neglected ideas and discourse altogether. Indeed, thanks to the 'new institutionalism' in particular, the role of ideas has experienced a comeback in the social sciences. But the standard approach is to treat ideas as resources that actors possess; that is, as properties. While some actors do possess more information than others—experts to be sure—this view taken alone neglects other, more fundamental aspects of policy discourse. Not only does it fail to capture how ideas and discourses can have a force of their own independently of particular actors, but also it misses the ways in which the actors themselves are properties of the discourses. Discourse, in this view, does more than reflect a social or political 'reality'; it actually constitutes much of the reality that has to be explained. In this respect, empiricists fail to appreciate the productive effects of communicative power. Instead of understanding power only in negative terms—such as the ability to control or manipulate others—the approach advanced here also emphasizes that discursive power can determine the very fields of actions, including the tracks along which political action travels. Discourse, for this reason, has to be recognized as a powerful meta-category of politics.

The emphasis on discourse and the politics of meaning put forward here does not naively take the world to move just because of words. But, unlike the empiricist tradition, words and language, especially when combined with power, are recognized themselves be a form of action, and thus important data for political and policy analysis. Whereas empiricism treats language and meaning as an ornament of social behaviour, a discursive approach makes clear that discourse and social meaning are internal to the very social systems we seek to research. Without them, the institutional practices of a society cannot be understood; indeed, they would not even function, if they could exist at all.

Given that empiricism in the social sciences has failed to produce the promised body of causal theory, it has persisted at considerable cost. Through its rejection or marginalization of interpretive inquiry, it has extricated much of the very lifeblood that drives politics and policymaking and has, in the process, distorted our understanding of the nature of the phenomena under investigation. But the solution is not to reject empirical research. A discourse approach, rather, seeks to show that we need a much more refined understanding of the interactions that construct reality, in particular the way the empirical is embedded in the normative. Indeed, we come to see that all research is located across a subjective continuum. This necessarily negates the possibility of the kind of rigorous causal theory sought by empiricists, but it opens the way to a much more textured, sophisticated understanding of social and political reality. Moreover, the constructionist view is not just a new idea about how to reconstruct our research methodologies; it provides in fact a better picture—even empirical description—of what social scientists already do. By stripping away the outdated pretences of empiricism, it makes it easier to deal with social scientific practices in a way that is both more cogent and more relevant.

In the pages that follow the reader should not expect to find a comprehensive theory. The discursive approach, with its resistance to unidirectional causal explanations, provides little in the way of methodological tidiness. Given that outcomes are seen to depend on contextual factors, universally applicable generalizations are not to be found. The contingent nature of contextual explanations means that discourses sometimes directly shape practices in ways that are relatively easy to identify, but sometimes also do so in a more subtle manner that is difficult to reconstruct. There is thus no possibility of a causal theory validly applicable across social contexts.

The book is organized in four parts. Part I introduces the re-emergence of interest in ideas and discourse (Chapter 2) and then turns to the postempiricist or constructionist view of social reality (Chapter 3). Public policy is presented here as a discursive construct that turns on multiple interpretations. Part II examines more specifically the nature of discursive politics and discourse theory (Chapter 4) and illustrates through a particular disciplinary debate the theoretical, methodological, and political implications of such a conceptual reframing of policy inquiry (Chapter 5). Taking up the epistemological and methodological issues raised by the discursive approach, Part III offers a postempiricist methodology for policy inquiry based on the logic of practical discourse (Chapter 6). The remaining three chapters of the part then explore specific methodological perspectives pertinent to such an orientation, in particular the role of interpretation in policy analysis (Chapter 7), narrative policy analysis (Chapter 8), and the dialectics of policy argumentation (Chapter 9). Part IV (Chapters 10 and 11) discusses the participatory implications of such a method and the role of the policy analyst as facilitator of citizen deliberation.

What is the policy analyst in the government agency supposed to do with a discursive approach, some will ask? The answer is evident throughout the chapters: to improve policy argumentation. This is already an acknowledged and accepted task of the analyst. Unfortunately, conventional policy analysis has too often only narrowly understood its mission as informing public managers and politicians rather than the broader range of participants. Moreover, the practice has limited its activities to generating empirical data presented as if they spoke for themselves. As we see here, the task of improving argumentation requires more that just supplying 'better' data. It must as well include a more sophisticated understanding of the relationship of social science to political deliberation, including how various types of knowledge fit differently into different kinds of policy arguments and how the discursive structure of an argument itself has an impact on the deliberative process. As discourses both frame and carry knowledge, they both supply the analyst's data with meaning and structure the way policy is discussed and decided. Although this is not designed as a 'how to do it' book—an approach to which an interpretive discourse analysis does not readily lend itself—much of the material for the more practical policy analyst is found in Parts III and IV.

Some will argue that a discursive approach with its emphasis on narratives and storylines can only land us in the swamp of political relativism. This criticism, countered in Chapters 6 and 7, hinges on an outdated neopositivist understanding of relativism. Before we get there, however, the reader should be clear that the discursive paradigm does not overlook or neglect the relation of ideas to power and interests. Indeed, a discourse approach of the type advanced here is grounded in a recognition that the distorting influences of power, ideology, manipulatory rhetoric, or authoritarian forces are basic features of political life. At the same time, the approach recognizes that decisions and actions are taken and that this always occurs in the context of ongoing stories about social and political phenomena, including the stories of the less powerful. Indeed, the decision-making process is generally driven by narrative accounts of problems and their causes. If communicative practices were only the manifestations of power and ideology, making decisions would mainly be a matter of determining whose domination we should accept. But some stories are more truthful, persuasive, and humane than other, as demonstrated by both common sense and the discursive logic of good reasons. Politics in a democratic society, as emphasized in the pages that follow, is a struggle for power played out in significant part through arguments about the 'best story'.

In advance of engaging with the topic, a few words in anticipation of postempiricism's critics are also in order. The main claim of the critics is that policy discourse analysis and the argumentative turn are themselves ideological in nature rather than objective and analytical (Lawlor 1996: 117). The postempiricist proponents of argumentation are said to advance a hidden agenda that is dangerous for both for democratic governance and the policy analysis profession—indeed, postempiricism has been described as so false as to be 'chilling' (Lynn 1999: 411). Such provocative words clearly miss the mark. Not only do the critics harbour their own ideology—that of a professional policy community and its claims to science—they seldom really consider the postempiricist perspective (even admitting to only a second-hand understanding of the approach). In this respect, they appear opposed to opening the door to a deeper understanding of how important aspects of the policymaking process work. With regard to professional concerns, postempiricist policy analysis does not belong to a particular group. It is more broadly interested in the political implications and consequences of using professional policy analysis as a method for informing and making policy decisions for the larger public. If the discussion is discomforting to some, postempiricists see no need to apologize. The discursive approach is designed to identify and bring in the neglected political voices, of which there are many. Should this be considered ideological, so be it. Postempiricist scholars oppose the overly top-down conception of governance upon which this critique rests. Rather than worrying about protecting a narrow understanding of the interests of the policy analysis community, or the steering capacities of elite decision-makers, postempiricists are more concerned about the current state of discursive deliberation in a democracy rampant with social injustices, many of which are widely recognized to be at the root of our most serious policy problems. It is the modest hope here to contribute to the advancement of that cause.

Finally, I would like to thank a number of people for supplying me with helpful comments along the way. They include Susan Fainstein, Maarten Hajer, Douglas Torgerson, Peter deLeon, John Forester, Barbara Czarninawska, Patsy Healey, Goktug Morcol, Kathrin Braun, Helga Putzel, Navdeep Mathur, Peter Bogason, Tim Luke, Hubertus Buchstein, Henk Wagenaar, Rob Hoppe, Michel van Eeten, Reinhard Blomart, Christoph Scherrer, Dvora Yanow, Gerald Miller, John Grin, Jeanette Hofmann, Kaifeng Yang, Eva Hartmann, Farrukh Salikov, Giuseppe Ricotta, Martin Benninghoff, and Ian Welsh. I also want to thank Jiajia Ma for assisting in getting the manuscript ready for publication. In addition, I extend my appreciation to Policy Studies Organization for granting me permission to publish a revised version of the essay that constitutes the foundation of Chapter 6, and Duke University Press for permission to use the material appearing in the box 'Beyond Textbook Myths' of the same chapter. I am also grateful to MIT Press for permission to reproduce the two figures in Chapter 9. And, finally, special thanks go to the editors with whom I worked at Oxford University Press, in particular Dominic Byatt,

Amanda Watkins, Stuart Fowkes, and Michael James. Along the way they gave me a good deal of much appreciated encouragement and assistance that helped make this book possible.

Frank Fischer

New York City
December 2002

Contents

1

Making Social Science Relevant: Policy Inquiry in Critical Perspective

During the past three decades, public policy studies has been one of the fastest growing specializations in the social sciences. The field emerged to both better understand the policymaking process and to bring scientific knowledge to bear on policy decision-making. To deal with the second of these two concerns, bringing knowledge to bear, a specific set of methods evolved, namely, the techniques of policy analysis. Following Dunn (1981: 35), policy analysis can be formally defined as 'an applied social science discipline which uses multiple methods of inquiry and arguments to produce and transform policy-relevant information that may be utilized in political settings to resolve policy problems'.

The development of public policy studies as a field unto itself has largely been an American phenomenon, especially so in the case of policy analysis.[1] To be sure, Canada (Torgerson 1986; Pal 1992) and a number of European countries have followed suite, the Netherlands being an important example (Van de Graaf and Hoppe 1996). But they remain highly influenced by developments in the United States. Great Britain as well has taken up the challenge, although the scholarly activities there have been less influenced by the American literature (Parsons 1995; John 1998).[2]

This is not to say that there has been little policy research in Europe. A great deal of it has been conducted within the various substantive specialties themselves, such as in the fields of economics, social welfare, or health care.[3] In this literature, though, there is little or no emphasis on developing policy studies or analysis as a field or discipline. Such policy specific research has seldom treated its topic with the kind of methodological self-consciousness that one finds in the development of the field of policy studies per se, where the concern goes beyond particular policy issues to examine the nature of policy generally, policy decision-making, and the relevant methodological and analytic issues.

---

[1] The term 'policy studies' is used here to designate the general field of inquiry. The term 'policy analysis' designates the application of a range of decision-oriented methodologies usually assumed under policy studies, cost-benefit analysis being an example. And 'policy research' is employed in this work to refer to the primary activity of scholars engaged in policy studies.

[2] In Great Britain policy studies has been and continues to be a topic of the field of social administration, which has its history in the Fabian reform tradition in the late nineteenth century.

[3] See for example Andersen and Liefferink (1997).

Short of having embraced policy studies or policy analysis as a separate field of inquiry, some European countries have made significant contributions to particular aspects of the policy process. German social scientists, for example, have made important contributions to our understanding of the policy implementation process, especially in the 1970s and early 1980s (Scharpf 1973; Mayntz and Scharpf 1973). Both Sweden and Denmark have produced a good deal of research on policy implementation and evaluation research. Moreover, in these countries there is a relatively small but growing number of scholars who formally identify with policy analysis (Windhoff-Heritier 1987; Saretzki 1998; 2003; Parsons 1995; Bogason 2000: 109–36). Indeed, many of them have made significant contributions to the development of the kind of postempiricist, discursive approach that is offered here. In fact, as the reader will see, a good deal of what follows comes from Europe rather than the United States. An important reason is that much of the theoretical foundations for the postempiricist policy analysis has been inspired by European social theorists, in particular the work of Habermas and Foucault, as well as the social constructionist movement as it has evolved in Britain and France.

In the American experience the roots of the policy analysis profession can be traced back to the progressive movement which called for increasing the role of expertise in government (Fischer 1990). What was then an emerging concern is now a modern-day imperative: government decision-makers need relevant information. Although there is nothing new about policy advice-giving—it is as old as government itself—the increasing complexity of modern technological society dramatically intensifies the information requirements of modern decision-makers. Policy decisions combine sophisticated technical knowledge with intricate and often subtle social and political realities. While scientific considerations are more central in issues related to environmental or technology policy, they become increasingly important in social policy as well. What, for example, does research tell us about how children learn in the early grades? Or how can we make decisions about social assistance policies that best assist the poor in becoming productive members of society? Often such questions involve sophisticated social analyses, sometimes even including social experiments.

But what, more specifically, does the policy researcher analyse? Precisely what is public policy? The question is not as easy to answer as one might assume. Some writers have simply understood policy to be 'whatever governments choose to do or not to do' (Dye 1984: 1). Others have worked out elaborate definitions that seek to spell out the exact characteristic of a public policy. Lowi and Ginsburg (1996: 607), for example, define public policy as 'an officially expressed intention backed by a sanction, which can be a reward or a punishment.' As a course of action (or inaction), a public policy can take the form of 'a law, a rule, a statute, an edict, a regulation or an order'.

The origins of the policy focus are usually identified with the writings of Harold Lasswell, considered to be the founder of the field. Influenced as much by his European experiences as by American politics, Lasswell envisioned a multidisciplinary enterprise capable of guiding the political decision processes of post-Second World War industrial societies (Torgerson 1985). Of special importance, in this respect, is the landmark book *The Policy Orientation*, edited in 1951 by Lasswell and Lerner. The book called for study of the role of 'knowledge in and of the policy process'.

The ambitions of the policy orientation were sketched out with no small modesty. The 'policy orientation' called for an overarching social science discipline geared to the task of adjusting modern democratic practices to the realities of a modern techno-industrial society. To deal with the policy complexities that accompanied the rise of big government and corporate capitalism, Lasswell sought to layout the framework for the development of the 'policy sciences' and the training of a cadre of policy experts capable of bringing the necessary knowledge to the decision-making table.[4]

Specifically, Lasswell wanted to create an applied social science that would act as a mediator between academics, government decision-makers, and ordinary citizens by providing objective solutions to problems that would narrow or minimize, if not eliminate, the need for unproductive political debate on the pressing policy issues of the day. His policy science orientation was defined by three characteristics: a multidisciplinary approach; a problem-oriented focus that was contextual in nature; and an explicitly normative orientation (Torgerson 1985). Normatively, Lasswell recognized the need to anchor such an approach in human values. Calling for an emphasis on human dignity in theory and practice, he foresaw a policy science that could assist in facilitating the development and evolution of democratic government in a corporate liberal society. It was, as he put it, to be a policy science of democracy.

Developed to cut across existing specializations, the field would include contributions from political science, sociology, anthropology, psychology, statistics, and mathematics, even in some cases the physical and natural sciences. Informed by both quantitative and qualitative methods, the specific research strategy was framed around two objectives: the study of the policymaking process and the intelligence needs of the policymakers. The first task was the development of a science of policy formation and execution; the second concerned improving the concrete content of the information and the interpretations available to policymakers. Or, as he put, a policy science 'in and of the policy process'.

Beginning with the promise of improving policy decision-making, both the process and the outcomes, the field was invested with considerable enthusiasm. Even today there remains a cadre of followers who continue to extend and institutionalize Lasswell's theory and practices.[5] For these policy scholars, further development of the policy orientation remains the way to bring greater social relevance to the research assignment. But the policy-analytic enterprise as a whole failed to take up Lasswell's bold vision, instead following a constricted path of evolution. Not only

[4] Lasswell spoke of the 'policy sciences' but, to avoid a certain awkwardness created by his use of the plural, we speak here of 'policy science' in the singular.
[5] These policy scholars are primarily associated with the journal *Policy Sciences*, which Lasswell himself helped to found.

has it emerged more along technocratic rather than democratic lines, the empirical and practical pay-offs have been far smaller than the original promise.[6]

Policy inquiry as it is known today, particularly what we call policy analysis, emerged in the 1960s and 1970s and took a narrower technocratic form geared more to managerial practices than to the facilitation of democratic government. On the surface, the contemporary policy orientation has met with considerable success. Not only is policy studies prominently featured in the social science curriculum, but the practice of policy analysis is widely distributed throughout our governmental institutions and political organizations. Beyond academia, policy analysts are found as staff analysts in government agencies at all levels of government, and as researchers in public policy think tanks, research institutions, management consulting firms, interest groups, and non-profit organizations (Stone 1996). They are even increasingly found in the public affairs departments of major private sector companies, especially those that engage in economic and regulatory policy analysis. While the specific practices differ from context to context, the job involves producing and transforming information and arguments relevant to policy problems (Radin 2000).

In contrast to the multidisciplinary methodological perspective outlined by Lasswell, the field has been shaped by a more limiting methodological framework derived from the neopositivist/empiricist methods that dominated the social sciences of the day. This has generated an emphasis on rigorous quantitative analysis, the objective separation of facts and values, and the search for generalizable findings whose validity would be independent of the particular social context from which they were drawn: that is, a policy science that would be able to develop generalizable rules applicable to a range of problems and contexts. In no small part, this has been driven by the dominant influence of economics and its positivist scientific methodologies on the development of the field.

In this view, policy analysis is mainly designed to inform a 'rational model' of decision-making, or what Stone (1988) has called the 'rationality project'. Rational decision-making is seen to follow steps that closely parallel the methods of scientific research. Decision-makers first identify empirically the existence of a problem, then formulate the goals and objectives that would lead to an optimal solution. After determining the relevant consequences and probabilities of alternative means to the solution, they assign a numerical value to each cost and benefit associated with the consequences. Combining the information about consequences, probabilities, and costs and benefits, they select the most effective and efficient alternative.

Basic to the method has been an effort to sidestep the partisan goal and value conflicts generally associated with policy issues (Amy 1987). Policy analysis, in this model, strives to translate political and social issues into technically defined ends to be pursued through administrative means. Vexing social and economic problems are interpreted as issues in need of improved management and better programme

---

[6] Lasswell contributed to this orientation himself. Although he advocated a contextual orientation, he played at the same time a major role in establishing the behavioural tradition in political science, which contributed significantly to the more technocratic orientation that was to emerge.

design; their solutions are to be found in the objective collection of data and the application of the technical decision approaches that have in large part defined the policy sciences since the 1960 (Williams 1998).

Associated with this belief in the superiority of scientific decision-making has been an emphasis on the calculation of the efficiency and effectiveness of means to achieve goals, with the result that policy analysis has in significant measure evolved as a strategy for a 'technocratic form' of governance. Reflecting a subtle antipathy toward democratic processes, terms such as 'pressures' and 'expedient adjustments' are used to denigrate pluralistic policymaking. If politics does not fit into the methodological scheme, then politics is the problem. Some have even argued that the political system itself must be changed to better accommodate policy analysis (Heineman *et al.* 1990).

Technocratic policy analysis is thus a matter of uniformly applying empirically based technical methodologies, such as cost-benefit analysis and risk assessment, to the technical aspects of all policy problems. The function of such a policy science has been likened to a modern fuel injection system in automobile (Hofferbert 1990: 12). The fuel injector's function is to keep the car running smoothly by merely adjusting the mixture of inputs, external temperatures, humidity, and vehicle operations; the mission of the policy scientists is the design of programmatic adjustments and regulatory mechanisms to guide the harmonious and efficient interaction of the social system's social and political components.

Of course, this is something of a caricature of conventional policy analysis. But the methods diverge surprisingly little from what is taught in most policy analysis curricula. To be sure, many policy writers, following Simon (1957), speak of the policy decision-making process as one of 'bounded rationality', given the limited availability of relevant policy information. In this view, they portray the decision-makers as a 'satisficer' (seeking only 'satisfactory' information that will 'suffice'). Nonetheless, the rational model still informs this process; it offers the standards against which satisficing can be judged (Kiser and Ostrom 1982: 184–6). What these scholars have generally failed to recognize or accept is that, while satisficing is a good description of what decision-makers actually do, it is in fact an inherently interpretive activity rather than a lesser form of the rational/empirical model, a point to which we shall return.

In the next section, we briefly examine the problems that have emerged with this technocratic practice of policy-analytic research. We do this by looking at the policy orientation in its broader political context. Given that it developed first as a uniquely American practice before spreading to Europe, we emphasize the American story. Moreover, it is the American experience that best illustrates the limitations of the practice as it has emerged.

TECHNOCRATIC POLICYMAKING: THE LIMITS OF THE EMPIRICAL

Despite Lasswell's ambitious call for a multi-disciplinary policy science of democracy generally, the major thrust of contemporary policy studies—policy analysis in particular—came in response to a specific political agenda, namely, the Great Society legislation of US President Lyndon Johnson in the 1960s. By the late 1950s, the inescapable fact that an intolerable number of Americans lived in poverty—a condition abetted and heightened by racial discrimination—finally moved national policymakers to take corrective political actions.[7] President Johnson declared a 'War on Poverty' and committed the considerable resources of the federal government to solving the poverty problem. Of the many manifestations to follow the challenge, one of the first was a flocking of policy specialists of all sorts to Washington, some of whom found their way into the inner circles of the policymaking process.

One could hardly imagine a more significant role for social scientists in policy initiation and formulation.[8] The policy community was in large part professionally consumed with the mandate of devising new programmes to alleviate problems identified in health care, urban renewal, housing, education, legal assistance, social welfare, and hunger. The emphasis was on quick action rather than long-term analysis. The strategy was to exploit existing knowledge about poverty. If Americans could put a man on the moon, it was said, the country should be able employ its expertise to solve the earthly problems of the ghetto (Nelson 1977: 6). A leading journalist captured the thrust in a series of articles in *Life* portraying the period as the 'Golden Age of action intellectuals', in which policy experts were portrayed as 'the driving wheels of the Great Society' (White 1967). The article described nothing less than an alteration in the system of power governing American politics. As a new generation with special problem-solving skills, these policy advisers sought 'to shape our defenses, guide our foreign policy, redesign our cities, eliminate poverty, reorganize our schools, and more'. One influential scholar approvingly, called it the 'professionalization of reform' (Moynihan 1965).[9]

---

[7] Seeking to complete the New Deal social agenda, President Johnson advanced a vast array of programmes to assist the poor in American. Calling for an end to poverty in America, the president asked leading social scientists to assemble and use the best available social science to design his poverty programmes. Johnson's turn to experts was in large part an extension of the practices that President Kennedy had initiated in his administration. Of particular importance was the role of the economist and the then dominant theories of macroeconomic management. During the Kennedy years, the president's Council of Economic Advisors put together the first 'Keynesian' tax cut designed to stimulate economic demand. This was seen to signify real progress towards the technical, if not scientific, management of economic affairs. Impressed with this possibility of engineering the economy, journalists and others spoke of the economists as 'the New Priesthood'. Suffering from a relatively acute case of envy, sociologists and political scientists were eager to join the ranks; they put forth a call for a similar Council on Social Indicators (Fischer 1990).

[8] During this period, many leading policy experts had direct access to those with political power (Wood 1993). They brought with them numerous strategies and practices that gave practical expression to technocratic strategies and an apolitical ideology. It was common to hear people say that social problems were now more a matter of correct policy strategies than a matter of politics (Bell 1973). As Kennedy (1962) put it, the country's problems were now technical rather than political issues.

[9] Research foundations and academic journals virtually celebrated the political significance of this new professional presence in Washington. Policy expertise, furthermore, became a growth industry for think tanks, university research institutes, and management consulting firms. All of this, in turn, shaped the field of policy studies, which was to emerge as a central focus of the social science curricula. Such activities, moreover, were interconnected through a revolving door that linked universities, government agencies and Washington think tanks, identified with the Democratic Party administrations of this period.

The study of public policy also received a dramatic boost through an unexpected secondary consequence of the War on Poverty. Almost as an afterthought, Congress tacked on formal reporting requirements to the vast array of poverty-related programmes. This made available large amounts of money for the assessment of poverty and other related social policies that, in turn, gave rise to a small industry. Universities set up policy institutes and doctoral students wrote policy dissertations. In the process, a great deal of attention was given to the development of theories and methods for analysing public policy.

By the late 1960s, it was clear that much of the War on Poverty initiative had in significant part failed to achieve the promised results. Various commentators argued—not without some justification—that the problem was more one of rising expectations than diminished levels of service. Others have maintained that without these programmes the situation in American ghettos would have escalated into a serious, long-term crisis. But the fact remained: there was far less to show for these programmes than the Johnson administration and its supporters had promised.

It is difficult to pinpoint the blame for the limited showing of such a complex undertaking, but one thing was obvious: little attention had been paid at the outset to the estimation and evaluation of these strategies. Few researchers had systematically examined the effects of such programmes. Almost everyone had been for increasing social welfare payments, but few considered the effect these payments might have on concerns such as family structure and unemployment. Rather than a programmatic assessment of actual impacts on the poverty problem, the overwhelming focus of policy analysts during this period was on problem recognition and policy formulation. Only later did the other phases of the policy process start to get attention. Topics like implementation and evaluation had simply been ignored.

But the search for answers changed that; the research focus shifted from policy formulation to the implementation and evaluation of policy outcomes. And as it showed, the neglect of implementation proved to have been be a critical error. All too often it was merely assumed that if the money and the political commitment were available, the poverty problem could be solved. Overlooked was the complex world of public bureaucracy situated between the resources and the commitment on the one hand and those in need of help on the other. Somewhat embarrassingly, this led to the rediscovery of public administration. Of such import was the problem that it led others to cast doubts on the very idea of assistance through public policy (Banfield 1970).

In their pioneering work on the implementation of federal job-training programmes in Oakland, California, Pressman and Wildavsky (1973) showed not only the ways policy remains tied up with the political process long after its legislative formulation, but also more specifically how it is often difficult to even recognize an outline of the original policy goals by the time the resultant programme reaches the implementation stage. In the Oakland case, the local policy politics that shaped the final job programmes to be implemented were so conflictual that the resulting changes made it difficult to know how to evaluate the outcomes of the policy. Were they be judged against the requirements of initial legislation drafted in Washington (which would surely mean declaring them failures)? Or were they to be judged in terms of the political understandings later shaped in the implementation process itself? Perhaps only one thing was clear: the unemployed remained the losers.

This realization led Majone and Wildavsky (1979) to develop an 'evolutionary theory' of policy evaluation. In this view, the content of a policy is seen to evolve as it moves through the policy process, rather than simply legislatively stated once and for all at the outset. As each group struggles to interpret a piece of legislation in a light favourable to its own interests, the content of the programme evolves through a seemingly endless set of negotiations between interested parties. For the rationalistic conception of policy analysis this politics of implementation has been something of an embarrassment, if not a disaster. As the policy goal proves to be a moving target, the question of whose interpretation of the goals and objectives to take as the actual public policy problematically remains open. Unless one holds firm to an outmoded top-down/ends-means conception of the administrative role, which is often the same as insuring an implementation failure, there is no way around a political approach to implementation. Given that the local bodies have to be committed to the implementation process for it to work, such actors have to be built into the shaping of the programme. And even here, as the failures in Oakland made clear, there are no guarantees. Beyond saying that the Oakland situation made all parties unhappy, it left us with a very challenging question: could another way be found to design the processes of both policy formulation and implementation? Indeed, we are still looking for the answer.

While implementation studies rediscovered the role of politics in policy administration, the search for alternative approaches largely emerged along technical lines. The dominant focus was on evaluation, particularly a rigorous empirical research methodology called 'evaluation research'. In large part, the evaluation research of that time (a technique largely developed by psychologists engaged in the evaluation of social problem, especially educational problems) featured precise empirical measurement of programme impacts. But it also included social experiments involving empirical evaluation under quasi-experimental conditions. In important circles in the 1970s, evaluation came to be considered the sine qua non of policy research (Fischer 1990: 161–4).

There were good reasons for the turn to evaluation. The fact that large amounts of money had at best made only a relatively small dent in the lives of poor people created a great deal of interest in what went wrong, in particular where the money went. Often in conjunction with implementation studies, in the form of process evaluation, a multitude of evaluation studies sought to determine which programmes were successful, which failed, and why. A fair amount of this research was conducted in conjunction with implementation studies, especially in the form of 'process evaluation'. For some writers the solution to the implementation quagmire was to be found by integrating implementation design with evaluation feedback.

Evaluation research led to a substantial amount of methodological innovation that has contributed significantly to our ability to measure programme results. But evaluation research proved to be no 'magic bullet'. As it emerged in the 1970s, it was guided by a technical understanding of programme research. Despite ever more precise measurements, evaluation research ran up against the same politics that thwarted the technocratic understanding of policy formulation. In short, the empirical results never spoke for themselves. The assessment of findings always depended on the criteria employed and the criteria were inevitably politically determined. Moreover, while liberal researchers designed their work to learn how to better pursue such social objectives in the future, conservatives just as easily used evaluation to discredit the use of government social programmes more generally. Evaluation itself got caught up in a politics of advocacy, as the Nixon administration declared the War on Poverty a failure and assumed the reigns of government. Indeed, the use of evaluation findings became part of a conservative strategy for budget-cutting (Fischer 1990: 162–4; Morehouse 1972: 873).

Then there was Johnson's other war. If the impact of the War on Poverty on policy analysis was mainly played out in professional circles, the Vietnam War tended to display more publicly the limits of technical analysis in the political realm. Indeed, public concern over the Johnson administration's technocratic approach to the war was one of the factors that turned many away from him, leading him to ultimately step aside.

The strategic analysis of the war, closely monitored by presidential administrations for more than a decade, was the joint responsibility of the Office of the Secretary of Defense and the various departments of the military services. At the time, policy planning in Vietnam was often portrayed as the paradigm of 'rational analysis'. Indeed, the defence community was consistently at the forefront of the development of analytical techniques for guiding management and policy. Methods of systems and cost analysis had been developed by the Rand Corporation for the US Air Force and other military agencies. Moreover, the much touted method of Planning-Programming-Budgeting-Systems (PPBS) was first designed and implemented in the Department of Defense, before being extended to the domestic executive agencies.

Despite these extensive analytical capabilities, however, Washington seriously miscalculated and mismanaged the Vietnam war. For many, the reliance on rational analytical techniques was a major factor contributing to the country's defeat. Not only did a heavy emphasis on quantitative analysis neglect critical social and political variables, but the analytical results seldom moved from the field back to Washington without political distortions. Moreover, policy debates in Washington almost always missed the moral dimensions of the war, which was to become the grist of the anti-war movement. This was particularly the case after the publication of the Pentagon Papers revealed the degree to which policy planners had deceived the public about both the purposes and the progress of the military effort.

The realization of these limitations was to shape the debates in the policy community for decades to come. Policymakers and analysts could, *ex post facto*, extract a variety of critical 'lessons' from Vietnam. One of the best discussions of these lessons is offered by deLeon (1988). First, as he shows, the experience made more than clear the deficiencies of 'rational' decision-making techniques in political forums. The Vietnam conflict pitted participants with very different cultural values against each other. The political and moral determination of Hanoi regularly defied the strategic logic undergirding the expert recommendations, invariably calling for further escalation of military measures against the North Vietnamese.

Second, quantitative measures proved unreliable for planning purposes. In significant part, the difficulty stemmed from the unreliability of the empirical data. In fact, as deLeon (1988: 64) put it, only well into the process did it become clear that 'the numbers coming out of Vietnam were just as subjective and open to manipulation as the more explicitly political and interpretive reports.'

Underlying both of these points was the problem of context. Vietnam was a constantly changing policy arena, 'a contextual chameleon which defied static analysis' (deLeon 1988: 64). Nonetheless, most official analysts of the conflict failed to see or refused to acknowledge the altering political landscape. Only after the evidence was unavoidable did this situational dimension get the attention it required. As a consequence, policy professionals had to confront the fact that the social context in which public policy was situated could no longer be ignored. The contextual setting, they had to learn, is always first and foremost a socio-political construct. Indeed, turning on the motives and beliefs of those involved, what appeared stable could quickly become conflictual, even turbulent. Rather than natural or given, a social context, it was discovered, was always subject to change. Its stability proved to be a function of the stability of the social and political alignments that shaped it in the first place.

All of these political and analytical realities have required conscientious policy analysts to reconsider their primary commitment to empirically based rational decision methods. Such experiences dramatically increased the appreciation of the social and normative elements inherent to the policy process. Coupled with the revelations of the Pentagon Papers and the Watergate hearings into the abuses of political power, it led many to call for a greater emphasis on the normative, ethical, and qualitative dimensions of policymaking.

In the 1970s these limitations were further corroborated by policy experiences on the domestic front. Perhaps the best example, as deLeon (1988) shows, was the attempt to use policy analysis to inform energy policymaking. Not only did the energy crisis offer policy analysts a dramatic opportunity to demonstrate their analytic proficiencies at modeling a complex technical policy problem, but the raw data for the calculations were at hand. What is more, their advice was eagerly sought out by top-level policymakers.

But the models proved to have nothing of their promised predictive power. And worse, as the shortcomings emerged, it became obvious to even the casual observer that, as deLeon (1988: 70) put it, 'the putatively "objective" nature of the modeling exercises and their computational opaqueness concealed the reality that their underlying and usually unspoken political and social assumptions were what actually "drove" the results'. Thompson (1984) captured the resulting charade by likening it to tribes engaged in rituals organized around their own assumptions. It was a realization that served to confirm the energy argument long advanced by the environmental movement, namely, that the problem was normative rather than empirical in nature. The energy problem, in this alternative view, had to be reframed in its normative social context. It was more about the American way of life, including foreign policy, than about a set of technical relationships between supply and demand (Lovins 1977). The effect was to cast considerable doubt on the policy analysis project. In the energy community, the much coveted access to power was dramatically curtailed.

These underlying analytic and political problems made it increasingly apparent that policy analysis lacked a sophisticated understanding of the relation of knowledge to politics. Simply stated, there was a general sense that better information would lead to better solutions, or what Collingsridge and Reeves (1986) have described as the 'overdetermined' conception of policy research. Some even believed that empirical research could itself find the answers. There was, in short, little sense at the outset that policy problems were as much the result of socio-political interpretations as they were concrete manifestations of relatively fixed social processes.

To compound matters, numerous studies emerged in the late 1970s and early 1980s that showed empiricist policy research was not much used. Research into the utilization of policy findings illustrated that at best a third of the administrators who received such information could identify a concrete use to which it was put, and then it often was not especially impressive (Caplan 1979; Rich 1979). Given the size of the investment in time and money, one could argue that the pay-off of policy analysis has not justified the cost.

This led some to look more deeply at the nature of social problems and their epistemological implications for a policy science (Mitroff and Pondy 1974). An emphasis on the inherently normative and interpretive character of policy problems was basic to this view. Policy analysis and policy outcomes, noted such scholars, were infused with sticky problems of politics and social values. Against this awareness the empiricist emphasis was naive. The profession had to open itself to a range of other types of methods and issues. Policy inquiry, in short, had to be restructured and the outlines of this new alternative framework were not so difficult to come by. They were to be found in ongoing debates over the nature of science taking place in the very 'hard' sciences that policy science had sought to imitate. Much of what follows in this book is an extension of this effort to reframe our understanding of public policy and its analysis, a project that has moved from the fringes of the field to a mainstream challenge.

THE POSTEMPIRICIST ALTERNATIVE: ARGUMENTATION AND DISCOURSE

The disciplinary soul-searching that these disappointments triggered led to determined efforts to gain a more sophisticated understanding of the relation of politics to knowledge, policy to social scientific expertise. Of special importance at the outset was Rein's (1976) call for a value-critical policy analysis that recognized the central role of social values, including the importance of taking seriously narrative storytelling about policy problems. A policy discipline that could not address a 'crisis of values' (for example, in the analysis of urban malaise of the 1970s), argued Rein and others, was less than useful, if not itself a part of the problem. What good was it to identify efficient policy solutions when the very issue was a clash of social values underlying the more basic question—namely, how we should live together? (Friedmann 1973). No matter how efficient a programme might be, if it fails to confront the basic value frames that shape our understandings of the problem it is bound to be rejected.

Others, stressing the interplay between the social and technical aspects of policy analysis, recognized the role of communication and argumentation in policy analysis and sought to supply the field with rules and procedures for regulated discourse (MacRae 1976). Some took the rigour of the discipline of law as their model, a mode of inquiry well respected for its rules of discourse. In search of logical rules for policy argumentation, they advocated drawing on the concept of rules of evidence in legal proceedings. Others urged borrowing and adapting the rules of normative discourse in political philosophy (Anderson 1978).

Similar concerns led Weiss (1990) to reformulate the goal of policy analysis in terms of 'public enlightenment'. She has argued that policy formulation and evaluation shouldn't be geared only to achieving specific administrative goals or programmatic uses, as generally approached. In her view, it is the impact an analysis has on the broader processes of deliberation and argumentation that counts the most. An important insight, it makes clear that the limitations of rigorous scientific policy research in no way renders the enterprise useless. Instead, it tends to serve a different kind of function, that of 'public enlightenment'.

Such contributions helped to open the door to a more thoroughgoing epistemological critique. Whereas the early critics argued for bringing in the normative, they tended to do so—wittingly or unwittingly—in ways that maintained the separation between empirical and normative activities. The later policy theorists, in contrast, saw them as inherently intertwined. Influenced by the contributions of critical theory, post-structuralism, social constructionism, postmodernism, and discourse analysis emerging in other fields, these scholars began to take a more distinctively epistemological approach, which can for general purposes loosely labelled 'postpositivism' or 'postempiricism'.[10]

Postempiricism is better described as an orientation than as a well-defined philosophy of science. Most generally, the term is used to refer to an epistemological orientation that seeks to move beyond an 'objectivist' conception of reality. Stressing the subjective foundations of social reality, postempiricist scholars seek to overcome the objective–subjective dualism imposed by 'positivist' or 'neopositivist' epistemological doctrines,[11] principles that spelled out the traditional scientific principles

---

[10] 'Postempiricism' and 'postpositivism' are terms defined differently by various scholars. In this introductory chapter, they should be read to refer generally to the search for an epistemology (or theory of knowledge) and a methodology that transcends the narrow focus on 'objective' empirical research that has been the goal of a 'value-free' positivist social science.

[11] For purposes of the discussion in this chapter, 'positivism', and its more modern variant 'neopositivism', can be taken to refer to the theory of knowledge underlying the traditional understanding of rigorous scientific research. A more detailed discussion of these terms are found in Chapter 6 on epistemology.

long serving to rule out or downplay the subjective foundations of social under-standing and, as we shall see, empirical inquiry itself (Bernstein 1976; 1983). In the postempiricist view, there are many valid forms of explanation, empirical-scientific/causal analysis being only one of them. Such scholars acknowledge the substantive and methodological diversity of the sciences, and commit themselves to the descrip-tion of social phenomena rather than methodological prescriptions (Bohman 1991). Adamantly rejected is the idea that a unified understanding of science methodology can be applicable to all research questions. Underlying this commitment is a rejec-tion of the possibility of a neutral observational vocabulary that can be used to test and conclusively prove or falsify explanatory hypotheses. 'Facts' are always 'theory-laden' and thus rest on interpretations.[12] Emphasizing the integration of normative and empirical modes of discourse, postempiricists understand the discurs-ive processes of confirmation and falsification as complex activities involving a whole network of assumptions, hypotheses, competing theories, even research pro-grammes, rather than singular hypotheses subject to direct empirical test (Sabia and Wallulis 1983: 15–16). The approach in this work, as we see in Chapter 6, emphas-izes those variants that combine a social constructionist view of social inquiry with the role of discourse in the shaping of social explanation and understanding.

From the social constructionist perspective, as we see in the following discussions, the social and political life under investigation is embedded in a web of social mean-ings produced and reproduced through discursive practices. Politics and public policy are understood to take shape through socially interpreted understandings, and their meanings and the discourses that circulate them are not of the actors' own choosing or making. As Sederberg (1984: 5) puts it, 'such ties cannot be transcended through a simple act of will; the meanings we reject continue to inform our responses, if only because we react against them'. Even when social groups succeed in loosening the hold of a particular social meaning, they necessarily do it by embracing a different one. Basic to the politics of policymaking, then, must be an understanding of the discursive struggle to create and control systems of shared social meanings. It is an understanding that works on two levels: an interpretation of the first-order meaning and interests of the social actors under investigation, and an assessment of the second-order theoretical interpretations of the analysts themselves.

More than just an epistemological challenge to social science, social construc-tionism and postempiricism generally are anchored as well in a critique of bureau-cratic culture and the positivist emphasis on 'technical rationality' supporting it. Perhaps the main problem with modern-day neopositivism, like its predecessors, is that it still deceptively offers an appearance of truth. It does so by assigning numbers to decision-making criteria and produces what can appear to be definitive answers to political questions. Conforming to the bureaucratic imperative of impersonality and

---

[12] The word 'fact' is problematic in the social sciences. As we shall see in the following chapters, the facts do not speak for themselves, as is commonly believed and affirmed by the positivist theory of know-ledge. The term 'fact' will be used throughout this text to refer to consensual agreements about particular events or states of affairs (that is, what is widely believed to be the case) rather than to refer to a hard, firm, uncontestable reality located in an objective world.

value-neutrality, it seeks to reduce emotional and conflict-ridden political questions by translating them into scientific and technical answers. In the administrative managerial realm they are processed by technical methods that treat them as questions of efficiency, performance, and predictability amenable to bureaucratic decision procedures. The positivist methods of policy analysis have thus served intentionally or unintentionally to facilitate and bolster bureaucratic governance.

Postempiricist writers, in this respect, argue not only that rationalistic policy analysis is impossible, but that it largely serves as an ideology that masks elite political and bureaucratic interests. These scholars call for the use of interpretive (hermeneutic) and discursive (deconstructivist) techniques to demonstrate that politics and policy are grounded in subjective factors and seek to show that what is identified as objective 'truth' by rational techniques is as often as not the product of deeper, less visible, political presuppositions. For postempiricist policy analysts, the social construction of 'facts' and their subjective interpretations are the stuff of policy politics. Towards this end, they emphasize the role of subjective presuppositions and assumptions that direct our perceptual processes in pre-shaping what are otherwise generally taken to be strictly empirical factors.

Stressing the theoretical construction of the empirical realm, the postempiricist policy analyst calls for the use of interpretive methods to probe the presuppositions that discursively structure social perceptions, organize 'facticity', and deem events as normal, expected, and natural. Greater sophistication is called for in analysing competing definitions, contestable findings, questionable explanations, and contentious arguments. This includes the theoretical assumptions that underlie political discourse and the ways they shape the apprehension of policy alternatives, and thus alter the available range of choice-delimiting decisions.

A policy analysis attuned to the theoretical constitution of facticity directs investigation toward aspects of policymaking that are overlooked or obscured by the 'myth of the given'. In reconsidering questions that are not asked by the prevailing models of policy inquiry, a theoretically informed policy analysis strives to identify the grounds for contentions that arise from the theoretical assumptions, conceptual orientations, methodological commitments, disciplinary practices, and rhetorical approaches closely intertwined in policy disputes (Hawkesworth 1988).

Like science generally, the postempiricist orientation is grounded in a sceptical attitude. But rather than anchoring this scepticism in the search for 'truth', such analysts start with the recognition that different discourses, definitions, and questions lead to different policy prescriptions. Focusing on the discursive social constructions of the political actors, policy institutions, and analysts, postempiricism—particularly its postmodern variants—focuses on the crucial role of language, discourse, rhetorical argument, and stories in framing both policy questions and the contextual contours of argumentation, particularly the ways normative presuppositions operate below the surface to structure basic policy definitions and understandings. Such research shows how our understanding of the social world is framed through the discourses of the actors themselves, rather than fixed in nature (Gottweis 1998).

Taking cognizance of the social and political characteristics of inquiry, as well as the range of contestable issues surrounding policy questions, postempiricism seeks to disarm the pretence of objective, neutral scientific policy analysis. As Hawkesworth (1988) explains, because of the theoretically constituted character of empirical assertions, and thus their essentially contestable nature, policy analysts have to understand and accept the need to explicate the multitude of dimensions inherent to deliberation and debate relevant to most policy issues. Identifying contentious issues related to theoretical assumptions and methodological approaches, as well as popular political principles, enables policy inquiry to facilitate rather than to supplant informed political choice.

Beyond serving the needs of bureaucratic decision-makers, postempiricist analysts seek to represent a wider range of interests, arguments, and discourses in the analytical process. Part of this is done by emphasizing political choice and citizen participation. It is also done by examining and clarifying the ways in which people's interests are discursively constructed, how they come to hold specific interests. Towards this end, the focus has to include an analysis of the often distorted nature of political communication in Western societies.

Such activities are grounded in important political realities related to both the nature of contemporary politics and the administrative state. Given the disturbingly thin relationship between the citizen and the legislator, the traditional conception of the administrative role limited to technically executing policies handed down by elected legislators no longer corresponds to basic realities. With politicians more and more engaged in symbolic politics, creating persuasive sound-bites, identifying wedge issues, and raising campaign funds, administrative decision-makers are left to deal with a good deal of both policy formulation and implementation (Fox and Miller 1998). Indeed, given the growth of the delegation of decision-making to administrative bureaucracies in the modern state, coupled with the increasing shallowness of electoral politics, decisions are increasingly shaped by the discourses of policy experts rather than elected officials. To recognize this and at the same time continue to employ positivist methods of rational, scientific, and neutral methods, argues the postempiricist, is to hide the nature of the actual decision process that is taking place. Policy analysis ends up serving an ideological function.

For the postempiricist, this means exercising much more political insight in the processes of policy definition and formation. Only by getting more deeply involved in the discursive and symbolic sides of politics, argue such theorists, can policy analysts help decision-makers and citizens develop alternatives that speak to their own needs and interests rather than those defined and shaped for them by others. Towards this end, they stress the need for participatory democracy and the development of techniques of participatory policy analysis, approaches that emphasize deliberative interactions between citizens, analysts, and decision-makers (Hajer and Wagenaar 2003). The goal is to provide access and explanation of data to all parties, to empower the public to understand analyses, and to promote serious public discussions. By supplying citizens with the information they need about their circumstances to make intelligent choices about the actions they can take, the postempiricist policy analyst adopts a methodological stance designed to dispel the mystique through greater citizen involvement (Danziger 1995). Seeking to reconstitute politics through collective deliberation, the postempiricist policy analyst serves as a democratic facilitator, a topic which we take up in Part III.

The argument for participatory policy analysis, moreover, is grounded in more than democratic theory. Such an approach opens the door to participation on epistemological grounds as well. In a relational conception of knowledge (that is, knowledge understood as a product of an interaction among competing views), the policy analyst has no privileged position from which to define the issues (Mannheim 1936). The case for participation, as such, is thus also built on an epistemological need to bring in the different points of view. Constituting the raw materials of a dialectical policy deliberation, as we see in Chapter 9, they are the stuff out of which a policy consensus has to be forged. Towards this end, such an analysis focuses on the crucial role of language, rhetorical argument, and stories in framing debate and, in the process, on structuring the deliberative context in which policy is made. It also brings in the local knowledge of citizens—both empirical and normative—relevant to the social context to which policy is applied.

CONCLUSION

The study of public policy, as we have seen in this chapter, emerged to bring the theories and methods of social science to bear on the pressing social and economic problems confronting modern society. Although the initial Lasswellian conception of a policy science represented a multidisciplinary project devoted to the norms and values of democratic governance, the practices that have defined policy analysis in the contemporary social sciences have been more narrowly empiricist, rationalistic, and technocratic.

Over the past 30 years the approach of this narrower orientation has raised serious questions about the relevance of such policy research. Even though empiricism has remained dominant, it has had to give some ground to more normative and qualitative perspectives, albeit mainly grudgingly. In the process of acknowledging its failures to make the promised pay-offs, illustrated here in part through analytic experiences associated with the Great Society and the Vietnam War, the mainstream approach still neglects to confront fully the socially constructed value-oriented nature of the political realities it takes as its topic. Most of the mainstream efforts at reform have introduced qualitative methods in ways that still subordinate them to the larger empiricist/rationalist project, more often than not in the hope that one day it will finally rise to the challenge.

It is against this backdrop that the postempiricist perspective has entered policy studies in Europe and the United States. Drawing in particular on European theories of discourse and social constructionism, postempiricists have sought to more fundamentally redirect the objectivist theory and methods of policy analysis. Beginning with a critique of the technocratic perspectives of conventional policy analysis, it has in more recent years advanced a qualitative understanding of the goals and tasks of the field. Although there is no one postempiricist perspective, and perhaps never will be, there is increasingly a convergent set of themes and approaches that define these efforts. Among the converging contributions, as we shall see in the ensuing chapters, have been discursive, interpretive, narrative, and argumentative-based approaches to policy analysis. Inherent to these discourse-analytic and interpretive methods has been an emphasis on participatory democracy, derived as much from the require-ments of a postempiricist epistemology as from the values and norms of democratic governance.

As this work stresses the postempiricist emphasis on discourse and argumentation, we turn in the next chapter to an examination of a renewed interest in the role of ideas and discourse in policy studies. Distinguishing postempiricist from main-stream perspectives, the discussion sets the stage for a more detailed presentation of the discourse-analytic approach and the deliberative practices to which it gives rise.

PART I

PUBLIC POLICY AND THE DISCURSIVE CONSTRUCTION OF REALITY

2

Constructing Policy Theory: Ideas, Language, and Discourse

The goal of social scientific research is to construct explanatory theory. In the policy and planning sciences, if not social science generally, such theory is taken also to serve as basis for guiding social action. But the nature of such explanation is scarcely straightforward. Whereas conventional social science has emphasized empirically rigorous causal explanations, postempiricists show that explanation in the social world can take numerous forms and that no one form is necessarily privileged. In large part, the form of explanation depends on the nature of the particular social reality to be explained. In this chapter we examine the interpretive or discursive understanding inherent to social explanation. Given the interpretative nature of such explanation, we can only justifiably speak of causal theory in social science in a loose sense—'quasi-causal' is the term we shall use in a later chapter— as opposed to the empirically rigorous form called for by neopositivists. Here we examine the implications of this perspective for a discursive approach to public policy.

Although the more recent work on ideas and discourse is neither directly nor tightly interwoven, as the various approaches come from different directions, each, has contributed or added something to the orientation. While all might not agree, from a postempiricist perspective it seems plausible to point to a pattern of development, one that emerges with ideas and shifts to discourse. Postempiricism, to be sure, originates with theoretical developments outside of policy studies, in particular social constructionism, critical theory, and post-structuralism. But in policy inquiry it has evolved in significant ways in critical debates with various policy theories, in particular pluralism, rational choice theory, neo-institutionalism, policy learning, and advocacy coalition theory. As these orientations have opened the door to ideas and discourse in policy studies, with the postempiricist perspective evolving in significant part as critique of their more limited understandings of discourse, we consider their contributions along the way towards a more critical, theoretically sophisticated discursive approach.

RECONSIDERING IDEAS

Social science, as we have seen, has laboured during the past 60 years or more to develop an empirically based causal theory of political behaviour. Empirical theory would offer 'realist' explanations that correspond to objective realities 'out there' in the world. Because they are seen to be independently anchored in concrete realities, such explanations would be accessible to all observers willing to employ the appropriate empirical methods of observation and measurement. In short, their validity and reliability could be independently verified.

The logic behind this objectivist orientation has been partly methodological and partly political. In methodological terms, non-empirical normative factors have been ruled out or downplayed by positivist social science as inherently subjective. Since the 1950s until sometime in the 1980s, ideas and values have taken a back seat to other variables. Involving interpretive explanations that turn on the subjective perspectives and political interests of the observer, they are seen to lead to the quagmire of relativism, which in turn can spawn political demagoguery and intolerance (although others argue that open debate has generally proved to be the best strategy against these vices). To circumvent political intolerance, variables such as ideas and values are to be eliminated or minimized to the degree possible. In those cases where they prove unavoidable, efforts should be made to find quantitative indicators that can stand in for them; such numerical values can then be plugged into the appropriate empirical model.

Other neopositivists responding to the newly emerging discourse-interpretive challenge have more recently sought to take ideas into consideration. Whereas rationalists have generally assigned ideas to such general categories as 'unexplained variance', various modern-day rational choice theorists try to integrate ideas and beliefs held by individuals or groups without giving up or modifying their basic contention that human beings behave rationally in the effort to achieve their self-interested ends. Goldstein and Koehane (1993), for example, see ideas as 'road maps' that assist agents in instrumentally following their own preferences in a complex world. Under conditions of uncertainty, ideas serve as guides to behaviour. When information is limited, or when the choices available to participants offer no readily beneficial course of action, ideas help actors come to grips with their situation. In the language of rational choice, it helps them choose a *reasonable* rational plan of action. Thus, ideas influence policy when their principled or causal beliefs guide policy participants in clarifying their goals and in understanding complex situations, and identify the end-means relationships for achieving them. But the approach remains based on self-interest, still considered the primary determinant of behaviour. Ideas, in short, can help to fill in gaps that interest-based explanations are unable to cope with. For these theorists, building in ideas adds to rather than challenges the rational actor model.

Although this is an interesting attempt to respond to obvious shortcomings of a narrow emphasis on self-interest, it is wrong to relegate ideas and beliefs to a secondary role as responses to uncertainty, especially when they are of principled nature (John 1998: 154). More specifically, such rational choice positivists fail to account for the fact that ideas often shape the interests themselves. Not only do these theorists neglect the fact that ideas affect how actors come to see—and change—their interests, they ignore the possibility of seeing things in altogether new ways, or what others have referred to as 'reality shifts'. The result, as Philpott (1996: 186) has put it, is that ideas in such work seem to function only as 'partial explanatory gadgets'.

Often in direct response to such a positivist/rationalist understandings of ideas, other approaches have emerged in the 1980s and the 1990s to deal with the limitations of such interest-based materialist explanations, particularly in explaining why political systems deal with some kinds of social problems and not others. As Howlett and Ramesh (1995: 109) put it, this concern led 'to another set of studies that focused on the effects of social and political ideas on defining the sorts of problems with which governments must deal'. Rejecting the attempt to reduce ideas to considerations of self-interest, these studies have sought to build on an older tradition of theorizing that accepts ideas on their own terms and assesses their impact on social interests and political decisions. Through these 'ideational prisms', as Howlett and Ramesh (1995: 109) refer to them, social actors conceive of social and political problems that are seen to be in need of governmental action. The problems that political systems attempt to deal with are not seen, in this view, as having altogether objective foundations in the material or economic base of society; rather, they are in significant part constructed in the realm of political discourse (Rochefort and Cobb 1993; Hilgartner and Bosk 1981). This is not to say that politicians do not attempt to rationally respond to objective factors. It is to stress that politicians and policy decision-makers, like the public generally, are engaged in the manipulation of signs and symbols that shape the way these objects are seen and understood, much like the author of a play. Viewed this way, the various actors, following the scripts of ideologically shaped discourses, emphasize different objectives, actors, and outcomes in competing prescriptions. Political action, like action generally, is shaped and controlled by the discourses that supply it with meaning.

Beyond recognizing that self-interest is unable to explain important changes in behaviour, we need to more specifically ask how ideas and beliefs can be integrated without subordinating them to the needs of instrumental rationality and strategic action (Mansbridge 1980). It may well be the case that ideas help us deal with uncertainty, but to leave it there is to miss much of the story, especially when it comes to explaining major social and political changes. For instance, how do we deal with the fact that historically significant world views such as individualism, socialism, religious fundamentalism, or post-material values fall through the analytical net of self-interest? How do we include the influence of principled beliefs that have changed the course of history, for example, the opposition to slavery or the spread of democratic ideals? Or, to take an especially poignant contemporary issue in search of explanation, self-interest has a hard time explaining the actions of terrorists willing to sacrifice their own lives for specific political or religious beliefs, not least of all those from comfortable middle-class backgrounds.

For millennia, philosophers and historians have wrestled with these questions. Despite the neopositivist dominance in modern social science, the influence of ideas has been debated in the enterprise as long as it has existed. In the main, the debate has tended to swing between two ends of a continuum. At one end, there have been the idealists who have often exaggerated the role of ideas in human affairs at the expense of economic and political interests (Schloming 1991). At the other extreme are those who have seen ideas as little more than rationalizations of political interests. This, in fact, is where the word 'ideology' gets the bad name generally associated with it (Mannheim 1936).[1] Ideology, in this view, is only propaganda or mystification. Competing elites are seen to seize on popular ideas to propagate and legitimize their interests, but the ideas themselves do not play a critical role. Both of these positions, those of the idealist and of the materialist, are exaggerations; the task is to find an appropriate balance between them. Indeed, as we argue in Chapter 5, ideas can have a causal influence, but seldom can they be altogether divorced from material interests or institutional processes.

All social actors, as we know from phenomenological and interactionist sociology (see Chapter 3), use normative concepts and images as the basis for formulating their actions. Ideas, as such, constitute the world as humans know it, understand it, and guide their actions. The question is thus not whether ideas are important, but rather *how* important are they? Do they have a clearly identifiable causal role in determining action? Or do they largely mirror events that happen for reasons related to social structures or group interests? Are ideas mainly rationalizations or legitimizations offered to explain what otherwise would appear to be strategic manoeuvres to satisfy one's interests?

It is not easy to move beyond these general perspectives on the role of ideas and beliefs generally.[2] One reason, as John (1998) points out, is that 'a large number of cognitive processes are classified under the term'. Ideas can be statements of value or worth; they can specify causal relationships; they can be solutions to public problems; they can be symbols and images, which express public and private identities; and ideas can be world views and ideologies. Theorists not only differ in the extent to which they think ideas influence or constitute actions, they refer to different things when they talk about ideas. Indeed, writers can—and typically do—refer to one, or any combination, of these definitions when they write about ideas.

BEYOND SELF-INTEREST: IDEAS MATTER

As is the case with numerous topics in the social sciences, a standard reference point for considering the role of ideas is the work of the famous nineteenth-century German sociologist Max Weber. Weber (1948: 280) formulated the relationship between ideas and material interests in this way: 'Not ideas, but material and ideal interests, directly govern men's conduct. Yet very frequently the "world images" that have been created by "ideas" have, like switchmen, determined the tracks along which action has been pushed by the dynamic of interest.'

Excellent examples of this in contemporary politics can be found in Thatcherism in Britain and its counterpart in the United States, Reaganism. Both political leaders introduced new ideas about governance and economy that switched the political

---

[1] The negative connotation associated with the word 'ideology' is attributed to Napoleon, who labelled his political critics 'ideologists'.

[2] The word 'belief' applies generally to things that people take to be true or given, including ideas. The word 'idea' refers here to both specific empirical beliefs about what 'is', including causal relationships, as well as to specific normative beliefs about what 'ought' to be the case, including moral principles.

tracks to neoliberalism. Indeed, Reagan's lasting influence, despite his many policy failures, was his impact on political discourse in the US. Whereas for more than 40 years the Democratic Party shaped the dominant political paradigm around economic regulation and social assistance in the name of the 'public interest' or 'common good', Reagan reshaped the contours of public discourse by replacing regulation and assistance with deregulation, free markets, and the interests of the individual, especially the individual as entrepreneur. In the process, the normative terminology of public interest was replaced with an emphasis on self-interest and personal gain. Today, it is scarcely possible to discuss new policy proposals without first explaining and legitimizing them in terms of the economic language of costs and benefits, a formulation that does not easily admit the traditional concept of the public interest. The public interest, as an emphasis on the larger common concerns of society, cannot be easily discussed in terms of cost and benefits; indeed, it is generally understood as morally transcending such narrow economic criteria. And, just as important, when a public interest claim succeeds in satisfactorily meeting the cost-benefit test, it is usually difficult—or impossible—to measure the outcome in terms of monetary values.

Looking closely at the enactment of historically significant legislation, we almost always discover that shared values are the forces behind the interest groups and social movements that struggled to achieve it—the end of slavery, women's right to vote, anti-communism, civil rights, environmental protection, and anti-smoking campaigns, to name some of the more obvious examples. More specifically, consider the passage of the Voting Rights Act of 1964. Only two years before this landmark legislative achievement for the civil rights movement, the prospects for the passage of such legislation looked very poor. In the short span of just a couple of years, views about equality of opportunity changed so dramatically that they cleared away the long-standing entrenched political opposition that had blocked the path of such legislation for more than 100 years.

Beyond the broad sweeps of historical change, moreover, there is plenty of evidence to show the importance of ideas in the ordinary course of public affairs. Research shows, as Orren (1988: 13) writes, 'that people don't act simply on the basis of their perceived self-interest, without regard to aggregative consequences of their action'. They are motivated as well 'by values, purposes, ideas, and goals, and commitments that transcend self-interest or group interests'. Indeed, over the past 30 or 40 years a good deal of support has steadily accumulated to support the contention that ideas and values can be relatively autonomous of interests and institutions. Although it is never easy to sort out these influences, such research makes clear that the values of individuals can arise quite independently of their life experiences and can exert an independent influence on their political behaviour (Verba and Orren 1985).

Consider some examples. People's attitudes toward war are found to be influenced more by their general views on foreign policy than by their experiences of war or military service (Lau, Brown, and Sears 1978). In similar respects, opinion surveys show that businessmen's attitudes towards foreign policy and military defence better correlate with their political ideas rather than with how closely their entrepreneurial activities are involved with defence or defence-related production (Russett and Hanson 1975). Counter-intuitively, being out of a job has less effect on people's political values and actions than do their attitudes towards unemployment. Again, social attitudes about school busing to achieve racial integration among blacks and whites have had less to do with a person's own experiences with busing in their neighbourhoods than with their beliefs and values about busing (Sears, Hensler, and Speer 1979). Such findings show that in addition to acting to maximize personal self-interest people also strive to achieve or affirm social and ideological goals (Kinder 1998; Kinder and Sears 1985).

Political research has also demonstrated that ideas often play a special role in the behaviour of political leaders, especially among those who are better educated about social and political issues (Mueller 1973; Polsby 1984). Political leaders frequently do not reflect the narrow self-interested orientations attributed to them by various political theories, rational choice in particular. Opinion research shows their beliefs to be explained by ideological orientations as well as, or better than, by social and demographic characteristics. Income also has surprisingly little influence on people's attitudes about economic redistribution policies. Instead, their views are often better explained by reference to their beliefs about the appropriate role of equality in society. Relatedly, there is also little solid evidence showing that political interest and participation arise mainly from individuals' calculations of the costs and benefits to them personally. Neither personal economic distress nor good fortune is a good indicator of active political engagement.

Because politics is grounded in disputes about the good life and the means of realizing it, policy politics by its nature centres around controversial ideas and beliefs about the best courses of action. Social democrats and free market conservatives, for example, clash over such basic policy issues as the primacy of social equality and state interference in the individual's freedom to acquire property. In the process, participants advocate differing ideas in an effort to win over one another, be they politicians, agency bureaucrats, professional experts, legislators, or members of interest groups. But even when the participants agree about general ideas, they often argue about how to best apply it to specific action contexts.

In this view, particular policies come into existence because people have beliefs about what they take to be the right course of action and struggle to influence and shape decisions in the light of them. Over and above the effects of political institutions and interests on policy, the political advocacy of ideas and beliefs is seen as a causal factor. This is especially the case when it comes to explaining policy stability and change. For a good illustration, we can return to President Johnson's War on Poverty.

Before Johnson denounced poverty as a stain on an affluent American way of life, there had been virtually no political thrust to fight poverty. Even though poverty was only a minor issue in public consciousness in the 1950s, by the 1960s it had become a central issue on the political agenda. The widely held belief that poverty was morally unacceptable in an affluent society gave impetus to the President Johnson's crusade against poverty, the most important social agenda since the New Deal. It was thus ideological commitment rather than political power per se that drove this historic legislation. Asserting that 'objective conditions are seldom so compelling and so unambiguous that they set the policy agenda', Majone (1989: 24) points to the fact that poverty in the 1950s was scarcely a matter of public consciousness in the US. But in the mid-1960s, despite no objective changes in the relations among rich and poor, poverty became the central policy issue. 'What had changed', as he puts it, 'were attitudes and views on poverty, and beliefs in the capacity of government to find solutions to social problems.'

The same can be said of Reagan's turn to 'supply-side economics' and the deregulation of transportation.[3] Supply-side economics, for example, was a little-known and little-respected theory among mainstream economists; it was taken to be more ideological than empirical. Indeed, before he lost his bid for the Republican presidential nomination to Reagan in 1979, George Bush regularly portrayed it as 'voodoo economics'. The work of a conservative 'policy entrepreneur', an economist named Arthur Laffer, the theory nicely fitted ideologically into Reagan administration's narrative about the problems plaguing the American economy. As a result, it was snapped up overnight and regularly featured as the new medicine for an ailing economy.

A major reason that policy theory has neglected ideas is the field's more general theoretical shortcomings. Much policy research has been guided by the relatively static concepts of the 'policy cycle' or the 'stages model' of the policy process. As a heuristic, the stages model has proved to be overly descriptive and lacking in explanatory power. While it does include the role of institutions and ideas in the policy process, especially in the agenda-setting process, the framework tells us little about their relationship to other political factors. In response to the theoretical limits—if not failures—of this and other similar lines of policy research, other approaches have sought to put policy studies on firmer theoretical ground (Sabatier 1988; 1999; deLeon 1999). Most importantly for present purposes, these lines of investigation have often featured a concern for ideas.

Of particular importance in rekindling this interest in ideas in policy theory has been the 'new institutionalism' (or 'neo-institutionalism', as it is also called), a theoretical orientation that has focused on the evolutionary relationship of ideas and norms to institutional practices.

NEO-INSTITUTIONALISM AND POLICY IDEAS

The reconsideration of ideas and beliefs in mainstream political and policy research owes much the 'new institutionalists' or 'neo-institutionalists', especially those in comparative politics and policy. Long concerned that the existing theoretical approaches to inquiry are insufficient for dealing with the variety and complexity of social and political change in modern societies, these scholars have argued that the

---

[3] Yet another example is found in the field of transportation deregulation. Research also shows that the drive for the deregulation of transportation during the Reagan era was preceded by a new consensus about policy regulation on the part of particular economists in leading American universities, a number of whom took important positions in the administration.

analysis of variations in public policy outcomes should more broadly examine the interplay of political elites, interest groups demands, institutional processes, and ideas in political and policy analysis (King 1973–4).

Today there are three varieties of neo-institutionalism: an historical institutionalism, a sociological institutionalism emphasizing culture and norms, and a rational choice institutionalism (Hall and Taylor 1996). With regard to policy discourse and ideas, it is important to emphasize the line of research initiated by March and Olsen (1984), which emphasizes both historical and normative dimensions, and the historical institutionalism of writers such as Hall (1986), Skocpol (1985), and Steinmo (1993). Such neo-institutionalism is first and foremost an attempt to overcome the limits of group-based pluralist explanations of political phenomena. 'It emphasizes', in the words of Howlett and Ramesh (1995: 27), 'the relative autonomy of political institutions from the society in which they exist; the organization of governmental institutions and its effects on what the state does; the rules, norms and symbols governing political behaviour; and the unique patterns of historical development and the constraints they impose on future choices.' The leading innovators of the neo-institutionalism in political science, March and Olsen (1984: 738), explain that the approach focuses on complex macro processes at the expense of micro sociopolitical processes, stresses the messy multi-dimensionality of historical change, and prefers to downplay metaphors of choice 'in favor of other logics of action and the centrality of meaning and symbolic action'.

It is not that institutions cause political action; rather, it is their discursive practices that shape the behaviours of actors who do. Supplying them with regularized behavioural rules, standards of assessment, and emotive commitments, institutions influence political actors by structuring or shaping the political and social interpretations of the problems they have to deal with and by limiting the choice of policy solutions that might be implemented. The interests of actors are still there, but they are influenced by the institutional structures, norms, and rules through which they are pursued. Such structural relationships give shape to both social and political expectations and the possibility of realizing them. Indeed, as Weick (1969) and others have shown, it is often the opportunities and barriers of such institutions that determine people's preferences, rather than the other way around, as more commonly assumed (Fischer 1990: 282–3).

Much of this work seeks to move beyond the narrower focus of traditional political analysis on the pluralist interplay of interest groups, which largely neglects elites, institutions, and ideas. To some degree the problem of elites is dealt with by the neo-pluralists, who emphasize the skewed play of power in the interest group process. But institutions and ideas are still neglected, at considerable cost to explanatory power. To be sure, pluralists can speak of a political marketplace of competing ideas, the structure of which reflects the balance of group power in society. But this has seldom been their primary interest or emphasis.

Even more problematic in pluralist theory is the absence of the power of institutions. For pluralists, institutions have mainly been understood as arenas where interest group politics plays itself out. Beyond that, institutions are seen to exercise no special role in shaping policy outcomes. Neo-institutionalists, in contrast, seek to show how institutions actually structure the play of power, often in ways hidden from view. Not only can they facilitate the ability of some groups to achieve their goals, they can block or hinder the attempts of others. And one of the key factors in this structuration of the process is the ideas embedded in the institutional structures and their practices. Neo-institutionalists see political and policymaking practices as grounded in institutions dominated by ideas, rules, procedural routines, roles, organizational structures and strategies which constitute an 'institutional construction of meaning' that shapes actors preferences, expectations, experiences, and interpretations of actions. As a dominant force determining meanings, they shape the ways people communicate and argue with one another.

One of the seminal examples of this line of institutional analysis is the work of Hall (1986; 1992; 1993). For Hall (1986: 19), institutions refer to 'the formal rules, compliance procedures, and standard operating practices that structure the relationship between individuals in various units of the polity and the economy'. Institutions, as such, do more than transmit the preferences and interests of groups; they combine and change group preferences, especially over time (Hall 1986; 1992). Supplying the political and organizational context in which actors interpret their self-interests, institutions play a major role in determining how interest groups, politicians, and administrators decide their policy preferences.

Examining the ways Western countries reacted to the economic crisis of the 1970s, Hall (1992) shows that a full explanation of why policymakers radically shifted their beliefs about economic management from Keynesianism to monetarism (that is, from the control of the aggregates of consumption and investment to the control of the money supply) requires an understanding of the ability of institutions to hinder or facilitate new ideas. Institutions, as Hall shows, facilitated the restructuring of economic policy by influencing the manner in which the new ideas emerged in political and administrative deliberations and were subsequently articulated in government policy decisions. In the early 1970s Keynesian ideas were dominant in the British treasury and other governing institutions. By mid-decade, however, an unemployment crisis and high levels of inflation created problems for the Labour government's emphasis on Keynesian policy ideas. Confronted with political discontent, and stymied by its inability to employ fiscal techniques to stimulate an economic recovery, the Labour government was unable to apply its established policy wisdom. This opened the door to new ideas, which the Conservative Party eagerly sought to exploit.

In response to what appeared to be an enduring recession, one that no longer seemed to respond to Keynesian fiscal techniques, conservatives deftly moved to reconfigure power in new decision-making institutions less entrenched in Keynesian ideology. At the same time, the conservative media took a more oppositional stance and helped, among other things, to promote new conservative policy think tanks emphasizing free-market solutions, in particular the free play of financial markets. These institutional changes, Hall shows, facilitated the discussion by shaping and advocating of a new set of ideas among party officials, the media, and members of public, and in doing so paved the way for a remarkably rapid adoption of these ideas by Conservative Party elites. Not only did this new institutional landscape and the ideas it proffered bring Prime Minister Margaret Thatcher to power in 1979, it offered her a dramatic political opportunity to shape and wield a new political coalition capable of scuttling the old economic orthodoxies with astonishing ease. And with no small impact. By combining technical economic arguments about monetarism with a narrative about the benefits of hard work and thrift, which she often told through stories about her father's grocery store, along with slogans such as 'Labour is not Working',[4] she managed to bring about a dramatic neoliberal transformation of the British political economy (Schmidt 2002). Indeed, Thatcherism switched the tracks along which British politics was travelling, the lasting effects of which one can easily detect in the more conservative 'third way' strategy of Prime Minister Blair's Labour government. The traditional left-oriented political language of the Labour Party was no longer perceived to be a viable electoral option.

Some contend that Hall has overemphasized institutions at the expense of the more general realignment of political forces that took place at the time (including the impact of the wing of the Conservative Party that put forward the new free-market philosophy, one of its members being Thatcher herself). Even if institutions are credited with too much influence, however, Hall clearly illustrates the ways they come into play. He has had, as such, an important influence on the study of institutions and ideas in comparative policy studies.

Building on this line of comparative institutional analysis, others have taken the relationship between institutions and ideas a step further by examining more specifically the functions of specific policy discourses. Policy discourse in this work can be understood as the communicative interactions among political actors that translate problems into policy issues. Schmidt (2001), for example, argues that 'discourse can provide insight into the political dynamics of change by going behind the interplay of interests, institutions, and cultures' to explain how change is brought about by 'an interactive consensus for change through communication' among the key political actors. This is not to suggest that discourse can be understood without the variables of interests, institutions, and culture. Indeed, as she makes clear, discourse is not easily separated from the interests that are expressed through it, or the institutional interactions which shape their expression, or the cultural norms that frame them. Discourse, she argues, can (and often does) exert a causal influence on political change, although the influence tends to that of an intervening rather than an independent variable. For this reason, as she explains, discourse cannot be *the* cause, but it is often *a* cause of political change (Schmidt 2002). Discursive communication is only one of a number of multiple causes or influences, but it can at times be the very variable or added influence that makes the difference, especially in the explanation of change. It can do this in a variety of ways, including the conceptual reframing of interests in ways that permit consensual agreement or through the reframing of institutional rules and cultural norms governing the play of power.

---

[4] To leave no symbol unturned, the slogan 'Labour is not Working' was accompanied with pictures of workers standing in the unemployment line.

In Schmidt's approach, discourse has two dimensions: the ideational and the interactive. In ideational terms, discourse supplies policy with substantive arguments, both empirical and normative. These arguments provide the logic and premises of a particular policy discourse, including statements of its normative appropriateness in terms of broadly held social values. They serve to define or redefine the actors' perceptions of both their self-interest and the general interest of society.[5]

Beyond the ideational dimension, the social interactive dimension of discourse is attached to different institutions and actors who carry out one or both of two discursive functions, which she calls the 'coordinative' and the 'communicative'. Coordinative discourse refers to those tasks at the centre of policy construction and development, including government agencies but also epistemic communities, advocacy coalitions, and discourse coalitions. The communicative function of the interactive dimension, by contrast, relates to discursive exchanges with the broader political system and takes place in its various deliberative policy forms. Concerned with policy issues of national political concern, its primacy function is to generate persuasion and confer political legitimacy on policy initiatives.

Perhaps most important from a neo-institutionally-oriented discourse perspective, Schmidt (2002) illustrates the ways different institutional contexts emphasize different aspects of the interactive dimension of discourse through an analysis of the impact of the European Union on national governance practices. In governance systems where political power is concentrated in the executive branch, she finds communicative discourse to be extensive. Its objective is to persuade the larger public of the appropriateness or necessity of policy decisions made by a policy elite and thus to circumvent political sanctions such as electoral defeat or public protests. In governance systems where power is more dispersed, coordinative discourse plays a bigger role. It is aimed at forging agreements among the wider range of policy elites involved in policy development who, in turn, must seek to communicate decisions to their political constituencies. In dispersed or decentralized systems, if the coordinative discourse fails to persuade, there is no agreement and sanctions tend to be immediate.

More recently neo-institutionalists' attention to institutionalized discursive practices has influenced various other theoretical orientations to reconsider the role of ideas, including the policy network scholars and advocacy coalition researchers interested in the formal and informal institutional relationships among those actively engaged in thinking about and making public policy in particular policy areas.

POLICY COMMUNITIES, ISSUE NETWORKS, AND LEARNING

In the 1980s an interesting and influential line of research emerged that built on Heclo's (1978) seminal conceptualization of issue networks. This work has moved

---

[5] This aspect of the definition, she writes, is closely related to the concerns of 'those who focus on the role of ideas in policy change, on policy narrative . . . or frame of reference, on discourse, national identities, norms and values, and collective memories' (Schmidt 2002: 210).

the focus in policy research to policy subsystems and their importance for policy formation in the policy cycle. Unlike agenda-setting, where interest group leaders and select members of the public are more readily involved, in policy formulation participation is much more restricted to the members of policy subsystems who have a working or professional knowledge in the substantive issues. Members of such subsystems actively participate in advancing solutions to policy problems and discussing the feasibility of the various options. Some serve as 'policy entrepreneurs', actively developing and pushing particular policy solutions, sometimes their own.

Heclo's purpose was to show that policy subsystems can be more fluid than recognized by traditional theories of agency-interest group relations. Where traditional descriptions focus on institutionalized systems of interest representation, particularly as reflected in the concept of 'iron triangles' (closed systems of interest groups, legislative committees, and agency leaders), other institutional forms have emerged that are better described as comparatively open systems with broader ranges of participants. This is especially the case with policy subsystems concerned with social and public interest-oriented policies, such as environmental, health, or consumer issues. Instead of just industry people, relevant agency personnel, and legislative committee members, it is now possible to identify many more actors in the process. In addition to these traditional constituencies, journalists, academics, state officials, policy entrepreneurs, and political activists, among others, are found to be actively engaged in particular policy subsystem processes. Unlike traditional sub-governments, which involve stable sets of participants who work to shape and control fairly narrow policies related to their own material interests, issue networks are characterized by various policy players moving in and out of them with regularity. Rather than groups united to ensure dominance over a policy or programme, no one in particular appears to have firm control of the policy issues. For these policy actors, a clear material self-interest is frequently subordinate to either an emotional commitment or an intellectual conviction (Heclo 1978). Policy issue networks are thus less stable, much less institutionalized than iron triangles, and have a higher turnover of participants. Since Heclo's initial formulation, the literature on policy networks has grown extensively, including considerable work in England and continental Europe more generally.

Policy network theory, to a greater or lesser degree, takes ideas as well as interests to bind together the groups and individuals in a policy sector. It assumes that what keeps networks functioning are common ideas about solutions to public problems. Some issue network theorists have gone further to maintain that alliances over policy can be primarily about sharing values. Without some agreement about what the main policy problems are and how to solve them, it is argued, networks cannot function. If there are major conflicts within networks, informal bargaining and the transmission of ideas among the participation will be difficult, as these processes can be blocked or impeded by inside groups holding on to the power (Smith 1993; Marsh and Rhodes 1992; Milward and Wamsley 1984).

Other scholars in the early 1980s drew a distinction between policy networks and policy communities. Although not everyone agrees on the distinction, it can be employed to identify an important characteristic of the politics surrounding policy subsystems and policy formulation. In this view, policy networks are immersed in larger policy communities. Such communities include a variety of policy actors who may or may not be represented in policy networks. All members of a policy community share a common interest and concern for a particular policy domain and are political engaged, in one way or anther, in bringing about policy reform. Policy community thus refers to a broader more inclusive category of actors and potential actors interested in policy formulation, who need not possess a hard and fast consensus about problems or the appropriate solutions. Members may be generally united around a central set of policy beliefs, but they may disagree over particular issues pertinent to the policy sector, including some fundamental issues (Brooks and Gagnon 1994). The concept of a policy network, in contrast, is more restricted to a subset of community members who interact with each other on a regular—even routinized—basis, sharing more specific knowledge-based understandings about problems and solutions. Such networks are based on the exchange of information and influence between participants, with those having little or nothing to exchange usually being relegated to the margins, if not excluded.

One of the important studies of policy communities and networks is that of Haas (1992), who identifies communities of experts in international environmental relations as 'epistemic communities'. Such epistemic communities (which others, following the distinctions above, might describe as networks) transmit and maintain beliefs about the verity and applicability of particular forms of knowledge. Ideas are important because 'the diffusion of new ideas and information can lead to new patterns of behavior and prove to be an important determinant of international policy coordination' (Haas 1992: 3). Haas's work illustrates the profusion of governmental agencies, policy analysts, and experts that have emerged since the mid-twentieth century as one of the driving forces behind these communities. Increasing complexity of public issues and more unpredictable policymaking environments have compelled decision-makers to more and more turn to—even participate in—epistemic communities to resolve policy dilemmas. Policy beliefs and the politics of expertise, in the process, assume a central role in the development and construction of policy, as decision-makers seek more certain knowledge to deal with complex and often risky problems.

Closely related to this literature is the notion of policy learning. Here, emphasis is placed on the ability of policymakers to make choices based on specific experiences rather than exclusively relying on pressure from electorates or institutional routine. Responding to different or changing social and institutional contexts, they are capable of learning from the implementation of policies and adjusting or changing future policy strategies accordingly. Policy implementation and evaluation, in this large and growing literature, are conceptualized as iterative processes of active learning on the part of policy actors about policy problems and the solutions to them.

Political and policy learning can be understood to have two dimensions. One involves voters and parties comparing 'the outcomes that are occurring with those they desire and placing renewed pressure on politicians and the bureaucracy to address the difference' (Steward 1992: 247). The second involves 'public officials and politics themselves adjusting their actions in the light of experience'. It is this latter concern with learning that has mainly been the focus in policy studies, particular as initially spelled out by Heclo (1974: 78) in his seminal and still influential work on the subject.

Policy learning for Heclo is 'a relatively enduring alteration in behaviour that results from experience' (1974: 306). The concept of policy learning captures the effort to 'reduce the gap between what is expected from a program and what government is doing'.[6] Towards this end, Heclo calls for an approach emphasizing knowledge acquisition and utilization that would produce better understandings and explanations of policy outcomes than the dominant theories stressing societal conflict. Without denying the importance of societal interests in periods of fundamental change, Heclo maintains that much of what is important during normal times can be explained in terms of policy decision-makers learning and applying lessons drawn from their experiences, a point drawn out as well by Hall (1992) in his work on the neoliberal transformation in Britain.

Identifying seven competing theories of learning, Bennett and Howlett (1992) set out a series of questions that policy-learning theories need to confront. The first pertains to who is doing the learning. Locating the agency of policy learning is a complex matter ranging in different theories from high-level politicians and civil servants generally 'to complex arrangements of state and societal actors in various types of domestic and transnational policy networks' (1992: 282). The second question focuses on what is learned. Here the task does not get much easier, as policy learning involves the growth of intelligence in government agencies and policy networks that pertains to formulating and implementing policies. And finally an evaluation of policy learning theories must determine the outcomes of the learning. Is it enough for learning to reflect a new way of thinking about a problem, or does it have to be reflected in a concrete change of policy?

A more recent influential contribution to policy-learning theory has been advanced by Sabatier and Jenkins-Smith (1993) in their 'policy advocacy coalition approach', which concentrates on policy subsystems and learning. A central feature of the model turns on the way members of different policy coalitions, organized around different policy beliefs, can learn from the technical research and debates in policy communities. As such, this work emphasizes the importance of the role of policy ideas and analysis in the policy process. Sharing knowledge, beliefs, and values, the members of policy advocacy coalitions differentiate themselves from their competitors along cognitive lines. While the core beliefs of policy communities do not easily change, argues Sabatier, policy learning can affect the more instrumental aspects of policy politics. This work has had an important impact on the field; for this reason, we return to it in Chapter 5. There we examine it against a postempiricist discourse perspective. Whereas much of this literature has treated policy learning as a form of empirical feedback from concrete experiences, learning from

---

[6] For a useful discussion see Rose (1993: 50).

a discursive perspective will be seen to involve interpretive reflection on such experiences as well. Because we deal with it in some detail, we shall postpone further discussion of the advocacy approach to policy learning until then.

Although this literature on networks, communities, and learning has represented an important advance over interest and materialist-based theories, it has in general maintained a distinction between politics and scientific expertise. Expert consensus can influence the politics of policymaking, but politics does not influence science (Litfin 1994). In the end, the relationship of expertise to policy learning is still largely understood as the rational application of knowledge rather than as an inherently political process. The recognition that scientific expertise is itself shaped by power and politics is the first step toward a discursive understanding of the policy process. Towards this end, we turn next to two more critical perspectives on discourse, institutions, and power, those of Juergen Habermas and Michel Foucault, both of which are essential contributions to a postempiricist discursive approach. With these perspectives, the evolution of the theoretical discussion makes the shift from ideas to a more radical focus on discourse.

CRITICAL THEORY: DISTORTED COMMUNICATION AND DISCURSIVE IDEALS

Although the critical theory of Habermas (1970*a*; 1973; 1987) at first seems quite removed from the more practical concerns of policy inquiry, it has stimulated a sizeable literature devoted to the critique and reconstruction of policy analysis. Habermas's (1987) goal is to supply a communications model of action. Missing from interest-based models, he argues, is a recognition that power is more than either the ability to achieve objectives through the mobilization of resources or the domination of the other participants through physical or manipulative means. Moving beyond a negative understanding of power as control and domination, his model of action emphasizes as well the positive or productive ability of communicative power to organize and coordinate action through consensual communication. Knowledge and discursive practices are thus a critical dimension of the struggle for power.

Habermasian-oriented critical policy inquiry starts from an investigation of what it understands to be the veiled ideological nature of mainstream policy analysis and its complicit relationship to the conservative implications of pluralist policy politics. Given the skewed distribution of power that characterizes Western capitalist democracies, professional policy analysis in this view can never yield an authentically representative or non-biased political consensus. In short, the political elites in this pluralist model of representation are unable to adequately represent the interests of ordinary citizens. Not only does the model neglect political interest groups lacking political power, professional experts, mainly employed to serve elite interests, can—and often do—have a strong motivation to conceal or downplay important information, including relevant normative perspectives. Working in settings largely removed from public view, experts can easily use a range of strategies to distort policy deliberations in ways that suit either their own purposes or the interests of their employers (for example, concealing important findings, exaggerating the significance of their own findings, under- or overstating the impact of consequences, or denigrating unfavourable arguments offered by their opponents).

The policy analysis profession is thus by and large seen as uncritically accepting the politics of the existing political system.[7] Described as technocrats, such professionals employ purportedly 'value neutral' positivist methods that contribute to and support patterns of distorted communications concealing social and political conflicts. Where Marxism has held that conflicts between labour and capital would invariably lead to a collapse of the liberal capitalist state, Habermas shows the ways in which the state and science have managed to divert this potential crisis from the public to the socio-cultural sphere. The domain of the public sphere, where citizens can openly discuss political agreements needed to resolve public problems, has been depoliticized through state interventions that conceal the dominant interests of capitalist business. A scientization of policymaking by the state through methodologies such as policy analysis and planning, argues Habermas, has been one of the primary strategies for carrying out this depoliticization.

This depoliticization is seen to threaten modern government with a destabilizing legitimacy crisis created by the inability of elite decision-makers to adequately address the interests and needs of the larger citizenry. The solution, in the Habermasian view, is a 'repolitization of the public sphere' to include the full range of interests and the development of a more authentic consensus through a renewal of the processes of discursive will formation in important political and policy issues. Such deliberation would to be conducted through the rules of communicative interaction governing argumentation. Towards this end, Habermas's theory of communicative interaction spells out a theory of 'ideal speech', designed to serve as a critical standard for assessing political discourse.

Critical theory commends, then, a continuous interchange of ideas, interpretations, and criticisms among social scientists and other political actors. Because the truth of a statement can be supported only through consensus on the interpretation of the experience to which it refers, truth claims have to be warranted through argumentation. As the grounds supporting statements are 'pragmatic' or interest-related, the focus of inquiry must be on clarifying the interests presupposed by the claim (which, in turn, collapses any firm distinction between theory and practice). Without denying the importance of empirical-analytic statements, they can be ascribed purpose or meaning only through dialectic deliberation. Towards this end, Habermas emphasizes 'communicative competence' through unfettered argumentation.

Communicative competence in this approach is based on a discursive ethics grounded in a 'counterfactual' concept of the ideal speech situation that spells out the standards and conditions for unconstrained discussion. In this ideal situation, no one would impose restrictions on who may participate, what kinds of arguments can be advanced, or the duration of the deliberations. The only resource actors would have at their disposal is their arguments, and the only authority would be that of the

---

[7] Mainstream policy analysts, of course, would make no secret of this. See, for example, Lynn (1999).

better argument. In the ideal, all actors would have equal chances to participate (including the chances to learn to participate) in the discursive process of consensus formation.

Although many of critical theory's opponents have criticized it as 'abstract theorizing' of little relevance to the practical tasks of a field like policy analysis, it is not without connection to important practical questions. Like pluralism, critical policy theory is concerned with the exchange of ideas and interests. But, unlike pluralism, it focuses on the question of the legitimacy of the communicative exchange of these ideas and interests. It seeks to specify the criteria governing an undistorted communication between the participants. In the process, it emphasizes the role of citizens as well as organized interest groups in the formation of a legitimate consensus. Critical policy analysts stress the need to develop institutions that extend the possibilities for citizen competence and learning (Forester 1985).

Those who reject critical theory as irrelevant to the task of building participatory policy institutions generally miss the point. Habermas has provided the philosophical foundations for building the alternative model, not a blueprint for a practical model itself. The ideal speech situation is not a formula for designing decision-making structures, as many critics have tried to make it out to be.[8] Instead, it offers a *counter-factual* that serves to generate standards for the assessment of participation. And, as ideals, these principles have served as a powerful inspiration for a group of critical policy scholars working to think through an effort to construct a non-technocratic, postempiricist model of policy analysis (Forester 1993; Dryzek 1990; Torgerson 1986; Luke 1987; Fischer 1990; 1995).

Critical theory also speaks directly to the question of how to rethink the technocratic practices of policymaking. It offers an unusually instructive conception of what is involved in a more comprehensively rational understanding of evaluation (Fischer 1985). It offers, in this respect, criteria for moving beyond the merely technical interest in empirical analysis that has shaped policy analysis to show how this conception is inherently connected to normative questions related to the social life-world, the social system, and what Habermas (1971) calls 'the emancipatory interest'.

Critical policy inquiry, then, emphasizing the social construction of reality and the indeterminacy of knowledge, represents a thoroughgoing critique of mainstream neopositivist methods. Most basic to the critique is the idea that the effort to eliminate subjectivity is futile. Using methods of critique and deconstruction to demonstrate this pervasiveness of subjectivity, such scholars show that the rational-analytic techniques of mainstream policy analysis tend more to serve an unwitting ideological function than as a method for assembling empirical truths.

DISCOURSE AS POWER

Where Habermas's critical theory supplies a normative ideal for communication and argumentation, Foucault (1972; 1973; 1977; 1980; 1984) focuses on the role of

---

[8] Part of the problem is that Habermas is himself not always clear about this point.

discourses as they have functioned in specific historical contexts, particularly in the development of modern medical policies and the administration of hospitals for the mentally ill, the shaping of criminology and the management of prisons, and the practices of educational institutions. Contemporary discourse analysis owes a large debt to Foucault's oeuvre.[9] Although highly abstract and often difficult to understand, his work is nonetheless widely acknowledged to be a major contribution to the study of discourse in the social sciences. While it has not been as influential among policy scholars as that of Habermas, Foucault's contribution continues to grow. Although it is impossible here to give anything more than a general orientation to his work, a basic understanding is necessary for grasping the discursive approach.

Like Habermas, Foucault understands truth to be founded on discursive conventions. But in his theory such conventions extend beyond objects and object relations to include the knowing subject as well. Whereas critical theory seeks to account for the way that subjective knowers come to construct their worlds, Foucault emphasizes the subjects themselves to be the creations of prevailing discursive practices. Rather than focusing on people making discursive statements, he emphasizes the ways in which discourses make people. Foucault, in this way, moves beyond linguistic and communicative analysis by anchoring discourse in societal processes. That is to say, discourse analysis is not limited to the study of language or communication. It is concerned with specifying socio-historic discursive formations, conceptualized as systems of rules that facilitate certain statements but not others at particular times, places, and institutional locations.

Elaborating on the relationship of discourse to power, Foucault focuses on the discursive construction of social subjects and knowledge and the functioning of discourse in social change. Towards this end, he explicates the way discursive practices are constitutive of knowledge, emphasizing the conditions under which knowledge is transformed into discursive formations (that is, disciplines) such as science, law, or politics. This includes the conditions that make discourse possible, the rules of formation that define the possible objects of discourse, and enunciative modalities, subjects, concepts and strategies of a particular type of discourse. Foucault's work, as such, is on the domains of knowledge that are constituted by such rules.

Especially important for social science is Foucault's *constitutive* view of discourse, which understands discourse to actively construct society along various dimensions—including the objects of knowledge, social subjects, forms of self, social relationships, and perceptual frameworks. In this work he delineates the interdependencies of the discursive practices of a society and its institutions. Such practices, understood as texts, always draw upon and transform other contemporary and historically prior texts. Any given type of discursive practice is thus generated out of combinations of others, and is defined by its relationship to them. In the

---

[9] Foucault's work on discourse analysis has its origins in the student revolt in Paris in 1968. Radical students and scholars turned their attention to the full spectrum of hidden means through which a social system conveys its knowledge to ensure not only its political control but ultimately its survival, in particular newspapers, television, high schools, and universities (MacDonell 1986: 9–23).

analysis of these processes, changing discursive practices are seen to be important elements in social transformations. The struggle for power is thus understood to occur both in and over discourse. Although Foucault's focus is upon the discursive formations of the human sciences, his insights are applicable to all types of discourse.

Basic to Foucault's analysis is a critique of the way in which the traditional state-centred theory of power has hindered our ability to recognize the discursively based expert powers dispersed through the social system. His work demonstrates how traditional analysis has blinded us to the more subtle but profound nature of professional power. Recognition that the most significant power of the professional is lodged in basic conceptual categories of thought and language opens the door to a discursive understanding of the role of professional disciplines and expertise in modern society, policy analysis not withstanding.

Foucault's critique of modernity—as a discourse orientation—is anchored in his analysis of the rise of extensive administrative forms of regulation—what he calls the 'disciplines'. From the seventeenth and eighteenth centuries onward, the emerging professional disciplines increasingly took charge of the complex processes by which individuals are made into objects of study—defined as social objects in need of organization and regulation. Such concerns—Foucault would say 'obsession'—with rational control epitomizes the goals of modernity. Modernity, in Foucault's analysis, can be understood as freeing individuals from the constraints of the Old Regime in order to subject them, for their own good, to the new disciplinary authorities of schools, factories, jails, hospitals, and state administrators. Forging together knowledge, profit, and power, the spread of the new disciplinary order provided a way of controlling large numbers of people, rendering their behaviour stable and predictable, without using uneconomical and ostentatious displays of sovereign power, in particular military or police force, which can risk open rebellion on the part of the masses.

Expert disciplines thus took shape at the intersections of words, things, and knowledge (Foucault 1973). Their regulatory discourses produce 'truth' in the sense that they supply systematic procedures for the generation, regulation, and circulation of statements. The knowledge produced is a part of the discursive practices by which rules are constructed, objects and subjects are defined, and events for study are identified and constituted. Such disciplines function in ways that can be almost totally appropriated by certain institutions (prisons and armies) or used for precise ends in others (hospitals and schools). At the same time, they remain irreducible to—and unidentifiable with—any particular institutional form or power in society. Rather, disciplines 'infiltrate' or 'colonize' modern institutions, linking them together, honing their efficiencies, and extending their hold. Professional disciplines, operating outside of (but in conjunction with) the state, are thus seen to predefine the very worlds that they have made the objects of their studies (Sheridan 1980).

For this reason, argue Foucault (1972) and his followers, the 'political' in the contemporary world can no longer be understood adequately in terms of dominant elites and centres of power. Whereas politics in modern political and social theory is largely explained in terms of institutionalized state power and law, mainly designed to impede or promote the action of individual citizens, from Foucault's point of view power is dispersed as well throughout the spectrum of social relations. Manifested in multiple and ubiquitous forms, political power no longer belongs to the state alone: it is everywhere. It is at work among psychiatrists who determine the social and medical status of homosexuality, the street-level social workers who interpret the categories of poverty, or the judges who decide the obligations of the father toward his family. Indeed, the very deception of modern politics, according to Foucault, is found in the practice of confining the location of power to the central government, filtering from awareness its many ever present forms (Foucault 1973; 1980). These newer forms of discursive power are basic to the professional discipline themselves. As the agents of expert discourses, professionals embody the techniques and practices that disperse power and social control away form the formal centres of governance.

Because this power is 'multiple' and 'ubiquitous', it is *exercised* rather than *possessed* per se. It cannot, in this respect, be identified as the privilege of a dominant elite class actively deploying it against a passive, dominated class. Disciplinary power in this sense does not exist in the sense of class power. Instead, it exists in an infinitely complex network of 'micro powers' that permeate all aspects of social life. The struggle against such power, Foucault argues, must be localized resistance designed to combat interventions into specific sites of civil society.

Foucaultians have generally been critical of the Habermasian emphasis on ideal discourse, portraying it as ahistorical and politically naive. From their historical-analytic perspective, as they assert, such an emphasis on ideal communication and better arguments can have little effect on the configurations of power in contemporary political systems. At worst, such discourses are themselves co-opted into the service of the very ends they seek to challenge. Habermasians, of course, are not without countercharges. They point to Foucault's neglect of the normative agency associated with discourse. In their view, he has theoretically structured himself into a corner that denies or underplays the role of discursive struggle against the pervasive nature of power. Indeed, Habermasians see this as historical naivety on the part of Foucaultians. Foucault (1984), in fact, later acknowledged this point, at least in part, and spoke of the need for resistance, although he mainly emphasized local resistances. Beyond this concession, in part in interviews before his death, he never worked this point out in any theoretical detail. Habermasians have, at the same time, had to recognize the implications of Foucault's deeper understanding of discursive power. There has thus been no shortage of debate—often strident in nature—between these two postempiricist perspectives. In Chapter 11 we will return to this question and offer a suggestion as to how these two theoretical perspectives might better understand one another, particularly as the issues pertain to policy deliberation and the practices of policy analysis.

At this juncture, we can leave behind the contributions of the competing policy theories and can pull together the primary threads of a postempiricist discursive approach to policy inquiry. While there is no firmly established body of principles underlying this perspective, it is possible to underscore the essential elements that constitute this relatively new theoretical orientation.

POSTEMPIRICISM AS DISCURSIVE POLICY INQUIRY

A discursive policy approach takes a more fundamental view of language and discourse. In contrast to the relatively moderate view of ideas-based researchers in the policy mainstream, who in large part see ideas to be one of a variety of competing explanatory factors (along with interests, institutions, culture, and so forth), the discourse approach sees the medium of language as constituting the very meanings upon which ideas are constructed. Instead of seeing ideas as one of the many variables influencing politics and policy, the approach sees language and discourse as having a more underlying role in structuring social action. In this view, the very terrain of social and political action is constructed and understood in terms of the languages used to portray and talk about political phenomenon. Discourse theory, in this respect, focuses as much on the meta-politics of institutions and action as it does on events and arguments as they more immediately present themselves (Shapiro 1981: 2–3). Focused as such on the commitments (political and intellectual) that are logically anterior to policy concepts, discourse analysts look first at the rules that govern and make possible a policy deliberation. Without denying the importance of the actual deliberation *over* competing ideas, they stress the ways in which policy argumentation is influenced or shaped by the languages of the different kinds of discourses within which they are framed—scientific, legalistic, or everyday.

On this view, the use of language—words and speech—is important, but not just in a linguistic sense. Discourse here is grounded in the awareness that 'language does not simply offer a mirror or picture of the world, but instead profoundly shapes our view in the first place' (Fischer and Forester 1993: 1). Linguistic discourse and communicative interaction are understood to be the primary reasons that the social world differs both ontologically and epistemologically from the physical world. Embedded in the practices of a society, the language of a discourse can never be understood as a fixed or closed set of rules. Always based on the interpretations of both those who speak it and those who receive it, discursive meanings, motives, and actions can never be determined by the words alone.

In this respect, it is also important to recognize that, while ideas fit into an overarching category of 'mind', discourse pertains to the category of language. As Torgerson points out, 'the shift to discourse involves a transfer of ideas out of the context of mind to the context of language'. Although the focus of most policy theorists on ideas moves—intentionally or unintentionally—beyond an empirical-analytic focus (as either apprehension of sense date or logical deduction), it still problematically tends to preserve the Kantian possibility of the 'individual mind' and the view that all ideas and actions originate with individuals (a position known as 'methodological individualism'). For the discursive turn, in contrast, language and ideas are irreducible to the individual. Whereas the focus on ideas still makes possible the separation of the subjective thinker and the object world, as Torgerson puts it, 'the discursive approach rejects this "subject–object" dualism by understanding that inquiry is part of the same discursive medium that it studies'. Thus, 'from the discourse perspective there is no safely privileged space for the inquirer, no place of autonomous reason beyond the discursive medium which all share in one way or another' (Torgerson 2002). This common connection, as we shall see, is also the epistemological link to democratic politics.

Rather than just reflections of action, speech and discourse are themselves on this view understood as forms of social action (Austin 1962). Through the signs and symbols of a language, people construct their social world and the political actions they undertake to influence it. As such, communicative power is also understood to be 'capacity-giving' (Litfin 1994: 15–23). In the framing of political questions and programmatic solutions, language and discourse exercise their own effects on the policy decision processes. While they can never stand altogether free from interests and institutions, ideas can be, as John (1998: 157) puts it, 'independent in the sense that discourse has its own rules which structure how the public and policymakers perceive policy issues' (an example being the logical structure of the story, to which we return in Chapter 8).

In a sense, one can draw an analogy here with a foreign language. As anyone who has learned a language knows, the names of objects and phenomena are constructed in different ways. In some cases you can find a directly corresponding word or phrase, but in others the concept is formulated in a different way—perhaps it has to be described in more words, perhaps it is approached from a different angle. In both instances, it often offers the foreign speaker a different way of looking at the phenomenon. The difference can be only a matter of curiosity, or it can present a very different way of seeing and understanding.[10] For the discourse analyst, the same can be true of the different languages of political discourse, whether of liberalism or conservatism, of the worker or the manager, or of the rich man or the pauper. Each supplies a different way of experiencing the world, which in turn is organized through a specific way of speaking. Educational psychologists, for example, have shown the ways in which different modes of talking, particularly in the form of dialects, serve to socially differentiate, categorize, or segregate groups of children in school (Labov 1972; 1982). Or take the contemporary example of hip-hop in the black community in the US. While educated highbrows find the words of hip-hop atrocious, it expresses a particular way of experiencing and knowing the world. Indeed, it serves as a medium for social solidarity in a struggle over personal recognition and identity.

Implicit in such speech is an elaborate set of understandings—both stated and tacit—that tell the story of a particular social situation, including who the good guys are and who is responsible for the social disadvantages. Parts of the story are condensed into particular symbols, such as a gesture or a way of walking, that very

---

[10] For example, the German language applies the word 'scientist' (*Wissenschaftler*) to both the physicist and the literary scholar. Whereas in English the word 'scientist' refers to someone who employs specific empirical methods, in German it refers more generally to systematic inquiry. Thus, in the German language the 'two cultures' distinction dividing science and the humanities is not as problematic as it is in English. Or take the French word for 'fact' (*fait*). Preserving in part the Latin meaning of 'factum' (defined as 'made'), *fait* means both 'fact' and 'made'. This serves to more easily draw attention away from 'fact' as hard or objective phenomenon. It is easily compatible with the social constructionist understanding of a fact as something made, understood as socially constructed.

economically reproduce them without ever having to be explicitly told.[11] In their
various forms, it is these underlying assumptions and presuppositions that determine
how different groups understand ideas and arguments and how they respond to them
in the world of action.

   To bring the point more directly to bear on contemporary political discussion, consider the fact that no one has ever seen a political system or economy, despite the fact
that we talk about them as if we had. A political system, for example, is a linguistic
concept discursively invented and employed to describe a set of relationships that we
can only partly experience—one goes to the voting booth, appears as a witness in a
court case, visits parliament, speaks with a political representative, and so on. But
no one ever sees an entire political system. While we can directly encounter parts of
a political system or discover its effects, the system itself remains a set of formal and
informal relationships that can be constructed and discussed only through language.
A political system, in this way, shares similar features with the physicist's molecule,
or the psychologist's concept of a personality, each of which cannot be directly
observed and have to be theoretically constructed. We see the parts of a political systems more through its effects than through the actual operations. To explain the operations of its components we must in large part rely on a combination of reports from
those who were there—as in most cases we ourselves were not there—measured
against various interpretations of what the outcomes mean. That is, we have to interpretively judge the behaviours of political actors in significant part against their outcomes. As interpretations rather than hard evidence, such judgements always remain
open to reconsideration. Even though we speak of these actions as if our understandings are hard and concrete, they are in reality the narrative stories we construct
as plausible explanations. What we take to be 'fixed truths' are only the stories that
have over time come to be consensually accepted as plausible by a significant number
of people, including influential interpreters of political events, such as journalists,
political elites, scholars, and the like.

   What does this mean for political inquiry? As Shapiro (1981: 231) puts it,
'insofar as we do not invent language or meanings in our typical speech, we end up
buying into a model of political relations in almost everything we say without
making a prior, deliberate evaluation of the purchasing decision'. Thus, given that
the languages of politics inscribe the meanings of a policy problem, public policy is
not only expressed in words, it is literally 'constructed' through the language(s) in
which it is described. To offer a simple but clear example, it makes an important difference whether policy deliberations over drug addiction are framed in a medical or
a legal discourse. That is, to say something one way rather than another is to also
implicitly say a whole host of other things, which will be grasped by some and not
by others. In this way, a political 'agenda is established out the history, traditions,
attitudes, and beliefs of a people encapsulated and codified in the terms of its political
discourse' (Howlett and Ramesh 1995: 110; Jenson 1991). A discursive approach not

---

[11] For a good example, see Mandela's (1994) discussion of how black South Africa prisoners communicated with each other in jail, deceiving their white Afrikaner guards.

only examines these discourses, but seeks to determine which political forces lead to their construction.

Whereas empiricist social science has mainly treated discursive meanings as 'the psychological icing on the cake of social behavior', the discursive approach understands these social meanings to be constitutive of and embedded in social behaviour (Gibbons 1987*a*: 140). That is to say, commonly accepted inter-subjective meanings are embedded in the very institutions and practices of society; and without them these institutions and practices would be dramatically different, if they existed at all. In short, these social entities cannot be discussed independently of them. Social meanings, in short, cannot simply be abstracted and treated as one of the various variables explaining institutions.

Gibbons (1987*a*: 139) illustrates the position with an examination of the legitimacy of the social welfare state. Standard approaches, he explains, treats legitimacy 'as a question that can be divorced from the description and explanation of the working of the polity'. When the question is raised, moreover, legitimacy is understood in terms of the individual actor's psychological orientations rather than being inherent to the larger social system. Instead of being just a set of subjective attitudes about political behaviour, these discursive meanings are an essential part of the way of life in the social welfare state. Not only do these social meanings make the social welfare state what it is, they are a necessary part of the explanation of the social and political action of the citizens within in.[12] As Gibbons (1987*a*: 140) explains, 'without these intersubjective meanings and the variety of political, economic, and social practices that they inform, the actions, behavior, and everyday life of the citizens within the... political economy would be radically different'.

Like neo-institutionalists, discursive policy analysts are thus interested in the way that ideas and values are embedded in discourses of institutions. Indeed, most discourse analysts are themselves neo-institutionalists in one way or another. But they mainly see such discursive patterns to reflect a much more pervasive system of power than do mainstream neo-institutionalists. Discourse theory moves in this respect from the ideas of actors influencing or shaping the play of interests in institutions to an understanding of discourse itself as a medium of power, or what Foucault (1980; 1984) called the 'politics of discursive regimes'. Depending on which neo-institutionalists one reads, the interpretation of embedded ideas and discourses can sound somewhat similar. For the discourse approach, as we examine in more detail in Chapters 4 and 5, ideas are not understood as an objective, separable component of an institution subject to empirical analysis or as the inherent, defining feature of an institution. For the discourse analyst the institution itself is constituted by the discourse. That is, the institution loses its established meanings outside of the discourse. There is no objective institution independent of these meanings. The discourse, as such, exercises its own independent power effect on institutional behaviour, which

---

[12] An interpretive account of the US social welfare state, for example, rests on various social meanings that are constitutive of the American way of life. They would include the democratic relationship between the state and the citizens; the promise of economic security and well-being; and a supportive family life (Gibbons 1987*a*: 140).

can be assessed only interpretively. For discourse theory the explanatory process associated with both institutions and discourses is inherently interpretive. From this perspective, the play of institutional politics, at both the micro and the macro levels, is situated within a competition over different understandings of socio-institutional reality. Empirical considerations come into play, but only as they are woven into the various narrative constructions. When factual understandings are founded on a wide consensus, they can help to make some constructions more plausible than others. But in political and social life they are never detached from the narrative constructions. This is the nature of the reality that the social sciences investigate.

As in the policy network literature, the importance of expert discourses is a central feature of discursive politics, especially among those who follow Foucault. But such professional discourses are seen as much more than a way to bring reason—in particular technical reason—to bear on the play of power. Whereas policy network theorists largely understand experts to exercise power by virtue of their possession of or access to information, discourse theorists understand experts to be part of a larger power–knowledge relationship who have, as such, the ability to constitute, control, and legitimize the very issues that we take to be the subjects of deliberation. Rather than understanding power and discourse to be properties of particular actors, which assumes that knowledge and interests are distinct, expert ideas and discourses can themselves be powerful entities. Network theorists perpetuate the fact-value distinction between causal knowledge and normative beliefs, but discourse analysts hold them together by looking at the ways experts frame and interpret information.

Social learning is also an important concept in discourse theory, but discursive analysis calls for a deeper understanding that allows for more than a narrow technical focus on the exchange of policy-analytic information and empirical findings. For such discourse theorists the most important part of social learning—in fact the things that make it 'social' learning—are 'reality shifts', or learning different ways to see the world. Indeed, such learning is the very thing that justifies speaking of 'social' learning. Such an approach insists on a much less instrumental and more political understanding of policy learning, as we shall see in Chapter 5. In this respect, postempiricist theorists are fundamentally interested in the question of rationality. Building on a critique of the technocratic understanding of rationality (exemplified, for example, in rational choice theory), they emphasize a more comprehensive approach that not only integrates empirical and normative discourse but is highly dependent on social context (a discussion spelled out more elaborately in Chapter 9). Indeed, in this view, rationality is itself embedded in social contexts.

For discourse scholars, then, political action is constituted by discourses, from hegemonic discourses embedded in the existing institutions (for example, the theories and practices of liberal capitalism) to the oppositional efforts of other groups attempting to create new discourses (for example, environmentalism). Public policies are not only influenced by the discourses of particular groups, they are shaped and supported by the institutional processes in which specific discursive practices are embedded, processes which can have a life of their own. Though such claims about the importance of discourse are not altogether unrelated to the concerns of interest-based or institutional explanations of public policy, discursive policy analysts see discourse as an alternative way to approach political action. In important ways, this work seeks to develop Weber's understanding of how ideas and images determine the paths along with action travels. Interests do not disappear but they are shaped and at times driven by ideas. In seeking to determine how ideas construct both material interests and social reality, the discourse perspective insists on conceptualizing these processes through the kinds of interpretive methods that Weber himself helped to spell out for the social sciences. They pose, in the process, a view of explanation that rekindles the classical debates in social science and philosophy about of the nature and origins of social structure and human agency.

The policy process, in this conception, is still about gaining and exercising power. But the process is mediated through competing discourses (including hegemonic and challenging discourses) that reflect—often subtly—the distribution of power. Without ignoring concrete actions per se, it places analytical emphasis on the struggle over the meaning of the ensuing political events and actions. Political struggle, including struggle about interests, is carried out through a fight about ideas, beliefs, and values. Interests are still very much present, but they are constructed by—or infused with—systems of ideas. In the process of struggle, as Stone (1988: 28) explains, participants seek to define, classify, and delimit the understandings of the concepts that bear on political action. Behind their competing policy arguments are ideas about responsibility and blame that mirror basic political power relationships underlying the social order.

In this understanding, policy analysts socially construct facts that, in the play of politics, are contested by stakeholders and other interested participants. The orientation of the discursive policy analyst, for this reason, is one of scepticism and critique rather than truth-seeking per se. In the process, it is argued, critical discourses can often do more than legitimize policy; they can also liberate it from the narrow play of interests. The process of argumentation can rediscover and rejuvenate the humane and democratic values implicit in modern liberal institutions. By unleashing the emancipatory possibilities embedded in such traditions, it can help to counter the manipulatory symbolic politics that define much contemporary politics, as well as technocratic approaches to both policymaking and policy analysis.

CONCLUSION

In this chapter we explored the return in policy studies of an interest in ideas and discourse. Much of this more recent work has emerged to deal with problems of explanations based on interests and structure. The discussion shifted to a focus on how political and social ideas define the kinds of problems that government come to deal with. Towards this end, we examined an array of perspectives. Drawing on Weber, we saw the way in which ideas can both determine and shift the political tracks along which self-interested action travels. We then surveyed the general social psychological findings about the effects of beliefs and attitudes on social behaviour, before turning to the theory of neo-institutionalism and the way in which ideas can become embedded in institutional practices. From there we saw the ways in which policy network theory, including epistemic communities and learning, draws attention to knowledge elites working in the various policy subsystem. Such a politics of expertise, particularly given its mainly technocratic character, often makes it difficult for other politicians and citizens to effectively participate in policy decision-making. From this orientation we explored how the dominant ideas of expert communities can significantly control the way other political actors think about and decide policy issues.

All of these perspectives, mainly emerging from the mainstream of the discipline, have largely understood ideas to be one of the various factors that have to be taken into consideration, along with interests and structures. For the most part, they have emphasized the role of ideas and beliefs in the processes of political and policy argumentation. It is here, as we saw, that postempiricists enter the picture. It is not that they deny these perspectives. Indeed, as we saw, they owe much to them as a platform from which they have launched a deeper, more constitutive conception of discourse. Drawing on the Habermas's critical theory of communication and Foucault's post-structural theory of discursive power, especially with reference to expert disciplines such as planning and policy analysis, we outlined the discourse approach's meta-theoretical emphasis on language and power.

On this view, the use of language is important, but not just in a linguistic sense. Discourse here is grounded in the awareness that language profoundly shapes our view of the socio-political world rather than merely mirroring it. Embedded in the practices of a society, the language of a discourse can never be understood as a fixed or closed set of rules. Always based on the interpretations of both those who speak it and those who receive it, discursive meanings, motives, and actions take their meanings from the institutional-discursive contexts in which they are uttered (a perspective which we examine more carefully in Chapters 4 and 5).

Finally, to anticipate an essential question, what does this admittedly unusual way of talking about policy and policy institutions mean for practicing policy analysts? How does the discursive policy analyst go about advising his or her client? These questions we take up in Parts III and IV. Before that we need to more fully clarify the socially constructed nature of reality and the symbolic sides of policy, as well as the discursive politics to which it gives rise.

3

to build or form putting together p frame; devise

Public Policy as Discursive Construct: Social Meaning and Multiple Realities

and have their worlds socially constructed by family, community (inherited)

The starting point for a postempiricist discursive alternative to contemporary policy inquiry begins with the recognition that the human and physical realms are inherently different. The reason has to do with social meaning. Whereas physical objects have no intrinsic meaning structures, human actors actively construct their social worlds. They do so by assigning meaning to events and actions, both physical and social. Human experience, as such, is enveloped in a non-material social, cultural, and personal realm of thought and meanings.

It is not that all people are constructing and reconstructing their worlds all of the time. On the contrary, most of the time we live in a social world into which we were born, a world of meaning generally taken for granted by the people who live in it. Given their socialization, it comes to them more or less as a given, fixed reality and they treat it as such. People realize, of course, the world was established before they arrived. The point is that many of the ideas and social understandings upon which their world was constructed are difficult to recognize or identify. They are typically buried in everyday practices and accepted as part of the nature of things. Indeed, for many, these ideas and beliefs come to give the impression of being natural, or perhaps obvious, in the language of the everyday world. Even when people do have an appreciation of these ideas and meanings, the original meanings of their forefathers are not immediately or obviously accessible to them. It may be the case that these ideas or meanings were appropriate at that time, but no longer relevant or right for a new generation and its social circumstances. For instance, it is common today in the Western world to accept that women are equal to men and should have the same rights. But, as feminists are quick to point out, numerous laws and practices still in existence have their origins in a time when women were seen as inferior.[1]

One of the main features of the politics of social change—indeed often the main feature—is the calling of particular meanings into question. Movements concerned with issues such as civil rights, women's liberation, or environmental protection have organized their struggles around calling attention to underlying social assumptions and their less obvious implications for contemporary life.[2] Thus, while most of us

---

[1] A good example is employment practices. Why, for example, do women still get less pay than men for the same job?

[2] Environmentalists, for instance, have shown that nature has been defined differently at different times by different people. Where industrialists have viewed the environment as a source of natural resources to be exploited for productive gain, American Indians and other aboriginal groups have understood the environment to be mother earth and sought to live in harmonious balance with its natural requirements.

are first and foremost products of our social environment, we also can be agents affecting the world in which we live. Not everybody assumes the role of agent of social and political change. But the activities of those who do are among the main objects of political inquiry.

If the first principle of a phenomenological or interpretive perspective is an emphasis on meanings in the construction and understanding of social reality, the second is that social meanings are always potentially open to reconstruction and change. The social world of the individual or the collective is constantly enlarged by new experiences and thoughts; it is continuously in the process of evolving through reflection, practices, and communication with others. Changing over time through the interaction of people's cognitive schemes with their social environment, the social world is an interpretive linkage of social perceptions, recollections, and expectations, all of which are grounded in subjective experience and understanding of the social and physical realms.

This understanding of social reality has profound import for the way we approach the study of social and political inquiry. Based on social meanings—motives, intentions, goals, purposes, values, and so forth—social action is constructed through language and, as such, its analysis has more in common with history and literature than with physical science. Rather than seeking proofs through formal logic and empirical experimentation, the investigation of social action requires the use of metaphoric processes that pull together and connect different experiences based on perceived similarities. The meaning of a social experience is assessed in terms of its position in the larger patterns of which it is a part, be it a situation, a social system, or an ideology.

Because social meanings change, there can be no fixed or lasting set of meanings associated with the actors and events that constitute social and political life. To be sure, some meanings can last for generations and be approached as relatively fixed. But there are no firm social categories in which positivists can empirically anchor their methods. Even when social meanings last for longer durations, they still have to be seen as related to a particular time and place. This is to say, there can be no universal interpretations that are applicable without reference to social context.

The neglect of this basic nature of social reality by empiricist social science has had profound implications for political and policy inquiry. The failure to carefully connect or relate empirical findings to the social understandings of those under investigation is a root cause of the problem. By treating the meanings of their findings as clear or evident, empiricist social scientists assign to them in effect the social understandings of the dominant social groups. In a world of dominant and subordinate groups, this practice wittingly or unwittingly supports the conception of the socio-political world advanced by social and political elites. This failure to translate empirical findings into a set of social meanings germane to the full play of politics underlies the charge of social irrelevance that has plagued sociology, political science, and, yes, even economics. If the pretence that empirical findings speak for themselves has managed to endure in ivory tower social science, it becomes a problem rather quickly in an applied field of inquiry such as policy analysis, where the explicit goal is to facilitate real-world decision processes. These processes, as we see below, are entirely interwoven with dominant and competing systems of social meaning.

Despite the continuing dominance of empiricism in the social and policy sciences, the implications of social science's neglect of the value-laden social meanings inherent in social and political action has long been understood by the critics, in particular political philosophers and interpretive social scientists. That this polemic still has to be engaged, despite recognition of the methodological implications associated with dealing with meaningful action, is more than a little astonishing. The endurance of empiricism in the face of the success of this critique only underscores the power of a scientific ideology.

Basic to the postempiricist critique has been an analytical differentiation between two fundamental traditions of knowing—causal explanation of the type sought by the physical sciences (concerned with establishing relations between causes and effects) and the kind of social understanding central to the social world. Because the arguments for scientific causal explanation are best known, coupled with the fact that we deal with them more extensively in Chapter 6, we concentrate here on the concept of social understanding.

THE PHENOMENOLOGY OF SOCIAL ACTION

Whereas positivist-oriented empirical analysis aims at causal explanation and prediction of behaviour, social understanding requires a teleological explanation related to goals and purposes. In the traditions of sociology, following the great German sociologist Max Weber, such explanation is referred to as the process of *Verstehen*. *Verstehen* identifies the process of rendering facts *understandable* by interpreting their meanings in the light of relevant social goals and values.

The origins of *Verstehen* sociology can be traced to philosophers and social scientists influenced by the philosophy of phenomenology. Although the label 'phenomenologist' captures a somewhat mixed group, by and large the works of Alfred Schutz (1967) and his followers, especially Berger and Luckmann (1966), have been seminal in the interpretivist debate with the positivist approach. The special value of the phenomenological movement has been its deep-seated critique of social science inquiry itself. No other theoretical orientation has devoted as much effort to the explication of the distinction between the social and physical worlds and the methodologies appropriate to each.

The crucial question of a phenomenological interpretive social science revolves around the applicability of objective, empirically oriented methods to the subjectively based problems of the social world. Concerned fundamentally with the role of social meaning, the interpretivist objection to the use of physical science techniques is that the physical world possess no intrinsic meaning structure. As Schutz (1962: 5) explained, it is up to the physical scientists 'to determine which sector of the universe of nature, which facts and which events therein, and which aspects of such facts and events are topically relevant to their specific purpose'. The data and events within the observational field of the physical scientist do 'not "mean" anything to the molecules, atoms and electrons therein'.

I agree!

The social realm, unlike the physical realm, is inherently laden with subjective meaning. For the social inquirer, the observational field has 'a particular meaning and relevance structure for the human beings living, thinking and acting therein. The human subjects have preselected and preinterpreted this world by a series of commonsense constructs which determine their behavior, define the goal of the actions [and] the means available—which help them find their bearings in their natural and socio-cultural environment and to come to grips with it' (Schutz 1962: 5–6). Thus, the social world is an organized universe of meaning experienced and interpreted by everyday social actors. Social knowledge is in significant part the product of these common-sense interpretations that, when combined with the social actors' personal experience, forms an orientation toward the everyday world that is taken for granted.

The social actor's constructs, as first-order constructs of social reality, pose a fun- ← damental methodological implication for social scientists. Unlike physical scientists, social scientists cannot establish from the outside which events and facts are interpretationally relevant to the actor's own specific purposes. The constructs of social science must take the form of second-order constructs. The crux of the problem, as such, is how to establish and maintain a systematic relationship between social scientists' second-order explanations and the everyday first-order explanations of the social actors under investigation.

The failure of the empiricist approach is its inability to incorporate an adequate account of the social actor's subjective understanding of the situation. By focusing on the observable dimensions of a social phenomenon, empiricists observe the social world from a different angle from that of their subjects. The empiricists' models, in short, tend to be constructed around the researcher's own implicit assumptions and value judgements about reality. They thus drift away from the social context by tacitly substituting their own view of the relevant aspects of the situation for the social actors' understanding of the social realities. These tacit value assumptions are usually difficult to observe since they are buried in the foundations of the empiricists' theoretical model.

To accurately explain social phenomena, the investigator must first attempt to understand the meaning of the social phenomenon from the actor's perspective. Such an understanding is derived by interpreting the phenomenon against the social actor's own motives and values. A good example is offered by the policy analytic approach of Schuman (1982). Following the theoretical insights of Schutz, Schuman conducted a phenomenological examination of higher education policy in the United States by letting the students speak for themselves.

Schuman's goal was to reveal the everyday meanings of going to a university for both college students and those who chose not to attend. After reviewing the standard kinds of statistically-based explanations about why students are said to go to college—mainly to earn a better living—he showed through extensive interviews that such objective analysis cannot capture the much more complicated sets of reasons and motives involved in decisions to both go to and stay in college. Economics-related statistics simply missed the intricate web of reasons and motives that bear on such decisions. Letting the students speak for themselves revealed the statistics to be accurate, but not right. As Schuman (1982: 29) puts it, they are not wrong, but at the same time you can't say that they are correct. The problem with such statistical explanations, he shows, is that they deal with only a very small part of the student's reality and thus go astray because of exclusion. In short, the meaning of these statistics as they relate to the students can be understood only by examining them in terms of the configuration of factors that structure their personal social context. To know what college means to people, he argues, we must get them to reveal both their way of seeing the world and the world in which they are living.

Despite the many misunderstandings that have surrounded this process of *Verstehen*, it does not signal a return to an explanatory technique based on empathy or intuitive understanding of the motives and reasons behind observed social action (Morrow 1994). From Schutz's perspective, *Verstehen* is not an instrument of explanation but rather a process of concept formation employed in arriving at an interpretive understanding of social phenomena. The focus of the interpretive process is on the social actor's meaning rather than the intuitive or empathic mental processes of the observer. Interpretive understanding, in this respect, does not deny the need for verification, as implied by intuitive conceptions of *Verstehen*. Instead, it calls attention to the fact that any method that permits the observer to select and interpret social facts in terms of his or her own private value system can never produce a socially relevant, valid theory.

A couple of illustrations can help to clarify this point. If the empiricist social scientist wants to explain why Mr X is more actively engaged in politics than Ms Y, he or she may appeal to an empirically established casual finding in the empirical literature: men are more active politically than women. The interpretive political scientist, however, is likely to ask whether this type of causal reference really provides sufficient information to enable one to understand the situation. Most people confronted with this question would ask to be supplied with additional information. What are Mr X's reasons and motives for his political involvement? Does he seek to gain moral approbation? Is he determined to protect certain strongly held beliefs? Does he think political involvement will further his business career?

The limitation of a causal explanation is even better illustrated in historical situations. Take the case of Neville Chamberlain's action at Munich in 1938. Would it be productive to ask: what always causes a Chamberlain at a Munich in 1938 to do exactly the sort of thing the actual Chamberlain did there and then? (Dray 1957). The interpretivist's contribution here is to show that the historian works to marshal the facts and norms of the situation to illustrate that Chamberlain's actions can be explained as the logical outcome of a specific configuration of factors. The task is to demonstrate that, given certain motives and purposes, it was (or was not) logical for the man to act in a specific way in such a situation.

Inquiring into social meaning is not to be dealt with as an uncontrollable or indeterminable aspect of social discourse. Aimed at mutual understanding through acculturation and commonly shared social learning, social understanding can in many cases be subjected to tests of valid inference. Because of the intermingling of factual and normative elements, though, such inferential tests generally follow a different path from those rendered by empirical analysis. The nature of the process can be nicely illustrated with a courtroom analogy. In a court trial, subjective perceptions of facts and reasons are submitted to a number of inferential and documentary tests. The judge and the jury, for example, do not simply impute reasons and motives to the defendant, however plausible they may sound. Documentary evidence and testimony must be produced in support of an explanation formulated in terms of 'reasons' for behaviour rather than causes in the strict sense of the term. The verdict is reached by bringing together the external evidence and the defendant's publicly stated subjective intentions. It is the task of the judge and the jury to interpret the defendant's social behaviour against a reconstruction of what they take to be the facts.

Following this line of argument, it can scarcely be said that interpretive understandings are arbitrary. Although answers are not worked out by rigid adherence to the scientific methods of demonstration and verification, interpretive understandings can be based on the giving of reasons and the assessment of arguments. In such analysis, the task is to show how certain circumstances *logically* entitle a specific opinion or way of viewing things. The relationship of the belief to a decision or action is not external and contingent (like causes) but internal and logical. Even though such argumentation is not based on certainty in the scientific sense, it is possible to have a significant degree of confidence in a well-reasoned interpretation of social action, a topic we examine in more detail in Chapter 7 on interpretive policy analysis.

THE SOCIAL CONSTRUCTION OF REALITY

Whereas phenomenology is basically a philosophical orientation that has shaped the interpretivist perspective in the social sciences, the interpretivist emphasis on multiple social realities has given rise to various theoretical lines of investigation. The contemporary variant most important to postempiricist policy analysis is social constructionism, also more simply referred to as constructionism. Social constructionism refers to the varying ways in which the social realities of the world are shaped and perceived (Gergen 1999). Although there are theoretical differences among those who call themselves social constructionists, they share a common concern for how people assign meaning to the world.

The idea of social constructionism has it origins in the sociology of knowledge (Berger and Luckmann 1967; Mannheim 1936). Most basically, it is an inquiry into the ways objects are seen through different mental structures or world views, how they are interpreted in different social circumstances and understood during different historical periods. Because social constructs are so much a part of our way of life, it is often difficult to recognize them as constructions. Their identification and explication, for this reason, relies heavily on the interpretive or hermeneutic methods of social inquiry, which we discuss in some detail in Chapters 6 and 7.

The social constructionist approach is of particular relevance to policy analysis for two reasons. One is its major influence on the field of science and technology studies, a focus of inquiry with direct bearing on the methods and techniques of policy science (Latour and Woolgar 1979; Jasanoff 1990). Such theorists examine the ways in which scientific facts, experiences, events, and beliefs are constructed and certified to be true or valid. As we see in more detail in Chapter 6, the most basic insight of such work is that the very objects of inquiry are constituted through a mix of physical objects and social interactions. Science, for this reason, is seen to be better explained as a social process with similarities to many other social processes, rather than an objective methodology removed from social and subjective concerns. For example, those things taken to be the concepts and theories of the field are the product of a social consensus process among elite members of the scientific community rather than discovery and proof of a fixed social reality per se. The facts of science are thus determined as much by the assumptions underlying them as they are by empirical observations. The point is derived from studies of the physical science, but applies even more to the social sciences.

The other relevant way in which social constructionism has played a major theoretical role is the focus on social problems in sociology, an area of study closely related to public policy (Best 1989; Gusfield 1981; 1989). In so far as public policies are designed to address social problems, it is in many ways the same topic only dressed up somewhat differently. Originally, social problem theorists assumed that the existence of social problems such as drug addiction or crime were the direct outcomes of readily identifiable, visible objective social conditions. Contemporary constructionists now see them to be the products of activities of political or social groups making claims about putative conditions to public officials and agencies, with the recognition of the grievance depending on the success of their rhetorical campaign. Whereas social scientists, in the first instance, were regarded as experts employing scientific methods to locate and analyse those moral violations and advise policymakers on how to best cope with them, such problems in the constructivist view result from a sequence of events that develop on the basis of collective social definitions.

Best (1989), for example, points to three primary foci in the studying of the construction of social problems: the claims, the claims-makers, and the claims-making process. In the case of environmental politics, Hannigan (1995: 54–5), following Best, shows the ways the environmental problem is socially constructed as a multi-faceted construction which welds together a clutch of philosophies, ideologies, scientific specialities, and policy initiatives. He argues that six factors are forged together in the construction of the environmental problem: (1) scientific authority for and validation of claims; (2) existence of a popularizer who can bridge environmentalism and science; (3) media attention in which the problem is framed as novel and important; (4) dramatization of the problem in symbolic and visual terms; (5) economic incentives for taking positive action; and (6) emergence of an institutional sponsor who can ensure both legitimacy and continuity. Put differently, even if ozone levels in the atmosphere increase, without an effective interplay of these six factors drawing public attention to it, the ozone hole will not be a worrisome topic of public concern, let alone make it onto the political agenda. That is, from a political perspective, the problem would not exist.

Such constructionist analysis of social problems closely parallels the concerns and considerations that come into play in the policy agenda-setting process generally, involving first how an issue comes to be identified and defined and, second, how it gets on the political and governmental agendas (Cobb and Elder 1972; 1983; Clemons and MacBeth 2001: 175–233). In this sense, the constructionist perspective on social problems analyses the first step of the policy agenda-setting process, especially problem definition. A useful analytic example in the policy literature is offered by Linder (1995: 208–30), who supplies a framework of categories for identifying the rhetorical and problem elements involved in the social construction of a policy problem. Examining the public controversies in the US over the health risks posed by living in proximity to the electric and magnetic fields created by power lines, he demonstrates how the rhetorical elements of problem construction can be identified in terms of four analytic categories:

- the nature of the argumentative appeals and warrants (for example, as moralist or paternalistic premises);
- how scientific claims are treated in the controversy (for example, as decisive evidence or partisan advocacy);
- the image of the public underlying the rhetoric (for example, as victims or potential issue activists); and
- the image of the electro and magnetic fields (for example, as toxic hazard or socially perceived risk).

Linder then delineates four policy-analytic elements embedded in each of the rhetorical constructions:

- the policy objective (for example, health protection or the public's right-to-know);
- the type of policy intervention (for example, regulatory control or research support);
- the policy instrument (for example, limits on exposures or a public information campaign); and
- the objectionable errors (for example, false negatives or false positives).

POLITICS IN A WORLD OF MULTIPLE REALITIES

As the foregoing discussion makes clear, politics is about social meanings. It is about politicians, interest groups, and citizens who hold multiple and changing social meanings about the political actions and events that transpire in the world in which they operate. Indeed, the creation of meaning is a crucial dimension in the political manoeuvre for advantage: the construction of beliefs about events, policies, leaders, problems, and crises that rationalize or challenge existing inequalities. Such meaning creation is basic to the mobilization of support for particular actions as well as to efforts to immobilize the political opposition. While intimidation and coercion help to counter political resistance, the most basic strategy for generating support in a democratic system is the evocation of social and political interpretations that legitimize the desired course of action. Designed either to threaten or reassure—or both, depending on the interests of competing groups—such interpretations encourage people to be actively supportive or at minimum to remain quiescent.

Despite the fact that symbols and their multiple meanings create problems for the systematic empirical study of politics and public policy, there is no escaping their central role in the world of political action. Even though politics is generally discussed and pursued in practical terms, particularly in terms of consequences, it is always at the same time about the social meanings of problems and events. As every politician, journalist, or historian knows, political controversy and strategic behaviour turns on conflicting interpretations of events and actions. Political leaders are judged to be tyrannical or benevolent, economic and social policies as exploitative or just, and so on. Although the process takes different forms, it is witnessed throughout the ages in all political cultures.

Where do these social meanings come from? This is not an easy question. One thing is clear, though: they do not spring from thin air. Social meanings are the products of interactions among social actors. People decide the meaning of statements by considering them from the perspectives of others significant to them, through either direct communicative encounters or the 'inner speech' process involving imagined conversations with their intended or would-be interlocutors.

The social meaning upon which political discourses turn are mainly derived from moral or ideological positions that establish and govern competing views of the good society. Although contemporary parties and groups go to considerable effort to avoid explicit use of ideological language—more so in the United States than in Europe—the struggle over the allocation of political benefits and costs is always enveloped in the ideological contest. A political claim thus reflects and reinforces an ideology, a subject, and a reality. For example, those who accept and support the electoral outcomes of contests between the Republican and Democrat Parties in the United States wittingly or unwittingly sustain a construction of a world that generally treats the issues of class, race, gender, and inequality as secondary concerns.

Both the material and social worlds get their specific social meanings from the symbols of a world view or ideology. The language, objects, and rituals to which those in politics respond are more than abstract ideas. A symbol typically carries a range of diverse, often conflicting meanings that are an integral part of particular social or material situations. The experience of the symbols stands for the material condition and vice versa. Although the social–psychological processes through which this happens are not fully understood, the material foundations of the symbol is generally evident. Languages, objects, and actions that evoke social meanings presuppose that the evocation is a function of particular material and social conditions. Every sign, as Edelman (1988: 9) puts it, exercises its effect because of the specific content of privilege, disadvantage, frustration, aspiration, hope, and fear in which it is experienced.

Recognizing the degree to which linguistic symbols structure our understanding of politics is the first step in seeing that political language *is* in important ways political reality itself. As the medium of symbols, it is generally the language about political events, not the events themselves, that people experience. Even the political events that we personally witness take their meaning from the language that portrays them. For both participants and observers there is no other reality.[3]

Thus the potency of political language does not stem from its mere descriptions of a real world, as empiricists have maintained. Rather, it comes from its reconstruction of the world—its interpretations of past experiences, its evocation of the unobservable aspects in the present, and constructions of possibilities and expectations for the future. These features make language a powerful constitutive force within politics. And, as such, the ability to use it effectively is an essential resource in the unfolding of the political process.

By compelling us to examine the subtle connections between social meaning and language, the constructionist perspective makes us aware that the potential ambiguity of statements about social action invariably carries different meanings in different settings. For this reason, the analyst must carefully attend to the speaker's political language. As Edelman (1988: 104) explains, the use of political language is a clue to the speaker's view of reality at the time, just as an audience's interpretation of the same language is a clue to what may be a different reality for them. If there are no conflicts over meaning, the issue is not political, by definition.

This position is in no way intended to imply that all political arguments are either equally valid or entirely relative, a question we examine more closely in Chapter 9. The point is to recognize and appreciate that social situations and the discourses about them create political arguments that cannot be finally verified or falsified. Because a social problem is not a verifiable entity but a construction that furthers ideological interests, its explanation is bound to be part of the process of construction rather than a set of falsifiable propositions (Edelman 1988: 18). In short, a society of multiple realities and relative standards are all we ever achieve (Edelman 1988: 111). It is a reality that social scientists must accept and learn to deal with.

In so far as the aspects of events, leaders, and policies that most decisively affect current and future social well-being are uncertain or unknowable, the political language that depicts them is necessarily ambiguous. Even when there is consensus about an action or a statement, there will be conflicting assumptions about the causes of developments, the intentions of interest groups and public officials, and the consequences of the specific event. It is thus not just what can be observed that shapes public action and political support, but what must be assumed, supposed, or constructed. Is the president or prime minister a well-meaning leader who represents the common people's aspirations against the elitist liberals and intellectuals, or is he a front man for mean-spirited corporate executives and a menace to the poor? The answer depends on political ideology and social assumptions.

Reason and rationalizations are thus intertwined. There is no way to establish the validity of any of these positions that can necessarily satisfy those who have a material or moral reason to hold a different view. Indeed, given the intertwining of facts

---

[3] To put it more concretely, although we organize disciplines around the study of political systems and political economies, nobody has ever seen one of these entities. We can only see various pieces of the whole. Our understandings of these broader systems are interpretive constructions based on these partial views.

and interests, the hallmark of political argument is the near-impossibility of marshalling evidence that can persuade everyone. Pervasive in such argumentation are contradictions, ambiguities, and rhetorical evocations that reflect the material situations and ideological orientations of the political participants. In short, it is not reality in an observable or testable sense that shapes social consciousness and political action, but rather the ideas and beliefs that political language helps evoke about the causes of satisfactions and discontents.

To be sure, language is only one aspect of a political situation, but it is a critical one. Through language political phenomena are interpretively fitted into narrative accounts that supply them with social meanings acceptable to particular audiences and their ideologies. Although they are susceptible to political criticism, firmly held narratives manage time and again in suspending belief or critical judgement, in sustaining opposition, or marshalling political support despite events that create doubts that put them in question (Edelman 1988).

Even though there is nothing new about the role of symbols in politics, this emphasis on symbols takes on special meaning in the modern age of the mass media. As postmodernists point out, politics today has become something of a spectacle. In the study of politics we are especially indebted to Murray Edelman (1988) for this perspective, who in many ways was a postmodernist ahead of his time.

THE POLITICAL SPECTACLE AS HYPERREALITY

Politicians and the media, as Edelman has shown, have turned contemporary politics into a political spectacle that is experienced more like a stage drama rather than reality itself. Based on socially constructed stories designed more to capture the interest of the audience than to offer factual portrayal of events, the political spectacle is constituted by a set of political symbols and signifiers that continuously construct and reconstruct self-conceptions, the meaning of past events, expectations for the future, and the significance of prominent social groups. As an interpretation reflecting the diverse social situations of its audiences and the language and symbols to which they are exposed, the political spectacle attributes meanings to social problems, political leaders, and enemies that rationalize and perpetuate political roles, statuses, and ideologies. The spectacle of politics is a modern-day fetish, a creation in part of political actors that come to dominate the thoughts and activities of both its audience and the actors themselves.

The best-known example of the political spectacle is the American-style presidential campaign, which focuses more on the horse race than on the issues themselves. For at least a year before a presidential election the media turn the contest into a virtual soap opera that comes to fascinate a large portion of the society, despite its banality. For many observers, it has led to the near collapse of the American political culture (Agger 1990).

Postmodern analysis identifies this spectacle as part of the hyperreality that characterizes much of contemporary American society and increasingly European youth culture as well. Hyperreality pertains to a situation in which words, symbols, and signs are increasingly divorced from direct experiences in the social world. It refers, as such, to a process in postmodern society in which 'symbols can be thought of as float[ing] away ... to procreate with other symbols' (Fox 1995).

This free play of signifiers is based on the marketing and advertising practices of post-industrial society, where the design of products to which symbols have been attached become too complex for the consumer to master (Jameson 1992). As symbols lose their moorings, marketers take advantage of this and manipulate them by attaching them to other symbols. Thus, as Fox (1995) puts it, machines become sexy, cleaning fluids repair dysfunctional families, and to purchase a particular brand of coloured carbonated water is to signify membership in a generation.[4]

As signs increasingly break away from the objects or events they were designed to denote, any sort of concrete or empirical conception of reality loses its influence over them. In the process, such signs can in a certain way be understood to have a life of their own outside everyday experiential reality. Like sports celebrities and movie stars, politicians increasingly operate in this realm, especially evidenced in electoral campaigns. As public relations consultants and spin doctors manipulate the symbols of a media-driven political process, political symbols increasingly evince tenuous relations to the objects and events traditionally taken to be reality. One of the most interesting images of this state of affairs is drawn by the French philosopher Baudrillard (1989) in his book *America*. More than a little cynically, he offers a portrait of the American family travelling along the open highway in an automobile whose windows have been replaced by television screens.

Not all citizens are duped by such linguistic manipulations, but many do seem to take hyperreality to be reality itself. For those who recognize these manipulations, it has the effect of turning many of them off to politics generally. A phenomenon of considerable concern to serious observers of the political scene, its manifestations are decreasing levels of citizen participation, dwindling levels of voter turn-out, indifference to important issues, poor understanding of the issues, and low levels of civic involvement, among other things.

THE SOCIAL MEANINGS OF PUBLIC POLICIES

Maynard-Moody and Kelly (1993: 71) describe the policy process as a struggle over the symbols we invoke and the categories into which we place different problems and solutions, because ultimately these symbols and categories will determine the action that we take. On this view, a political community is made up of citizens who live in a web of independent associations fused together through shared symbols. In such a community, people envisage ideas about the good society and struggle for common, shared interests as well as their own personal interests (Stone 1988). Unlike contemporary policy analysis, such an interpretive policy analysis rejects the idea that individual interests are simply given. The analyst needs to account for how

---

[4] Fox applies this provocative perspective to the 'reinventing government' effort to reform public administration during the Clinton administration.

citizen get their images of the world in which they live, how they are socially constructed, and the ways these images shape individual interests and policy preferences.

Earlier we defined policy as a political agreement on a course of action or (inaction) designed to resolve or mitigate problems on the political agenda. This agreement, as Heclo (1972) explains, is an intellectual construct rather than a self-defining phenomenon. Discursively constructed, there can be no inherently unique decisions, institutions, or actors constituting a public policy that are only to be identified, uncovered, and explained. Public policy, as such, is an analytical category with a substantive content that cannot be simply researched; more fundamentally, it has to be interpreted. Hence, as Majone (1989: 147) adds, our understanding of a policy and its outcomes cannot be separated from the ideas, theories, and criteria by which the policy is analysed and described.

From a constructivist perspective, the basic political agreement upon which a policy rests refers to an understanding based on a set of normative and empirical beliefs. As Stone (1988) makes clear, the standard production model of policy fails to capture the nature of this understanding. The essence of policymaking, as she writes, is the struggle over ideas and their meanings. Recognizing that shared meanings motivate people to action and meld individual striving into collective action, ideas are the medium of exchange in policymaking, a mode of influence even more powerful than money, votes, or guns. As such, policymaking is a constant discursive struggle over the definitions of problems, the boundaries of categories used to describe them, the criteria for their classification and assessment, and the meanings of ideals that guide particular actions.

Each policy-related idea is an argument, or rather a set of arguments, favouring different ways of looking at the world. The task of the analyst is to examine the multiple understandings of what otherwise appears to be a single concept, in particular how these understandings are created and how they are manipulated as part of political strategy. Uncovering the hidden arguments embedded in each policy concept, Stone (2002) explains, can illuminate and even at times resolve the political conflicts that would otherwise only appear to be on the surface of the issue.

Conventionally, policy is described in instrumental terms as a strategic intervention to resolve or assist in resolving a problem. From this perspective, as we have seen, policy is analysed objectively in terms of efficiency or effectiveness. And this is not entirely wrong. But it neglects the fact that the very same policy is a symbolic entity, the meaning of which is determined by its relationship to the particular situation, social system, and ideological framework of which it is a part. As Yanow (1996) puts it, policies are neither symbolic nor substantive. They are both at once. Even purely instrumental intentions are communicated and perceived through symbolic means (Yanow 1996:12). The creation and implementation of a policy is about the creation of symbols, with programme names, organizations and rituals, with even the design and decor of buildings being part of the language. In this formulation, notions of cause and effect need not disappear, as critics of interpretive analysis often suggest, but the focus on such relationships does not take precedence over interpretive analysis.

Much of the best constructivist research has to do with determining what is considered a policy problem and what is not, or what in policy studies is usually discussed as agenda-setting. In the constructionist view, the problems which governments seek to resolve are not just considered to have an 'objective' base in the economy or material structure of the society, but are also constructed in the realm of public and private discourse. They do not come into existence simply because they are there, or for their implications for well-being. As Edelman puts it (1988: 12), such problems come into discourse and therefore into existence as reinforcements of ideologies, not simply because they are there or because they are important for social welfare.

The ideologies and values underlying policies are often reflected in symbols. Created through language and communicative interaction, such symbols signify the meanings of particular events and offer standards for judging what is good and bad. Edelman (1977; 1988), for example, illustrates how words such as 'welfare' generate images that cause people to reject the claims of groups in need of social assistance. Because the interests of competing groups give rise to diverging meanings, as Edelman (1988: 15) puts it, national security is a different problem for each of the parties concerned with it, such as the various branches of the arms forces, the General Dynamics Corporation, that firm's workers, the Women's International Leagues for Peace and Freedom, and potential draftees. In this sense, a problem is the result of negotiations among groups with competing definitions. This can, of course, be understood as interest group politics, but it differs from the standard approach that sees each group pursuing its own interest in a particular context. Here groups have different interests, but they also define the problems and interests differently.

Given these subjective and less observable dimensions of policy, it is difficult to justify the conventional modes rational analysis. On those rare occasions when social well-being is not closely linked to value differences and objectives are comparatively non-controversial, the standard technical approach to policy analysis—adjusting efficient means to political ends—can play a role. In the real world of policy politics, though, the majority of the situations involve much more than the logic of effective means to achieve social goals. Moreover, means and ends are often inherently connected in such ways that make it difficult to see which is which. Is, for example, the death penalty a means to a necessary end, or it is an evil end unto itself? It depends on whom you ask.

What is more, the reasons political actors generally offer for their policy objectives are rationalizations designed to persuade particular audiences. Ideological arguments, writes Edelman (1988: 115), are typically advanced through a dramaturgy of objective description, which masks the performative function of political language. In the name of such description, the acceptability of the policy argument ultimately depends on how effectively it succeeds in rationalizing the situation of its intended audience.

Although conventional policy analysis is devoted to uncovering and deciding objective facts, policy turns less on the *facts* of a controversy than on the meanings that it generates. Indeed, it is precisely that events are assigned different meanings by different groups that makes them politically controversial. Even when groups can come to an agreement on disputed facts, the question of what these facts mean to the situation is still open. A question such as whether drug addiction originates from the social inadequacies of the drug addicts themselves or is the product of particular social pathologies of life in poor neighbourhoods does not lend itself to unambiguous empirical answers.

To be sure, political news coverage and politicians' speeches about policy issues lead people to believe that policies are about factual problems and solutions. But the political construction of policy problems attaches them, both explicitly and implicitly, to normative symbols of right or wrong, good and bad. Conservatives, for example, often search for and insist on policy solutions that fit their ideological emphasis on free market-oriented solutions, regardless of the characteristics of the particular problem. Independently of its demonstrated effectiveness in dealing with a problem, a solution that emphasizes a greater role for government will be opposed as leading to the wrong kind of society. It is in this sense that a solution often goes out looking for a problem to solve.

Rather than taking the actions and assertions of politicians and policymakers as straightforward statements of intent, accounts of policy problems and issues are thus seen as devices for generating varying presuppositions about social and political events rather than factual claims. While the concept of a fact is not rendered meaningless, policy actions have to first and foremost be seen as resting on interpretations that reflect and sustain particular beliefs and ideologies. To be sure, empirical data and information play a role in policymaking, but their meaning is determined by how they fit into the particular arguments of an ideological framework. While the policy analyst can investigate the empirical dimensions of a problem and inform the political players of their findings, these research findings cannot be confused with an explanation of policy politics. The meaning of the 'facts' to the political actors is determined by political discourses and these meanings are what the political struggle is first and foremost about. The social problems that enter the policy process are thus social constructions built on an intermingling of empirical findings with social meanings and ideological orientations. To understand how a particular condition becomes constructed as a problem, the range of social constructions in the discourses and texts about it need to be explored in the situational context from which they are observed.

Furthermore, problems and the policies designed to deal with social problems are important determinants of which actors will have the authority and power to deal with the issues they raise.[5] As Baumgartner and Jones (1983) point out, when a policy is presented as dealing with a technical problem, professional experts will tend to dominate the decision process. When the political, ethical, or social dimensions are seen to be the primary characteristics, a much larger group of participants usually becomes actively involved.

Often social conditions fail to become problems because powerful political groups can strategically manoeuvre to block measures that benefit a particular group. The

---

[5] Cobb and Elder (1983) write that the question of who communicates what to whom, and how, and with what effects goes to the crux of the political process.

effective long-term strategy, however, is ideological. When the ideological premises for or against an action are embedded in the existing discourses, people will accept them as part of how the world works and not recognize them as ideological. To people who see black people as inferior, discrimination is not a problem.

Because there are generally long-standing agreements on many social practices, only a limited number of the many potential problems actually become problems. Perhaps the most powerful influence of news, discussion, and writing about policy problems is the immunity from notice and criticism they provide for serious conditions that are not on the accepted agenda for political consideration. By naming a policy one way rather than another, diverse and contradictory responses to a spectrum of political interests can be either revealed or hidden. Because an emphasis on policy inconsistencies and differences can generate unwanted political conflicts, policy names are often designed to reassure or assuage citizens and politicians. Politicians, for example, speak of peace-keepers rather than deadly missiles. In this way, policies portray accomplishments, while masking problematic actions and counter-productive strategies that offset or reverse claims of success. Similarly, Edelman (1971) has shown the ways in which political elites and opinion-makers frequently respond to social and economic problems by symbolic political actions designed to reassure the public without dealing concretely with the problems. Through the symbolic manipulation of political language, political leaders at times create public expectations that can be satisfied by symbols of political action rather than action itself.

Finally, it is important to recognize that ambiguous meanings often have important political functions. Seeking to satisfy different interest groups at the same time, government policies often comprise a sequence of ambiguous claims and actions that contain logical inconsistencies. Given the would-be irrationality of the process, policy scientists have devoted a good deal of energy to developing strategies for circumventing this inconvenient aspect of political reality. What they have generally missed, however, is the degree to which such work enables conflicting groups to find ways to live with their differences. By helping to bring together citizens with varying policy preferences, ambiguity often facilitates cooperation and compromise. Enabling politicians to blur or hide problematic implications of controversial decisions, ambiguity can assist in sidestepping barriers that otherwise block consensus-building. People who benefit from the same policy but for different reasons can more easily find ways to agree. As Cobb and Elder (1983) explain, the ambiguity of symbols provides a vehicle through which diverse motivations, expectations, and values are synchronized to make collective action possible.

Numerous studies have shown the way legislatures seek to satisfy demands to do something about problems by passing vague statutes with ambiguous meaning. Legislators can placate both sides in a conflict by rhetorically supporting one side of the issue but making the actual decision more in the favour of the other side. By helping both sides feel better off with a policy agreement, legislators can facilitate negotiation and compromise by allowing opponents on both sides of an issue to proclaim success from a single policy decision. Because ambiguity allows participants to read themselves into collective programmes and actions, individuals can reconcile their own ambivalent and inconstant attitudes. In this way, the ambiguity of symbols helps coalitions form where pure material interests would divide potential members. It can quell resistance to policies by reassuring at the same time as the actual policies divide.

In the remainder of the chapter we illustrate this perspective with three cases of policy research that explicitly employ a constructionist approach to public policy. Both demonstrate the usefulness of the perspective in dealing with problems confronting policy research.

MEANING CONSTRUCTION AND THE POLICY PROCESS: THE TYPOLOGIES OF PUBLIC POLICY

The first example comes from the work of Peter Steinberger (1980), who has shown the ways in which a phenomenological perspective can both reformulate and research a problem long associated with one of the most influential contributions to policy research, namely, Lowi's typological classification of public policies. In one of the seminal works in the field of policy studies, Lowi (1972) has described public policies as serving distributive, regulatory, redistributive or constitutive functions in the political process.[6] While there can be no question that his work zeros in on important issues, from an empirical perspective the approach has proved to be frustrating. Stated simply, the problem is that most policies, upon empirical analysis, prove not to be easily pigeon-holed in terms of Lowi's categories. Every policy, as Lowi has himself noted, tends to have a redistributive impact of some kind. Steinberger sums up the problem by arguing that, while the literature on the scheme offers clear insights, it appears to be less than useful in empirical terms.

Steinberger suggests that Lowi's theory can be rescued with a phenomenological constructionist approach. In view of the complex and ambiguous nature of public policies and their meanings, the very problem that makes it hard to classify policies with Lowi's scheme, Steinberger argues that the task is impossible. Such ambiguity, he argues, is not a defect of understanding; it is instead a central and unavoidable feature of public policy. It is a basic defining component of analysis, rather than a barrier or obstacle.

Because policies are understood and defined in a wide variety of ways, they can never be self-explanatory. Seldom do policy controversies involve relatively easy questions of pros versus cons, or positives versus negatives. Instead, they typically turn on several very different and competing understandings or definitions of the same policy, of its purposes, its substantive content, and potential consequences. Stated in terms of Lowi's scheme, an issue may be a matter of regulation for one

---

[6] Lowi (1972) classifies public policies according to whether they are policies that *distribute* subsidies and tariffs, such as monies to build a bridge over a river; *regulatory* policies designed to control competitive activities, such as granting a licence for a television station; *redistributional* policies that shift resources from one group to another, such as progressive income taxes; or *constitutive* policies that determine the organizational and procedural rules governing politics and policymaking.

group and better understood by another in terms of the redistribution of resources. The implications are that each policy is likely to have different meanings for different participants; that the exact meaning of a policy, then, is by no means self-evident but, rather, is ambiguous and manipulable; and that the policy process is—at least in part—a struggle to get one or another meaning established as the accepted one. Steinberger, in fact, suggests that we can go a step further and say that no policy has a relevant meaning until it is attached to a particular individual or group.

From this perspective, it is not the actual policy outcomes but rather the *expectations* of outcomes that determine policy issues and shape their politics. Some, for instance, saw the War on Poverty as an attempt to adapt government practices to meet the needs of poor people (Kramer 1969), while others saw it as a series of control policies designed to co-opt the poor by buying off their political protests, without offering any real change in the redistribution of resources (Piven and Cloward 1971). Lowi offered his scheme with the hope that it would serve as a sound theoretical approach for exploring the relations between substantive policy issues and the political processes associated with them. Although the scheme has generated little empirical progress, Steinberger shows that it can be theoretically revitalized by recognizing the multiple meanings of public policies. Not only does his approach make clear that the potentially relevant social meanings of policies are more numerous than initially theorized, he offers a research strategy that integrates the phenomenological approach into one of the important mainstream policy research agendas. Towards this end, the phenomenological orientation addresses itself first to the question of problem definition. It asks, for example, whether certain policies tend to be defined in characteristic ways. And if so, are they developed and disseminated in particular ways? Do some groups tend to see all policies in terms of particular policy characteristics? Can business groups be shown to see policy issues in terms of substantive impacts, while environmental groups speak in terms of exhaustibility, and so on?

Focused on the decision-making process, the approach asks whether we find characteristic juxtapositions of meaning. Does the adoption of one particular meaning by group A tend to lead group B to adopt an alternative meaning? And if so, does the nature or intensity of political conflict correlate with the juxtaposed definitions? During the course of the decision process does the number of competing meanings tend to multiply or diminish? And finally, such an approach asks to what extent policy implementers prove to be conscious of, and concerned with, policy meanings. Does the administrative discretion of public agencies include leeway in terms of which particular policy meaning are adopted? Or do implementers tend to ignore the meanings generated by the political process and redefine policies to suit themselves? To what degree do the ambiguities of meanings make it difficult for policy actors to carry out their assigned tasks?

Such hypotheses, Steinberger writes, can help to turn Lowi's typology into a guide or checklist for the phenomenologically-oriented policy researcher. By determining the ways different groups assign political meaning to different types of policies— distributive, redistributive, and so on—the approach can provide a starting point for policy analysts interested in pursuing more fully the insights of the typological tradition.

POLICY DESIGN: CONSTRUCTING TARGET POPULATIONS

A second line of investigation concerns the groups targeted by public policies. As signifiers pointing to specific characteristics or conditions as opposed to others, policies specify—directly or indirectly—which players are virtuous and which are dangerous, which actions will be punished or penalized, and which will be encouraged and rewarded. At the same time, citizens and politicians are constituted as subjects with particular sorts of self-conceptions, self-aspirations, fears, and beliefs about the relative importance of events and objects. Moreover, they construct immunity for some social situations by treating them as non-problems. Policies thus define the shape and contours of the world of the citizen, although not in the same ways for all (Edelman 1988). They do it in the light of the diverse experiences and situations from which people react to the political events of the time.

An important example of such constructive policy research is that of Schneider and Ingram (1993*a*; 1997; 2003). Drawing explicitly on a constructivist perspective, they offer a detailed analysis of the ways the very target populations that policies are designed to a deal with are socially constructed. One of the reasons for many policy failures, they argue, is that politicians in search of political support strategically manipulate the social constructions of policy issues and their target populations.

The construction of potential target populations refers to the images, stereotypes, and beliefs that confer identities on people and connect them with others as a social group who are possible candidates for receiving beneficial or burdensome policy.[7] For example, 'advantaged' populations (business, veterans, scientists), as Schneider and Ingram (1993*b*: 2) write, 'have considerable political power and are positively constructed as meritorious and deserving', while 'contending' groups (Wall Street investors and big labour) 'are constructed as undeserving or greedy'. 'Dependent' groups (children and the disabled), in turn, 'lack power and are constructed as good people, although not as highly meritorious as those in the advantaged category'. And

---

[7] The social construction of a target population', Schneider and Ingram (1993*b*: 2) write, 'refers to the cultural characteristics or popular images of a group that is (or could be) eligible for the enabling or coercive application of policy. Social constructions are constituted by values, symbols, images, and beliefs about the characteristics of the group... Target populations may be constructed as 'deserving' or 'undeserving'; as 'intelligent' or 'stupid'; as 'honest or 'dishonest'; as 'public spirited' or 'selfish' and so on. Some constructions survive for decades, such as the portrayal of Communists as evil persons; but many are fluid and manipulated by media, political leaders, literary and artistic leaders as well as social scientists. For example, the social construction of homeless people is a matter of considerable debate. Some believe that the homeless are good people, down on their luck, and simply in need of a job to get back on their feet. Others believe that homelessness is a lifestyle choice by persons who wish to avoid the discipline and hard work necessary to hold a regular job. Current policy often implies through policy treatment of target groups that the homeless are needy people who deserve to be helped, but who are largely incompetent at managing their own lives.'

the 'deviant' members of society (criminals, child abusers, and flag burners) 'lack power and are negatively constructed as undeserving and dangerous, and generally bad people'. Politicians and public officials in a political system driven by self-interest, accordingly, are 'under considerable pressure... to provide benefits to advantages populations' and 'to provide punishment to deviant populations'.[8] And in the process, the differing policy messages sent to 'the target populations powerfully impact the orientations and political participation of the target populations'. As Schneider and Ingram (1993*b*: 3) put it:

Advantaged groups are taught that their interests coincide with the public interest. They see themselves as good... are supportive of government... participate at high levels [and] pay careful attention to what government does, and are quick to criticize expenditures on other populations... Deviants receive messages that they are bad people and that they can expect to be treated with disrespect or even hated. They are responsible for their problems and must fend for themselves. Deviants become angry and feel oppressed.

Social constructions of groups are influenced by a wide range of factors: politics, culture, socialization, history, the media, literature, and religion. For example, by separating target populations into the deserving and undeserving groups, politicians are able to legitimize the bestowal of beneficial regulations or subsidies on the former and punishment or neglect on the latter. Such characterizations of target populations become embedded in a particular policy design itself and send messages to people about whether their interests are legitimate and how much (or little) they are valued by society. In Schneider and Ingram's (1993*a*) view, the divisive, valued-laden social construction of target populations interacts with the power the target groups have over the future of careers of political leaders.

These messages transmitted by public polices, along with the accompanying political orientations and patterns of participation, exacerbate many of the policy crises that confront modern society. As Schneider and Ingram (1993*b*: 3) explain it:

Public officials too often are unable to deal with complex problems in an appropriate manner because to do so would provide advantages to the 'wrong' people... or inflict costs on advantaged groups. The contention of pluralists that an open, participatory system results in competition among interests, thereby producing good public policy doesn't work when social constructions teach some people that their interests are not legitimate. Problems are not resolved when policies are designed to reinforce stereotypes that increase social divisions and lack empathy rather than accomplish goals.

---

[8] In a democracy driven by the pursuit of self-interest, political and government officials experience substantial pressure to supply beneficial policies to advantaged citizens groups. 'Such policies will become oversubscribed and overfunded as benefits will be extended to these groups far beyond those needed to achieve instrumental goals and far beyond what would be a "fair share" of governmental largesse. The policies are legitimated by claiming that broad public purposes are served... Indeed, there are may instances where national interests have been... defined simply to justify continued provision of beneficial policy to powerful, positively constructed groups.' Moreover, 'there also are strong electoral incentives to provide punishment to deviant populations. Indeed, such policies contain extraordinary political advantages, as those who are punished are too weak and discredited to combat either their image or the policies directed toward them, and the public can easily be persuaded that such policies serve both

An excellent example of the political uses of target constructions concerns poverty policy in the United States, although the example can easily be generalized to other countries. Much of the politics of poverty between the Great Society's War on Poverty and the Reagan Revolution's efforts to eliminate the welfare state has been a struggle over the interpretive framing of the public's understanding of the poor. Indeed, the Reagan administration's success in branding the poor as undeserving was one of the salient characteristics of the American political landscape in the late twentieth century. Chronically poor mothers with dependent children were, for instance, stigmatized by conservatives as welfare queens (while the liberal complaint about corporate welfare got little attention).[9]

More specifically, Schram (1993) shows how social welfare policy in the post-industrial United States is involved in the construction and maintenance of social identities that shape or influence both the distribution of public programme monies and economic opportunities in the private sector. Mired, as Schram (1993: 249) puts it, in old, invidious distinctions (for example, independent/dependent, contract/charity, family/promiscuity), welfare policy discourse today helps to recreate the problems of yesterday, keeping many women trapped in poverty.

The ability to make clear diverging interpretations of policy meanings advanced by different groups, as well as understanding the elements through which these meanings are transmitted, allows the policy analyst to assist in identifying the underlying sources of policy conflict and to reformulate the issues in ways that can move the dispute towards an acceptable, constructive resolution. By revealing the taken-for-granted assumptions that underlie citizens' everyday understandings and behaviours in problematic social situations, the analyst can help citizens to reflect on the conflicting frames inherent in policy controversies, permitting them a better comprehension of the relationships among hidden premises and conclusions.

CONCLUSION

In this chapter we examined the socially constructed nature of the realities that policy studies seeks to explain. Recognition that human actors discursively construct their social worlds is basic to the critique of the objectivist approach of empiricism; it means taking seriously the fact that important parts of the social world do not lend themselves to direct empirical observation and measurement. A socially relevant approach to policy inquiry has to include the subjectively oriented goals, motives, and intentions of the policy actors. As such, it has to be grounded in an interpretive analysis. This is not to argue that empirical research should be abandoned, but rather

---

justice and public safety. Policies toward deviants also will become oversubscribed in that there will be constant search for new target populations who can be constructed as deviants and punished accordingly. The overrepresentation of minorities in the criminal and juvenile justice systems is an example... Such policies are often ineffective and inefficient' (Schneider and Ingram 1993*b*: 2).

[9] The effort of the political left to refer to corporate welfare is largely ignored, as the corporate world constitutes the 'good guys' (Baker 1985).

to make clear that empirical research itself has to be embedded in an interpretive-oriented discursive perspective, a point elaborated in Chapter 6.

In the course of the chapter we saw how purposes, values, and motives function in the explanation of social action. Constructed through language, such normative explanations have more in common with literary and historical understanding than with the kinds of causal explanation sought in the physical sciences. The failure of the empiricist approach to incorporate an adequate account of the social actor's understanding of the action situation is tantamount to seeking to explain political behaviour by excluding the very forces driving it. The exclusion is especially problematic when it comes to understanding political and policy change, processes often driven by new or evolving social meanings. Politics and policy, as we saw, are as much a competition over social meanings as they are empirical outcomes. As a struggle over the definitional categories into which we place problems and the symbols we attach to them, policy is seen to evolve as a diverse, often contradictory, and shifting set of responses to a spectrum of political interests. In this sense, public policy is a discursive construct rather than a self-defining phenomenon.

A postempiricist discursive approach has to be grounded in the theory of social constructionism, particularly as developed in the fields of science studies and social problems. Of particular importance is its relevance for problem construction and agenda-setting. But social meanings are not limited to a particular phase of the policy process; they are infused throughout. Towards this end, we saw that the types of proposals generated in the policy formation stage carry different meanings for different social actors, as well as the ways in which target populations are socially constructed.

Having laid out social constructionism as the groundwork for the development of a discursive approach to policy inquiry, we turn in Part II to a more detailed examination of the ways in which social constructions are produced and negotiated in politics through the medium of discourse.

what did I get out of this reading?

1. I like the notion that empirical research does not provide enough explanations to social problems.

2.

PART II

PUBLIC POLICY AS DISCURSIVE POLITICS

4

Public Policy and Discourse Analysis

Discourse is not easy to define. Many authors in the primary anti-positivist traditions of discourse analysis—hermeneutics, post-structuralism, and post-Marxist—use the term differently, making it difficult to offer a fixed or commonly accepted definition. Various characteristics of discourse, however, are relatively clear. Discourse, as Howarth (2002: 9) writes, refers 'to historically specific systems of meaning which form the identities of subjects and objects'. Discourse theory, as such, starts from the assumption that all actions, objects, and practices are socially meaningful and that these meanings are shaped by the social and political struggles in specific historical periods. Through a range of linguistic and non-linguistic materials—verbal statements, historical events, interviews, ideas, politics, among others—the goal of discourse analysis is thus to show how these actions and objects come to be socially constructed and what they mean for social organization and interaction. Included among the methods for doing this are the tools of rhetorical analysis, hermeneutics, deconstruction, and genealogical approaches to discourse analysis. The discussion that follows draws on these various approaches without adhering to a particular school of analysis.

Clearly, then, discourse is more than just synonymous with discussion or talking. The meanings of the words used and the statements employed in a discourse depend on the social context in which they are uttered, including the positions or arguments against which they are advanced. At the level of everyday interaction, discourses represent specific systems of power and the social practices that produce and reproduce them. MacDonell (1986: 2) illustrates the point by showing how discourses function in different social settings: the kinds of speech appropriate on the factory floor differ sharply from those in the corporate boardroom, just as doctors in a hospital speak differently from their patients. Different social groups, especially groups with differing degrees of power and authority, may use the same words differently in their interpretations of social and political situations.

For Hajer (1995a: 44) discourse is 'a specific ensemble of ideas, concepts, and categorizations that are produced, reproduced, and transformed to give meaning to physical and social relations'. As such, discourse and discursive practices circumscribe the range of subjects and objects through which people experience the world, specify the views that can be legitimately accepted as knowledge, and constitute the actors taken to be the agents of knowledge. Through such discursive delimitations, as Shapiro (1981: 130) puts it, a discourse establishes 'norms for developing conceptualizations that are used to understand the phenomenon'. Discursive practices, which Foucault took as his basic unit of analysis, are the widely held and oft-repeated interpretations of social conduct that produce and affirm behaviours. Over time these interpretations become unreflectively taken for granted; they are scarcely noted by the actors who employ them. As generally accepted presuppositions, they become embedded in the institutional deliberations and practices that produce and govern basic societal relations.

Focused on virtually all research concerned with language in its social and cognitive context, including scientific disciplinary discourses, legal discourse, everyday narrative discourse, and so on, discourse analysis has given rise to numerous approaches. Basic to these orientations, though, is a concern with defining the units of analysis in various modes of deliberation and inquiry (Meinhof 1993). A discourse, in this respect, is not just any collection of words or sentences. Rather it is an integration of sentences—spoken or written—that produces a meaning larger than that contained in the sentences examined independently. Each kind of discourse links the sentences that compose it according to distinct *patterns* of reasoning. Physics, for example, is one kind of discourse; social science another; and law still another. And there are, of course, many others, including everyday discourses.

Fairclough (1992) offers a method that combines elements of hermeneutic, post-structural, post-Marxist and rhetorical approaches to discourse analysis. Following his approach, a 'discursive event' can be at once be seen as text, discursive practice, or social practice (Fairclough 1992: 4). 'The "text" dimension attends to language analysis of texts.' Focus on this aspect of discourse is the primary activity of linguistics (Johnstone 2001). Here a basic task is to understand how a discourse links together its utterances according to distinctive discursive forms—for example, referential, narrational, persuasive, expressive, or poetical (Kinneavy 1971). A discursive practice, of particular interest to literary scholars, focuses the processes of text production and interpretation. The analysis of discursive practices involves, among other things, an examination of which types of discourses are employed in particular contexts, especially which discourses are privileged in particular areas of policy-making and which are excluded. And as social practice, discourse refers to issues such as the institutional and organizational circumstance of the discursive event and how that shapes the nature of the discursive practice (Fairclough 1992: 4). Here one would focus on the kinds of assumptions that underlie practices of particular policy institutions—for example, the way an office of education might be governed by a particular educational philosophy, or the way in which a particular methodological orientation might be embedded in the rules and procedures of a political science association and its official journal. This concern with social practices is a primary interest of the social scientist.

Whether directly expressed in discussion and debate among speakers, or embedded in the practices of societal institutions, discourse communicates on two basic levels: the broad cultural level and the everyday level of communicative interaction. Although perhaps somewhat simplistically, these two levels can be usefully thought of in terms of micro everyday (first-order) and macro socio-cultural (second-order) discourse, which is the primary concern of this chapter. At this socio-cultural level, macro discourse transmits basic values and gives cohesion to shared beliefs, similar to what Schmidt (2002: 210) describes as 'communicative' discourse in Chapter 2.

Among other things, it supplies society with basic stories that serve as models of behaviour, both positive and negative.

Examples of discourse at the macro level are not difficult to find. Perhaps the best example in Western countries is Christianity. In Christian cultures, the most profound illustration is the story of Jesus of Nazareth, which provides insights for all members of society, even including people who are not especially religious. Such discourses convey to a society its basic socio-cultural identity, that is, where it comes from, how it got there, and what its goals and values are. Or take the case of modern-day Israel. It exists in significant part because of the Holocaust and the story is told and retold to remind Jews of who they are and why they must defend themselves. In Germany, of course, the same story conveys a very different message of shame and guilt.

At this cultural level, discourses function epistemically to regularize the thinking of a particular period, including the basic organizing principles of social action (such as the rules of feudalism or capitalism). Functioning as deep socio-linguistic structures, discourses organize the actors' understandings of reality without them necessarily being aware of it. In the Foucaultian sense of the terminology, such epistemic discourses have formative or constitutive power that structures basic social definitions, meanings, and interactions in a socio-cultural system. As large encompassing systems of meaning embedded in and transmitted by culture, macro discourses constitute the 'residua' of a society's or group's collective memory. They do so primarily in the form of stories that can be taken as the engrams basic to our modes of thinking and action.

Consider a couple of examples. Basic to French history and culture is idea of the French nation as carrier of civilization to other parts of the world, an idea grounded in the French Revolution and extended by the far-flung missions of Napoleon. This contrasts with the English tradition that emphasizes the establishment of a parliament and the rights of Englishmen. Whereas French political discourse stresses the universal rights of man, English political discourse is grounded in the particular rights of Englishmen and a concern about parliamentary encroachments. Such larger discursive themes serve as points of orientation and departure in more concrete political and everyday discourses in these different political cultures, especially when it comes to dealing with each other. Under these broadly structuring discourses, political stories and narratives are told which not only reflect these general systems of meaning but also work them out in the concrete practices of the everyday world of social action. In the politics of the European Union, for example, these differences offer underlying reasons why the British are reluctant to turn over their sovereign powers to a continental governing body (Schmidt 2001). For the French, they constitute grounds for advancing the European Union, so long as the French government is one of its leading directors.

An even more deep-seated example of such cultural residua is found in the way common everyday phases of a language can carry and sustain more fundamental norms which speakers no longer recognize as such. For example, consider the expression '*alles in Ordnung*' in the German language, which is regularly repeated in the course of the most mundane events. No one thinks about it, but the phrase no doubt has roots in the emphasis on discipline and authority that runs through

Prussian history. (A famous story is told of the Prussian king who fired his generals because they failed to follow his orders to the letter, although their actions enabled them to win the Franco-Prussian war.) Contemporary Germans today do not attach such deep meaning to the regular repetition of '*alles in Ordnung*', which can be likened to Americans casually asking someone 'how it's going?' A discourse analysis would nonetheless take note that the phrase is still there and resonates, even unintentionally or unconsciously, with part of German history. In this way, it carries forward important aspects of a culture. One would not want to draw immediate consequences from such an utterance, but would nonetheless want to ask about the way such an expression still tends to influence contemporary cultural orientations, including important social constructs such as efficiency or cleanliness.[1] Albeit always in new ways, a culture constantly reproduces itself. The process of reproduction is one of the ways a people show or reveal themselves.

DISCOURSE ANALYSIS

Discourse analysis in politics begins with the recognition that discourses are distributed across institutions. In addition to the dominant discourses, competing discourses struggle to gain recognition and power. A key task for the analyst is to account for the viewpoints and positions from which actors speak and the institutions and processes that distribute and preserve what they say. As MacDonell (1986: 2–3) writes, a discourse 'may be identified by the institutions to which it relates and by the position from which it comes and which it marks out for the speaker'. The speaker's position, however, does not stand alone. It can only be understood 'as a standpoint taken up by the discourse through its relation to another discourse', as when the owners speak to the workers.

The discursive constitution of society, as Fairclough (1992) makes clear in his very useful explication of the theory and methods of discourse analysis, does not stem from a free play of ideas in people's heads. Rather, it emerges from practices that are rooted in and oriented to basic social structures and ideological practices, particularly the tensions and conflicts to which they give rise. This connects discourse to practices that constitute—and naturalize, sustain, and change—the basic social and political significations of the world. Politically, such practices not only construct but also support and alter specific power relations between collective entities (classes, groups, communities, and so on) through which they are expressed. The ideological significations of these entities, as Fairclough makes clear, are generated within power relations as part of the exercise of and struggle over power. Discourse in politics is thus not only an activity in a power struggle, but also a stake in it as well.

The question of the relations among discourse, power, and ideology is the subject of complicated debates. Indeed, the term 'discourse' was in part introduced to deal

---

[1] No contemporary German would deny that an emphasis on order and efficiency is embedded in Germany's institutional culture, but many complain that it is not always that easy to find in practice.

with problematic issues related to particular theories of ideology.[2] Here, though, there is no widely accepted statement in the literature. Although discourses are not ideologies, they do intersect with ideologies, which supply the words of a discourse with different meanings. Built into the various meanings of discursive practices, ideologies—as interpretive constructions of reality—contribute to the production or transformation of power relations and political domination (Fairclough 1992: 86–91). Pecheux (1982) argues that discourses, which have their basis in language, nonetheless are always uttered in the social sphere, which is constructed ideologically. They always find their social meanings by reference to an ideological position (MacDonell 1986: 43–55). Even though they are not ideologies per se, discourses will generally have an intentional or unintentional relationship or position to one. Drawing on Althusser (1971) and Pecheux (1982), as MacDonell (1986: 102) writes, a discourse 'is pinned down where it serves as a weapon in an ideological struggle'. It is in these struggles that a discourse finds its social meanings.

A first-rate example of the relationship of discourse to ideology is found in the academic discourse of economics. Western industrial societies are organized as capitalist systems; thus it is difficult to render any statement completely outside the realm of capitalist ideology. Nonetheless academic economics presents itself as a value-free scientific discourse independent of capitalist or socialist ideologies. It purports to identify and describe casual economic relations, often portrayed as 'natural', and offers an apolitical way to discourse about them. Despite the fact that modern-day 'neo-liberal' capitalist discourse can arguably be defined as the hegemonic discourse of our time, many contemporary introductory economics texts never—or almost never—mention the world 'capitalism', thus extracting the discourse from its historical and ideological context. A socialist, however, is correct to identify the capitalist understandings embedded in these discourses. The key words of such the discourse—'management', 'workers', 'profit', and 'corporations', and so on—are interpreted to have very different meanings by socialist ideology. Where a capitalist reads the economic text and unreflectively takes the word 'profit' for granted, the socialist reads the same word against a concern for exploitation.

Because ideologies reflect basic material and social relations in a society, they also supply people with different social identities. The various groups in society thus orient themselves ideologically in different ways to particular discourses. To stay with economics, the British Labour Party, or at least the left wing of the party, keeps its distance from the free-market discourses of contemporary economics. In this respect, as Pecheux (1982) has argued, people construct their consciousness in terms of three basic orientations to the dominant discourses and their ideological orientations. Some freely consent to and identify with the social image held out to them by

---

[2] Initially, the concept of political discourse was introduced to understand the historical evolution of social systems by analysing the nature, origins, and evolution of its discursive formations. In particular, it has been developed to escape the problematic aspects of the concept of ideology, especially its relationship to the Marxist concept of 'false consciousness' and the limits of more materialist approaches that assigned cultural and other ideational dimensions to a secondary status. In the process, though, this relationship of discourse to ideology has become a complicated theoretical question.

the dominant ideology, for example, working class or upper class (they are the 'good subjects'). Others refuse the social categories that are offered, adopting a 'counter-identification'. These 'trouble-makers' include criminals, but also often liberal reformers. The third group, Pecheux argues, takes the orientation of 'disidentifica-tion'. Whereas the counter-identification position defines itself in oppositional terms ('what *you* call the political crisis'), this third group sets out a new discourse. Although the identifications established by the dominant ideology can never be entirely evaded, this orientation seeks to transform and displace them. A traditional example is the Marxist theory of capitalism; a contemporary illustration is radical ecology. It here that one can understand the revolutionary Sartre's argument that the trouble with being radical reformer is that the opposition always sets your agenda. The alternative, he argued, is to be a revolutionary and seek to set the agenda yourself.

Gramsci's concept of hegemony provides a fruitful way of conceptualizing and exploring these interrelated ideological and political aspects of discourse, in particular the ways they both contribute to and are shaped by wider processes of social and political change (Laclau und Mouffe 1985; Fairclough 1992). Hegemony, in Gramsci's (1971) work, emphasizes domination across the economic, ideological, cultural, and political domains of society. It refers to the power over society by one of the economically defined classes in political alliance with other societal forces. For Gramsci, though, this does not mean a fixed or firm social equation. Hegemony, as he defines it, is an unstable equilibrium that always remains partial and temporary. For this reason, the focus is on the strategies of political leadership required to sustain the hegemonic balance of forces. Constructing and maintaining the alliances necessary to sustain the equilibrium, as discursive power, involves integrating rather than simply dominating subordinate classes to win their consent. Through a combination of ideological means and material concessions, hegemonic politics emphasizes the constant struggle around the points of greatest instability between classes or groups, in an effort to build, sustain, or block alliances. Hegemonic struggle, as Fairclough (1992: 92) explains it, 'takes place on a broad front, which includes the institutions of civil society (education, trade unions, family), with possible unevenness between different levels and domains'.

Gramsci (1971: 324) offers a conception of political groups as structured by the diverse ideologies implicit in their discursive practices. Given the sometimes conflicting or contradictory components that make up such understandings of groups, Gramsci speaks of their 'strangely composite' character. Basic to these composites is the way in which common-sense knowledge serves as both 'a repository of diverse effects of past ideological struggles' and a regular target for restructuring in social and political struggles. In common-sense knowledge, 'ideologies become naturalized, or automatized' (Fairclough 1992: 92). On this view, ideologies are understood to be fields of 'conflicting, overlapping, or intersecting currents or formations', or what Gramsci referred to as an 'ideological complex'. This necessitates an examination of the processes that articulate and restructure ideological complexes. In more recent years, a newer group of 'neo-Gramscian' scholars have sought to revitalize Gramsci's insights in the area of international relations and foreign policy (Gill 1993; Cox 1994; Sinclair 2000).

Such an approach to political struggle offers a dialectical perspective on the relationship between discursive structures and events. Viewing discourses as the relatively unstable and often contradictory configurations that hold together the equilibria of political hegemony, 'the articulation and rearticulating of orders of discourse is correspondingly one stake in hegemonic struggle' (Fairclough 1992: 93). Furthermore, 'discursive practice, the production, distribution, and consumption (including interpretation) of texts, is a facet of hegemonic struggle which contributes in varying degrees to the reproduction or transformation not only of the existing order of discourse, but also to the reproduction of existing social and power relations.'

To illustrate the relationship between discourse and social change Fairclough offers a number of examples. His concern is with broad tendencies in discursive change affecting the societal order of discourse, which are related to more general directions of social and cultural change. One of his examples to explain the ways that language and discourse are used to facilitate social change is that of 'commodification'. This involves analysing a process whereby a social domain and its institutions, whose concern is not producing economic commodities in the narrower economic sense of goods for sale, come nevertheless to be organized and conceptualized in terms of commodity production, distribution, and consumption. 'In terms of orders of discourse', he writes (1992: 207), 'we can conceive of commodification as the colonization of institutional orders of discourse, and more broadly of the societal order of discourse, by discourse types associated with commodity production.' Specifically, the process of commodification is used to show the way in which a language text can be employed to mediate a social transformation to a more entrepreneurial market-oriented culture, a phenomenon of no minor importance. Since the Thatcher years in Britain and the Reagan period in the USA, such a process of commodification has been increasingly extended to one institutional domain after another.

Education in both countries is an important example. Towards this end, Fairclough concretely illustrates the role of the commodification discourse in mediating the process of social change through the example of the transformation of the traditional liberal educational curriculum to a more practical training orientation for the labour market. In the process, he shows how education is increasingly reconceptualized as an 'industry' or 'enterprise' concerned with producing and selling cultural or educational commodities to their student 'clients' or 'consumers'. A widespread feature of contemporary educational discourse is the wording of courses or programmes of study as 'commodities' to be 'packaged' by curriculum designers and 'marketed' in a competitive bid for 'customers'. (See Appendix.)

In order for a specific discourse to become hegemonic, according to Laclau and Mouffe (1985), a particular set of 'nodal points' must be established in the discursive field. Given the 'surplus of meanings' that characterize the discursive fields of most policy issues, as illustrated in Chapter 2, a candidate for hegemony must compete with a wide range of potentially relevant but different discourses. Within the discursive field, as Battistelli and Ricotta (2001: 4) write, 'to become hegemonic the specific discourse needs to dominate the field in which it was formed, blocking the flow of differences in meaning and setting itself up as the center of interpretive processes'. This happens as the discourse succeeds in the 'structuring of privileged discursive points, or nodal points of discourse' that facilitate discussion about some things and not others: that is, when its concepts and definitions have succeeded in fixing specific meanings to be employed in interpreting a wide spectrum of social issues, problems, objects, actors, and situations.

For Fraser (1989: 164) such discourse politics is understood in terms of struggles over the interpretation of issues rather than over substantive questions. This 'politics of conflict interpretation, includes not only the interpretations of the problems, but also the types of discourses they should involve' (Braun and Herrmann 2001: 2). This involves examining questions such as whose interpretation becomes authoritative, as well the reason why. Are the dominant forms of political discourse available for interpretive argumentation shown to be acceptable and fair to the parties involved? Do the arguments favour the dominant political groups or do they assist challengers in making their oppositional claims? To get at these questions the interpretive analyst has to examine the social and institutional logics that underlie the interpretive processes. In which societal institutions are the interpretations developed, and what forms of social relations bind interlocutors together?

Towards this end, discourse analysis must also include a focus on the available discursive resources in a given social situation and how they are stratified in accordance with societal patterns of dominance. Discursive resources involve accepted idioms in which claims can be advanced, such as talk about rights, or economic talk; available vocabularies, such as medical, religious, or feminist vocabularies, frameworks of argumentation (especially as they pertain to debates among citizens, experts, politicians, and others), and narrative approaches or conventions that are available for the construction of stories and their telling. Especially important in Fraser's scheme is an emphasis on modes of subjugation. How do different discourses position or subjugate participants in a communicative exchange (for example, are they experts or citizens, politicians or businessmen, and so on?).

Such an orientation would also require us to examine the distribution of discursive capabilities across a society (Beck 1986; Schiller and Symthe 1992). Some people can speak regularly, while others can hardly ever be heard, unless they threaten violence. A key aspect in modern society is the role of the media, particularly how it is controlled. As is well documented, the media in the United States and Europe is increasingly controlled by smaller numbers of people and the content is more and more influenced by the advertisers who pay for the programmes. This strongly supports the ideological complex with a distinctive consumer-oriented business bias. Moreover, much of the news is limited in the perspectives it offers. Consequently, such research shows that modern citizens are socialized more into roles as passive members of the audience than active participants. From this perspective, education and access to information and information technologies, such as computers and the Internet, become important topics. Some writers such as Beck (1995) have, in this respect, described the defining tensions of the twenty-first century in terms of a conflict between those who have expertise and those who do not.

Fraser distinguishes between the dominant means communication and interpretation that are officially approved or sanctioned, and the subordinate discourses that are normally denied easy access to the primary discursive arenas. Discursive politics, from this perspective, is an essential strategy of political resistance (Fraser 1989: 165). The arguments of the subordinate groups, argues Fraser, cannot be 'translated into the dominant discourses without being redefined in ways that shed important meanings'. Towards this end, Fraser calls for the development of 'social spaces' where groups with unequal discursive (and non-discursive) resources can deliberate about different ways of talking about social issues and problems.

Discursive understanding of power and political struggles, as Fraser's Habermasian focus also makes clear, holds open the possibility of moving beyond the traditional negative connotations associated with ideology and power. In much of social science power and ideology are understood negatively; they refer to domination, manipulation, and control. Missing from this view, as we noted in Chapter 2, is the more positive understanding of discourse. Communicative power, as Habermas and others have made clear, can create new consenses that open the way to alternative identities and courses of action. Moving beyond domination or the mobilization of resources, discursive power is productive power. It is, as Litfin (1994) puts it, 'capacity-giving', a topic to which we return in later chapters.

POLICY DISCOURSE AND ARGUMENTATIVE STRUGGLE

Can we apply the discourse model more directly to the policy research? Such work is increasingly emerging. In *Governing Molecules*, for example, Gottweis (1998; 2002), has examined the discursive construction of genetic engineering in Europe and the United States to show that the genetic controversy is a process inseparable from the social construction of political, economic, and scientific worlds. Calling for a 'poststructural policy analysis', Gottweis employs discourse-analytic methods based on insights from Derrida and Foucault to demonstrate the need to examine how discourses and narrative stories that create orientation and meaning constitute the policy field of genetic engineering. Critical of the assumption that political science can simply assume the 'existence' of actors and structures in politics, as well as the narrow understanding of politics that has informed conventional political studies, he argues for 'conceptualizing the process of policymaking as situated at the intersection between forces and institutions deemed "political" and those apparatuses that shape and manage individual conduct in relations to norms and objectives but are deemed "nonpolitical," such as science or education.' Rather than 'assuming stable boundaries between sectors such as politics, the economy, and science', he calls for the study of 'the micropolitics of boundary drawing' (Gottweis 1998: 27).

Through this perspective Gottweis (1998) shows that the politics of genetic engineering cannot be reduced to citizens demanding the regulation of recombinant DNA technology. The politics of genetic engineering also takes place when scientists carry out specific experiments in genetic engineering and subsequently make claims about the importance of their research for the understanding of both nature and

social behaviour. This approach allows Gottweis to identify a much more sophisticated regime of 'governability', a system of fields and sites ranging from research
laboratories to legislatures that negotiate and deploy approaches designed to control
and manipulate genetic materials, or as he puts it, 'to make them governable'.

In *Ozone Discourses*, Litfin (1994: 3) offers a discourse or 'reflective' approach to
the 1987 negotiation of the Montreal Protocol (on substances that deplete the ozone
layer). Essentially, it is a story about how a dominant anti-regulatory discourse succeeded in supplanting a new environmental regulatory discourse. Through the narrative discourse she illustrates how mainstream functionalist, agency-centred, and
epistemic community approaches downplay, even ignore, the ways in which the information of scientific experts mainly reinforces or reinforces existing political conflicts.

On the surface of the matter, this landmark ecological treaty would seem to be the
outcome of a rigorous risk analysis process and astute diplomatic negotiations. With
complex atmospheric models as the scientific basis for negotiation and decision-
making, this account has led writers such as Haas (1989; 1992) to explain the
Montreal process in terms of an epistemic community composed of atmospheric scientists. In this view, knowledge is taken to be a body of concrete and objective facts
that were not only relevant to the actors' perceived interests, but were fundamentally
implicated in questions of interpretation and policy framing. Knowledge provided
the means that reoriented actors' understandings of their own interests, thus making
the agreement possible.

Litfin (1994: 46–51), in sharp contrast, offers a very different picture of what happened. The 'knowledge' at issue was itself 'framed in light of specific interests and
preexisting discourses so that questions of value were rendered as questions of fact,
with exogenous factors shaping the political salience of various modes of interpreting that knowledge', including the discovery of an ozone hole of the Antarctic that
helped to empower the subordinate regulatory discourse. By neglecting issues of
interpretation and legitimacy, mainstream theories offer explanations that fail to capture the multi-dimensional interpretive and interactive processes that link science to
politics. In so far as these reflective elements are essential to knowledge-based
power, she argues that standard accounts have to be extended to include a discursive,
productive, or capacity-giving conception of power.

In *The Politics of Environmental Discourse*, Hajer (1995*a*) has analysed the politics of the acid rain controversy to show how different applications and understandings of acid rain have generated very different types of politics in two countries.
Because Hajer's concept of discourse coalitions most directly engages the analytical
and methodological debates in policy analysis, particularly in terms of his critique of
the influential work of Sabatier and Jenkins-Smith on advocacy coalitions, we turn
to a more detailed examination of his contribution in the discussion below.

Devoted to a comparison of acid rain policies in Britain and the Netherlands, Hajer
offers a full-scale study of discursive policy analysis. Building on Foucault's theoretical work, Hajer labours to translate this lofty theoretical contribution into a framework for the analysis of concrete policy problems. The task, as he explains, is to
understand how particular discourses in a distinct political domain come to influence

discourses in other domains. Towards this end, he draws on discursive concepts developed by the social psychologist Billig designed for a less abstract 'level of interpretive interaction'. The result is a 'social-interactive discourse theory' geared to the analytical tasks of policy analysis.

In Hajer's scheme, as in Foucault's, the dominant discourses supply social actors with 'subject-positions' that define their social and power relationships in terms of a principal narrative or narratives (1995a: 65). Discourse analysis shows the way in which actors attach meanings to other actors in terms of the positions assigned or attributed to them in the dominant or counter-discourses. Actors are 'positioned' with regard to specific social attributes such as blame, and responsibility. In this view, social actors mainly make sense of the world by borrowing terms and concepts from the discourses made available to them in their social groups and the society generally. That is, to be understood and considered relevant, a speaker has to situate his remarks in—or relate them to—the recognized discourses in use at the time. A speaker's statements must say something in terms of the ongoing flow of discursive exchanges.

Ideas that do not draw on or interact with the available discourses will be dismissed as strange or irrelevant. To take an example, before Adam Smith came along and offered a fully developed discourse on the virtues of the free market, it was difficult, as economic historians show, for the small businessman to express or convey such interests and concerns. Now capitalist discourse has long been one of the available discursive themes to which one can appeal—approvingly or disapprovingly—in an effort to be understood. Today, one can say the same of environmental discourse. Forty years ago it was difficult to express concern about the environment without confronting furrowed brows. Now it is more than clear what is at stake when one refers his or her argument to environmental concerns.

Actors in this discourse-analytic approach are constituted by discursive practices, meaning they have to be understood through the concepts and languages employed to describe their activities. In the case of the public administrator, for example, conventional social science typically defines a public administrator in terms of his or her functional role in the agency. But a discursive analysis would examine the other stories co-workers tell that interpret the administrator's behaviour in different ways, for example as party functionary, dedicated man of the people, or small-minded bureaucrat, or perhaps all three, depending on the occasion.

Rather than a set of ritualized roles, social interaction is thus conceptualized as an exchange of arguments, of competing, sometimes contradictory, suggestions of how one is to make sense of reality. For political and social research this means exploring discourse practices through which social actors seek to persuade others to see a particular situation or event. In this dialectical or perspectival view of knowledge, it is important to know the counter arguments and positions of the others involved (MacDonell 1986: 43–59). As discursive arguments always take their meaning in opposition to other positions, the analyst always has to pay attention to the dialectical tensions among rival positions, a point to which we return in Chapter 6. The discursive fields in which communicative exchanges take place thus need to be a central interest of analysis. 'Language', as Shapiro (1981: 14) puts it, 'becomes part of data analysis for inquiry, rather than simply a tool for speaking about an extra-linguistic reality.'

Underlying this approach are two basic analytical tasks, one concerned with the substantive content of discursive statements and the other related to their implications for institutional practices. With regard to discursive content, one can easily grasp the point by comparing the discourses of physics and environmentalism. Physics is a discourse, produced, reproduced, and transformed through practices like academic teaching, laboratory experiments, and peer-reviewed journals. Environmental discourse, in contrast, is produced through activities such as practising of alternative life-styles, engaging in political demonstrations and protests, making references to pristine forests, reciting folklore about nature, and the rejecting consumer culture. Both discourses have their own context or domain. No one can successfully use the language or modes of argument of physics in everyday discourse. And the same holds true of the language of environmentalism; it does not get one very far in the physics laboratory.

Hajer's specific concern is with the discursive content of environmental policy discourse, yet another kind of discourse with its own characteristics. While we can identify a rational or systematic basis for policy discourse, it lacks the kind of coherence of content found in formal discourses such as physics or law. Legal discourse, for instance, is a highly structured, internally consistent mode of deliberation with its own inherent criteria of credibility. It's systematized, institutionalized practices are reflected in the procedures of lawsuits, the preparation of legislation, appeals processes to higher courts, and the like. Policy discourse is also dependent on its institutional environment, but it cannot achieve the kind of internal coherence of a discourse such as law, or even political theory for that matter. This has to do with its position at the intersection of various discourses, combining a range of discursive components—empirical, institutional, pragmatic, and normative factors—that give it its unique character and requirements. In the case of regulatory policy, for instance, Jasanoff (1990; 1995) has captured this in her concept of 'regulatory science', which she juxtaposes to 'science' per se. Where the later follows the logic of empirical causality, regulatory science involves an interdisciplinary interaction between legal, economic, scientific, and administrative discourses. Each contributes to what can become consensually established as a set of rules designed to judiciously govern over a particular policy domain.

In Hajer's (1995a: 53) social-interactive approach, the interplay of such discourses is not to be conceptualized as 'semi-static plays in which social actors have fixed and well memorized roles such as environmentalist, policy-maker, scientist, or industrialist', or the firm belief systems stereotypically attached to these roles. To the contrary, politics becomes an argumentative struggle in which actors not only try to make their opponents see the problem according to their view, but also seek to position or portray other actors in specific ways (for example, by showing the relationship of a particular argument to the interests of an industrialist) that open up new possibilities for action. Grounded in qualitative methods, the discourse-analytic task is geared to the real world of social action. The evidence for this is found in the actors themselves. Discourse is not a category merely imposed on them by social scientists; rather, it is something social actors constantly practice.

A significant part of the task is to identify the elements in argumentative interactions that are essential to explaining the emergence and persistence of particular discursive constructions. How, for example, do concepts such as 'sustainable development', 'acid rain', or 'globalization' get constructed and shaped? What kinds of forces—both political and rhetorical—are brought to bear to establish such discursive formations, and how do they affect the behaviour of both individuals and social groups? Once established, how can such constructions establish discursive hegemony over a particular policy domain?

A social-interactive discourse approach takes social actors to be actively engaged in choosing and adapting thoughts, shaping and fashioning them, in an ongoing struggle for argumentative triumph over rival positions. Taking here a position that would seem to draw as much or more from Habermas than Foucault, Hajer sees the task of the discursive policy analysis as uncovering the defining claims of a particular position. That is, we need to examine the structure, style, and historical context of an argument to determine why some modes of argumentation serve to effectively justify specific actions in particular situations and others fail. The discourse analyst needs to examine a particular conception of reality as something that is upheld by key political actors through discursive interaction, as well as how the oppositional forces seek to challenge these constructs.

Most fundamental to these discursive interactions is the question of how a particular framing of an issue can bestow the appearance of problematic on some features of a discussion while others seem proper and fixed. The task of the analyst is to show whether particular definitions 'homogenize' a problem, that is, render the problem understandable by situating it is a wider social frame, or whether definitions lead to a 'heterogenization' that opens up established discursive categories and hence the possibility of new courses of action. In the process, the opening up, or 'deconstructing', of a policy discourse can show how it emerges as the unintended consequence of a confluence of events and ideas. It can also show how seemingly technical issues can conceal normative commitments, as well as what sorts of institutional arrangements make this possible. Discourse analysis, in this way, helps us see which institutional dimensions are firmly entrenched and which structural elements are more open to change.

Important to understand is how social actors can contribute to the production and potential transformation of a discourse. In this respect, Hajer (1995*a*: 55) adopts an 'immanentist' view of language. Like Marx, Hajer argues that discursive actors can shape their own history, but not under conditions entirely of their own choosing. Given that they are operating in pre-existing social structures, the political context of interaction has to be situated in a discursive construction that offers both possibilities and constraints. Oppositional groups must recognize that various modes of expression have meaning or effect only to the extent that they are appropriate to the context in which they are uttered. Because the rules and conventions that constitute the social order have to be constantly reproduced and reconfirmed in actual speech situations— whether in documents, media coverage, or public debates—the challenge for such groups is to find ways to break open these routines. In general, this happens through the discovery of contradictions or paradoxes.

In view of the complex multi-dimensionality of a given social configuration, the particular conceptions of reality that ruling groups advance to legitimize existing institutions must necessarily cover up contradictions and paradoxes. The task for the opposition is to open and exploit these ideological tensions and contradictions by showing how they function to hide or conceal other realities (Mannheim 1936). At times, such openings are facilitated by the emergence of exogenous crises or shocks to the social system that make these tensions either visible or difficult to conceal. However, unlike Sabatier's (1988) emphasis on external shocks, which tend to play a quasi-deterministic role, the crucial issue from a discourse perspective is the kind of strategic communications to which the such a crisis gives rise.

Discursive responses to a crisis are in no way automatic. The ways in which they are portrayed can vary widely, with very different implications, ranging from 'there is little that can be done; we must accept it' to 'dramatic action must be taken—those responsible for allowing it to happen must be punished'. Compare here the rhetoric of President Herbert Hoover during the Great Depression with that of President Franklin Delano Roosevelt. Where Hoover could only ring his hands in despair ('There is nothing more we can do'), Roosevelt energized the nation to rally around a new set of institutional arrangements ('There is nothing to fear but fear itself'). Without the strategic discursive responses of a dynamic new leader, as Houck (2001) shows, the course of American history would have surely been quite different. Nothing is given in such political developments. How discursive responses will unfold are case-specific, depending on a wide range of factors from how those who have power choose to exercise it, to the personal characteristics of the particular actors on the stage at the time, what sort of orientation the media is disposed towards, the mood of the public, the resources of different groups, other related contextual factors, and more. The point is that a systems crisis itself does not determine what follows; rather, it is only the trigger for discursive responses that open or close off possible courses of action.

POLICY STORYLINES

The basic linguistic mechanism for creating and maintaining discursive order, or responding to a destabilizing jolt to the discursive order, is the concept of the story-line. A storyline, Hajer (1995a: 56) writes, 'is a generative sort of narrative that allows actors to draw upon various discursive categories to give meaning to specific or social phenomena.'(For example, 'there is nothing we can do' or 'we must take immediate action'.) The primary 'function of story-lines is that they suggest unity in the bewildering variety of separate discursive components parts of a problem' that otherwise have no clear or meaningful pattern of connections.

To understand the world around them, most people do not draw on comprehensive discursive systems for their cognitions. Instead, they rely on storylines. That is, they do not appeal to well-developed theories of ecology or political philosophies for cognitive assistance, but rather turn to discursive storylines as short-hand constructions.

Storylines, in this way, function to condense large amounts of factual information inter-mixed with the normative assumptions and value orientations that assign meaning to them. As social constructions of particular events, storylines serve to position social actors and institutional practices in ongoing, competing narratives. In the process, they

---

Globalization as Storyline

For the purpose of clarifying the concept of a storyline, the current politics of global-ization provides an excellent illustration of the struggle to define and interpret reality. Consider the anti-globalization protests that have taken place in Seattle, Gothenburg, Genoa, New York, and so forth. Political elites portray or 'discursively position' pro-testers as irresponsible anarchists hostile to an inevitable good that cannot—and should not—be impeded. The actions of such people, according to President George W. Bush's political narrative, will only deny the poor of the underdeveloped world the economic benefits of globalization. Against this dominant storyline, which is widely supported by the media, opponents of globalization and others sympathetic to their views argue that the demonstrators are not simply anti-global, if anti-global at all. Rather they protest against a particular capitalistic version of globalization that currently is beyond control. In this view, the dominant political leaders are seen to only speak for transnational cap-italists, whom they themselves cannot control, as the globalization process transcends the nation state. Since globalization is taking place in the total absence of democratic institutions, where the discussion of the development of globalization could take place, the demonstrators turn to the only forum available to them, namely, the streets.

The point here is that there is no objective or fixed narrative construction of the demonstrators and what their actions mean. Indeed, both interpretations of the actions of the protestors may have truth to them. Much of the politics surrounding the issue, however, involves a discursive struggle to establish a working definition of these people and what they are up to. Regardless of what the final outcome will be, these meanings are at present up for grabs and the outcome will depend on more than who has the most power. In this respect, the ability to cleverly shape the discursive space can have an import-ant and even decisive impact on how this struggle with evolve. The media will provide the principal form for these debates, as that is where most of us will follow these events. Each side will vie to place its own linguistic tropes on the events seen on television.

In the case of the protests in Genoa, the first media reports on German television simply showed people throwing stones and referred to them as 'chaotic' people. This was a clear expression of the hegemonic position, which a few days later waned as evidence of police brutality began to emerge and movement leaders began getting the alternative story across in the media. Prominent politicians, especially those supportive of the demonstrators, began to call for an investigation of the Italian police force in Genoa.

The winner of the discursive struggle defines what will be taken to be reality with cat-egories that at the same time suppress alternative conceptions. Through the delineation of categories and practices, for example, the defenders of globalization will seek to extend and expand a discursive field that will enable the continuing expansion of the transnational-capitalist approach to globalization. Those who speak an oppositional discourse will continue to be portrayed as either outmoded or anarchist. In the process, their questions and arguments will be suppressed.

stress some aspects of an event and conceal or downplay others (covering over potential problems—tensions or paradoxes—that might be embedded in the story).

Maintaining the social order depends on the successful reproduction of particular understandings of the relevant actors and institutions—that is, the capitalist and the free market economy require legitimization and active participation. At the same time, critical tensions in the free-market storyline ('the capitalist is only interested in his profit margin') coupled with the emergence of counter storylines based on new problematic events or revelations (such as a sudden and dramatic increase in oil prices) open the way for efforts to introduce stronger market regulations. Finding or reconstructing the appropriate storyline becomes a central form of agency for the political actor. Effective communicative skills and argumentative strategies are thus important resources that play a significant role in determining the shape of events. Like an art form, such communicative skills hold out the possibility of making people see things differently, and, in the process, shifting the course of political struggle.

The relevance of discursive strategies is particularly evident in environmental politics. The environmental movement has long been haunted by the dilemma of whether to argue on the terms set by the government or to insist on their own mode of expression. In the latter case, of course, the movement runs the risk of losing its direct influence and therefore often trades its expressive freedom for influence on the policymaking process.[3] Given a hegemonic discourse, people who try to challenge the dominant storyline are often expected to position their contribution in terms of established categories. Indeed, this is the primary way a hegemonic discourse exercises it power. The concept of 'sustainable development' is a good example of the process.[4] Because the earlier environmental storyline, 'limits to growth', proved to be a non-starter for the industrial community (as capitalist industry exists to grow), there was a need to innovate a new storyline capable of working for both environmentalists and industrialists. The response was the concept of 'sustainable development'. Shaped by leading industrials, it refers to environmental protection but without sacrificing industrial development, which environmentalists have long defined as the very source of pollution.

Environmentalists can—and often do—reject the terms set by the dominant discourse, insisting on the importance of their alternative discourse. The disciplinary

---

[3] The point is well illustrated by the Green Party in Germany. The party gained political influence by joining with the Social Democratic Party to form the governing coalition in 1998. But the Greens' position as junior member of the coalition caused the party to soften its more critical political positions, such as opposition to military engagements, at considerable cost. In response, many party loyalists resigned their memberships, charging the leadership with having politically sold out in the interest of gaining power. In the process, the party created political identity problems for itself that have led many voters to see the party as a superfluous feature of the German political landscape.

[4] The concept of sustainable development was advanced by the Bruntland Commission and was the focus of discussions at the second international Earth Summit in Rio de Janeiro. The Commission defined sustainable development as a 'framework for the integration of environmental policies and development strategies—the term "development" being used in the broadest sense of the term'. Sustainable development is designed to meet 'the needs of the present without compromising the ability of future generations to meet their own needs' (World Commission on Environment and Development 1987: 42).

force of discursive practices, as Hajer (1995*a*) explains, often depends on the implicit assumption that subsequent speakers will respond within the same discursive frame. Such discursive challenges may consist of rejecting an understanding of events and actions in terms of established categories or, often even more powerfully, in establishing new combinations with the operative, routinized discursive structures. Indeed, this is what much of contemporary environmental politics is about.

Although this social-interactive theory of discourse focuses on how people take up or deny particular positions, it also recognizes the ways in which power is embedded in the reifications of a discourse and, as such, remains hidden. People use particular terms without giving much thought to the way they sustain a specific social order. Merely consider the difference between saying 'Negro' and 'Blackman'. Both words refer to the same physical person, but each rests on and reproduces a very different conception of power relations between the races. Many people simply assume that such a word is a formal name for such a person with a particular skin colour, or that it is 'just the way one talks' on particular occasions, without being explicitly aware of (or taking into account) the social implications embedded in the language. In such cases, people can support a given power structure while explicitly denying that they are necessarily doing so. They do not use the specific words, but their listeners read racist meanings into them. Because routine forms of accepted discourse generally express continuous but opaque power relationships, they can also be especially useful to particular groups seeking to convey particular social messages while avoiding direct confrontations.[5]

Through an analysis of the social meanings embedded in the discursive practices of the societal and political institutions, the analyst can thus investigate the nature and reproduction of the power structure. At the 'macro' level of analysis, the investigator is able to focus on how political and economic elites construct and maintain a societal-wide hegemonic discourse that makes clear what is on the agenda and what is not, as well as how oppositional groups seek to make their voices heard. Today we can easily understand this in terms of the construction of a market-oriented neo-liberal ideology that now dominates not only Western industrial countries, but much of global discourse as well. The success of such a hegemonic discourse is in significant part measured in terms of the difficulties it poses for those who argue for government interventions in both the economy and the provision of social redistributive programmes. At the 'micro' level of analysis, the focus turns to the relationships between discourse and specific institutional practices. The goal, following Foucault, is to undercover the ways that discourses embedded in institutional practices function to reproduce the existing power-structure relationships from the bottom up. Here, through the workings of professional expertise, ideas and knowledge can serve as an independent force stabilizing or cementing society together. In terms of neo-liberalism this can take the form of cost-benefit oriented policy analysis in agency

---

[5] A good example here is the political rhetoric of Joerg Haider, the right-wing Austrian politician, who uses words employed by the Nazis. The words say nothing about Nazis but they serve to recall specific memories of a particular political past.

bureaucracies, which implicitly insures the primacy of market criteria, over in preference to social agency practices that emphasize 'workfare' counselling. One the surface, cost-benefit analysis looks like—and is presented as—a scientific technique for rational data collection and decision-making. But most people do not see that the data collected by the methodology channels discussion in directions biased toward a market orientation of society (Fischer 1987: 117).

Emphasis on institutional practices also helps to clear up the widespread misunderstanding that such argumentative research just deals with languages and, in the process, loses connection with the 'hard' institutional realities of policymaking. To the contrary, for the kind of discourse analysis advanced by Fairclough and Hajer, understanding what the relevant utterances mean requires approaching the institutional setting as an 'argumentative field' in which statements are made. The focus is thus not simply on the language or discursive constructs but on the ways utterances relate to the specific institutional contexts and practices in which they can be meaningfully stated and understood. Indeed, Hajer (1995*b*) takes the point a step further and argues that we need engage in 'institutional constructivism'. This involves analysing which sorts of practices actually produce or facilitate particular policy changes. In the acid rain case, for example, one of his most interesting discoveries is that, after the environmentalists had succeeded in publicly winning the policy debate—at which point everybody began speaking the environmental language, or a version of it—no policy change could be detected. Why? Because the technically oriented practices of the environmental agencies remained unchanged. Although the public political discourse had accepted the environmental understanding of acid rain, the environmental ministries continued to monitor the problem with their traditional methodologies (Hajer 1993). The practices themselves determined the policy, despite the new environmental discourse.

CONCLUSION

Discourse, as we have seen in this chapter, is an ensemble of ideas and concepts that give social meaning to social and physical relationships. Operating at both the macro and micro levels of society, discourse both transmits the cultural traditions of society and mediates everyday social and political interactions. Focusing on the relationship between discourse and social practices, the task of the discursive analyst is to explain how specific discourses become hegemonic, explicate the characteristics of discursive fields (including the nodal points that privilege some arguments over others), identify the defining claims of the particular positions, clarify how individual discourses come to influence others, determine the structure of the arguments, identify which styles of discourse make them effective in given contexts, uncover the ways that the discursive resources are distributed across social systems, and show how particular socio-historical constellations serve to justify specific courses of action. Emphasizing the ways discursive production socially constructs reality, such analysis examines the way hegemonic conceptions of reality are upheld and reproduced by key political groups, while oppositional groups seek argumentative strategies to challenge these dominant social constructs. Although discourses take place in pre-structured contexts that limit or impede the range of possible actions, persuasive discourses can even in the face entrenched social and material forces open new paths to action.

More specifically, we saw the ways discourses establish the terrain on which political struggle takes place. Assigning subject-positions to social actors in both cultural narratives and ongoing storylines, they define the actors' social and political relationships, attributing to them various social attributes such as virtue or blame. In argumentation at the micro or practical level, participants exchange competing and sometimes contradictory arguments to make sense of social reality, including the interpretation of political conflicts themselves. Operating in a field of existing narrative discourses, social and political actors are seen to choose and adapt thoughts and ideas in an ongoing effort to triumph over rival arguments.

The nature of these discursive interactions is further explored in the next chapter, which presents a comparison of Sabatier's theory of advocacy coalitions with Hajer's theory of discourse course coalitions. Of particular importance, the comparison offers the opportunity to take a closer look at the essential role of discourse and interpretation in understanding the processes of social change. Where the former seeks to advance an empiricist theory of policy change, the latter details the postempiricist discursive alternative. The two approaches are compared in terms of a concrete policy issue, environmental protection.

Finally, it should be noted that most of the points in the discussion were made or illustrated through policies pertaining to environmental politics. In significant part, this is because the fields of environmental and science studies, given their close relationship to social constructionist perspectives, have generated a great deal of the research about policy discourse. But this should not be taken to limit the value of the perspective. In the expert-oriented information society in which we live, the role of discursive politics in policymaking is expected to become increasingly apparent in other policy areas as well. If, as some have argued, the struggle between those with and those without knowledge is one of the key socio-political dynamics of this new century, the discourses of knowledge in their various forms will be a central aspect of political conflict across the policy spectrum.

APPENDIX
DISCOURSE AND SOCIAL CHANGE:
COMMODIFYING EDUCATIONAL POLICY

Fairclough's (1992: 207–15) analysis of educational commodification begins through a textual analysis illustrating the way particular words and images are mixed together to create a social meaning. Towards this end, Fairclough focuses on the how the word 'skill' is employed in a university catalogue designed to attract and inform students. The text is structured to implicitly—if not explicitly—inform the students that they need skills to get ahead in their lives and that the educational institution in question is well prepared to supply them with the appropriate skills.

After having analysed the linguistic presentation of the text, Fairclough then turns to the analysis of discursive practices to show the way the word 'skill' is given a double meaning. By strategically overlaying a term of business discourse on an educational discourse, educational planners and curriculum designers create a rhetoric of skills that can be interpreted in more than one way. As a commodified educational discourse becomes 'dominated by a vocabulary of skills, including not only the word "skill", but a whole wording of the processes of learning and teaching based upon concepts of skill, skill training, use of skills, transfer of skills, and so forth', the concept permits 'two often contradictory constructions of the learner to coexist without manifest inconsistency, because it seems to fit into either an individual view of learning, or an objectivist view of training'. In addition to the semantic history of the word, as Fairclough writes, 'this ambivalence is reflected in the history of the concept within liberal humanist and conservative economic discourse'. The concept of skill, on the one hand, 'has active and individualist implications: skills are prized attributes of individuals, individuals differ in types and degree of skill, and it is open to each individual to refine skills or add new ones'. The concept of skill, on the other hand, 'has normative, passive and objectifying implications: all individuals acquire elements from a common social repertoire of skills, via normalized training procedures, and skills are assumed to be transferable across context, occasions, and users, in a way which leaves little space for individuality'.

Drawing on laissez-faire, market-oriented economic discourse, 'the message to teachers and course planners is a subtle version of the marketing axiom of consumer sovereignty: "Give the customers what they want"'. This juxtaposing of 'wordings facilitates the metaphorical transfer of the vocabulary of commodities and markets into the educational order of discourse'. But, at the same time, 'this commodified educational discourse is commonly more self-contradictory that this might suggest'. A clue to such contradictions in the blurring of clients and consumers is an ambiguity about to whom educational packages are being sold. Who is doing the learning? Is it the students or the companies that are likely to hire the students? The company may in fact need clients 'in the direct sense of paying the learner to take a course'. In this way, 'learners are contradictorily constructed'. They are constructed 'in the active role of discerning customers or consumers aware of their "needs" and able to select courses which meet their needs'. But they are constructed, at the same time, 'in the passive role of elements or instruments in the production processes, targeted to train in required "skills" or "competences", courses designed around precise "attainment targets" and culminating in "profiles" of learners, both of which are specified in terms of quite precise skills'. This subtle intermingling of active and passive constructions of student learners 'facilitates the manipulation of the learners through education, by overlying it with what one might call an individualist and consumeristic rhetoric'.

From the perspective of social practices the university has conflated these separate discourses in such a way that, while they benefit different participants differently, they gradually come to be taken as the same thing. That is, obtaining skill comes to be seen as the essence of education, although the curriculum for these skills is no longer shaped around the liberal arts components, but rather the needs of industry. Instead of the traditional understanding of education as a way for the individual to broaden his or her relationship to the world in which he or she lives, thus opening up new possibilities, it is in fact narrowed down to a package that is shaped to meet the needs of business and industry rather than the individual per se. This is not to say that the individual cannot gain from this restructuring, but it is to say that the choices are dramatically limited to those that also fit the interests of the employers. Subtly, though, in the process the two come to be conflated. The university tries to say at the same time, 'come to us and get a well-rounded education', but at the same time it is saying 'come to us and get a job'. The two are not the same and the tension has to be mediated. This happens through the concept of skill, which blurs the tension in subtle ways. In the process, the university gets restructured. It becomes increasingly of a training centre for industry, with the business school more and more emerging as the primary faculty, rather than a traditional centre for knowledge and learning for itself. Whereas the traditional university was administered by the faculty, as they possessed the knowledge of the curriculum and could best decide the issues of learning, today the deans become managers and the faculty members are increasingly their subordinates. The facade of faculty governance remains, but it increasingly serves to hide the real nature of institutional power and control.

5

Discourse versus Advocacy Coalitions: Interpreting Policy Change and Learning

Perhaps the most widely discussed contribution to the field of policy studies during the past decade has been the Advocacy Coalition Framework (ACF) developed by Sabatier (1987; 1988) and his associates, Hank Jenkins-Smith in particular (Sabatier and Jenkins-Smith 1993). This work was advanced as a response to what they see as the main failure of the field. Policy studies, they argue, has failed to produce a systematic body of rigorous empirical research findings, a point about which there can be little disagreement. In particular, they single out the 'stages model' of the policy cycle for failing to generate rigorous policy research.

Missing from the stages heuristic, as Sabatier and Jenkins-Smith (1993) argue, is a causal model that offers a clear basis for empirical hypothesis testing. Basic to their critique is an explicit call for empirical causal explanations of policy change capable of building the foundations of a predictive policy science. Towards this end, Sabatier (1987) has advanced his policy advocacy coalition framework, which in every way is a rigorous call for the rejuvenation of the empiricist research agenda in policy studies. Designed to set the field on firmer scientific foundations, there is no better example of the empiricist project in contemporary policy studies.

To the credit of Sabatier and his colleagues, the policy advocacy coalition framework has not only managed to generate a more interesting set of research questions than its predecessors, the stage model in particular,[1] it has succeeded in capturing the minds of a considerable number of scholars in both the USA and Europe. Presented as an integrative model that builds on a range of theoretical contributions, in particular work on the socio-economic correlates of policy outcomes, policy network theory, policy learning theory, ideas-based empirical research, and institutional rational choice theory, there are few discussions of policy theory today that do not devote attention to the advocacy coalition framework.

Basic to the ACF is the importance of policy sub-systems in policy formulation and implementation. Like many US and European policy scholars, Sabatier and

---

[1] Although some have treated the stages model of policy research (that is, the sequence of steps through agenda-setting, policy formulation, adoption, implementation, and evaluation) as if it were a research model, particularly as it relates to rational problem-solving, it is better understood only as a general heuristic for delineating the kinds of issues that have to be researched. See deLeon (1999).

Jenkins-Smith (1993) emphasize the significance of relationships within policy sectors for understanding how policy decision-making functions. As such, the ACF framework has roots in the work on policy communities and policy issue network theory. Moreover, as with policy network theory generally, the ACF takes policymaking to be an ongoing process with no clearly demarcated beginnings or terminations. The advocacy coalition, though, involves a broader set of processes than the policy network perspective. An advocacy coalition is conceived of as an alliance of political groups in a policy subsystem sharing the same interests and ideas that come together to argue against other policy coalitions concerned with the same policy issues. Involving more participants than the traditional policy sector decision-makers—administrators, congressional committee members, and relevant industry lobbyists—advocacy coalitions, like policy communities more generally, include journalists, interested politicians, public interest groups, policy analysts and researchers, state and local officials, among others. All play a role in the dissemination of policy ideas. In contrast to policy-network theory, advocacy coalition members bargain and form alliances within a policy subsystem. Rather than consensus dominated by relatively stable political patterns of negotiations, which tends to characterize the European focus on networks, the ACF emphasizes cross-cutting networks of political elites.

The goal of the ACF is to empirically explain policy change through the interaction of competing advocacy coalitions. An advocacy coalition, according to Sabatier and Jenkins-Smith, refers to coalitions of 'actors from a variety of... institutions at all levels of government who share a set of basic beliefs... who seek to manipulate the rules, budgets, and personnel of governmental institutions in order to achieve these goals over time' (1993: 5). In this scheme, between two and four coalitions are involved, each with its own policy belief systems, which compete for dominance in a particular policy sector. Because the political struggle for policy control or change is played out through the argumentative interactions of the actors holding these policy belief systems, knowledge plays a basic role in the struggle. In so far as public policies are seen to rest on implicit theories about how to reach their goals, they themselves can be conceptualized in the same way as belief systems generally. In addition to basic value priorities, they offer perceptions of important causal relationships, ideas of world states (including the magnitude of the problem), positions on the efficacy of policy instruments, and so on. This cross-mapping of beliefs and policies is seen to offer a way of evaluating the influence of various political actors over time, including the role of technical policy-analytic information on policy change.

Towards this end, Sabatier has modelled the structure of a policy belief after Lakatos's (1971) theory of knowledge. A policy belief system is conceived as being hierarchically organized around a deep core of fundamental empirical and normative axioms, a secondary policy core that contains information about basic policy practices, and a range of instrumental considerations pertinent to the implementation of the policy core.[2] Drawing on Lakatos's distinction between core and subsidiary

---

[2] Some epistemologists argue that a belief system is more like a web than a hierarchy. For present purposes, however, we shall ignore this point.

elements of scientific belief systems, the ACF lays out 'three structural categories: a deep core of fundamental normative and ontological axioms that define a person's underlying political philosophy, a near (policy) core of basic strategies and policy positions for achieving deep core beliefs in the policy area or subsystem in question, and a set of secondary aspects comprising a multitude of instrumental decisions and information searches necessary to implement the policy core in the specific policy area' (Sabatier 1993: 30). The three basic structural categories 'are arranged in order of decreasing resistance to change, that is the deep core is much more resistant than the secondary aspects'.

Underlying the ACF conceptualization of policy belief systems are three fundamental theoretical foundations. The first is an 'expected utility model' introduced to account for the way political actors weigh their alternative courses of action against their contributions to a particular set of goals and objectives. In this view, decisions are largely instrumental in nature. Second, rationality is understood to be limited rather than perfect. Decisions are thus the result of 'satisficing', the process of dealing with the cognitive limits on rationality that emphasizes limited searches for information.[3] Third, Sabatier and Jenkins-Smith (1993) maintain that because policy subsystems are composed of and dominated by policy elites, as opposed to members of the public at large, there are credible reasons for believing that most political actors engaged in the policy process will have fairly complex and logically consistent belief systems in the policy sectors that interest them.

A policy position is thus grounded in claims about causal knowledge. The essential core axioms and many of the policy practices are, according to the theory, resistant to change. Core axioms and stable secondary propositions, for this reason, give rise to stable coalitions. Ideas, in this scheme, remain stable unless there are major external disruptions. Only large-scale external shocks to the policy system (such as an oil crisis in the case of energy policy, serious and enduring recession in economic policy, or war in foreign policy) are seen to be capable of shaking the core of a policy belief system.

Why are core beliefs so resistant? The reason, argue Sabatier and Jenkins-Smith (1993), is that policymakers always seek to interpret new events in ways that do not disturb their basic axioms of knowledge. Only a serious crisis holds out the possibility of shaking basic policy beliefs. By making it at times impossible to avoid or overlook the fact that specific beliefs fail to explain key events, a severe 'reality' shock can jolt policymakers into examining and rethinking the basic beliefs that guide their actions. Here the process is seen to be analogous to the process of paradigm change envisioned by Kuhn (1970) in scientific research. Under stable or 'normal' periods, policy beliefs, like scientific beliefs, are understood and adjusted within an established paradigmatic framework. As in the case of 'normal science', it is only when such dominant frameworks fail to explain crucial events that researchers begin to question the paradigm itself and the search for its successor begins sooner or later to follow.[4]

---

[3] See Simon (1957).

[4] Kuhn (1970) developed a theory of scientific change which shows that the replacement of one theory with another does not happen simply on the basis of the accumulation of evidence against

Taking cognizance of such patterns, Sabatier and Jenkins-Smith recommend that, in determining how policy-relevant knowledge shapes the agenda, as well as how learning takes place, policy researchers focus on the influence such coalitions have on a policy issue for the duration of at least a decade. From their cognitive fortresses competing coalitions advance their strategic arguments. The primary independent role of knowledge, according to the model, is through policy learning, played out in the debates in the policy networks, especially expert debates. Policy learning thus mainly impacts on the secondary core aspects of policy belief systems.

Although the primary focus is structured around a synthesis of ideas about networks and beliefs, Sabatier and Jenkins-Smith bring in other dimensions of the political system. Institutions are said to play a role through the levels of government and the interaction of government agencies and committees, though this discussion remains quite general and underdeveloped. Nor does the framework have much to say about the role of actors' exercising political choice. ACF theorists see interests and ideas moulding individual actors into patterns of political behaviour, with strategic political interaction and social choice scarcely coming into play, a point to which we return.

More important than either institutions or strategic choice is the role of economic change. Policymaking in the ACF depends on stability and change in the wider socio-economic system. Changes in the economy or society flow into public opinion, affecting the policy orientations of interest groups and political parties and thus the ideas and social preferences of policy decision-makers.[5] This is, in a sense, a equilibrium model of policy change.[6] 'While Sabatier and his co-researchers are careful to reject a deterministic model of policy change', as John (1998: 171) explains, 'they argue that rapid change in the external world gives "shocks" to the policy-makers by disrupting stable patterns of interests and exchanges.' Although social and economic conditions external to the policy-making system generally serve as stabilizing factors for relatively long durations, major disruptions of these conditions can alter the meanings and salience of the pertinent policy ideas. The economic crisis created by the 1973 oil embargo, for example, is seen to have precipitated rapid policy changes that culminated in the major policy regime shift ushered in by President Ronald Reagan in the 1980s. Although it is difficult to find fault with the example per se, standing alone it overlooks the discursive role played by the neoconservatives in bringing about those changes.

The advocacy of new solutions to policy problems in such situations can unsettle or disrupt the pattern of political interests that glue together an advocacy coalition,

---

a theory. Rather, irrational resistance against new theories often comes from researchers with a vested interest in the existing theories, or what he called 'normal science'. Frequently, a science has had to await for the demise of an older generation of scientists to finish the process of a 'scientific revolution'.

[5] Here the approach draws on Hofferbert's (1990) funnel model. The framework also bears resemblances to a general equilibrium model of political change.

[6] John (1998) argues, for example, that, when a crisis event (such as an economic crisis) occurs, it redistributes the resources within the coalition and this makes it difficult to determine if it is the ideas about the crisis or the changing interests in the coalitions that creates the response. It is a charge that Sabatier and Jenkins-Smith acknowledge, but essentially don't deal with.

creating in the process new relationships among crucial political actors. The out-come can be policy change, but there is no way to empirically predict which direction it will take. For instance, the first response to the oil crisis was the Carter Administration's energy-saving programmes in the 1970s, to be followed in subsequent years by Reagan's very different market-based measures. The result of the Reagan changes was a very different approach to the energy problem, supported by a stable conservative 'neoliberal' advocacy coalition.

What the ACF tries to answer is this: 'what will happen when experience reveals anomalies—such as internal inconsistencies, inaccurate predictions, and invalid assertions—among beliefs' (Sabatier and Jenkins-Smith 1993: 30). Beginning from the assumption that actors feel social-psychological pressures to hold valid and consistent belief systems, Sabatier (1993: 30) ask whether 'conflicts are resolved in a essentially random process—that is, with all beliefs accorded the same logical status—or are some beliefs more fundamental than others and thus more resistant to change?'

From this conceptualization of the ACF, Sabatier (1993: 27–34) outlines a series of empirical hypotheses to be tested. For illustrative purposes, five of the basic hypotheses are listed below.

Hypothesis 1: In major controversies within a policy subsystem when core beliefs are in dispute, the lineup of allies and opponents tends to be rather stable over periods of a decade or so.

Hypothesis 2: Actors within an advocacy coalition will show substantial consensus on issues pertaining to the policy core, although less so on secondary aspects.

Hypothesis 3: An actor (or coalition) will give up secondary aspects of a belief system before acknowledging weaknesses in the policy core.

Hypothesis 4: The core (basic attributes) of a governmental program is unlikely to be significantly revised as long as the subsystem advocacy coalition that instituted the program remains in power.

Hypothesis 5: The core (basic attitudes) of a governmental action program is unlikely to be changed in the absence of significant perturbations external to the subsystem, that is, changes in socio-economic conditions, system-wide governing coalitions, or policy outputs form other subsystems.

Towards this end, Sabatier and Jenkins-Smith have developed empirical research strategies for mapping the structures of such coalitions over time. Unfortunately, though, this extensive research effort proves only the most straightforward and common-sense hypotheses. Sabatier and Jenkins-Smith do engage a number of scholars who offer more traditional qualitative case studies in *Policy Change and Learning*, an edited volume designed to explore empirically the PAC. While they acknowledge that qualitative methods can help, such work is posited as secondary to the quantitative analysis. Its use is primarily in assisting the empirical worker with the process of hypothesis formation and concept formation. The fact that the qualitative studies in the volume tend at best to give the ACF mixed reviews is largely shrugged off in their final assessment of the value of the model.

A primary contribution of ACF research is the finding that the role of interests over time is not strong enough alone to explain change. Policy ideas and beliefs clearly play a role. Despite the stimulation that the ACF has brought to a rigorous analytical policy discussion, however, it has been criticized from numerous quarters. The main criticism concerns its inability to explain policy change. On its own, it seems better at explaining policy stability. This is especially the case given its reliance on external events to explain political changes in and among coalitions.

It is also argued that the ACF may overemphasize external factors through its use of the time-series method. External shocks are easy to measure in time-series analyses, but this emphasis may be misleading. It would appear to have led Sabatier and associates to neglect the role of strategies of coalition-formation, including the role of rhetoric or discourse in their development (John 1998). Moreover, the results of their empirical efforts are not entirely supportive of a shock model, as they acknowledge. Sometimes external events fail to have the expected effect on coalition formation, suggesting other possible explanations. One of them is that political elites can discursively interpret such events in ways that manage and reduce public concerns, minimizing demands for policy responses.

It is also possible that a style of group interaction that features a large number of policy actors—particularly new ones such as policy analysts and journalists—is not entirely suited for policy explanations outside the USA. The policy communities of Western European countries are more closed than those in the USA, although these communities are themselves starting to change in similar directions. Not only are European policy issues becoming more complex, they are showing greater fragmentation as the number of players increases in the policy decision-making process. While this trend has begun to manifest itself at the national level of politics, such developments are especially evident in the policymaking processes of the European Union. In this regard, the policy advocacy coalition approach may be more useful for analysing EU policymaking than policymaking in the member countries, as new ideas and a greater fluidity of policy networks are basic to the European Commission.

With regard to the structure of policy belief systems, there is considerable evidence that the process of discursive argumentation follows something like the Lakatosian model. But discourse analysts criticize Sabatier and Jenkins-Smith's emphasis on technical considerations advanced through expert discourses. While there is ample evidence to show that different groups seek first to protect the core components of their belief systems by deflecting challenges to argumentation at the peripheral levels, it is not the case that such challenges, or even effective challenges, occur only at this level. Indeed, illustrating this point is a central concern of Hajer's discourse coalitions approach, to which we turn in the next section.

Finally, it is interesting to note that throughout the efforts to empirically demonstrate the ACF, there are regular references to the absence of the kinds of data important to the various analyses. In some cases it is suggested that the missing empirical data will not create a problem for the findings, even though such data often appear to be central. In other instances, proxy data of various sorts are employed, with the argument that it should be good enough or that it is the best one can do. There is scarcely any mention that such absences jeopardize the possibility of creating the kind of predictive causal theory called for.[7] Moreover, there is no apparent recognition that the justification for eliminating or substituting various indicators raises just the kind of interpretive issues social constructionists describe as basic to the conduct of science in general. That is to say, despite the aversion to interpretive methods, the empirical analysis of the ACF is, like scientific analysis generally, infused with interpretations. Rather than acknowledging the process as basic to the practice of such analysis, Sabatier and Jenkins-Smith invariably seek to downplay such interventions as unproblematic or unimportant. What they fail to concede is that their own work remains as much in the realm of interpretation as in that of empirical proof.

Despite these problematic criticisms, however, one can still say that the ACF framework has significantly expanded the purview of policy studies in the direction of policy debate and argumentation. This approach to policy coalitions brings into play a much larger range of participants than traditional institutional, group, or network accounts. Experts, analysts, technicians, journalists, television programmers, researchers, and academics all have a role. In the end, the arguments about norms and evidence advanced by this range of participants play an identifiable and, at times, important role in structuring policy outcomes. Bringing these factors together both theoretically and empirically is an important theoretical advance in the study of public policy. But, beyond a synthesis of theoretical perspectives, the advance is jeopardized by Sabatier and Jenkins-Smith's empiricist approach. While they offer the framework with the intent of promoting the development of a rigorous empirical causal model of policy change, this is not a workable approach from a constructivist perspective. The problem is not so much the theoretical framework per se, but rather the neopositivist methodology with which they approach it, as we shall demonstrate in the next section. As an extension of the discussion of discourse analysis in Chapter 4, we examine these concerns through the lens of Hajer's 'discourse coalition' model of policy change.

DISCOURSE COALITIONS: CRITIQUE OF THE
ADVOCACY COALITION FRAMEWORK

To recall the discussion in Chapter 4, it is clear that Hajer provides a very different model of policy change from Sabatier's. Although his analysis of discourse coalitions focuses on environmental policy, as does much of Sabatier's work on advocacy coalitions, the discourse coalition approach is similarly designed to explain policy

---

[7] At various junctures in their efforts to empirically support their claims that the advocacy coalition framework is a rigorous causal theory, Sabatier and Jenkins-Smith point to the problems of missing data needed to prove their theory (see, for example, Sabatier and Jenkins-Smith 1993: 155). But this never seems to have an influence on their positive conclusions. Invariably, they find reasons to proceed without the data, while a social constructionist would use this as an illustration of the interpretive element in the social scientific research project (see Chapter 6). In other places, they disagree among themselves about the implications of the empirical findings for major theoretical issues at the theoretical core the advocacy coalition framework (Sabatier and Jenkins-Smith 1993: 225). Rather than entertaining the possibility that these differences might jeopardize the validity of the model, they simply say that the reader should decide.

change generally. These factors, coupled with the fact that Hajer's analysis includes a discussion and critique of the ACF, facilitate a discursive-analytic critique of Sabatier's model.[8] Though Hajer's approach is multifaceted and could take the discussion here in several directions, the primary objective is to use his critique to show the limits of Sabatier's neopositivist objectives and to illustrate a discourse-analytic alternative.

Most fundamentally, Hajer's critique is built around his contention that the advocacy coalition framework is too thin analytically to adequately account for the interactive dynamics of policy change. He acknowledges that the ACF identifies and describes important aspects of policy change, but argues that the key issue from a discourse perspective is that the ACF is unable to explain *why* and *how* changes come about. When the ACF tries to explain change, as Hajer (1995*b*: 5) writes, 'it takes refuge in very general statements that help very little in understanding the time and space dynamics of change'. That is, it neglects the social and historical context in which such change takes place. Such contextless statements are essentially a consequence of Sabatier's empiricist desire to develop empirical hypotheses that are universally applicable to the widest range of social contexts. To engage in this kind of science, however, important explanatory factors have to be put in 'black boxes'. In short, they have to be placed outside the analysis. Moreover, the items that the ACF black boxes are precisely those symbolic, normative concerns that a discourse analysis takes as its primary subject. The material that discourse analysis identifies as key to understanding why and how specific policy changes come about is methodologically excluded from the neopositivist analysis.

The first problem, in this respect, is the ACF's understanding of environmental politics. An environmental advocacy coalition is structured as a relatively unified coalition of groups with a commonly shared set of beliefs. Such an interpretation is necessary for the purposes of organizing the empirical data into distinct categories, but it neglects or defies critically important differences inside the environmental movement, from those taking a basic reformist perspective (who are willing to negotiate in corporate boardrooms) to those who oppose industrial society more generally (including those who chain themselves to trees). Such tensions within the movement have often had important impacts on the political strategies advanced by environmental leaders (Dowie 1995). More specifically, they can determine the kinds of negotiations that a policy advocacy coalition is willing to entertain, especially over time.

Sabatier and Jenkins-Smith basically attempt to ignore or circumvent this problem by selecting a narrow set of environmental groups and recording their contributions to policy argumentation as if they represent the movement as a whole. It might increase the chances of coming up with empirical correlations, but it puts in doubt the relationship of any such correlations to reality. (It could also in itself be read as

---

[8] Part of the discussion in this section draws on a debate over advocacy coalitions versus discourse coalitions between Sabatier and Jenkins-Smith and Hajer and Fischer at the annual meeting of the American Political Science Association in 1995, including the paper Hajer (1995*b*) prepared for the occasion.

a political statement or judgement about the environmental movement: some groups are to be taken seriously but not others.) In any case, the respective importance of the different groups has to be decided by events over time, not by the operational-ization of variables.

Beyond this most basic concern, Hajer finds the concept of an advocacy coalition to rest on false assumptions about both how policy coalitions are structured and how they function. An 'advocacy coalition', according to Sabatier (1993: 25), refers to a group of actors sharing a set of basic beliefs who seek through a 'non-trivial degree of coordinated activity' to achieve their policy goals over a period of time. The ques-tion is, asks Hajer, what is the essential variable here? Where Sabatier and his col-leagues emphasize policy beliefs, Hajer points to narrative storylines rather than cognitive beliefs. Instead of being constructed around preconceived beliefs, policy coalitions are held together by narrative storylines that *interpret* events and courses of action in concrete social contexts.

This is not to say that there are no beliefs systems. Rather, it is to argue that it is not the knowledge in belief systems per se that holds the members of such coalitions together, but the 'storylines' that symbolically condense the facts and values basic to a belief system. To be sure, many professional experts in a policy coalition are inter-ested in the validity of core cognitive factors, particularly those in the professional 'policy networks' relevant to the issue area. But the broad majority of the members of a politically oriented policy coalition respond to simplified storylines that sym-bolically reflect the concerns of core beliefs rather than the beliefs themselves. For the kind of empirical research that Sabatier wants to conduct this poses a major prob-lem. Storylines, as symbolically constructed discursive structures, cannot be object-ively analysed like particular beliefs, which can at least in principle lend themselves to particular hypotheses. Aspects of storylines, to be sure, can be empirically exam-ined, but their meaning and role in change is qualitative in nature and has to be inter-preted in the specific contexts of action (that is, the social context which are black-boxed by the ACF).

To better understand how narrative storylines work, consider how individuals adopt them in the first place. Most people come to their basic ideological orientations and political identities through a combination of socialization and emotional responses to important life-situations. Take, for example, the case of people who identify themselves as conservatives. Attracted emotionally as much as intellectually to a particular orientation to the world, such people join with other like-minded indi-viduals who share a set of conservative views about both how the world works and how it should work. While they adopt the conservative position on political issues, the choices are typically more a response based on an emotional orientation than specific facts underlying the position. What is more, the basic beliefs that they espouse are generally adopted second-hand.[9] Having never carefully examined these facts themselves, they simply accept and hold them. Maintained through discursive

---

[9] There is an extensive literature in social psychology on this point, including the way people use short-hand heuristics to make decisions rather than the actual information itself (Kinder 1998).

reproductions—repetition—such positions operate to a considerable degree independently of factual investigation (as they are typically not adopted because of the facts alone). Hence, it is not the validity of the facts per se that motivates a person to reconsider his or her views on a political issue. A person will seldom necessarily or quickly change his or her beliefs because of purported problems with the facts if they contradict his or her ideological orientation. Individual preferences are thus less well defined and much more fluid than the ACF suggests. As Reich (1988: 5) has argued, instead of merely responding to pre-existing and firmly held public wants, the art of policymaking involves in significant part 'giving voice to these half-articulated fears and hopes, and embodying them in convincing stories about their sources and the choices they represent'.

The beliefs that citizens and their politicians hold are generally rooted in two fundamental concerns. The first is the human desire for social solidarity, for belonging, for attachment, and for approval. In this sense, as Kinder and Sears (1985: 672) put it, 'political ideas are "badges of social membership"'. Both concretely and symbolically, they reflect complex social allegiances and animosities. People have few preconceived preferences and interests divorced from their group affiliations and social relationships. Moreover, the political and policy-oriented ideas and beliefs that they do have are typically based on rather general knowledge of issues and purposes. Although many people cling to specific values, and may even have strong positive or negative feelings toward politics, few citizens show much interest or appetite for coherent ideologies or abstract principles. In most cases, the links between people's self-interests and specific beliefs appear to be skewed—even sometimes overwhelmed—by emotional factors. From this perspective, as Orren (1988) argues, politics has more in common with religion than with science. The search for policy-relevant facts is not unimportant, but it takes a back seat to storylines that offer social orientation, reassurance, or guidance.

Thus, what people in an environmental discourse coalition support is an interpretation of threat or crisis, not a core set of facts and values that can be teased out through content or factor analysis. Rather than a stable core of cognitive commitments and beliefs, they share storylines that often tend to be vague on particular points and, at times, contradictory on others. This is not to argue that there are no core policy beliefs undergirding a storyline; instead it is to say that beyond the relevant professionals working in a field, most people do not possess enough of the concrete knowledge required to justify referring to their commitment to a core belief system in any empirical sense of the term. Consequently, it not a set of specific facts of a belief system that constitutes the critical dynamic holding a policy coalition together. Moreover, even when we can map out the belief system underlying a storyline, the storyline itself is more than a set of facts and normative orientations. It involves a melding of these components into a persuasive narrative structure that provides orientation more than specific pieces of information. It is, in this way, more a way of thinking about a problem than it is an assemblage of facts. As a way of thinking, it can also permit people with somewhat different core beliefs to continue to be part of the same coalition. If, for instance, the primary storyline is the need to

accept a 'precautionary principle' to govern environmental protection, one can disagree on important facts without switching over to a coalition that sees the precautionary principle a threat to the capitalist system.

Equally important, storylines are not just about a given reality. While they typically give coalition members a normative orientation to a particular reality, they are
as much about changing that reality as they are about simply understanding and
affirming it. They are, in short, about 'world making' (Goodman 1978). In this sense,

---

Global Warming and its Discourse Coalitions

A contemporary example of discursive politics is the controversy that has surrounded the
attempt to ratify the Kyoto Treaty on global warming. Although European governments
and more than 100 additional countries around the world have agreed to support for the
treaty, the Bush administration has refused to sign it, arguing that it suffers from various
technical problems related to its implementation. According to the administration's argument, the treaty is bad policy because it is grounded in faulty empirical assumptions
about its ability to achieve success. This would seem to support the ACF model of
environmental politics. But supporters of the treaty generally don't take issue with these
factual contentions. Rather they have struggled to keep the treaty alive because it signi-
fies a continuing commitment to global environmental protection. In this sense, it a way
of thinking about global environmentalism rather than a hard core set of accepted beliefs.
That is, the basic issue is not the facts alone. Problematic for the Bush administration, at
the same time, is its failure to come up with an alternative storyline.*

Given that the Bush administration has done little more than argue for more research,
as if getting better facts was alone the issue, it finds itself increasingly positioned as the
bad guys in the contemporary environmental narratives. One need not argue here that
facts don't count in politics to recognize that it is first and foremost storylines that drive
this matter. Facts are important but only as they fit into storylines. As is evident from a
closer look at the Europeans' argument for supporting the Kyoto Treaty, the conflict is
over a storyline about global warming and the narrative that supports it.

The storyline says there is a crisis and something has to be done; the situation requires
attention. Even though we don't know all of the causal relationships that create global
warming, holding to the commitment to take action together preserves the possibility of
continuing to work on finding a solution. The Bush counter-argument implies that
the problem isn't so urgent and that it is unwise to make a commitment before
knowing the facts. What the Bush administration neglects is the powerful symbolic
dimension that the treaty offers, independently of whatever effects it might or might not
have. Kyoto, it fails to recognize, has become a symbol that creates a powerful emotive
response. It is this emotive response that has generated the politics against the United
States, not the facts. Factually, the United States is not necessarily wrong, but that is not
what drives policy change, at least not alone.

*This is an essential issue in Roe's (1994) discussion of narrative policy analysis, that is, the
necessity to supply alternative narrative storylines, a topic we take up in Chapter 8.

their objective is to bring about a set of circumstances that does not yet exist. The fact that it does not exist does not mean that it is without significance. If people believe in and act upon a particular utopian conception of the world, it can be very real in its consequences. To reject such beliefs as subjective, as positivists do, is to throw out the very stuff that is driving the struggle for change.

Facts can, of course, create problems for storylines. But storylines have a resilience, like Sabatier's advocacy coalitions. Indeed, this is what Sabatier points to himself when he argues that coalitions can be stable and unbendable over substantial periods of time. The reason he gives is that the actors in a coalition can for long periods of time interpret the facts according to their own interpretive schemes. And when these facts are problematic for the scheme they can be denied or even ignored for substantial periods of time. But ACF theorists fail to recognize the implications of this. Rather than seeing the interpretive schemes—or what we call here 'storylines'— as the primary dynamic driving the process, they treat them as secondary to the empirical cognitive dimensions. Instead of taking these interpretive frameworks as the primary focus of analytical interest, they are treated more as subjective factors that tend to get in the way of knowledge-based cognitive changes. Cognitive policy beliefs do exists, but they are more the stuff of academic research rather than political struggle. In this sense, one can argue that ACF researchers have substituted their own academic policy focus for that of the everyday world actors they are investigating.

Given the interpretive nature of storylines, debates about issues like environmental pollution turn out to be as much about the social order as they are about measurable things like bad air and dirt. To illustrate this, Hajer employs Douglas's (1988) famous definition of pollution as 'matter out of place'. Anthropologist Douglas coined this succinct phrase to demonstrate the ways in which the concept of pollution relates to more than a set of physical characteristics. Even more fundamentally, it possesses a social meaning that is determined by the specific sociocultural context in which it is uttered. To analyse pollution as a quasi-technical reality, as Hajer (1995a: 18) puts it, 'misses the essential social questions that are implicated in such debates'. Pollution 'is not only a technical-administrative affair in which the objective reality of expert discourse determines what is out of place and which solutions are selected that respect the implicit social order of the expert discourse.'

Storylines also have important implications for understanding the coordination and operation of policy coalitions. For Sabatier and Jenkins-Smith (1993: 5), advocacy coalitions involve individuals who get together (in 'non-trivial' ways) to coordinate their political activities in specific, identifiable ways. From the perspective of a discourse coalition approach, policy coalitions, as discursive phenomena, 'are reproduced and transformed through a variety of political actors that do not necessarily meet but through their very activities reinforce a particular set of *story lines* in a given policy domain'. A policy coalition, for this reason, can be much larger and more flexible than Sabatier's advocacy coalition concept would indicate. People in India, Germany, and the United States, for example, can all share, sustain, and reproduce the sustainable development storyline without having met each other, let alone having coordinated their political activities. The same, of course, can be said of people in the

United States who send financial contributions to the Friends of the Earth. They support the environmental storyline of Friends of the Earth without having ever gone to a meeting, or necessarily knowing exactly the organization's policy positions. Such a discursive understanding of policy coalitions means that the interactive dynamics of a discourse coalition does not involve the kinds of objectively identifiable activities that Sabatier and Jenkins-Smith take as their units of measurement. Important defining features of such coalitions can be described, but not nailed down with the sort of empirical precision required of a rigorous scientific explanation.

The goal of the discursive-analytic approach is to show that argumentative interaction operates as a relatively 'independent layer of power practices' governed by a logic far more complex than the analyses of conventional realists recognize (Hajer 1995*b*). Where the empirical realist relegates the politics of discourse to the expression of power resources through language, which in part it surely is, the discourse analyst also recognizes the process to create structures and fields of action by means of narrative storylines, which position the relevant actors and selectively employ discursive systems such as law, economics, or physics. New discourses can—and at times do—have the power to alter existing commitments. They supply people with new ideas about their potential role and possibilities for change that can create new capacities to act. In the process, actors are by no means completely autonomous: they are constrained not only by conventional understandings and agreed-upon rules of the game but also by mutual positioning, existing institutional routines, and changing contexts. From the analysis of discourse coalitions we see how these practices can mutually influence and reinforce one another.

In addition to helping political actors constitute coalitions in policy domains, storylines are instrumental in the constructing of the policy problems in the first place. Drawing from his research on acid rain, Hajer (1995*b*: 3) puts it this way: 'Dead fish or dying trees might have been well established physical phenomenon but it the acid rain story-line that relates them to human action and first presents the forester and fisherman with an alternative understanding of a natural phenomenon and indeed first allows the dead fish to become a policy problem.' Hence, 'acid rain can be seen as a way of defining air pollution that was emblematic of environmental discourse in the 1980s, which has now yielded to ozone concentrations and global warming.' 'This issue of defining and refining', Hajer (1995*b*: 3) writes, 'is the sort of issue the ACF argues it wants to address but its insistence on anchoring the analysis to a "given" reality stands in its way of doing so.'

In the ACF, problems and solutions present themselves as relatively well-defined and the analysis focuses on the identification of the coalitions arguing for the particular understandings and approaches to them. In contrast to well-defined problems and solutions, Hajer argues that the analyst needs to examine how different coalitions struggle through argumentation to define and redefine the problem, the solutions, and their own orientations to them. Moreover, whereas the ACF researchers emphasize the positive benefits of quantitative indicators in helping to solve policy controversies, discourse theorists investigate why these particular indicators are seen as legitimate and appropriate for the role.

Hajer's (1995*a*) own work on air pollution policy offers a good example of such argumentation over definitions. Acid rain started off in Britain as a new storyline that tended to destabilize the existing patterns of environmental argumentation. Suddenly air pollution was no longer a localizable health issue, as initially defined, but now was concerned with nature as well. In the process, the definition of the air pollution problem defied the ability of existing arrangements to categorize it in ways that made it easy to regulate and manage. Hajer could in fact identify a coalition that argued precisely this case. Yet, as his research showed, it was by no means the sort of an advocacy coalition that Sabatier and Jenkins-Smith speak of. Absent was the well-coordinated advocacy process that centred around Lakatosian-like policy belief systems. Rather, he found a great many different policy actors often with differing beliefs systems uttering a wide variety of bits and pieces of knowledge and ideas that made up the discursive construct of acid rain. In fact, it was the introduction of the acid rain concept and the storyline to which it gave rise that first brought the majority of these actors together, instead of the other way around. What is more, they came together not so much physically but as 'co-authors' contributing their pieces to the acid rain story.

Thus, where the ACF defines policy coalitions in terms of 'core beliefs' shared by conspiring actors that coordinate their undertakings, Hajer finds that coalitions are based on the shared usage of a set of storylines. In the initial phases of the policy process, he argues, these storylines tend to be more effective the more they are *multi-interpretable*. Multi-interpretable storylines, not shared knowledge, were the glue of acid rain coalitions.

The argumentative alternative to the ACF is to speak of *discourse coalitions* whose members share a particular way of thinking about and discussing environmental issues. Instead of an 'objective' environmental problem that can be nailed down empirically, the discourse analyst has to dig out the different ways of talking that can be found in the environmental domain. Hajer shows, in this respect, that the career of the acid rain storyline moved in tandem with the career of a much more elaborate and new way of thinking about the environment, namely, 'ecological modernization'.

In effect, the acid rain controversy was a struggle between competing ways of framing environmental pollution problems that had dramatically different institutional implications. It was not the objective, measurable facts of the problem but rather the way of seeing the facts that became important. In this way, the acid rain controversy is interpretively read by a discourse analyst as an argumentative struggle to position other actors in terms of a particular policy discourse (assigning responsibility, blame, trust, and the like). It was framed as an effort to make others actors *see* that the environmental problem should be shifted to a higher level of societal deliberation, one that discursively engaged the legitimacy of basic social and political arrangements, rather than merely seeking pragmatic solutions for a particular pollution phenomenon, as the ACF conceptualizes the problem.

A basic problem with the ACF conceptualization of policy belief systems is that individuals are seen to have their own clearly defined value preferences that are stable over time (a position theoretically identified as 'methodological individualism'). From a discourse perspective, we see that the same actor can in fact say very different things at different times and places. For instance, Hajer shows how the UK environmental minister spoke the language of policy pragmatism in his official role as minister, but in other political contexts drew heavily on the very different discourse of ecological modernization that included an attack on pragmatist thinking. The same was largely true for the Swedish environmental minister as well.

Was the British minister schizophrenic, asks Hajer (1995*b*: 5)? 'Did he just think X, but was forced to say Y in some situations? Was one statement only rhetoric and the other concerned with "true beliefs?"' The answer, he tell us, is both 'yes' and 'no'. From discourse analysis we learn to recognize how some actors can position other actors in ways that compel them to say things in one place they might not have uttered in another.[10] Because all of these statements become part of the discursive space, they can have their own unintended political effects in argumentative struggle. For Hajer, it is just such seemingly contradictory statements that we need to focus on. The danger with empirical research, he argues, is that, 'once we start to clear out our data set to get some sort of coherence', we run the risk of 'throwing away the most valuable material since it is precisely in the contradictions in written and spoken statements that we can [begin] to see policy change materialize' (Hajer 1995*b*: 5).

An argumentative-oriented discursive approach thus requires detailed case-specific analyses of how policy is made. 'Open the black boxes and get dirty fingers in the stacks of governmental archives, at the disorganized shelves of Friends of the Earth, in the reconstructive expert-interviews in which the point is to follow the problem definitions of the interviewee and precisely avoid that he or she starts to answer according to the pre-conceived categories that we have in mind' (Hajer 1995*b*: 5). Instead of organizing research to facilitate the search for empirical generalizations, the key to explaining how change comes about has to be grounded in a detailed contextual examination of the circumstances at play in specific cases. For this purpose quantitative methods have to take a back seat to qualitative research.

Finally, a few words concerning the stability of policy coalitions, an issue central to the ACF. Although Hajer's view that policy coalitions are based on shared story-lines might suggest that coalitions can change rapidly—thus raising the question how longevity is achieved—he recognizes the stability of discourse coalitions and emphasizes the need to explain it. In the ACF, stability is explained through the distinction between core and secondary beliefs. Because the core beliefs are deeply embedded and highly protected by secondary forms of knowledge, the difficulty encountered in trying to change them explains their stability. But for Hajer this stability is more a function of trust and credibility than entrenched core beliefs. In this view, stability is the function of successful discursive reproduction of institutions by reliable and trusted members of policy coalitions. More than just a question of what is said, it is

---

[10] For instance, many political officials feel compelled to speak about protecting the environment in public circles, but criticize environmentalists when they talk to industrial leaders behind closed doors. Even more to the point, they may speak to public groups about need to protect the environment, but to other groups about balancing environmental protection against economic growth, a position designed to cater to business leaders.

also a matter of who said it. The right thing said by the wrong person can, and often does, have no cognitive impact whatsoever. Instead of institutions simply functioning on their own, as he nicely puts it, 'institutional hardware needs discursive software to be operative' (Hajer 1995*b*: 6). Thus, while scanning policy documents for signs of change, the analyst also needs to examine the reiterated commitments that serve to maintain the institutional arrangements in a given policy domain.

POLICY LEARNING

Central to the ACF, as we saw in Chapter 2, is the concept of policy learning. Much of the policy-learning literature has featured a rather rationalistic, technocratic understanding of learning, a tendency evident in Sabatier's work as well. Positing learning across policy belief systems as one of the central questions of the ACF, Sabatier (1987) offers a number of explanatory factors, all of which exhibit the rationalistic bias behind his concept of cognitive change. First, learning is seen to be facilitated by informed debate. In general, one cannot dispute this point. But Sabatier's conception of debate is largely technical in nature. Emphasizing the need for both sides of the debate to have the appropriate technical capacities, learning is seen to require a relatively apolitical forum 'in which the experts of the respective coalitions are forced to confront each other' (Sabatier 1987: 679). Central variables governing the operations of this form are professional criteria: professional prestige, the norms of expertise, and peer review.

For debate in these expert forms to be successful, in Sabatier's view it has to avoid engaging core questions, as such discussions are seen to give rise to defensive responses that hinder reasoned deliberation. For this reason, learning is said to be easier when it involves problems for which quantitative performance indicators can be found. In particular, such learning is easier if the research questions concern natural or physical systems. In these systems, which offer greater possibilities for controlled experimentation, the critical variables are not prone to behaving strategically, as they often do in social systems.

Taken together, Sabatier's explanatory factors spell out a technocratic conception of policy learning that neglects the social and political aspects of learning. Scientific debate based on the exchange and comparison of objective findings rather than political deliberation is the mechanism for creating policy consensus. Although change occurs among secondary rather than core components, enough change in the secondary level is said to have the ability to affect long-term core beliefs, despite their strong resistant to change.

There are two basic problems here, one scientific and one political. The scientific approach underlying ACF policy learning, as social constructionism makes clear, rests on an outmoded understanding of how science works. Many of the objects of inquiry that the ACF singles out for technical debate are as much social constructions as they are objective realities, in the conventional sense of the term 'objective'. Moreover, the scientific process is governed by norms and principles that are grounded in the social consensus of the various scientific communities rather than anchored to an objective reality itself. This means, as we show in Chapter 6, that such a debate is shaped by the presentation of the data as much as or more than it is by the best technical data. Resting on the idea that the scientific method is general and applies the same to all fields, the ACF overlooks the fact that the different disciplines that come into play in policy research often work from different and often competing premises (or what has been called 'contradictory uncertainties'). There can be—and often are—major problems in reaching a consensus, especially in a complex and multi-faceted problem area such as the environment. As Hajer's work illustrates, the various disciplinary discourses involved in the acid rain controversy constructed their arguments so differently that they had trouble reaching an agreement about the nature of the problem. Indeed, as social constructionists show, disagreements between biologists and physicists frequently stem from very different conceptions of science and its practices.[11] Scientific ideology aside, different disciplines have different modes of reason. The idea that 'science is science' and that all scientists, using the scientific method, can come to reasonable consensus has proved to be erroneous (even when working for the same employer, as Hajer sardonically notes). In short, science alone is not the answer. In matters of policy, professional experts, like policymakers generally, need external social influences to come to closure.

What is more, the types of technical instruments and modes of argument that Sabatier would feature in his policy learning forums have in fact been shown to frequently serve as instruments of social regulation and control rather than learning per se. For instance, in his study into the Windscale Inquiry in Britain, Wynne (1982) has demonstrated how the demands of rationalism and objective science served to facilitate the formulation of some types of beliefs and values while ruling out others as irrelevant.

Against this technocratic cognitivism of the ACF, a social-constructionist discourse analysis emphasizes the role of credibility, acceptability, and trust instead of just 'empirical evidence' in the explanation of policy change. Whereas the ACF claims that science can bring about a consensus on policy matters based on exchange and comparison of objective findings, social constructionists point to a wealth of research showing such findings, particularly in policy forums, are intermingled with discourses about political acceptability and social trust (Fischer 2000: 133–42).

In his examination of the British effort to retrofit power stations with sulphur dioxide scrubbers, Hajer gives us a glimpse of this 'constructionist moment' in the forging of a scientific consensus in environmental science. Here policy change was made possible because the manager of the electricity utilities met with the scientists who had conducted the research and, in the process (walking through the laboratories, looking at some papers, having dinner, and so on) developed a trust in the men behind the data. Persuaded of the credibility and trustworthiness of these scientists, the manager wrote something of a paper explaining his 'findings'. Arguing that the evidence was now compelling and recommending the installation of the

---

[11] Unlike physics, for example, biology does not strive to be a predictive science. Biologists, for example, do not predict the appearance of new species.

scrubbers, he sent his conclusions to Prime Minister Thatcher (herself a science graduate). Hajer (1995*b*: 8) summed up the inquiry this way:

This means that there was a lot going on that was not objectively reported. People leaving the track of purely cognitivist criteria of persuasion, people taking the roles of the other, people showing that they respected the preferred self-understanding of the other, etc . . . [I]t illustrates how evidence is constructed and underlines the need to examine the dynamics of how credibility, acceptability and trust develops since this is essential for the sort of policy changes that is called for in intractable controversies.

The expectation or 'hope that learning will be facilitated by the erection of new professional forums is thus misplaced' (Hajer 1995*b*: 8). Moreover, Hajer takes the argument a step further and asserts that 'learning requires the invention of new types of reflexive institutions in which various actors meet and discourses can be pitted against one another'. The goal 'of such institutions would be to construct the policy problem'. Essentially, 'this would require a liberation of political judgment among experts and enhance technical and political understanding among other participants' (Hajer 1995*b*: 8).[12]

Political judgement brings us to the second problem. Much of the emphasis on policy learning, like that found in Sabatier's ACF, focuses on what he calls 'secondary learning'. Technical in nature, it overlooks the political dimensions that influence what comes to be understood and accepted as learning. In short, learning for one person may not be learning for another person with a different political ideology.

No amount of data, regardless of how well tested and verified it might be, will convince a person that anything important or useful has been presented if, in his or her view, the findings lead to policy judgements that take him or her in the wrong direction, or at least down a road he or she is unwilling to travel. For such a person, the findings will not be considered learning per se. Or, alternatively, if they are, they will not be viewed positively. Indeed, they are as likely to harden the positions as to trigger a new reflective process that leads to change.

We can often see this in contemporary politics today. For example, modern-day conservatives have no interest in social programmes administered by the state, regardless of how successful the programme might have proven. From a conservative perspective, the only fully accept programmes are those that are administered by private or market-based institutions. In such cases, no amount of evidence will change hardnosed conservative opinion. Advancing a market society will remain the conservative commitment. Only programmes that can meet this criterion are judged to have the potential to contribute to policy learning. For conservatives, relevant learning takes place only if it moves along this ideological track. Positive findings about public programmes can be considered information, but they can represent learning only in so far as they help to teach how to foster and further a society organized around private,

---

[12] Fraser (1989) similarly speaks of the establishment of 'social spaces' where groups with unequal discursive (and non-discursive) resources can deliberate about different ways of talking about social issues and problems.

market-based institutions. The same principles apply, of course, to liberal thinking about the uses of government intervention.

Nowhere in the ACF framework does this dimension of learning come into play. Indeed, experts are advised to ignore it, staying away as far as possible from questions pertaining to core beliefs. But this advice defies much of what goes on in professional policy institutes and think tanks. In fact, in many of these organizations the goal is to find or generate support for core normative and empirical beliefs. That is, in the political world, technical information is largely valued only in so far as it helps to promote particular conceptions of policy learning. Much of what passes for 'counter expertise' in a field such as environmental policy works just in this way. Here we can find countless instances where scientists representing one coalition or the other simply tailor their arguments to the particular coalition for which they work (Rampton and Stauber 2001).

To be sure, social and political learning doesn't occur every day. But when it does it is often the stuff of history. For example, the modern social system, following the collapse of the feudal system, can be understood in terms of political elites introducing new political ideas for organizing and regulating the social order, such as parliaments and free market economies (Habermas 1973). We can see it as well in the transformation of the former Soviet Union. While we don't know important things about the specific events that led up to the decisive rethinking of the Soviet experience, given the secretive nature of the process, the societal transformation introduced by Gorbachev through perestroika certainly reflected a long process of political learning that slowly made its way through elite political circles. Yet another contemporary example is the efforts of European welfare states to consider how they might introduce market reforms in ways compatible with their own political cultures. Despite much lecturing on the part of the United States, countries such as Sweden, Holland, Greece, and Germany have been very reluctant to simply accept American free-market ideology on its own terms. Instead, they have sought new ways to combine social welfare systems with free markets that preserve their own social values while revitalizing their economies.

CONCLUSION

This chapter has compared Sabatier's empiricist-oriented advocacy coalition framework with Hajer's interpretive discourse coalition approach. Although the ACF importantly emphasizes a wider range of participants in policy subsystems engaged in policy debate and argumentation, its problems stem from the attempt to employ the model as the basis for a rigorous causal theory of policy change. Setting aside questions concerning the availability of appropriate empirical data for such analysis, the pursuit of such a theory requires Sabatier and Jenkins-Smith to 'black-box' important explanatory factors in the social context in which the action takes place, thus placing essential elements outside of the reach of the analysis. This has led the ACF to conceptualize environmental movements and environmental policy beliefs systems in a way that brackets out the kinds of discursive dynamics that govern argumentative struggles in policy sub-systems.

It is, as Hajer illustrates, narrative storylines rather than policy beliefs and empirical evidence that drive institutional practices and the advocacy argumentation process. Problematizing the idea that analysis should be rooted in individuals with their own well-formulated beliefs systems, he seeks to understand how individuals interact with other individuals to create webs of meaning with which they can make sense of a complex reality.

In contrast to evidentiary arguments, storylines emphasize the complex ways that cognitive elements are located in the competing normative interpretations of political phenomenon. Ambiguous storylines that relate to varied value commitments of actors hold such coalitions together. As condensations of facts and values, they are seen to be the basis for coordinating and operating policy coalitions. Because such storylines can easily be shared, discourse coalitions cannot only be larger and more extensive, they can also be more flexible than advocacy coalitions. As they are less tied to concrete phenomena, storylines lend themselves to multiple interpretations. Although storylines are not always easy to change, especially when they are embedded in institutional practices, they are generally more accessible to new conceptualizations that can innovate the way to creative change, often more quickly and in more unexpected ways than advocacy coalitions (more narrowly dependent on the largely technical and instrumental debates in policy sub-systems).

The discursive-analytic approach takes argumentative interaction to operate through an informal interpretive logic more complex than seen in the empirical-deductive logic of the ACF framework. Whereas empiricists sees the politics of discourse as a mere expression of power resources through language, discourse analysis recognizes that narratives go beyond the expression of existing resources to structure the very fields of action itself, positioning the relevant actors and the selective employment of discourses and modes of argumentation. Whereas problems and solutions in the ACF are seen to present themselves as relatively well-defined with analysis focused on the identification of the coalitions arguing for particular understandings and approaches to them, storylines are discursive elements that create particular 'takes' on policy problems in the first place, as is illustrated by the acid-rain example. Discourse analysts ask which picture of environmental realities the narratives depend on, and who benefits from them.

The discursive alternative to the ACF thus speaks of policy coalitions as particular ways of conceptualizing and thinking about environmental issues instead of cognitive communities seeking to provide solutions to pre-established problems. Everything about the history of the environmental problem shows it to be fundamentally about ways of *seeing* the relationship between nature and industrial society. Such transformative politics, being itself interpretive in character, is beyond the reach of the ACF's empiricist perspective. To the degree that the ACF can offer causal explanation of policy change—a question viewed here with scepticism—it can do so only for the 'normal politics' organized around established but contested conceptions of the environmental problem. Moreover, it cannot account for the fact that the persuasiveness of particular argumentative strategies will determine the course of such political change, rather than objective factors such as external events. Both technical evidence and external events can be interpreted in different ways. As such, there can be nothing automatically predictable about the responses to environmental crises. The courses of action that emerge are shaped by the creative responses of skilful communicators to marshal the relevant facts and values. Only through a discourse-analytic approach is the understanding of such change accessible.

Finally, the discourse perspective makes clear the need to move beyond a technocratic conception of policy learning. Such an understanding of policy learning misses not only the socially constructed foundations of expertise, but also the ways it can serve as an instrument of social regulation and control rather than learning in the broader sense of the term. In this view, emphasis is placed as much on the role of credibility, acceptability, and trust as on empirical evidence in the explanations of policy change. As the discourse-analytic approach emphasizes a dispersed system of power, extending beyond the state and interest groups to particular institutions and expert disciplines, change is understood to be much more dependent on shifts in orientations in a variety of sites than is suggested by the ACF. Clearly, then, learning extends beyond the secondary technical nature to encompass as well broader changes in the very way of seeing. Emphasizing the ability of ways of seeing to create new realities capable of shifting the configuration of policy discourses, they can open up forms of change—sometimes dramatically so—in places where arguments otherwise seemed deeply entrenched and immovable.

Thus, underlying a discourse-analytic approach is an emphasis on interpretive analysis. The complexity of the problem, the uncertainty of the available data, the absence of other data, the different social contexts in which it takes place, as well as competing rhetorics, make clear that the task of explaining environmental politics and policy will remain a task for interpretation. An empirical, predictive causal theory is not one of the possibilities, a point we further elaborate in Part III concerned with methodological issues.

PART III

DISCURSIVE POLICY INQUIRY: RESITUATING EMPIRICAL ANALYSIS

6

Postempiricist Foundations: Social Constructionism and Practical Discourse

Why has policy science had so much trouble generating a body of knowledge capable of playing a significant role in solving the pressing social and economic problems that confront modern urban-industrial societies? An important part of the answer can be traced to discredited, but often still operative, empiricist epistemological assumptions. Drawing on newer developments in epistemology and the sociology of science, particularly social constructionism, the discussion outlines a postempiricist conception of policy science designed to address the multidimensional complexity of social reality. As a discursive orientation grounded in practical reason, the approach situates empirical inquiry in a broader deliberative, interpretive framework. More than just an epistemological alternative, a postempiricist interpretive approach is offered as a better description of what social scientists actually do in practice, a point nicely illustrated by Ball's (1987: 104–8) reinterpretation of Allison classic analysis of the Cuban missile crisis.[1]

The social sciences emerged in the main as an effort to develop a rigorous empirical-analytic science patterned after the methods of physics and the natural sciences. Today all but the diehards are willing to admit that this programme of 'neopositivist empiricism' has failed to payoff on its promises (Giddens 1995; Lemert 1995; Gulbenkian Commission 1996). Neither have the social sciences developed anything vaguely resembling the promised causal, predictive 'science' of society, nor has the policy science sub-field been able to provide indisputably effective solutions to pressing social and economic problems (deLeon 1988; Baumol 1991). The solutions to these problems, as Polkinghorne (1988: ix), writes, 'clearly

[margin handwritten note: the theory of know-ledge, esp. w/ regard to its meth-ods, validity, and scope]

---

[1] As Ball (1987: 104–6) shows, Allison (197: 105) explicitly states that all satisfactory social scientific explanation must be deduced from premises containing a general law or law-like generalization, but in the course of his analysis he himself nowhere alludes to or provides such a law-like generalization. Taking this scientific logic seriously, one would have to conclude that Allison's analysis is a failure. Ball, however, proceeds to show that, in the absence of such a generalization Allison has in fact explained a good deal. 'Misunderstanding the logical and epistemological character and import of his own implications', his analysis of the three explanatory models of the Cuba missile crisis are in fact 'interpretations of distinctly hermeneutical sort'. That is, 'he supplies his reader with second-order interpretations...of the actors' interpretations of their situation, which are in turn constituted by their understandings of Soviet and American intentions, interests, strategic objectives, hopes and fears.'

[handwritten annotation: A convicted criminal who reoffends]

involve more than just insights from the social sciences; nevertheless, our inability
to provide the promised "scientific" knowledge that would contribute to this project
is noteworthy. From criminal recidivism and drug addiction to educational and welfare
reform, social scientific advice has had little direct impact on policy effectiveness.
Although this is not to say the social sciences have nothing to offer, as we will see
below, it has raised serious questions about the adequacy of their epistemological
assumptions and methodological practices. Here it is argued that the long-sought
usable information cannot be generated by more sophisticated applications of empiricist approaches. Rather it will require subsuming empirical research to approaches
more sensitive to the unique characteristics of the social world. Before turning directly
to the alternative approaches, it is important to clarify the basic epistemological issues.

POSITIVISM, NEOPOSITIVISM, AND EMPIRICISM

Positivism can be dated back to the eighteenth century, but its more modern-day
influence on the social sciences dates back to the logical empiricism of the so-called
Vienna Circle at the beginning of the twentieth century. For this group the only kind
of knowledge that could be entertained by science were empirical statements about
things 'in the world', along with the analytical statements of logic and mathematics.
All statements that could not be organized and verified by this understanding of the
scientific method were meaningless (Morrow 1994).

More specifically, 'logical empiricism' (also called 'logical positivism') is an epistemology—a theory of knowledge—holding that reality exists as an objective phenomenon and is driven by laws of cause and effect that can be discovered through
empirical testing of hypotheses and deductive statements. Such inquiry has to be
empirically objective and value-free, as the laws or generalizations exist independently of social and historical context. Science and its methods (particularly as they
pertain to the physical sciences) are the only way to obtain valid knowledge.
Objective, empirically defined facts are understood to be the objects of scientific
observation. Empiricism emphasizes the need to rigorously separate facts from values in the pursuit of valid, testable causal propositions about both physical and social
reality. The goal is to find and apply the general principles common to all of the sciences. For the social sciences this has meant employing the principles as guides for
both the understanding of social conduct and the organization of social and societal
relationships generally. Social science, as such, does not possess its own unique
methods of conduct, different from physical or natural sciences.

The terms 'neopositivism' and 'empiricism' are used to identify the present-day
empirical-analytic legacy of more traditional positivist theories. While the term
'positivism' serves today more to fuel a polemic than to identify a distinct epistemological theory or movement, 'neopositivism' is employed to refer to modern
empiricist concepts, theories, and techniques introduced to reform positivism, for
example, Popper's (1959) theory of falsification. As an epistemological orientation,
empiricism refers here to the pursuit of empirical regularities (particularly in causal
form, 'when A occurs, then also B') on the basis of which future phenomena can be

[handwritten annotation in left margin: a strong verbal or written attack]

explained and predicted. Empiricism, in this regard, is not to be mistaken with the word 'empirical'. Rather, we take it here to refer to an orientation that puts its dominant emphasis on the empirical (especially the empirical in a particular form) at the expense of other forms of knowledge.

Much of positivism in policy science has been shaped by the theory and methods of modern economics. McCloskey (1985: 7–8) has formulated the basic 'Commandments' of modern economics as follows:

1. Empirical prediction and social control are the primary goals of science.
2. For data to be relevant to the truth of a theory they must be observable.
3. Observations must be verifiable through reproducible experiments.
4. Rigorous objectivity is crucial; subjective observations have to be avoided.
5. The tasks of methodology is to differentiate scientific from nonscientific reason.
6. Scientific explanation of a phenomenon requires relating it to a covering law.
7. Scientists should in their professional capacity have nothing to say about values or morality.

McCloskey has demonstrated the various ways these principles have produced many 'crippled economists'. She put it this way: 'Many are bored by history, disdainful of other social scientists, ignorant of their civilization, thoughtless in ethics and unreflective in methods. Even the wise and good among their congregations, who are numerous, find it hard to reconcile their faiths with the ceremonies required of them on Sunday.'

A STRAW MAN ARGUMENT?

It is not uncommon for mainstream social scientists to argue that their postempiricist critics pick on a straw man—that no modern-day social scientists would recognize themselves in the caricature drawn by the likes of McCloskey and others. But the criticism misses the mark. While recognition of many or most of these shortcomings is scarcely new, it has not meant that positivist inclinations underlying the empiricist project have been discredited and banished from the enterprise (Boyte 2000). For a start, positivist-oriented social and political research remains very much alive in important quarters, rational choice theory being the most important example (Kiser and Ostrom 1982). Indeed rational choice, especially as borrowed from or practised by economics, is very much on the ascendancy (Cohn 1999). It now constitutes one of the leading theoretical orientations in political science and sociology.

Equally important is another basic reality. Although few describe themselves as positivists in traditional terms, many of positivism's basic tenets are still well embedded in both our research practices and institutional decision processes, a point well documented by Morcol (2002). An empirical conceptualization of reality that neglects the normative sides of social life (those of both the actors and the researchers), the neopositivist concept of objectivity, the separation of facts and values, and value neutrality are still very much the kinds of things that social scientists are expected to take seriously in one form or another. Not only are they the sorts of things that graduate students at leading universities are compelled to acknowledge, if not respect, they still frame an understanding of social science that is explicitly or implicitly offered to the public. They embody as well the kinds of empiricist language that the funders of social science research look for in the grant applications they consider.

To believe that such practices have no effect on the way social scientists look at the world is to fail to understand the sociology of social science. More than a set of epistemological principles, as Kolakowski (1968) has put it, positivism is first and foremost an attitude towards knowledge that extends from a scarcely formulated conception of reality to a way of speaking about knowledge and action. 'In practice', in the words of Hajer and Wagenaar (2003), 'this means that positivism does not restrict itself to the conduct of the social science, but also, and more importantly, includes normative beliefs and habits of governance and policymaking.'

Most troublesome, though, these positivist residuals continue to impede the effort to get on with the pressing task of developing alternative postempiricist practices that better speak to the broader needs of contemporary social and policy science. Even if we were to adopt the view that the empiricist practices of positivism need no longer be taken seriously, we would still be left with the task of articulating the alternative conception of social and political knowledge that should replace it. It is to this task this chapter seeks to contribute.

Those who have sought to address these failures of policy analysis have spelt it out in different ways. One of the important approaches has been to speak of the search for a 'value-critical' policy science capable of generating 'usable knowledge'. More concretely stated, these scholar have asked: how can we keep the endless flow of research reports from gathering dust in the file cabinet? Since the 1970s writers such as Rein (1976), Lindblom and Cohen (1979), Torgerson (1986), Dryzek (1990), Forester (1993), Fischer (1980; 1995), Miller (2002), and Hajer and Wagenaar (2003) have devoted considerable thought to the question of what a socially relevant postempiricist alternative might look like.

None of these writers argues that the social sciences have had no impact on public issues. To the contrary, the influence of social science is everywhere to be found in contemporary political discourse. But the role has been more to *stimulate* the political processes of policy deliberation than to provide answers or solutions per se to the problems facing modern societies. While such deliberation is generally acknowledged to be important to effective policy development, this 'enlightenment function' is not the formal analytic mission policy science has set for itself (Weiss 1990). More ambitiously, policy science has traditionally dedicated itself to the development of methods and practices designed to *settle* rather than stimulate debates. This traditional understanding of the policy-analytic role, it is argued here, represents an epistemological misunderstanding of the relationship of knowledge to politics. Further, the continued reliance on the narrow methodological perspective that informs this orientation is seen to hinder the field's ability to do what it can and should do: improve the quality of policy argumentation in public deliberation.

Towards this end, the chapter proceeds in four sections. In the first section it briefly identifies the problematic epistemological features of empiricist practices. It then outlines the theoretical origins of the search for a 'postpositivist' or 'post-empiricist' approach to social science generally.[2] Third, it examines more explicitly the nature of the alternative. Such social science is based on a turn from the dominant emphasis on empirical proof and verification to a discursive, contextual understanding of social knowledge and the interpretive methods basic to acquiring it. Instead of merely suggesting postempiricism as an alternative epistemological orientation, this 'argumentative turn' is offered as a better description of what social scientists already do (Fischer and Forester 1993). Finally, drawing these strands together, the fourth section examines the more concrete implications of the approach for policy inquiry. Instead of rejecting the empirical methods of the social sciences, the chapter argues that the issue is how to situate them within the context of normative concerns that give their findings meaning.

MAINSTREAM POLICY ANALYSIS: EMPIRICISM AND ITS TECHNOCRATIC PRACTICES

*Neo*positivism supplies the empiricist ideals of the social and policy sciences (Hawkesworth 1988). 'Positivism', a theory of knowledge initially put forth to explain the concepts and methods of the physical and natural sciences, lives on in modified form as 'neopositivism', a term designed to acknowledge various reforms and correctives in the theory and practice of positivism. Neopositivism undergirds the contemporary pursuit in the social sciences of a body of knowledge empirically organized as replicable causal generalizations (Fay 1975). Most easily identified as the principles spelled out, both explicitly and tacitly, in the research methodology textbook, this 'empiricist' orientation emphasizes empirical research designs, the use of sampling techniques and data gathering procedures, the quantitative measurement of outcomes, and the development of causal models with predictive power (Miller 1991; Bobrow and Dryzek 1987). Sliding past or ignoring the normative sides of inquiry, such an orientation is manifested in policy analysis through quasi-experimental research designs, multiple regression analysis, survey research, input–output studies, cost-benefit analysis, operations research, mathematical simulation models, forecasting, and systems analysis (Putt and Springer 1989; Sylvia, Sylvia, and Gunn 1997).

As leading empiricists such as Hofferbert (1990) and Sabatier and Jenkins-Smith (1993: 231) argue, the only reliable approach to knowledge accumulation is empirical

[handwritten margin note: provide support or a firm basis for.]

---

[2] There is no standard definition of 'postempiricism' or 'postpositivism', two terms taken here to be interchangeable. Postempiricism, as employed in this work, accepts the idea that something called 'reality' exists, and that parts of it lend themselves to objective analysis. But this reality can never be fully understood or explained, especially in the social world, given both the multiplicity of causes and effects and the problem of social meaning. The concept of objectivity can serve as an ideal, but as a criterion for the conduct of research it depends on the assumptions and agreements a critical community of interpreters. Given the multitude of causes and meanings involved, none of which speak unambiguously for themselves, the postempiricist orientation emphasizes the social construction of theory and concepts, and qualitative approaches the discovery of knowledge (Guba 1990). This postempiricist orientation has an institutional affiliation with the American Political Science Association through the Conference Group on Theory, Policy and Society, www.cddc.vt.edu/tps

falsification through objective hypothesis-testing of rigorously formulated causal generalizations. The goal is to generate a body of empirical generalizations capable of explaining behaviour across social and historical contexts, whether communities, societies, or cultures, independently of specific times, places, or circumstances. Not only are such propositions essential to social and political explanation, they are seen to make possible effective solutions to societal problems. Such propositions are said to supply the cornerstones of both theoretical progress and successful policy interventions.

Underlying this effort is a fundamental positivist principle emphasizing the need to separate facts and values, the principle of the 'fact-value dichotomy' (Bernstein 1976; Proctor 1991). According to the most rigorous interpretation of the principle, empirical research should proceed independently of normative context or implications. Because only empirically based causal knowledge can qualify social science as a genuine 'scientific' endeavour, social scientists are instructed to eschew normative orientations and to limit their research investigations to empirical or 'factual' phenomena. Even though adherence to this 'fact-value dichotomy' varies considerably in the conduct of actual research, at the methodological level the separation still reigns in the social sciences. To be judged as methodologically valid, empirical research must at least officially pay its respects to the principle (Fischer 1980). Or, put in other words, it remains part of the rhetoric of social science.

In the face of limited success in building a rigorous positive science, empiricists have had to give some ground. Although they continue to stress rigorous empirical research as the long-run solution to their failures, they have had to retreat from their more ambitious efforts (Peters 1998). Today their goal is more typically stated as aiming for propositions that are at least *theoretically* provable at some future point in time. An argument propped up by some with the promise of computer advances, it serves to keep the original epistemology intact.

Another common argument is to accept the other methodologies—case studies, textual analysis, ethnographies, and so forth—but to hold them accountable to the logic of experimental and quantitative analysis (King, Keohane, and Verba 1994; Peters 1998). In this view, qualitative methodologies remain adjuncts to the task of building rigorous empirical theory. If such research is conducted with empirical theory in mind, it can serve as a source of hypotheses for further testing. But the modification misses the point, as postempiricists are quick to point out. The failure to make such scientific progress is more fundamentally rooted in the empiricist's misunderstanding of the phenomenological nature of the *social* rather than in a lack of empirical rigour. As we shall see, the misunderstanding is lodged in the very concept of a generalizable, neutral objectivity that empiricists seek to reaffirm and more intensively approximate.

THEORETICAL DEVELOPMENTS: HISTORY OF SCIENCE AND SOCIAL CONSTRUCTIONISM

The postempiricist challenge is rooted in developments in the natural sciences, the history and sociology of science, and contemporary cultural studies. With regard to the natural sciences, the advent of quantum mechanics and chaos theory in physics and evolutionary theory in the biological sciences has led growing numbers of scientists to reject the Parmenidean world view in favour of the Heraclitean conception of flux (Toulmin 1990).[3] In short, the traditional understanding of the *physical* world as a stable or fixed entity is no longer adequate. For neopositivist empiricists, this poses a fundamental problem: they lose their firm epistemological anchor.

On the heels of these discoveries arrived new historical research observations about the nature of scientific practices. From these postempiricist studies we have learned that both the origins and the practices of modern science are rooted as much in social and historical considerations as they are in the disinterested pursuit of truth. Historical studies of science, for example, have shown the origins of positivist epistemology to be a response to the ways in which the Reformation and the religious wars of the fifteenth and sixteenth centuries destroyed the foundations of certainty, dictated up to that time by the church (Wagner 1995). In an effort to establish a new basis for the determination of truth, which could serve as a new foundation for social stability, Descartes and his followers sought to anchor knowledge in the confirmation of empirical experience.

Revealing the interplay of these social and technical concerns, critical historians of science have not only shown how what we call knowledge is socially conditioned, but also how other historical periods have defined knowledge in quite different ways.[4] In short, having emerged to address problems in a specific socio-historical context, neopositivist epistemology is not necessarily relevant to all other contexts. *gov. by an elite* That is, it should *not* be taken as a universal grounding for scientific practice as a whole. Its historical role in the development of modern industrial society and its contemporary technocratic variant, post-industrial society, in no way offsets the *of tech. experts* point. Rather, it demonstrates how a particular conception of knowledge can condition or mediate the very shape of societal development.

Beyond the historical and cultural dimensions, sociological investigation has shown the elements of empirical inquiry—from observation and hypothesis formation through data collection and explanation—to be grounded in the theoretical assumptions of the socio-cultural practices through which they are developed (Rouse 1987). In this view, science is itself a form of human activity. As it is basic to the approach advanced here, we turn to a more detailed examination of this perspective, known as 'social constructionism'.

Since the seminal work on the sociology of knowledge by Berger and Luckmann (1966), many authors acknowledge 'reality' to be a social construction, although there are many disagreements over exactly what that means (Lincoln and Guba 1985). In the meantime, owing to the newer sociology of science and the social study

---

[3] Such research has also led some physicists to argue that the explanation of the behaviour of a particle depends in significant part on the vantage point from which it is observed (Galison 1997). That is, in explaining important aspects of the physical world, *where* you stand can influence *what* you see. Relatedly, chaos theory has demonstrated that an infinitesimal change in any part of a system can trigger a transformation of the system at large (Morcol 2002; Kellert 1993; Gleick 1987).

[4] For a discussion different historical understandings of knowledge in relations to the concerns of policy analysis, see Mitroff and Pondy (1974).

of science generally, social constructionism has spread to the study of science. Instead of simply uncovering reality, scientific work is better understood a mix of discovery and construction of reality.

Social constructionism, as we have already seen, starts with the recognition of the theoretical ladenness of facts. This interpretivist position holds that social reality and empirical observations of it only exist in the context of a mental framework (a construct) for thinking about them. Social constructs or mental frameworks are grounded in values that determine our perceptions of reality. The findings of an inquiry are, as such, not a report of that which is 'out there' but rather part of a process that creates that particular version of reality. Knowledge, social knowledge in particular, 'is a human construction never certifiable as ultimately true but problematic and ever changing' (Guba 1990: 26). Thus, knowledge and theory can never be fully probed. Combined with the fact that knowledge is never value-free, it becomes clear that there can be no definitive criteria for preferring one theory to another. Theory and knowledge, as such, remain 'underdetermined'.

The methodological implication, as Lincoln and Guba (1989) explain, is that knowledge has to be acquired through a process of hermeneutic dialectics. Hermeneutics refers to the interpretive role in the formulation of subjective interpretations about reality. Basic to this interpretive process, as Gadamer (1976: 15) puts it, is an appropriation of 'the unknown with the known through a process of constructive understanding'. Stated simply, we understand things by fitting them into patterns of knowledge, events, and actions that we already possess, typically in narrative form, or that are at least available to us as members of a particular society.

Dialectics is a logic that seeks to represent the confrontation of subjective interpretations with other interpretations. The goal of a dialectical clash among various interpretations is a constructive synthesis that leads to a new inter-subjective understanding. Dialectic hermeneutics is a process whereby 'groups must confront and deal with the constructions of all others' in pursuit of a new consensual understandings (Lincoln and Guba 1989: 41). Knowledge for the social constructionist is thus forged through dialectically generated consensus. Such consensus, however, does not rest on a reality independent of those who shape and share it. As long as there remains the possibility of further confrontation with other points of view, the construction of a consensus is never finished or complete. The continuing confrontation with other constructs is the essential epistemological principle of constructionist methodology. There can be progress in the production of consensus, but such knowledge can never be proved in the standard scientific sense of the concept.

Applied to the scientific community itself, social constructionism is a direct challenge to the empiricist understanding of science. The sociology of science, devoted to exploring the human activity called 'science', in particular describing the practices that lead to the production of certified knowledge, initially worked from the empiricist perspective. Assuming that progress was driven by the process of uncovering the physical world, it took seriously the rules and criteria that separate scientific work from metaphysics. Over time, however, sociological and historical observations revealed that what scientists do departs distinctly from the epistemological rules on which positivist science was supposed to be based (see box). Social interest and

Beyond the Textbook Myths: What Studies into Science, Engineering, and Medicine Have Found

1. *Myth*: Scientific inquiry is neutral in terms of matters pertaining to social, economic, ethical, and emotional issues.

   Finding: The research process is discovered to take place within—and at times even depends on—a particular socio-cultural framework.

   Finding: Political and social priorities can influence both the discovery and the interpretation of findings.

   Finding: The selection of the research agenda can be highly influenced by available monies and other resources rather than just intellectual interest and curiosity.

2. *Myth*: The scientific research process has its own logic.

   Finding: There are numerous modes of inquiry referred to as science; no single methodology holds together the various disciplines—biology and physics conduct research in significantly different ways.

   Finding: The types of reasoning employed by research communities to interpret the responses collected from their research apparatuses include all of existing modes of reason—with mathematical analysis playing only rather small part of the process.

   Findings: The definition of what constitute good science is frequently determined by the elites—economic and political as well as scientific—empowered to make available research resources for investigations they deem to be scientifically importance—for example, national health institutes, the Pentagon, or major oil companies.

3. *Myth*: Scientific research objectively eliminates the biases of the investigators.

   Finding: The scientific establishment is a social structure with its own interests and hierarchy of authority.

   Finding: Scientists often have vested interests in the results of specific research activities.

   Finding: Although the theories and attitudes of the particular scientist is seen to be important in determining both the conduct of the inquiry and the interpretation of findings, the style employed in scientific writing has converged over several hundred years into a format that minimizes mention of any active role on the part of the investigators.

4. *Myth*: Scientists isolate and control all variables in a research experiment.

   Finding: Scientific experimenters identify and control only those variables emphasized by the theory guiding their research.

   Finding: Scientific papers do not reveal the entire process involved in carrying out an experiment, as a publication is usually intended more to make known a claim to the researchers' findings than to precisely clarify the procedural conduct of the experiment in accordance with the theory of replication.

5. *Myth*: The advance of scientific knowledge proceeds cumulatively and progressively.

   Finding: Scientific research frequently advances in zigzags, at times offering little reference to earlier findings.

   Finding: The advance of science, in contrast to the standard 'building blocks' theory of science, is the result of new findings that break out of the established theoretical moulds, giving rise to new and very different research programs.

6. *Myth*: Scientific findings are accepted when they economically explain more experimental data than alternative findings and theories; conversely data and theories are dismissed when experimental attempts to reproduce them fail.

   Finding: Determining which data to accept as facts or which theories to accept as valid is a process carried out by those empowered—explicitly or implicitly—with the authority to decide such matters; all practicing scientists in the field are not included.

   Finding: The establishment of theories and data as valid or true is not determined by their status as 'proof', but rather in terms of a consensus formed by those permitted to participate in the deliberative process.

   Finding: Availability and access of scientific information are at times restricted.

7. *Myth*: Scientific reasoning is guided by induction and deduction; experimental hypotheses are deduced from research data that have been inductively collected.

   Finding: Experiments supply signals that scientists have to interpret rather than prove in the commonly accepted understanding of the term.

   Finding: There is little experimental replication of most scientific research.

8. *Myth*: Advances in the quality of life over the last two centuries are mainly the result of application of scientific findings.

   Finding: Although scientific research has led to no shortage of important technical and social advances, it has also brought many dangerous problems such as such environmental crisis and the cloning of life.

Adapted from Sharon Traweek (1996).

politics, it became apparent, play a role in what is otherwise portrayed as the value-neutral conduct of science. Kuhn (1970), among others, saw the scientific community as a social structure that functions in many ways more like a political process than an impartial or disinterested body in the pursuit of truth for its own sake. In the process, novelty and deviance are often seen to be suppressed in efforts to sustain the views of the authoritative gatekeepers of knowledge. The result has been a newer social study of science that investigates the practices of natural science, including actual laboratory practices, much in the same way that social scientists study other social systems. Of particular significance, social context is always found to impinge on the practices of science and plays an important part in determining what counts (and is certified) as scientific knowledge by the scientific community.

From such investigations we see the degree to which the application of scientific methods to particular problems involves social and practical judgement. The model form of the experiment, for example, proves to be more than a matter of applying a causal research design to a given reality. In many cases, as Latour (1987) has shown, reality is discovered to be fitted to the empirical instrument. In others, science gets its results by identifying and organizing those parts of reality that are amenable to the research design. And in yet others, it goes beyond such selection processes to restructure the social context (Rouse 1987). These critical investigations make clear that a proper assessment of research results has to go beyond empirical data to examine the practical judgements that shape both the instrument and the object. Although such judgements structure and guide the research process, they are almost never part of the research paper. The formal write-up of the results is organized to conform to the official judgement-free logic of science.

Nowhere is this assumption-laden character of social reality more problematic than in the case of the principle of falsification (Popper 1959). With the recognition of the socially constructed character of a given reality, the empiricist's neopositivist theory of falsification loses its fixed anchor in the social world. Because the empirical object the researcher seeks to measure is rooted in his or her own understanding of it (that is, assumptions, expectations, and experience of the very object), efforts to treat the world and its representations as isomorphic easily lead to distorted conceptualizations (Hawkesworth 1988; Bernstein 1976). In the absence of firm connections between theoretical assumptions and empirical correspondence rules, that which is taken to be the 'brute data' of the social realm must itself take its meanings from theoretical constructions, often the same ones undergoing the empirical test (Hawkesworth 1988). Because there can be no complete 'factual' description entirely independent of the social circumstances under which it is made, science in effect measures an *interpretation* of the object rather than the object per se (Natter, Schatzku, and Jones 1995). Under such circumstances, the possibility of conclusive *dis*proof has to be largely ruled out.

Added to these difficulties is the problem of complexity. Because of the ocean of phenomena and experiences that constitute the social realm, empirical research proceeds through the isolation and correlation of a small number of variables. Empirical social science proceeds, in this respect, from the idea that a social phenomenon can be explained by locating the 'independent variable' which makes something happen. That is, the variable, which when added to or removed from a causal chain, will change the social outcome. To find such a single cause, shows Gaddis (2002), we would need to have a hierarchical ranking of causes. But causes in a complex social world cannot be separated out and ranked, as each variable is interlinked with and thus dependent on others. For this reason, such an analytical approach is unable either to explain past events or to predict future outcomes.

Given both the inconclusiveness of available data and the complex interdependencies of the variables, it is thus technically impossible to fully isolate an 'if-then' hypothesis from the vast realm of untested ancillary propositions and statements that make the deduction of such a hypothesis possible (McCloskey 1985). Put in a different way, without a fully tested theory from the outset, researchers can never be entirely sure of what they have predicted and measured. Under these conditions, as Scriven (1987: 28) argues, most of what goes by the name of scientific generalization can be rejected only by a rigorous application of the falsification principle. Although seldom acknowledged in the methodology textbooks, social scientists can only *interpret* the meaning of their results against a range of explanations and understandings that themselves are products of other interpretations. Social and political theories, for this reason, remain radically empirically 'underdetermined'.

Finally, the critique of falsification penetrates the conduct of the scientific community itself. Basic to the theory of falsification is the contention that science represents a critical, non-dogmatic attitude guaranteeing the constant surveillance of empirical propositions. But the claim scarcely corresponds with the historical evidence. Historical studies of scientific practice have documented the scientific community's reluctance to disregard or reject discredited propositions (Rouse 1987). Neither persistent empirical anomalies nor unresolved problems turn out to be enough to ensure the rejection of specific theories. Like other forms of inquiry, science is found to be rooted in the human conventions of the community of scholars struggling to resolve particular problems under specific historical conditions. Offering no ready court of appeal, the promise of inter-subjective reliability can offer no insurance against either human fallibility or social convention. Falsification fails not only as a guide to empirical research design but as a theory of professional conduct as well.

None of this means that science, whether physical or social, should not be taken seriously. It means rather that the thing we call 'science' has to be understood as a more subtle interaction between physical and social factors. Whatever constitutes scientific truth at any particular time has to be seen as more than the product of empirically confirmed experiments and tests. Such theoretical truths are better described as scientific *interpretations* or *beliefs* based on an amalgam of technical and social judgements. In some cases, the technical judgements are more decisive than in others, but both technical and social considerations are always involved (with the mix between the two remaining a question to be empirically examined case by case). Influenced by many more factors than 'the pursuit of truth', such claims have to be understood as the relative product of a community of practitioners who establish the evidential criteria and guide the research processes through which truth claims are decided. The communities that render these opinions, as historical and sociological analysis makes clear, constitute hierarchies of practitioners organized in significant part around their own internal power structures, interests, and status claims (Kuhn 1970).

Such studies also help us to recognize that scientific communities are not the only bodies capable of making judgements about the same reality. From competing perspectives, alternative groups grounded in other forms of rationality can make relevant judgements about the same phenomena. Historically, the determination of whose rationality prevails has largely been decided by those wielding the most influence or power. Invariably these determinations are subject to future challenges and new technical findings have always played an important role in such confrontations. But their role has generally been mediated by changing beliefs. Contrary to the official story, new findings alone have seldom been decisive. The advance of knowledge, in short, cannot be understood as a linear process driven by the better experiment.

In this understanding, facts, in the natural as well as the social world, depend upon underlying assumptions and meanings. What is taken to be a fact is in effect the decision of a particular community of inquirers who work within the set of theoretical presuppositions to which they subscribe. Customarily, of course, we simply accept a particular view of the world; the presuppositions that undergird it seldom come into question. This makes it possible, at least most of the time, to treat large parts of the world as natural and given. While such an organization of reality facilitates communication and understanding between social actors, it cannot in and of itself serve as an adequate basis for social research. Beyond seeking to explain a 'given' reality, social science must also attempt to explain how social groups construct their own understandings of that reality. Not only do such constructions constitute the most basic level of social meanings relevant to the world of social action, their implications are fundamental to an understanding of the processes of social change, without which we would have little need for social science. The thinness of modern social science can in significant part be attributed to the neglect of these subjective processes.

Nowhere are the implications of this critique more important than in the study of politics and policy. As the network of presupposed assumptions underlying social and political propositions are reflections of particular social arrangements, they themselves are influenced by politics and power. As Mannheim (1936: 72) put it, politics is always in a state of 'becoming'. Not only is one of the basic goals of politics to change an existing reality, much of what is important in the struggle turns on the socio-political determination of the assumptions that define it. Policy politics, as we saw in Chapter 3, is itself about establishing definitions of and assigning meaning to social problems (Edelman 1988; Gusfield 1981; Best 1989). The effort to separate out meaning and values thus removes the very heart of politics from social inquiry. In search of value-neutral generalizations, neopositivist/empiricist social science detaches itself from the very social contexts that give its findings meaning, a point to which we return later in the discussion.[5]

Seen in this light, the outcomes of such research can at best be relevant only to the particular socio-historical understandings of reality from which they are abstracted. Moreover, neopositivism's empiricist attempt to fix a given set of social and political arrangements tends to reify a particular reality. In so far as empiricist social science's emphasis on 'objective reality' diverts attention from the struggles grounded 'in other realities' that challenge existing arrangements, social science—wittingly or unwittingly—serves as much to provide ideological support for a configuration of power as it does to explain it.

Both the interpretive nature of the social object and the meaning of the empirical findings themselves render neopositivist science an easy target for those who wish to dispute the validity of specific experiments or tests. At best, neopositivist empirical research can offer a rigorous and persuasive argument for accepting a claim. But such an argument cannot *prove* the issue. Those who prefer to dispute a claim can easily find problems in the myriad of social and technical interpretations and assumptions embedded in both the research design and practice (Noble 1987). Nowhere is this more obvious than in the endless confrontations over the validity of environmental science's findings, which has given rise to a full-scale politics of 'counter-expertise'. Working with the same findings, groups on both sides of an issue easily construct their own alternative interpretations of the data. Each side, in the name of the 'facts', seeks to offer a better social construction of the evidence (Hannigan 1995).

It is here that the constructionist view helps us see that in such policy debates it is often the deeper social and cultural factors, rather than the 'facts' of the arguments, that play a decisive role in citizens' assessments of the competing views. By drawing our attention to the socio-cultural contexts that underlie the citizen–expert relationship, the constructionist approach shows how citizens interpret the 'objective' assessments of professional experts within the context of their own normative cultural experiences and the social dependencies inherent to them. In so far as these socio-cultural meanings are inaccessible to the neopositivist's empirical methods, such research often tends to underestimate the degree to which lay persons are ambivalent towards or alienated from professional experts and their institutions.

From this perspective, an understanding of the social world depends on knowing what social actors believe reality to be. While, as Innes (1990: 32) puts it, 'this does not require us to accept a shared meaning as the only way to understand something, such meanings are essential "data" for any analysis'. What we call 'knowledge' of the social world is the outcome of a negotiation between those with more 'expert knowledge' and the actors in the everyday world, including the experts themselves.

---

[5] Perhaps the most important example is the discussion on the part of the social actors over the proper distribution of wealth and other resources in society. Such discussion are taken to have no rational foundation, even though the actors themselves take them to be the most essential questions of political engagement.

For this reason, the process of investigation necessarily deeply involves the expert in the normative understandings and processes of everyday life. Thus the process of knowing cannot be understood as the exclusive domain of the expert.

To recognize this deeper interpretive role of the cultural context underlying social research is not to argue that it is never worth carrying out an empirical test. The postempiricist objective is not to reject the scientific project altogether but rather to recognize the need to understand properly what we are doing when we conduct one. Postempiricism, in this respect, is best explained as an attempt to understand and reconstruct that which we are already doing when we engage in scientific inquiry. Recognizing social reality to be a human construction, the focus shifts to the circumstantial context and discursive processes that shape the construction. We turn at this point to a closer examination of the epistemology of this alternative approach.

POSTEMPIRICISM: FROM PROOF TO DISCOURSE

In view of the constructionist understanding of scientific practices, postempiricism focuses on science's *account* of reality rather than on reality itself. This is not to say there are no real and separate objects of inquiry independent of the investigators. Rather than on the objects or their properties per se, the focus is on the vocabularies and concepts used by human beings to know and represent them. The goal is to understand how these varying cognitive elements interact discursively to shape that which comes to be taken as knowledge. As such, postempiricism emphasizes the ways that scientific accounts are produced by observers with different ideational frameworks, types of educational training, research experiences, perceptual capacities, and so forth.

Postempiricism's reconstruction of the scientific process is founded on a 'coherence' theory of reality that emphasizes the finite and temporally bounded character of knowledge (Brown 1977; Stockman 1983). In contrast to 'correspondence' theory, which takes scientific concepts to directly correspond to the empirical referents of reality, coherence theory addresses the indeterminedness of empirical propositions.[6] Attempting to describe a world that is richer and more complex than the empiricist theories constructed to explain it, coherence theory seeks to capture and incorporate the multiplicity of theoretical perspectives and explanations that bear on a particular

---

[6] On the 'correspondence theory' of truth see Lincoln and Guba (1985: 22). In this view, 'The scientist...can capture the external facts of the world in propositions that are true if they correspond to the facts and false if they do not. Science is idealistically a linguistic system in which true propositions are in one-to-one relation to facts, including facts that are not directly observed because they involve hidden entities and or properties, or past events or far distant events'. The truth of a proposition is established through deduction, following upon certain assumptions. Rational choice theory, based on 'given' assumptions about rational action, is the most rigorous contemporary representative of this 'hypothetico-deductive model' of explanation. 'Coherence theory', by contrast, judges the truth of a proposition in terms of its fit (or coherence) with experience as a whole. Unlike correspondence theory, coherence theory insists on investigating and rendering judgements on the 'givens'. For a classical example of a coherence concept of reality, see Marx's analysis of the concept 'commodity'. Following Hegel, he provides an analysis of the social roots, meaning, and role of the term as it is situated in the larger context of capitalism.

event or phenomenon. To use Toulmin's (1983: 113) words, postempiricist coherence theory seeks to bring to bear 'the range and scope of interpretive standpoints that have won a place'. Alongside quantitative analysis, the postempiricist orientation includes the historical, comparative, philosophical, and phenomenological perspectives (Morrow 1994). Quantitative empirical research, in the process, loses it privileged claim among modes of inquiry. While it remains an important component of theory construction, it no longer offers the crucial test.

Given the perspectival nature of the categories through which social and political phenomena are observed, knowledge of a social object or phenomenon can better be understood as something that emerges more from a discursive interaction—or dialectical clash—of competing interpretations. Whereas consensus under empiricism is inductively anchored in the reproduction of objective tests and statistical confirmation, consensus under postempiricism is approached through the discursive construction of a synthesis of competing views (Danziger 1995). For postempiricists, the empirical data of a neopositivist consensus can be turned into knowledge only through interpretative interaction with the other perspectives. Only by examining the data through conflicting frameworks or standpoints can unrecognized and hidden suppositions that give it meaning be uncovered or exposed. From this perspective, the crucial debate in politics is seldom over data per se, but rather the underlying assumptions which organize them. Such deliberations produce new understandings in a process better framed as a 'learned conversation' than the pursuit of empirical proof (Oakeshott 1959: 488–541). In this view, scientific theory is itself a conversation (McCloskey 1985: 27–30).[7] As Oakeshott (1959: 199) famously put it, 'As civilized human beings, we are the inheritors...of a conversation begun in the primeval forest and extended and made more articulate in the course of centuries'. Rather than just a matter of learning an accumulated body of information, scientific education 'properly speaking, is an initiation...in which we acquire the intellectual and moral habits appropriate to the conversation.' In the conversation, writes Czarniawska (1998: 7–8), 'scientific texts are its voices'. And, as in any conversation, to follow the discussion 'it is important to know who is talking to whom, and who is answering whose questions'.

Knowledge, in this evolving conversation, is understood more accurately as consensually 'accepted belief' than in terms of proof or demonstration.[8] Such beliefs

---

[7] The structure of an analytic discursive practice typically involves a 'complex blend of factual propositions, logical deductions, evaluation, and recommendations.' In addition to 'mathematical and logical arguments it includes statistical inferences, references to previous studies and to expert opinion, value judgments, and caveats and provisos of different kinds.' Such 'unavoidable complexity rules out the possibility of any formal testing—of proving or refuting the final conclusions. Whatever testing can be done will have to use a variety of criteria derived from craft experience, including the special features of the problem, the quality of the data, the limitation of the available tools, and the requirements of the audience. Only a detailed examination of the different components of the tasks of the analysts qua craftsman can help the producer or user of analysis steer a reasonable course between unhelpful counsels of perfection and methodological anarchism' (Majone 1989: 44–5).

[8] Data, as the raw material necessary for the investigation of a problem, are often 'found' rather that produced. As Majone (1989: 47) put it, 'This fact requires craft skills that are rather different from, and

emerge through an interpretive forging of theoretical assumptions, analytical criteria, and empirical tests warranted by scholarly communities (Laudan 1977). Instead of understanding these beliefs as the empirical outcomes of inter-subjectively reliable tests, the postempiricist sees them as the product of a chain of interpretive judgements, both social and technical, arrived at by researchers in particular times and places. From this perspective, social scientific theories can be understood as assemblages of theoretical presuppositions, empirical data, research practices, interpretive judgements, voices, and social strategies (Deleuze and Guatarri 1987). One of the primary strengths of a theory, in this respect, is its ability to establish discursive connections and contrive equivalences among otherwise disparate elements, as well to incorporate new components.

The emphasis thus shifts from the narrow concerns of empirical theory to a multi-methodological orientation and the development of 'a rich perspective' on human affairs (Toulmin 1990: 27). Such a multi-methodological perspective is especially appropriate to the study of politics and policy. The sorts of things political scientists and policy analysts explore tend to differ from one another so much that only rarely will one methodological approach suffice (Shapiro 2000).

While the standards of relevance and assessment of a postempiricist social science cannot be formulated as fixed methodological principles, this should not be taken to mean such research lacks rigour. In many ways, the adoption of a multi-methodological approach opens the door to a more subtle and complex form of rigour. Instead of narrowly concentrating on the rules of research design, combined with statistical analysis (which usually passes for empirical rigour), the postempiricist approach brings into play a multi-methodological range of intellectual skills, both qualitative and quantitative. Basic is the recognition that an epistemology which defines rationality in terms of one technique, be it logical deduction or empirical falsification, is too narrow to encompass the multiple forms of rationality manifested in scientific practices. The interpretive judgements that are characteristic of every phase of scientific investigation, as well as the cumulative weighing of evidence and argument, are too rich and various to be captured by the rules governing inductive or deductive logic (Collins 1992). Formal logic, in short, is too confining for a methodology that needs to meaningfully combine quantitative and qualitative orientations. For this reason, postempiricism seeks a new methodological configuration through an informal deliberative framework of practical reason.

in many respects more difficult to acquire than those needed for the analysis of experimental data.' For instance, 'when data are obtained by sampling, the sampling process may be influenced by the method used, the skill of the sampler, and a host of other factors that could lead to results quite unrepresentative of the general situation.' Data collected with particular categorical descriptions rarely conform precisely to the aims of the investigation. Given this impossibility of producing perfect data, 'the standards of acceptance will have to be based on crafts judgment of what is good enough for the functions the data perform in a particular problem.' As such, the acceptance of a judgement hinges on both rules and criteria internal to the discipline and to the nature of the problem, such as environmental protection or job training and so on. Thus, judgement of soundness of data and evidence depends on personal judgements, accumulated knowledge of institutional criteria, and experiential practices and practical experience that the analysts bring to the job.

PRACTICAL DISCOURSE AS REASONING-IN-CONTEXT

The construction of a postempiricist alternative begins with the recognition that the formal models of deductive and inductive reason misrepresent both the scientific and the practical mode of reason. As Scriven (1987) explains, the classical models of inductive and deductive reason provide inadequate and largely misleading accounts of both academic and practical reasoning. Most of such reason—for example, that of the judge, the surgeon, or the historian—has been falsely assessed as an incomplete version of the deductive reasoning of logic or mathematics, long aspired to in social scientific explanation. They are more appropriately conceptualized as forms of informal logic with their own rules and procedures. In pursuit of an alternative methodological framework, postempiricists have returned to the Aristotelian conception of '*phronesis*' and the informal logic of practical discourse that connects theory to practice and action (Fisher 1989; Flybjerg 2000: 55–65).

Informal logic, designed to probe both the incompleteness and the imprecision of existing knowledge, reconceptualizes our understanding of evidence and verification in investigations that have either been neglected or mistreated by formal logics (Scriven 1987). Countering social science's emphasis on generalizations, informal logic probes the argument-as-given rather than attempting to fit or reconstruct it into the confining frameworks of deduction and induction. Towards this end, it emphasizes an assessment of the problem in its particular context, seeking to decide which approaches are most relevant to the inquiry at hand. By expanding the scope of reasoned argumentation, the informal discursive logic of practical reason offers a framework for developing a multi-methodological perspective.

Most fundamental to practical reason is the recognition that the kinds of arguments relevant to different issues depend on the nature of those issues: What is reasonable in clinical medicine or jurisprudence is judged in terms different from what is 'logical' in geometrical theory or physics (Toulmin 1990). Basic to such judgement is a sensitivity to the contextual circumstances of an issue or problem. The reason of practical discourse, as *phronesis*, distinguishes contextually between the world of theory, the mastery of techniques, and the experiential wisdom needed to put techniques to work in concrete cases. In doing so, it supplies a conception of reason that more accurately corresponds to the forms of rationality exhibited in real-world policy analysis and implementation, concerns inherently centred around an effort to connect theory and techniques to concrete cases.

Policy analysis, from this perspective, can be better understood as a 'craft' than as a science in the positivist understanding of the term. In this view, we can best account for the ways the professional analyst employs skills and knowledge acquired more through imitation, experience, and practice than formal methodological training. The work of the policy analysis depends, as Majone (1989: 43–4) puts it in words that echo a social constructionist perspective, 'more on "knowing how" than "knowing that"': it is 'a social process, rather than a purely logical activity'. The repertoire of craft skills exercised by a researcher constitutes procedures, conventions, and judgements that are a combination of social, institutional, and personal factors. In determining 'whether specific data is of acceptable quality', writes Majone, 'the scientist applies standards that derive from his own experience but also reflect the professional norms of teachers and colleagues, as well as culturally and institutionally determined criteria of adequacy'. As is the case in the traditional crafts, successful practice is dependent on an intimate knowledge of tools and materials, as well as a 'highly personally relationship' between the craftsman and analytical tasks. Rather than working with concrete materials such as wood or stone, the policy analyst qua craftsperson, works with data, technical tools, concepts, and theories to structure arguments and evidence that support specific conclusions (Majone 1987).

From this perspective we learn that the job of the policy analyst is guided by all sorts of informal judgements and inferences concerning the various aspects of a particular problem. Although the basic principles and precepts of the craft can never to fully spelled out, the good craftsman generally has no problem in determining good from back work (Majone 1989: 66). In order to properly appreciate and understand these craft-oriented dimensions of policy analysis and to be able to competently assess the quality of the end product, one must learn how to explore the microstructures of a policy argument, the levels of policy evaluation being an example of such work. In Majone's words, 'such detailed examination would have only academic interest if it were possible to assess the quality of a policy analysis simply by comparing its conclusion with policy outcomes'. But complexity and uncertainty prohibit the reliance on such simple synthetic criteria. In addition to outcome-oriented criteria, process criteria of adequacy are also necessary, even though they themselves are insufficient for assessing the final quality of the analytic product. In the final analysis, Majone argues, a policy analysis can be judged if it stands the tests 'appropriate to the nature, context, and characteristic pitfalls of the problem' (Majone 1989: 67).

Policy analysis, as deliberative craft, thus seeks to bring a wider range of contextually sensitive evidence and arguments to bear on the problem or position under investigation. As Hawkesworth (1988) explains, the reasons provided in support of alternatives organize evidence, marshal data, apply explanatory criteria, address multiple levels of argumentation, and employ various strategies of presentation. But the reasons given to support one theory over another seldom, if ever, offer definitive proof of the validity of a competing alternative. Through the processes of deliberation and debate, a consensus emerges among particular researchers concerning what will be taken as valid explanation. Although the choice is sustained by reasons that can be articulated and advanced as support for the inadequacy of alternative interpretations, it is the practical judgement of the community of researchers and not the data themselves that establishes the accepted explanation. Such practical judgements, rather than supposed reliance on proof, provide the mechanism for not only identifying the incompetent charlatan but for investigating the more subtle errors in our sophisticated approximations of reality. To be sure, the informal logic of practical reason cannot guarantee the eternal verity of particular conclusions, but the social rationality of the process is far from haphazard or illogical. Most important, it supplies us with a way of probing the much neglected contextual dependence of most forms of argumentation (Scriven 1987).

As a contextual mode of reason, practical reason takes place within a hermeneutic 'circle of reason' (Bernstein 1983). To probe specific propositions requires that others must be held constant. Such analysis, however, always occurs within a context of reference grounded in other sets of presuppositions. Moving outside of each framework to examine it from yet new frames permits the inquirer to step beyond the limits of his or her own languages and theories, past experiences, and expectations. This increases the number of relevant perspectives, but need not lead to a hopeless relativism, as is often argued. Because the hermeneutic process is typically initiated by external stimuli in the object-oriented world, critical interpretations can never be altogether detached from the world (Williams 1985: 145). That is, in the words of Bernstein (1983: 135), the process 'is "object" oriented in the sense that it directs us to the texts, institutions, practices, or forms of life that we are seeking to understand'. Such external stimuli cannot compel definitive interpretations, as the empiricist might have us believe, but they do work to limit the number of plausible interpretations. While the possibility of multiple interpretations remains, there are thus boundaries or limits to what can count as an adequate understanding. An interpretation that bears no plausible relationship to the object world has to be rejected.

Given the limits imposed by fallibility and contingency, the informal logic of discourse speaks directly to the kinds of questions confronted in most political and policy inquiry. Bringing together the full range of cognitive strategies employed in such inquiry, it judges both the application and the results of such methods in terms of the contexts to which they are applied. Recognizing social context to be a theoretical construct, as well as the under-determination of our available knowledge, practical deliberation probes the competing understandings of particular problems and the range of methods appropriate to investigating them. Framing the analysis around the underlying presuppositions, postempiricist analysis seeks to anticipate and draw out the multiple interpretations that bear on the explanation of social and political propositions.

From this perspective, the function of the postempiricist expert is that of an interpretive mediator operating between the available analytical frameworks of social science and competing local perspectives. In the process, a set of criteria is consensually derived from the confrontation of perspectives (Innes 1990). Such criteria are employed to organize a dialectical exchange that can be likened to a 'conversation in which the horizons of both the social scientists and the local citizens are extended through confrontation with one another' (Dryzek 1982: 322). Thus, interactions among analysts, citizens, and policymakers are restructured as a conversation with many voices (Park *et al.* 1993). Given the reduced distance between the experts and the citizens, the role of both can be redefined. Whereas the citizen can take on the role of the 'popular scientist', the analyst becomes a 'specialized citizen' (Paris and Reynolds 1983).

As specialized citizen, the expert can never remove political choice from the analytical process. The task is, as Hawkesworth (1988: 192) makes clear, to enlarge the range of political possibility through a greater 'awareness of the dimensions of contestation, and hence, the range of choice, but it cannot dictate what is to be done in a particular policy domain'. The 'rational judgment' of the analyst can never substitute for the choices of the political community. Postempiricism thus requires a participatory practice of democracy. 'By encouraging policy-makers and citizens to engage in rational deliberation upon the options confronting the political community', as Hawkesworth (1988: 193) puts it, postempiricist analysis 'can contribute to an understanding of politics which entails collective decision-making about a determinate way of life.'

Local contextual knowledge and participatory inquiry are thus an inherent part of a postempiricist practice. In this respect, the postempiricist critique not only accounts for the normative limits of conventional practices, but offers an interpretive model of practical discourse geared to the normative contexts of social action. This practical model of reason not only situates empirical research within a larger framework of normative concerns, it also provides an alternative perspective on the problem of competing methodologies.

THE PROBLEM OF RELATIVISM

As an interpretive approach, postempiricism is often associated with relativism, which many people find disturbing. Relativism arises when the knowledge and social meanings of the observer are seen to be a function of their social positions or normative orientations. A long-standing issue in the social sciences generally, relativism has also been a specific source of controversy in the theory of policy analysis (Bobrow and Dryzek 1987: 149–82). Relativism's opponents advance both moral and empirical arguments against it.

From the empirical perspective, neopositivist critics argue that relativists can never offer a decisive test of their assumptions and conclusions because they are always relative to something else. The empiricists' belief in the separation of facts and values and their methodological emphasis on verification (or falsification) of empirical observations have in significant part been a strategy for avoiding this problem of relativism. It is designed to cut through a deeper kind of knowledge independent of social values or normative positions.

But relativism is not necessarily as problematic as empiricists would have us believe. Putting aside the nihilistic theories of relativism, it means only that relativists cannot establish in a conclusive way the truth of their beliefs. But this can be said also of empiricist statements. Given the tentativeness of all explanations in the social sciences, as social constructionists have shown, relativists are in no particularly awkward position with regard to the problem of verification or falsification. Good reasons for support or rejection are the best we can hope for. The search for definitive answers is left to the dogmatic ideologues.

The moral argument for rejecting relativism maintains that relativist arguments can be used to morally support any sort of behaviour, given its lack of universal ethical criteria. But historical evidence and moral logic cast this view in doubt. A relativist stance by no means compels one to argue against a need for moral standards. Instead, the relativist position, recognizing that interpretations of actions vary with changing social contexts, is often more relevant to the moral context of real-world decision-making. While relativist judgements require careful examination of the implications of a particular application, often leading to tentative qualifications, this does not in itself undermine the validity of the moral and ethical standards held by particular groups or individuals. Indeed, it can be argued that the commitment to certainty has motivated more harm than has relativism. The long list of moral injustices—from genocide to religious and racial persecution—have been committed by people who were certain that truth and righteousness were on their side. In this light, the reflective stance of relativism serves as a counterweight to those who dress up their political rationalizations in moral language.

Nor does an emphasis on the social construction of beliefs mean that all moral ideas are equally valid and acceptable. Because of differences in human situations and social goals, multiple realities necessarily characterize the social world. Moreover, the social construction of a world view, whether deemed right or wrong, is a challenging intellectual and emotive task. Coming to terms with a world view, especially one involving a competing view of reality, can in powerful ways further our understanding of the human condition. Contributing at the same time to our own self-understanding, many philosophers have emphasized its socially liberating effects.

For the postempiricist, this worry about relativism is an outmoded relic of neopositivist/empiricist epistemology. They simply turn the question around and charge the neopositivist with erasing the very social contexts that make meaningful judgements possible. In this view, the pursuit of universal knowledge necessarily depends on the systematic narrowing and obscuring of social categories. In the name of an abstract language, it eliminates or subjugates other forms of knowledge. Such knowledges are subordinated to or substituted by the social categories of the elites who establish the 'official meanings' of the dominant society. The empiricist critique thus falls into its own trap; universal knowledge is itself an ideology built upon relative social concepts, the concepts of those on top.

For a postempiricist such as Haraway (1991), the issue of relativism can be redefined as a question of location rather than criteria. Following Haraway (1991), the key practice that grounds all knowledge is 'position', or where to see from. A way of seeing, or 'vision' to use her term, involves 'a politics of positioning'. Rejecting the possibility of a universal vantage point, she argues that only 'the dominators at the top of the social structure can see themselves as self-identical, unmarked, disembodied, unmediated, [or] transcendent'. At the bottom of the social hierarchy, the political struggles of the oppressed are invariably grounded in a politics of positioning; they emphasize the capacity to see from the peripheries. To be sure, such groups have often romanticized the vision of the less powerful, failing to recognize that such positions are themselves never exempt from critical examination. But from an epistemological perspective, according to Haraway (1991: 188–201), the local knowledge of those on the periphery provides the key. Peripheral positions, she argues, are preferable as they offer more adequate and transforming accounts of social reality.

Similarly, Foucault (1972) urges us to focus on the 'marginal man' standing outside the mainstream of events; local resistances are seen as holding key insights into the real nature of the system. Because of their partiality, subjugated vantage points can remain as vigilantly hostile to the various forms of relativism as the most explicitly totalizing claims to scientific authority. Thus, the alternative to the single-visioned relativism of universal theory is the partial, locatable, critical knowledge capable of sustaining the kinds of connections that we call solidarity in politics and shared conversations in epistemology. Knowledge claims that are 'unlocatable', Haraway (1991) argues, are irresponsible as they cannot be called directly into account. From this dialectical perspective, it is precisely the politics and epistemology of partial perspectives that make possible sustained, objective inquiry. Struggles over what constitutes the rational, objective account are always struggles over how to see. Basic to the development of an alternative practice of expertise is just such a shift in the way of seeing, a topic to which we return in Chapter 11.

CONCLUSION

This chapter has examined the problems of policy research from an epistemological perspective. Focusing on the empiricist and technocratic aspects of policy analysis, the discussion first offered a critique of the neopositivist premises that have shaped and guided the enterprise. Then, drawing on the theories of social constructivism and practical discourse, it set out the foundations of a value-critical postempiricist framework for policy inquiry emphasizing the need to integrate empirical and normative inquiry (which we examine more specifically in Chapter 9).

In the course of the analysis we saw the way in which what we understand as 'science' is influenced by the socio-historical context in which in emerges and that social meanings and value judgements are built into scientific practices otherwise described as 'value neutral'. In particular, we saw that in a world of multiple realities there is no 'objective' reality in which a scientific social science can anchor itself. None of this was taken to mean that there is no point to scientific research, but rather that both its activities and products have to be understood in terms quite different from those offered by standard neopositivist explanations of scientific inquiry. Rather, social science—like science generally—is a social activity and its products are based more on consensus than proof in the traditional understanding of the term. Towards this end, postempiricism offers a craft-oriented discursive or deliberative approach to policy science, one that better explains what social scientists are already doing. In this view, the analyst functions as an interpretive mediator between the available analytical frameworks of social science and the competing local perspectives.

The chapter closed with a discussion of the problem of relativism traditionally associated with intepretivist approaches. Instead of a problem standing in the path of truth, permitting the justification any sort of behaviour, the relativist stance is shown to offer a critical reflective orientation that can guard against ideology and dogmatism. Following Haraway, the problem of relativism was redefined as a question of where one sees from rather than criteria. Such a view not only leads to richer accounts of the world, it offers the dialectical foundation of a postempiricist interaction between theoretical and local knowledges.

7

Interpreting Public Policy: Normative Frames and Methodological Issues

Social meaning, as we saw in Chapter 3, is basic to the study of public policy. Unlike the realm of physical objects, social meaning lends itself only in part to the methods of empirical analysis. In contrast to the physical world, social meaning poses special problems of access. Each person has only direct access to his own realm of meaning (Polkinghorne 1988; 1984). As meanings are not directly observable, the realm of meaning has to be approached through reflection and interpretive analysis.

Social meaning is an integrated ensemble of connections among images and ideas that appear in various modes of presentation, such as perception, remembrance, and imagination. Meaning operates in a complex of interaction involving different levels of awareness, abstraction, and control. Complex social patterns, folding back on each other through processes of symbolic displacement and condensation, interconnect the interpretive elements in ways that make it difficult to empirically investigate the realm of meaning. For this reason, despite their concern with human activities, the social sciences have in significant part left these interpretive dimensions of meaning to the humanities.

This is not to say that meaning has received no attention in mainstream empirical research. In large part, it is identified as 'attitude research' and represents one of the central concerns of empiricist quantitative social science. In this research the emphasis is on the measurement of ideational variables—attitudes, opinions, or ideologies—and efforts to coordinate them with variables related to social structures (for example, income, education). Positivist-oriented research has also employed the narrative form, in both written and spoken forms, through the methods of content analysis. An empirical method designed for the systematic quantitative study of communications, content analysis involves counting the incidence of particular items belonging to a set of predetermined categories, generally determined by the researcher.

Common also to mainstream social science is case-study research, which can include an emphasis on the social meanings held by the actors under investigation. This is especially so for case-study research based on interviews and participatory observation. The problem with much of this research, though, is that it is typically employed as an adjunct to conventional empirical research and is thus primarily geared to the ends of empirical research. Qualitative interpretive case studies are often used to pilot empirical studies by collecting information that helps to design appropriate research strategies. The aim is to obtain greater descriptive depth with a small sample of a larger population that has been surveyed with empirical measures.

Such applications of qualitative research are not without their uses, but from an interpretive perspective the exploration of social meaning begins from a very different set of assumptions from those of empiricism. Neglected has been the more fundamental role of interpretive analysis in rendering meaningful the categories employed in understanding real life-problems. To better grasp the difference, we need to appreciate the epistemological distinctions that separate the qualitative from the quantitative approaches to the study of social meaning.

The exploration of meaning in the social sciences has its origins in a variety of non-empiricist approaches to interpretive understanding. Of particular importance here are the methods of ideology critique and critical hermeneutics in the Hegelian and Marxist traditions (later elaborated by Gadamer and Habermas), followed by approaches to interpretive understanding developed in the theories of *Verstehen*, phenomenological sociology, and the tradition of symbolic interaction. While phenomenological and hermeneutic theories have played a central role in establishing the foundations of interpretive social science, the early theories were limited in important respects by the absence of an adequate theory of language. The revival of such issues, as we saw in Chapter 2, came under the headings of poststructuralism, discourse analysis, and narrative theory, approaches linked to the influence of various types of linguistic theory in use in the humanities, particularly literature. Especially important to these newer approaches to meaning has been an emphasis on narrative analysis.

In recent decades, thanks in large part to the postmodernists and ethnographers, emphasis on narratives has become an important part of interpretive inquiry. Indeed, it now plays a vital part in the epistemological challenge to the neo-positivist methods that have dominated physical science, social science, and philosophy. As a cognitive mode, narratives have the ability to bring together things that at first seem unconnected and distant. In particular, they are used to organize and understand problematic situations. Without an interpretive narrative that offers an explanation of how things work, social actors have trouble comprehending or synthesizing chains of meaning (a topic examined in more detail in Chapter 8).

While empiricists have sought to restrict the focus to the observable dimensions of social reality, the interpretive orientation on meaning requires the social scientist to pursue the unobservable as well. Because language is able to carry and transmit meanings among people, access to the realm of meaning often can be gained through the study of communication, both spoken and written. But such meanings are generally only indirectly made available through such communications. Thus it is necessary for the analyst to move beyond empirical methods—such as content analysis—to an interpretive reconstruction of the situational logic of social action. This involves inferring other people's meanings by identifying patterns that emerge through an examination of the verbal and non-verbal messages they give about their beliefs and experiences. Narratives, for example, offer a way of making the subjective dimensions of verbal actions more accessible. While the process is scarcely exact, it does work. Indeed, the social world is in significant part organized and interpreted through narrative exchanges in their various forms. The remainder of this chapter is devoted to a discussion of how policy analysis can investigate these interpretations.

INTERPRETIVE POLICY ANALYSIS

The interpretive policy analyst, Yanow (1993; 2000) explains, cannot stand outside the policy issue being analysed. Indeed, analysts have to immerse themselves in the beliefs (ideas, values, feelings, and meanings) of both the participants and the researchers. They have to try, as it were, to get inside the heads of the particular players in an effort to figure out the thinking behind the actions at issue. Put differently, he or she has to do what political actors are themselves trying to do—namely, determine what their opponents have in mind. Kaplan (1993: 170) illustrates this with an example from the budgeting process, typically taken to be a very empirical activity. As he put it: 'A central feature of [budgeting] involves predicting how other actors in the budget process will respond to a particular budget proposal. Agency budget officials thus frequently ask themselves, "How will this Budget Bureau (or OMB) official react to the proposal?"' The ability to predict the reaction inside of the head of budget reviewer is in fact a highly prized skill, and it is at its core an interpretive act.

How then does an interpretive policy analysis confront this analytical task? As Yanow (2000: 6) explains, interpretive policy analysis shifts the focus away from instrumental behaviour (values as costs, benefits, and choice points) to the expression of social meanings (based on ideal values, beliefs, and feelings). The social knowledge of an interpretive inquiry, as we saw in Chapter 3, is defined as the understanding of events and actions in relation to the subjective meanings, motives, or purposes that lie behind such actions or events, particularly those held by the relevant participants.

To illustrate this role of understandings and motives, consider Moffat's (1989) anthropological study of gender rules and policy practices in co-educational student dormitories at Rutgers University. By living in the dormitory with the students for a year, Moffat readily encountered students who openly argued that no one should feel guilty about having sexual relations, and that women students are just as entitled as male students to have sexual pleasure. This was in fact widely seen as the 'new sexual orthodoxy'. But, getting closer to the students, both men and women, he discovered a very different, contradictory set of subcultural understandings governing actual sexual relations. Hidden from view was a picture that looked much more like a battle between aggressive male students who viewed women students as objects of sexual conquest and women who found they had to negotiate their identities within this framework of meanings. Despite the widespread support for women's new sexual freedoms, many women reluctantly felt they had to barter sex for love or acceptance. The male aggressors, in the process, tacitly placed the women in one of two categories: those who stayed clear of these new sexual freedoms were 'good', while those who practised this new sexual orthodoxy were considered 'sluts'.

While postempiricist interpretive analysis is interested in concrete events and their empirical causes, Moffat's research serves to make clear the need to learn what social actors themselves *really* think about particular events, why they believe they occurred, especially what those who did them had in mind at the time, independently of their publicly expressed intentions or motives. In the world of politics, the 'real' reasons and motives for an action—as opposed to those officially offered—are as important as the action itself. People want to know whether things happened for the reasons given. Were there underlying motives? Were they well-meaning? Or were the statements part of a strategic rhetoric designed to advance a particular group's interests? And so on. From the interpretive perspective, as well as that of the political actor generally, such knowledge is basic to political action.

This does not mean that social scientists should not employ technical or theoretical concepts that are not part of the world they are researching. As Fay (1996: 117) puts it, 'Businesspeople may function quite successfully without the concept of liquidity preference even though this concept captures some important dispositional aspects of their economic lives.' Economists can use it to understand these and other parts of the businessperson's economic behaviour. But the interpretive analyst argues that social scientists should not use such theoretical concepts altogether independently of the intentional vocabularies and social understandings of the actors under investigation. They must first determine whether the social actors have such a concept without necessarily being able to explicitly identify or explain it. And, second, they must logically formulate social scientific concepts in such a way that they can be related to and translated into the vocabularies of the actors themselves. The failure to establish such relationships, as Fay argues, constitutes a failure 'to capture the phenomenon they wish to explain', as the activities at issue easily 'slip through the conceptual net' the social scientists have constructed.[1]

To correct for these potential failures, interpretive approaches to policy inquiry focus on the social meanings that policy concepts have for the variety of policy-relevant publics, including but not limited to clients, legislators, agency administrators, programme implementers, and the voting public (Yanow 2000: 8). By examining the processes through which the policy meanings are transmitted, which audiences for the meanings are intended, and how the 'readers' interpret, interpretive policy analysts seek to determine not only 'what' a particular policy means, but 'how' it means (Yanow 1996). In doing so, they consider the actions of legislatures and executives to be as central in communicating policy meanings as the enabling legislation itself. Human actions and artefacts are, in this respect, understood to be more than instrumentally rational. They are also expressive of meanings, including those of identity, individual or collective, local or national.

The process is well recognized in the legal process. Courts are at times required to decide what legislators meant by a particular statement in a statute over which

[1] Or consider another example. Many political scientists, as Fay (1996 : 118) explains, are 'bent on making some general claims about the nature of politics.' Assume, as he writes, 'that they employ a technical concept of politics which defines politics in a highly theoretical manner. But to what does this technical concept apply? The nature of social activities, including politics, depends on the intentions which the agents within a realm at least implicitly share. But this means that whether some behavior falls under the political scientist's technical concept "political" depends on how the agents of this behavior conceive of politics. The nature of behavior can profoundly differ depending on whether the activity occurs in an Africa tribe, and ancient *polis*, Elizabethan England, or twentieth-century America. Political scientists cannot know the extent to which an activity is indeed political by their definition without paying strict attention to the deep concepts, beliefs, and practices of those whose behavior they are studying.'

disputing parties attach different meanings. In such cases, especially those involving laws passed by legislators no longer alive, the judges are compelled to return to the original legislative debates and to interpret what the law actually means in the historical context in which it was established, the prevalent social and political meanings of the words used at the time, as well as the political motives of the speakers. The task is difficult and uncertain, but no one calls the effort irrational or unnecessary. There is, in short, no alternative.

As is the case with the judges, the central question for the interpretive policy analyst is: how is the policy issue being conceptualized or 'framed' by the parties to the debate? How is the issue selected, organized, and interpreted to make sense of a complex reality? The framing of an issue supplies guideposts for analysing and knowing, arguing and acting. Through the process, ill-defined, often amorphous situations can be understood and dealt with (Rein and Schoen 1993). As Yanow explains, frames highlight some issues at the same time that they exclude others. That which is featured and stressed is generally that which the framing group values, often giving rise to 'frame conflict'. Frame conflict occurs not only because different groups focus on different elements of a policy issue, but because they value different elements differently (Gusfield 1981). Competing frames reflect the contestation of competing groups for ascendancy or advantage.

Hofmann (1995) offers an especially insightful illustration of the policy consequences of such tacit, hidden frames, or what she interprets as 'implicit theories'. In a study of the German government's effort to facilitate technology development and transfer through enhanced interactions between universities and businesses, she shows the ways in which the major actors in the process—government, business, and the universities—all formally and publicly accept the idea of such cooperative efforts, but harboured different understandings of what the policy did or should mean. What would at first appear to be a relatively straightforward transfer of technology from university research centres to business firms is found to involve very different frames—assumptions and premises—that each group brings to its understanding of the policy. For this reason, no one could figure out why technology transfer was lagging, why the policy was not leading to the desired effects. The answer, as she shows, was found in the failure to recognize the discrepancies underlying the actors' 'implicit theories'. In fact, each group's interpretation of the roles of the others proved to be quite different from the understandings those groups had of their own activities, interests, abilities; and it is just these misunderstandings and misperceptions that created hidden barriers to effective policy development and implementation.

Through the analysis of such understandings we come to recognize the degree to which interest groups, policy constituencies, scholars working in competing disciplines, and citizens in the various contexts of everyday life perceive and structure social problems. Not only do they see things differently, they have different interpretations of the way things are, support conflicting courses of action concerning what is to be done, by whom, and how to do it. In short, such analyses recognize that beliefs and expectations shape the world we live in. They understand that, when people who see the world differently act on their views, the world itself changes.

Even when what people believe is wrong, as sociologists have long recognized, if they act upon their beliefs, the beliefs will be real in their consequences.

INTERPRETIVE FRAMES

The metaphor of the frame in interpretive social science can be traced to the work of Goffman (1974: 10–11), who defined frames as a principle of organization 'which governs the subjective meaning we assign to social events'. Although there is no definitive definition of a frame, we can usefully follow van Gorp (2001: 5) and take a frame to be an 'organizing principle that transforms fragmentary information into a structured and meaningful whole'. As such, frames—like metaphors generally—select out some parts of reality at the expense of others. A 'frame indicates which elements become more meaningful and consequently...can more easily be noticed by the audience'. Through the frame's link to familiar cultural symbols, both material and discursive, communication is not only facilitated, it is literally made possible.

Framing is a dynamic process by which producers and receivers of messages transform information into a meaningful whole by interpreting them through other available social, psychological, and cultural concepts, axioms, and principles. Elaborating on the social framing process, Entman (1993: 52) points to a frame's ability to define problems, state a diagnosis, pass judgement, and reach a conclusion. In a specific social context, these cognitive tasks generate substantive questions concerning the responsibility for a situation, the interventions that are acceptable or possible, and what can be done about the problematic situation (Gamson 1995). Explicitly or implicitly, the meaning of an incident or situation is structured by the evaluation that logically connects cause, responsibility, and remedy.

In their seminal work on 'frame reflection', Schoen and Rein (1994) point to the ways that public policies rest on frames that supply them with underlying structures of beliefs, perception, and appreciation. A policy frame, in this view, is understood as 'a normative-prescriptive story that sets out a problematic policy problem and a course of action to be taken to address the problematic situation' (Rein and Laws 1999: 3). Socially constructing the problem situation, a frame 'provides conceptual coherence, a direction for action, a basis for persuasion, and a framework for the collection and analysis of data—order, action, rhetoric, and analysis' (Rein and Schoen 1993: 153). Frames, as such, determine what the actors will consider the 'facts' to be and how these lead to normative prescriptions for action. Moreover, one cannot simply compare different perspectives for dealing with a problem without recognizing that frames change the problem. To illustrate the point, Schoen and Rein (1994) provide various examples of how policymakers employ frames to perceive problems, manage preferences, formulate solutions, settle disputes, and come to compromises.[2] In the process, they show as well that policymakers turn to 'reframing' as a primary

---

[2] Rein and Schoen (1993:153–4) explain the impact of frames through a discussion of poverty policy. 'Someone', they write, 'cannot simply say...."Let us compare different perspectives for dealing with poverty", because each framing of the issue of poverty is likely to select and name different features of

way out of or around situations in which conflicting frames have paralysed the decision-making process.

A main activity of policy analysts engaged inside and outside of public bureaucracies, particularly in the roles of policy entrepreneur and ideas broker, is the development and refinement of policy frames. Much of their work consists of naming the policy terrain and offering arguments as to how policy frames, policy designs, and policy actions can and should be linked. A good deal of their labour as technical specialists can be described as 'debugging the problems that emerge in the framing of a policy issue and in the process of bringing it into good currency'. Such work combines 'research and experience in the use of symbols, communicative metaphors, and simplifying assumptions' (Rein and Schoen 1993: 158).

Policy frames and their underlying appreciative systems can be uncovered through the analysis of the stories of the various participants are disposed to tell about policy situations. Problem-setting stories, frequently based on generative metaphors, link causal accounts of policy problems to particular proposals for action and facilitate the normative leap from 'is' to 'ought' (Rein and Schoen 1977). Because the reality of a policy situation is generally too complex to be grasped through any particular account, policy controversies are inherently subject to multi-perspectival accounts. As conflicting frames always carry the potential for multiple interpretations, there are often no commonly accepted frameworks available to facilitate problem resolution. The very process of attempting to elaborate and work out frames can bring analysts to the limits of their frames, initiating the process of 'frame reflection'.

Frame reflection, write Schoen and Rein (1994), can offer a way of revealing the ways in which social actors actually deal with the epistemological predicaments posed by frame conflict. Towards this end, they see the need for an empirical epistemology to clarify the criteria that are actually employed in judgements of frame adequacy and by what processes people actually approach frame conflicts in the absence of an agreed-upon framework for resolving them. Such research would address itself to the question of frame shifts: how the problem-setting frames of public policy change over time. This would help to make clear the properties of a possible frame-reflective discourse in which participants would reflect on the policy frame conflicts implicit in their controversies and explore the potentials for their resolution.[3]

---

the problematic situation. We are no longer able to say that we are comparing different perspectives on "the same problem," because the problem itself has changed. While we may be able to agree, for example that poverty is a lack of resources, the nature of what is lacking may be quite unclear. Income transfers aimed at responding to the lack of resources may create problems of dependency or an underclass that derives its income from governmental largess. When poverty is seen in terms of inequality, there is concern with the relative distribution of resources, so that in providing aid for the poor we are also compelled to consider the economic position of society's middle- and upper-income groups. In each case, the name given to the problematic situation or poverty selects different, at best overlapping, phenomena for attention and organizes them differently.'

[3] Identifying a frame as a member of a conceptual category does not identify its relationship to and effects on other frames in the same manner as the categorical identification of a natural or physical object. In the realm of social meaning elements are fundamentally related in terms of comparison and contrast, instead of by exclusion or inclusion in specific categories, as is the case in the positivist approach. Thus, categorizations and typologies are useful only for making comparative analyses, not for creating firm or fixed categories.

Postempiricist policy analysis, from this perspective, is frame-critical policy analysis. Uncovering the multiple and conflicting frames involved in a given policy dispute, it inquires into the sources of conflicting frames by examining the histories, roles, institutional contexts, and interests of those who advance them. Such analysis explores the assumptions, ambiguities and inconsistencies underlying conflicting frames, along with the consequences to which their uses may lead (Fairhead and Leach 1998).

It is in 'the participants' "conversation with their situation" that frame reflection and a resulting shift of frame may occur' (Rein and Schoen 1993: 163). Such a shift, caution Schoen and Rein (1994), is unlikely to happen before one actually takes some action. It is more likely to occur over time, as actors apprehend and respond to the changed situations in which they find themselves. In the process, a frame shift can occur thoughtfully or thoughtlessly. In the case of the former, frame shifts most typically take place at a particular 'juncture' or 'joint' in a participant's 'dialectical conversation' with the policy situation. In discourse with one another, policy participants 'subject their conflicting frames to conscious thought and control, and, in partial consequence, reframe the situation' (Rein and Schoen 1993: 164). In the latter case, one may simply find oneself having come to think about things in a different way. A mismatch between people's beliefs and their actual behaviour, or what psychologists call 'cognitive dissonance', may gradually and tacitly cause people to readjust their beliefs to accommodate changes in their situations. This means that cognitive work can take place, but without conscious awareness and reflection. Once such a change takes place, however, the actors may thoughtfully labour to supply it with justificatory arguments (Rein and Schoen 1993: 163).

The process of frame-reflection depends in particular on the orientations of the participants: their relative distance from their objects under consideration, their willingness to look at things from other perspectives, their propensity toward 'cognitive risk taking', coupled with their openness to the uncertainty associated with frame conflict. Given this interplay of social and cognitive components, underscore Rein and Schoen (1993: 164), 'the work of frame reflection is affective as well as cognitive; it involves both feelings and work on feeling'.

The framing of a policy issue always takes place within what Rein and Schoen (1993: 154) describe as a 'nested context'. Policy issues tend to arise in environments that are always part of some broader political and economic setting, which in turn is located in a particular period of history or time (a point to be expanded in Chapter 8). When some aspects of the nested context change, policymakers often learn that the rules or formulas upon which they have depended no longer usefully address the situation. In such cases, they write, 'the perceived shift of a context may set the climate within which adversarial networks try to reframe a policy issue by renaming the policy terrain, reconstructing interpretations of how things got to be as they are, and proposing what can be done about them' (Rein and Schoen 1993: 154).

The debate about protecting the environment is a case in point. When the environmental issues emerged in the late 1960s and early 1970s, the main focus was on the 'limits of growth' (Meadows *et al.* 1972). Western countries had to learn to tame the material tendencies of industrial society. Though this debate remained a dominant feature of the environmental movement throughout the 1970s, it proved to be something of a non-starter for the business community. As growth is the basic tenet of capitalist industry, the limits of growth frame left little room for business to manoeuvre. Throughout this period business leaders mainly sought to either stall or deny the environmentalists arguments, which did nothing to offset the increasing recognition that the environment was in serious trouble and getting worse (with new problems such as the ozone hole and global warming piling on). There was no serious attempt to talk across these two frames.

In response, the Brundtland Report (World Commission on Environment and Development 1987), which was put forth in advance of the 1992 Rio de Janeiro conference on the environment, proposed a new concept, that of 'sustainable development'. Sustainable development, as an alternative frame, opened up new possibilities. By drawing on the discourses of both business and the environmental movement, sustainable development opened the way for both groups to sit down at the same table. Whereas the environmental movement could interpret the emphasis on sustainability to be a discursive victory, business could focus more on the meaning of development. Regardless of how one judges the resulting movements around these concepts—there are indeed differing interpretations—the new discursive frame led to an outpouring of conferences, government initiatives, training programmes in sustainable development to train experts, and so on. It can be described as a 'discourse hegemonic shift' that gave new life to the environmental thrust. The fact that it may have served to co-opt many Greens, given the imbalance of power between environmentalists and business, is not to overlook the fact that it created a new discourse coalition that has allowed all sides to claim to be environmentalists (Hajer 1995*a*).

METHODOLOGICAL STRATEGIES

Yanow (2000: 22) outlines four basic methodological steps for interpretive policy analysis, based on her interpretive-analytic research. The first step is to 'identify the artifacts (language, objects, acts) that are significant carriers of meaning for a given policy issue, as perceived by policy-relevant actors and interpretive communities.' The second involves 'identifying the communities of meaning/intepretation/speech/ practice that are relevant to the policy issue under analysis.' Third, the analyst seeks to identify the relevant discourses and their 'specific meanings being communicated through specific artifacts and their entailments (in thought, speech, and act).' The final step is to 'identify the points of conflict and their conceptual sources (affective, cognitive, and/or moral) that reflect different interpretations by different communities.'

With regard to the first step, one way for the policy analyst to begin is by seeking out the relevant 'interpretive communities' in a particular policy space—that is, those people who share understandings of policy ideas and language different from those of other groups. In the policy literature, these are often referred to as policy 'issue networks' or 'communities' through which influential policymakers move and conduct business with one another (including policy decision-makers, professional experts, academic specialists, policy entrepreneurs, administrators, journalists, state and local officials, and so on).

The Israel Corporation of Community Centers:
An Interpretive Case Study

The typical analysis of policy implementation focuses on a set of factual propositions about observable phenomena. Yanow, however, shows that other aspects of implementation are not fully understandable through observation and factual analysis. They can be known only through interpretations. 'Agency staff, clients, and other policy stakeholders', writes Yanow (1993: 42) may form interpretations of policy language, legislative content or implementing actions; and these interpretations may differ from one another and may diverge from the intent of the policy legislators.' Because such multiple interpretations can either impede or facilitate the policy implementation process, they need to be taken into account. In so far as they are not altogether open to empirical analysis, their meanings have to be obtained through interpretive investigation.

Yanow provides an excellent example of the role of social meanings in public policy through an analysis of the Israeli Corporation of Community Centers (ICCC) established by the Knesset (Parliament) in 1969 as a government-sponsored, independent public organization to implement educational and social policies. These Centers were ' "to improve the quality of leisure time" for residents of urban housing projects and geographically isolated development towns' (Yanow 1993: 43) , and to integrate the different 'ethnic' groups in those towns. Towns built in the 1950s had failed to provide the range of social services and other facilities necessary to attract new residents, as well as hold on to the community members already there, especially the youth.

Yanow was interested in the fact that the ICCC, despite having not accomplished its stated goals twelve years after its establishment (including reducing the income gap between various inhabitants of the towns), was not perceived as a failure. Neither residents of these settlements areas nor the public more generally argued that the ICCC had failed. 'On the contrary, residents of center-less development towns and city neighborhoods marched in the streets calling on the government to build them community centers' (Yanow 1993: 45). How could this be explained?

The explanation, as she shows, was found in the fact that 'ICCC had succeeded in creating not only an agency and its physical embodiment, but also an identity which embodied a certain status as a desirable, attractive entity' (1993: 46). This 'meaning captured part of the tacit mandate of the agency's enabling policy—elements which were known and shared by legislators, agency members, clients, and policy-relevant publics, but which could not be expressed explicitly because there was no explicit social consensus to support them.' As she argues, 'had they been made explicit, they are likely to have raised explicit opposition.'

The corporation, as a new governing body, had to develop and communicate its organizational meanings from the outset. The founders did this by creating a specific set of 'organizational artifacts—agency names, its building and programs, Annual Reports and Annual Meetings'—which embodied the culture values and beliefs of the organization. The design of the agency buildings, writes Yanow (1993: 48–9) 'set the community center apart from its surroundings in every town or neighborhood where a new building was constructed', helping to create a message of 'difference through otherness.'

This message of otherness, facilitated by ballet classes, tennis lessons, photography instructions, theatre performances, classical music, and the like, worked to create an image that the Center and its programmes belonged to a world of higher middle-class western lifestyles and aspirations. These programmes mainly 'echoed the message of foreignness and distance which the buildings and landscaping communicated, rather than creating a common ground' (1993: 49). Instead of narrowing the socio-economic gap, 'they emphasized it'.

Thus, while the ICCC failed to ease the divide between the two primary populations, it managed to validate the 'underdog claim' to government recognition while also sustaining the values and image of the establishment. From this perspective, 'the policy's tacitly known elements were implemented successfully: community centers became identified with a particular quality of life that . . . became seen as desirable. The implementing body successfully used symbolic artifacts in their many forms as representations the values of the identity and status it wanted to communicate, and the various stakeholders, including many clients, came to share the meanings and the underlying values of those symbols' (1993: 53). The existence of 'a community center in a neighborhood became itself a symbol of a certain status and, thereby, of individual and group identity, without the individual or group necessarily having attained the status.' As a result, the community centre led the people to feel that they belonged to the respectable elements of Israeli society.

The Corporation's policy coupled 'with the interpretations may be "read" . . . as a text about conceptions of the desired Israeli identity.' However, the nature of this identity was 'never explicitly stated, because to do so would have meant making certain social goals explicit in the absence of general consensus to do so.' On the other hand, reducing the gap and improving the quality of leisure activities were accepted public goals that could be openly stated, despite the fact that they were not dealt with.

In addition to examining these communities, the interpretive policy analyst would identify the artefacts through which these meanings are expressed, communicated, and interpreted. The policy and its relevant artefacts—in the forms of language, objects, and acts—symbolically represent the meanings (values, beliefs, and feelings) that the policy issue in question holds for various policy-relevant interpretive communities (Yanow 1996). Interviewing, observing, and document analysis are the primary methods for collecting data. Most commonly, the investigation starts with the analysis of documents, in particular media coverage (both print and electronic). In some instances, it might involve the examination of transcripts of committee hearings. These are supplemented by open-ended interviews with the main actors (politicians, interest group leaders, community members, and so forth) identified through documents and other relevant sources. In these interviews the analyst seeks to test his or her assumptions about the boundaries of the interpretive communities, the significance of particular artefacts, and the meaning of stories that community residents share with one another. Those interviewed are requested to supply the names of others with whom the analysts might speak, with the transcripts of these interviews themselves becoming materials for additional analysis. Interviews, documents, and texts are supported by observation of political deliberations, interest and community group activities, and the undertakings of implementing agencies (Yanow 1996).

With this information the analyst builds an interpretive context for analysing social and political actions. Knowing which words or actions have importance can come only from such familiarity with the situation—understanding what is significant to political stakeholders and other policy-relevant publics. This familiarity is obtained through social interaction with the participants, in particular with the help of methodological techniques such as participant-observation and ethnography. Yanow (2000: 8–9) describes the goal as teasing out of everyday 'sensemaking' the puzzles and tensions which have presented themselves through actions and events that contradict the analyst's knowledge and expectations at the time.

Yanow (2000: 8) refers to puzzles such as the difference between 'what the analyst expects to find and what she actually experiences in the policy or field agency'. The various 'expectations that one brings to a policy analytic project derive from one's prior experience, education or training'. If there is a 'mismatch', the resulting tension or puzzle presents the opportunity to explain why the policy or administrative agency takes a different course. Rather than simply focusing on right or wrong, an interpretive approach emphasizes the treatment of differences as 'different ways of seeing, understanding, and doing based on different prior experiences'. Such discrepancies between 'expectations and present experience are a potential source of insight'. As Yanow (2000: 8) puts it, the conflict 'is produced in the juxtaposition of the analyst's "estrangement" from the analytical situation and his or her growing familiarity with that situation'. By probing 'the balance between "strange-ness" and "insider-ness", the analyst is able to move back and forth between seeing things as they are and as they are not'.

The tensions at issue here generally show themselves through the disparities between words and deeds. The interpretive analyst, in this respect, focuses not only

on the specific language of a policy document but also on what people do in response
to it. He or she 'explores the contrasts between policy meanings as intended by
policymakers—"authored texts"—and the possibly variant or incommensurate
meanings—"constructed texts"—made of them by other policy-relevant groups'
(Yanow 2000: 9). Policy analysis 'cannot be restricted to policy language or ideas as
understood and intended by their authors. Others whose understandings of the
policy are or will be central to its enactment are also of analytical concern.'

The literature of qualitative research offers a wide range of methodological tools
or techniques to help make sense of these puzzles or anomalies. As aids to rigorous
reflection and analysis, they are methods of exploring the available data. Such tools
enable a process of making these insights and understandings more explicit
(Erlandson *et al.* 1993). Of particular importance is the ethnographic approach to
participatory observation emphasizing social interaction and unstructured talking.
Basic to all of them is what Geertz has described as 'thick description'.

POLICY ANALYSIS AS THICK DESCRIPTION

The focus on social meaning draws much from the disciplines of anthropology and
ethnography which has long taken cultural meanings to be their central focus. One
of their basic methods for getting at such meanings is what Geertz (1973) has called
'thick description'. Thick description is an approach for exploring and discovering
the meanings embedded in the language and actions of social actors. Because meanings are attached to the actors being described, the process is both descriptive and
interpretive (Maxwell 1992: 288).

The depth of such meanings, writes Geertz, can be revealed only through detailed
descriptions of the social context of the situation in which communication and action
take place. In describing the context of an action, anthropologists make their field notes
'thick' with underlying inferences and implications relevant to their descriptions. As
Geertz (1973: 6) puts it, the descriptions go 'right down to the factual base but also to
the hard rock' of the events and relationships being explicated; thick description even
includes 'explication upon explications'. The anthropologist, he writes, confronts 'a
multitude of complex conceptual structures, many of them superimposed upon or
knotted into one another, which are at once strange, irregular and inexplicit , and which
he must contrive to somehow grasp and then to render (1973: 10).

Geertz's most famous example of thick description concerns cock-fighting in a
Balinese village. While it would appear that only the cocks are fighting, they are
discovered in fact to be fighting because the men are fighting. Geertz (1983) sets his
detailed description of the strange features of cock-fighting against the holistic background of Balinese culture, including its understanding of social relations, traditional beliefs, and religious practices. Placing his contextual interpretation in
ever-widening concentric circles, he reveals the 'common world' in which the practice of cock-fight betting makes sense to its participants. In the end, what appears to
be an economically irrational game of betting for financial gain is disclosed to be
about social structure and status relations in the village community.

Interpretive policy analysis thus seeks, in the words of Jennings (1987: 145) 'to transform thin particularity into thick particularity'. Such thick particularity, in Denzin's (1989: 83) view, has four characteristics: (1) it sets an act in context; (2) it specifies the social meanings and intentions underlying an action; (3) it explicates the development and evolution of the action; and (4) it portrays the action as a textual narrative that can be interpreted by the readers of the description. Through these steps the task is to render an understanding by traversing the layers of meanings that create or constitute an event or action. Beyond presenting the reader with factual information, as Denzin (1989: 83) explains it, thick description presents 'the voices, feelings, actions, and meanings of interacting individuals'. Basic to the process is the 'triangulation' of the range of conflicting voices, relevant connotations, and interpretations to offer a credible synthesis of human interactions. While the anthropologist uses thick description to describe ongoing relationships, the method of presentation bears a close relationship to historical writing and various forms of biography and documentary literature.

Thompson (2001) has examined the uses of thick description for policy analysis, applying the approach to the field of communications policymaking. He sees the method as offering two interrelated advantages. First, it can uncover and reveal the underlying complexities and connections that are typically glossed over by empiricists. Because it can reveal deeper meanings, the policymakers obtain a better understanding of the problems they are trying to solve. And secondly, resonating better with public perspectives than mainstream empiricist approaches, it can facilitate democratic policymaking. By offering detailed policy descriptions, thick description can make transparent to citizens the elite 'agendas that may be hidden deep within bureaucratic structures or behind a veil of scientific jargon'. In the process, such description also give a voice to citizens. Employing ordinary language descriptions, it renders policymaking more accessible. The method enhances the chances of meaningful citizen participation in the public deliberations.

IS IT OBJECTIVE?

Today the question is not so much about the importance of the role of the subjective in social action; rather, the disagreements are over how to do deal with it methodologically. In particular, as we saw in Chapter 6, the issue is about the relation of the subjective to the empirical. While empiricist sociologists and political scientists have tried in the past to find ways to ignore or sidestep the subjective dimension—that is, to establish explanations that can stand independently of social meanings, or to treat meanings as manifestations of objective phenomenon—their stance today tends to concede and accept the relevance of subjective data but, at the same time, to subordinate it to—or situate it in—the larger empirical project. For postempiricists, as we shall see here, the task is just the opposite, namely, to situate the empirical in the interpretive framework.

There are various views on the relationship of the empirical to the interpretive, the quantitative to the qualitative (Lin 1998). While some see the relationship as incompatible, and yet others as complementary, the social constructionist view advanced here takes all research to be grounded in a subjective dimension. Whether classified as quantitative or qualitative, all knowledge can be located across a continuum according to the degree to which it is based on subjective assumptions. Recognizing this common thread running through both quantitative and qualitative inquiry allows us to see that the divisions are less clear than generally presumed.

No one illustrates this point better than Kritzer (1996), who identifies and elaborates the interpretive dimensions of quantitative analysis. Kritzer, himself an empirical analyst, seeks to point out the neglect of this critical dimension in quantitative work. Towards this end, he offers a 'reconstructed logic' of the interpretation process in quantitative data analysis. His objective is to demonstrate that both quantitative and qualitative analysis involve extensive interpretation, each employing similar tools of interpretive analysis. In this work the lines between the two modes of inquiry are shown to be far less clear than generally presumed.

Utilizing concepts from modern literary and linguistic theory, Kritzer demonstrates the ways in which interpretation in statistical analysis resembles interpretive analysis in other intellectual contexts, such as literature, history, or ethnography. Only in the most *un*interesting cases, as he shows, do the brute data speak for themselves (for example, what percentage of the students are boys rather than girls?). The more interesting and important empirical questions of social science relate to theoretical questions that require interpretations of both methods and data (for instance, do the teachers favour the boys over the girls?). In this respect, Kritzer identifies three basic 'orders of interpretation' in quantitative analysis. The most basic concerns technical questions which are seldom asked or answered: for instance, what is the meaning of the statistical tests employed? What does the value we get from an F-ratio mean? The typical response—'the bigger the outcome the better'—does not answer this question.

The second order of interpretation involves the use of statistical outcomes to identify problems in the data and analysis, some of which are related to the data, some of which merge theoretical and data issues, and some of which mainly result from theoretical complexities inherent in substantive models. Such problems can, for example, result from a small number of extreme outliers along a statistical regression-analysis line (that is, data that would appear to be anomalously distant from a more generally cluster set of data), leading to unexpected correlation coefficients. How does one interpret the meaning of these divergent points? And, based on these interpretations, should they be retained or discarded?

The third order of interpretation is the most complex. It involves connecting the statistical results to broader theoretical patterns. Here the task is to use the data to assess and develop theoretical propositions. This generally involves employing contextual elements and 'side information' available to the analysts, as well as substantive theory. The sophisticated quantitative analyst has to be adept at recognizing the key contextual elements surrounding the data, as well as at using models to link specific findings to such contextual elements.

Kritzer (1996: 11) makes clear how the quantitative analyst, like the literary theorist, uses contextual and tropological paradigms 'to express a thought or describe a reality that is complex, inconsistent, and even contradictory.' Tropes are needed by the empirical analysts as well as the literary scholar to facilitate interpretation and to standardize the communication of those interpretations. Of special importance is the metaphor, a trope that makes an implied comparison which allows us to see something from another perspective or point of view.

Placing the emphasis on statistical analysis, McCloskey (1985; 1994) makes the same argument. In her view, if we look at what economists actually do with statistics rather than at what they say they do with them, we discover that statistical findings are shot through with uncertain, subjective judgements. A judgement that a statistic is 'significant', or that a value is high or low, depends on the rhetorical conversation that accompanies it. A contemporary example is found in the discussion of the war against terrorism. The United States points to nearly 3,000 deaths resulting from the attack on the World Trade Center in New York. But opponents of the United States, from the leaders of the Attac movement against globalization to oppositional groups in the Middle East, point to the deaths of 30,000 children every day from poverty and hunger. By all standards, both figures represent large numbers of victims. But clearly the meaning of these numbers depends on the conversation of which they are a part. Is the United States selfishly insensitive to the plight of the rest of the world, the great majority of whom live in abject poverty? Or does calling attention to the 30,000 figure misrepresent or neglect the intentions of those who carried out the attack, given that many hungry children die every year under regimes in Afghanistan and elsewhere in the Middle East? The point is that it is the rhetoric of the beliefs, not numbers, that determines the significance of these arguments. Yet, for all of our emphasis on numbers, we seldom take seriously the responsibility to be candid about our underlying beliefs. Both sides put out the numbers as if they spoke for themselves.

McCloskey (1985: 140) explains how two groups of economists can look at the same statistically reliable results and draw different conclusions. She gives the following illustration: 'Some economists ... reject the statistically solid result that oil prices appear in regressions explaining inflation, while accepting the flimsy result that money alone causes inflation.' At the same time, 'others do the reverse, believing oil prices to be flimsy and money solid'. But 'both groups justify their beliefs by claiming that *they* look at the evidence'. For all of the talk about Bayesian statistics, as she puts it, a typical response of such economists is to look at firm statistical results that they do not like—despite their apparently irrefutability by the rules of positive economics—and simply dismiss them with a statement like 'I can't believe it'. Few economists, like social scientists generally, take seriously the need to be candid about the beliefs that lie behind such judgements.

This does not mean that there can be no such thing as 'objectivity'. It just means that we need a more sophisticated understanding of objectivity that acknowledges the concept's reliance on social definitions. This involves recognizing that objectivity typically means that we converse with people who agree with our standards of comparison. To make this point, McCloskey (1985: 152) cites the mathematician Armand Borel, who put it this way (1983: 13): 'something becomes objective ... as soon as we are convinced that it exists in the minds of others in the same form that it does in ours, and that we can think about and discuss it together.' For this reason, we need to look more closely at the concept of objectivity and the related concept of validity.

VALIDITY AS CREDIBILITY

Normally, to speak of the degree of confidence in the 'truth' of a finding of a particular empirical analysis is to speak of 'validity'. Within the prevailing empiricist research paradigm, 'truth value' is objectively defined in terms of 'internal validity', described as the isomorphic relationship between a set of data and the phenomenon those data are believed to represent. But in a world of multiple realities the concept of an objective assessment of an isomorphism loses any rigorous meaning that neo-positivism assigns to it. More relevant is the compatibility of the constructed realities that exist in the minds of the inquiry's respondents with those that are attributed to them. This relationship is best termed 'credibility' or 'trustworthiness' (Mishler 1990).

Credibility needs to be established with the individuals and groups who have supplied data for an inquiry. Adopting credibility as the standard for policy analysis, Bozeman (1986: 528) writes that the 'chief requirement for an articulated assessment of credibility is that another interested party should be able to follow (not necessarily agree with) the decision procedures of the individual providing the assessment.' It is assessed by determining whether the description developed through inquiry in a particular setting 'rings true' for those persons who are members of that setting. Because these persons represent different constructed realities, a credible outcome is one that adequately represents both the areas in which these realities converge and the points on which they diverge. As Erlandson *et al.* (1993: 30) put it, 'A credible inquiry generally has the effect on its readers of a mosaic image; often imprecise in terms of defining boundaries and specific relationships but very rich in providing depth of meaning and richness of understanding.'

Because the major concern in establishing credibility is interpreting the constructed realities that exist in the context being studied, and because these realities exist in the minds of the people in the context, attention must be directed to gaining a comprehensive interpretation of these realities that can be affirmed by the people in the contextual setting. Qualitative theorists have developed a series of strategies for accomplishing this (see, for example, Lincoln and Guba 1985; Erlandson *et al.* 1993).

A qualitative inquiry should also provide its audience with evidence to show that, if it were replicated with the same or similar respondents in the same or similar context, its findings could be repeated (Lincoln and Guba 1985: 290). In the prevailing empirical-analytic research paradigm this quality is reflected in a concern for 'reliability', which refers to a study's (or instrument's) consistency, predictability, stability, or accuracy. The establishment of reliability depends on replication, the assumption being that repeated applications of the same or equivalent instruments to the same subjects under the same conditions will yield similar measurements. Reliability is a precondition for validity. Quite apart from the fact that few empirical findings are tested for their replicability, as we saw in Chapter 6, there can be no empirical assumption of an isomorphic relationship between observations and reality if attempts at replication yield different results.

The interpretive researcher, however, believes that observed instability may be attributed not only to error but also to 'reality shifts'. Thus, the qualitative researcher's quest is not for invariability but for 'trackable variance', that is, variability that can be ascribed to particular sources (error, reality shifts, better insights, and so on). Consistency is conceived in terms of 'dependability', a concept that embraces both the stability implied by reliability and the trackability required by explainable changes. One procedure for doing this is the 'dependability audit'.[4]

From an interpretive perspective, we can see similar processes operating in both quantitative and qualitative inquiry. While the quantitative analyst uses the rigorous language of validity and reliability, much of what actually goes on in such an analysis is infused with interpretive judgements that disappear in the final research report. Indeed, as we saw in Chapter 6, the qualitative inquirer's concept of credibility is a more accurate conceptualization of what goes on in quantitative research under the labels of validity and reliability. In this view, the degree of interpretation is more a function of the particular problem under investigation rather than a matter of a type of inquiry. The primary difference is the communities in which the analysts seek to establish credibility. Where empirical analysts turn to their body of peers in the relevant scientific community to establish the credibility of their research, the qualitative researcher takes the subjects themselves as a reference point. Although the processes operate on different levels, in both cases they follow the same general logic. It is the logic of interpretation and persuasive argumentation rather than proof and demonstration per se.

In the view here, both qualitative and quantitative research methods have their place in the social sciences. Instead of getting rid of or downplaying quantitative research, the argument here is to elevate interpretive analysis. Indeed, it would appear that interpretation is the link between them. In this case, interpretation should be the prior category, rather than the other way around. This, of course, would have a significant impact on both the teaching and the conduct of research methods. With regard to teaching, only a few social science programmes give much attention to qualitative methods. And those that do still tend to treat them as adjuncts to empirical methods. Instead, it is suggested here that this relationship should be turned around. Social science should be understood to be anchored to the interpretive narratives of the social world it seeks to explain and would turn to empirical methods as particular empirical questions arise in those accounts, including the possibility of larger structural relationships of which the actors are unaware. Not only does this free the social sciences from the narrow 'methodism' that has dominated it over the

---

[4] The dependability audit, write Erlandson *et al.* (1993: 34), provides for 'an external check . . . on the processes by which the study was conducted. This is done by providing an "audit trail" that provides documentation (through critical incidents, documents, and interview notes), and a running account of the process (such as the investigator's daily journal) of inquiry'.

past five or six decades, it would return them to the substantive materials that give them relevance.

There has been some recognition of this need to build in the qualitative dimension in recent years. In particular, the willingness of leading scholars such as King, Koehane, and Verba (1994) to concede ground to qualitative methods has been the source of renewed interest and discussion. Given that quantitative social scientists have long denied or denigrated the validity of qualitative methods, interpretive theorists have some reason for optimism. But it can be only a qualified optimism. While acknowledging qualitative methods, authors such as King, Koehane, and Verba have sought only to incorporate them on terms amenable to the logic of empiricist research (Buethe 2002). That is, qualitative research has to be designed and conducted in such a way as to render its results empirically testable. Indeed, affirming their basic commitment to neo-positivism, they argue in positivist language that the link between them has to be established through the logic of empirical science, which they describe as the single unified logic of inference (King, Koehane, and Verba 1994: 3) . In short, other logics of inference do not lead to real knowledge.

But, as should hopefully be clear by now, the primary goal of qualitative inquiry is not to draw out empirically testable hypotheses for empirical researchers; rather, it is examine the narrative understandings of the actors. While qualitative research can indeed serve as a corrective or a corroborative perspective for the mainstream project and its problems, the approach offered by King, Koehane, and Verba mis-understands and mistreats qualitative research. More than just another way of collecting data, such interpretive research rests on an altogether different epistemo-logical understanding of social reality and its construction. To the degree that social constructionism accurately conceptualizes the process of social explanation, this attempt to neo-positivize qualitative research only reproduces the very problems it has set out to solve. As such, these new efforts are best understood as an attempt to patch up the cracks in a troubled endeavour.

Although empirical methods have proved effective in many contexts, they remain of limited usefulness when applied to the study of social meaning. Failing to recog-nize that all reality is not of the same type, it has faltered on the idea that all know-ledge in the human disciplines could develop through a single unified approach. As a consequence, approaches must be designed specifically to the study all the kinds of reality, since the use of a single approach to knowledge requires a translation of the aspects of one reality into incommensurate categories drawn from another realm. For example, when social meaning is translated into categories derived from descrip-tions of objects in the material realm, crucial dimensions of the social experience are lost, including the experience of temporality. In addition, translation across realms of social existence requires reduction of complexity and loss of information, as for example when narrative intricacy is reduced to only those structures or operations that are recognized in the organized or material realms.

Even though the material realm can be studied by the use of quantifying procedures and statistical estimates, the realm of meaning is to be captured only through the qualitative nuances of its expression in ordinary language. The disciplines of history and literary criticism have developed procedures and methods for studying the realm of meaning through its expressions of language. The social sciences need to look to those disciplines rather than to the physical sciences for a scientific mode for inquiry of the realm of social consciousness.

SOCIAL MEANING AND THE QUESTION OF CAUSALITY

A major objection to interpretative social science has been its neglect of the question of causality, the central focus of empirical-analytic social science. For neo-positivist social science the goal is to develop a causal science of social relations. In such a theory, there is a clear statement that something happened because of something else. Although the social sciences have mainly succeeded in producing only correlations among events—A and B occur at the same time—a causal theory requires showing that the cause A precedes the effect B. Such explanations are next to impossible in the social world, as it is seldom possible to orchestrate events in ways that will reveal the temporality of the occurrences. Scientifically this requires the use of experimental methods that permit the introduction of A before B occurs. The discovery of such relationships is essential to the development of a social science capable of successfully predicting events, a basic goal of the empiricist orientation.

Many interpretive theorists, it has to be conceded, have simply replaced the issue of causality with meaning. For some interpretivists, the social sciences are only about uncovering and understanding social meanings. Meanings are not causes but, as they explain it, this need be of no particular concern. The social world is laden with meaning and meaning is a different kind of social knowledge. Many of these writers see these two types of knowledge as mutually exclusive; they cannot be combined in any simple or straightforward fashion, if at all. In this view, the goal of a relevant social science is to identify social knowledge and interpret it.

None of these answers sits well with the critics of interpretive social science. How, ask the critics, can the social sciences explain social phenomena if they ignore the causal relationships underlying them? Without causal explanations, for example, how can we come to know why people hold the ideas and beliefs they employ to interpret events? What social conditions—for instance, the conditions of the wealthy or the poor—lead people to see the world one way or the other? Seeking firm causal knowledge, empiricists have generally argued that meanings cannot be causes. Social scientists, in accord with positivist doctrines, must therefore turn away from the problem of meaning (Rosenberg 1988: 109). For these social scientists, interpretive understanding of meaning is incapable of explaining social and political phenomena and is thus unnecessary. Indeed, it is not even a mere link in a causal chain, as inter-subjective understandings are seen as epiphenomenal by-products of external forces. Moreover, as Smith (1988) sees it, the social actor's own understanding of an issue or event is a matter of 'underdetermination'. Stated more explicitly, actors are said to be unable to supply adequate accounts of their own behaviours and the events to which they relate, a point which often cannot be denied. But does it mean that actors never know what they are up to?

Other interpretivists, while agreeing that meaning is another kind of knowledge, reject such a dichotomy between explanation and understanding. Some, such as Gibbons (1987*b*: 3), argue that 'the attempt to understand the intersubjective meanings embedded in social life is at the same time an attempt to explain why people act they way do'. Or even more simply, as Whyte (1956: 40) put it, people sometimes do things for the reasons they think they are doing them. From this perspective, meanings can often reflect views of the world that can function as 'causal conditions for agency' and thus can be the foundation for explanations. Moreover, it is difficult to identify the rules that supply an action with social meaning without noticing that the recognition of these rules is in some part a cause of the action. In this respect, the strong variant of the interpretivist counter-response follows two lines of argument.

The first argument is to make a distinction between causal 'relationships' and causal 'mechanisms' (Lin 1998: 162). While empiricist social scientists stress the analysis of cause-effect relationships, they seldom establish any such relationship. Empirical analysts generally uncover statistical correlations between events, but are unable to prove that one caused the other (that is, that A appeared before B and thus made B happen). Statistical correlation can show only that two or more variables move together in a particular way, but it offers no evidence about causality. The basic reason is clear: the social world is simply too complicated to permit isolating variables in ways that permit determinations of what caused what. Despite this well-known fact, empiricists continue to posit causal analysis as the sine qua non of the enterprise. In reality, such analysis is not in a position to meaningfully organize and guide the disciplines. The proof of the pudding is in the eating: empiricist social science have largely failed to produce an interesting and relevant body of knowledge.

To move beyond the empiricists' statistical relationships in an effort to have a closer look at 'what causes what', that is, the 'causal mechanism', we have only one alternative—namely, interpretive analysis (Lin 1998). Whereas a causal (or statistical) relationship tells us which variables are involved, and something about the direction in which they move, only a closer qualitative analysis can offer us statements about how and why these variable are connected. Only through interpretive methods can we discover the various possible explanations of what particular actors thought they were doing when they engaged in the actions pertinent to the causal relationships. Because such reasons are generally discrete and context dependent, they seldom permit empirical generalizations of the type sought by the empiricist. But such knowledge, as Lin (1998) makes clear, is essential for public policy. Without it, policymakers cannot know which factors to address.[5]

---

[5] Lin (1998) illustrates this point through welfare policy examples. For instance, empirical research has established a strong correlation between previous work experience and employability. But such research cannot tell us whether the correlation results from the fact that people with previous work experience are simply favoured by employers, or whether these workers have the motivation and have gained skills that help them find new jobs. If those with work experience have more access to job possibilities because of their acquired knowledge and skills, a policy solution might be to hire job developers to assist job seekers lacking such experiences. But if employers don't hire people without experience because they don't

Contrary to the empiricist's emphasis on causal relationships, then, the actual causal mechanism is explained through qualitative research. Whereas empiricists such as King, Koehane, and Verba see the role of qualitative research as generating hypotheses for quantitative analysis, the interpretivists turn the argument around and argue just the opposite. Empirical findings are useful in identifying the relationships that the interpretivist has to explain.

Given that the interpretive analysis of the causal mechanism does not take the rigorous form of causal explanation—that is, A caused B—some interpretivists have offered the alternative conceptualization 'quasi-causal' analyses of social actions. As Fay (1975: 84–5) explains this line of argument, 'men act in terms of their interpretations of, and intentions towards, their external conditions, rather than being governed directly by them, and therefore these conditions must be understood not as causes but as warranting conditions which make a particular action or belief more "reasonable", "justifiable" or "appropriate", given the desires, beliefs, and expectations of the actors.' Thus, as Yee (1996: 97) explains, 'intersubjective meanings quasi-causally affect certain actions not by directly or inevitably determining them but rather by rendering these actions plausible or implausible, acceptable or unacceptable, conceivable or unconceivable, respectable or disreputable.' Here, to offer a hypothetical example, one might argue that a particular anti-abortion policy argument finds political support because it resonates with or makes sense in the context of a nation's religious-oriented political culture and the dominant discourses to which it gives rise.

While this is not the place to go into a detailed analysis of the problem, in the view promoted here the strong resolution of this epistemological conflict would be for discursive interpretivists to offer quasi-causal accounts of the effects of subjective factors like beliefs, intentions, and purposes. This would remain consistent with the kind indeterminacy that interpretivist theorists associate with the multiplicity of perspectives and the problem of semantic instability resulting from varying social meanings (emphasized in particular by postmodernists). In so far as interpretive analyses of inter-subjective meanings and discursive practices can be recast to offer some sort of causal or quasi-causal explanations, as Bohman (1991: 13) puts it, indeterminate causal explanations can account both for 'the protean character of reflective, social agency and for the possibility that all explanations might be unstable and impermanent at some future conjuncture'. In this way, as Yee (1996: 103) writes, 'even indeterminate causal explanations can be reasonably assessed because at any one moment their causal mechanism can be identified and evaluated'. The place of interpretive indeterminacy can, in this way, be incorporated through 'the reasoned assessment of indeterminate causal effects within specified parameters'.

---

trust them (perhaps seeing them as lazy or unreliable), the job developer will be of little help. To find out why the employer and the job seekers are doing what they are doing, the policy researcher has to enter the actual situation.

CONCLUSION

Social meanings, as we have seen, are basic to the understanding of public policy. Beyond technical rules and requirements, they convey essential meanings inherent to social and political interaction and are thus deeply involved in policy decision-making. This reality requires us to transcend the standard empirical focus of policy analysis to include the methods and practices of interpretive inquiry, which in turn means entering the social and political context of action to examine the specific motives, intentions, and purposes of the policy actors we study. In the language of phenomenology, as we discussed in Chapter 3, we need to examine the logic of the situational context that defines and shapes our understandings of policy problems.

Basic to interpretive analysis is the study of the frames that define policy problems and the ways different participants understand them. To get at these frames we have to examine a range of objects and activities to detect and tease out the social meanings that they embody or carry. In particular, we have to look at the various interpretive communities in a given policy arena to understand how they frame the situational contexts that attribute social meanings to the problems under investigation. Of special importance are the ways the languages such groups use call attention to points of conflict that reflect their different world views. Towards this end, the discussion pointed to the method of 'thick description' in explicating the core norms and values that permit us to understand their policy beliefs systems.

The chapter concluded with a discussion of various methodological issues closely related to interpretive analysis, in particular the relation of empirical or quantitative analysis to normative interpretive analysis. In this regard, the discussion took issue with the standard dichotomies that separate quantitative and qualitative analysis, arguing that all research is fundamentally interpretive. Interpretation was seen to bridge the empirical/normative dichotomy as it is the intellectual task inherent to both forms of analysis. The question, then, is not whether or not there is interpretation, but rather how much interpretation is involved in a particular analysis, determined in large part by the nature of the problem under investigation. This issue was also seen to redefine the conventional neo-positivist understandings of objectivity, as well as to reconsider the nature of causality in social scientific explanation.

In Chapter 8 we turn to the topic of policy narratives. The social meanings uncovered by the interpretive analysis are typically embedded in a policy narrative, designed to portray the fuller picture of a policy problem and the potential solutions. Built around interpretations, the narrative represents the policy situation, and offers a view of what has to be done and what the expected consequences will be.

8

Public Policy as Narrative: Stories, Frames, and Metanarratives

In this chapter we extend the discussion of discourse and interpretive methods by examining more specifically the narrative form of discourse and narrative analysis, an emerging and promising orientation in policy analysis. While there is a fair amount of conceptual overlap between the concepts of discourse and narration, we use narrative analysis in this discussion to refer to the analysis of stories.[1]

The contemporary focus on storytelling and narrative analysis owes much to the focus on language in poststructural and postmodern theories, particularly in literature and the humanities (Czarniawska 1997: 11–29). The emphasis of these approaches on narrative and discourse has played a vital part in the epistemological challenge to the dominant empiricist orientation. This influence is reflected in the postempiricist policy literature in numerous ways, the most explicit example being Gottweis' (2000) call for a 'poststructural policy analysis'.

Within policy analysis generally, narrative analysis is most closely aligned with problem-definition and problem-setting, arguably the most crucial step in analytic process (Clemons and McBeth 2001: 175–216). Such research has made clear not only the subjective and conflictual character of problem-definition, but even more specifically the key role of language and narrative stories in the negotiation of such definitions. But the focus on narrative analysis of stories should not be confined to the study of problem definition. It has an important role to play in the analysis of the policy cycle as a whole, in particular implementation and evaluation.

Narrative analysis concerns itself with stories, told in oral or written form, that reveal or convey someone's experiences (Fisher 1989). In this chapter, we focus more on narration that operates mainly at the everyday level of communicative interaction than macro-discourse concerned with the large structuring themes that shape and organize society.[2] To be sure, the narrative storylines employed to communicate in the everyday world draw on the vocabularies of the macro-epistemic level of discourse, as we saw in Chapters 4 and 5. But here we examine the more familiar micro-narrative form as a discursive practice subsumed under but shaped by these broader epistemic formulations.

---

[1] Narration and discourse are closely related. Discourse can—but need not—take the narrative form which we identify here with storytelling, in both oral and written form.

[2] Whereas discourse functioning at the level of social action generally takes the narrative form, discourse at the socio-cultural level can take a broader range of forms.

At the outset, the chapter examines the general features of a narrative story, emphasizing its uses in both the social sciences and everyday social contexts, and discusses the basic epistemological issues involved in the production of a text. The second half of the chapter turns to a survey of two prominent approaches to narrative discourse analyses that have emerged in the field of policy analysis per se.

THE NARRATIVE TRADITION AND
THE SOCIAL SCIENCES

There is, to be sure, nothing new about narrative storytelling; the narratives of the world are without number. We find storytelling in the pictures on the walls of the caves of early humankind. It was—and still is—the way we make meaning in our lives. From infancy we learn how to interpret and understand new narrative stories through older ones acquired in the course of socialization and lived experience. At the cultural level, narratives serve to give cohesion to shared beliefs and to transmit basic values. At the individual level people tell narratives about their own lives that enable them to understand both who they are and where they are headed.

The narrative form—or storytelling—is the domain of the spoken exchange in the everyday interaction (Riessman 1993). Through narration individuals relate their experiences to one another. It is the cognitive form with which people convey what they think and feel, and understand one another, in writing as well as speech. Structured sequentially with a beginning, middle, and end, as Czarniawska (1998: 2) explains, the narrative tells us about an 'original states of affairs', an action or event, and the consequent state of events. As a mode of thought, the narrative furnishes communication with the particular details that constitute the stuff of which meaning is made. 'Details, particular and familiar', as Tannen (1989: 136) puts it, 'enable speakers and hearers to create images' and 'it is in large part through the creation of a shared world of images that ideas are communicated and understanding is achieved.'

Stories, by their nature, are inherently joint social productions. All of the elements of a story—plot, structure, meaning, resolution, and so forth—are created by people conversing and arguing with others. As Wagenaar (2001: 4) puts it, stories 'are the products of the social groups in which they emerge; the thoughts, beliefs, affects, and passions they express and construct are not private properties inaccessible to the outside observer, but instead are situated at the interface of the individual and his wider environment.' It is through the act of storytelling that individuals assess their social positions in their respective communities, grasp the goals and values of their social groups and communities, internalize their social conventions, and understand who they are vis-à-vis one another. It comes then as no surprise that the growing literature on identity politics relies heavily on narrative storytelling (Mottier 1999).

Narratives create and shape social meaning by imposing a coherent interpretation on the whirl of events and actions around us. A good narrative, as Kaplan (1993: 172) explains, 'grasps together' a variety of disparate information and thoughts by weaving them into a plot. Stringing together the beginning and middle of a story with a conclusion, a narrative pulls together a variety of component—metaphors, categories, markings, and other sense-making elements—to come to a conclusion that flows naturally out of these factors. Good stories, Kaplan (1993: 176) writes, have the possibility of creating 'a tapestry that is both lovely and useful and helps make sense of complex situations occurring within an environment of conflicting values'.

The narrative scheme configures a sequence of events and actions into a unified happening by identifying the larger patterns to which they contribute. As we saw in the discussion of Hajer's (1995*a*) analysis of environmental discourses, the thread that weaves these components of narrative discourse together is the storyline. The storyline, as plot, shows the part an individual action contributes to the experience as a whole. The ordering process operates by connecting diverse happenings along a temporal dimension and by identifying the effect one event has on another. In the process, the storyline typically forges the unknown with the known patterns. A narrative is thus different from a chronicle, which simply list events according to their place on a time line (Kaplan 1993).[3] A good narrative, as such, not only conveys a meaning to the listener, but offers the listener or reader a way of seeing and thinking about events that points to implications requiring further attention or consideration.

At the same time, stories encourage us to 'ask about the authors and story-tellers, readers and listeners, plots and storylines, settings and characters, and to see how authors, readers, and settings, may also be characters in their own stories' (Wagenaar 2001: 5). In listening to narratives, the analyst encounters metaphors, categories, markings, and other sense-making elements that connect language to action. The structures, sequences, and conflicts that unravel a story's plot reveal the significance the events have for the relevant social actors. Typically, this significance is derived from the moral in the story, unravelled through the normative argument that weaves through the plot and sequences (McCloskey 1990: 27–9). Underlying storytelling is a demand for moral reasoning (White 1981: 20). As McCloskey puts it, a good story has 'moral weight'.

Connecting actions and events into understandable patterns, the narrative is a cognitive scheme. Bruner (1986) describes the narrative form as one of the two means of knowing and explaining. Like the scientific mode of knowing, the narrative has its own distinctive ways of ordering experience and constructing reality. As an interpretive mode, it possesses its own operating principles and criteria for judging a well-formed narrative explanation. Whereas the scientific mode looks for particular types of empirically based causal connections between events, the narrative mode seeks to explain in terms of social intentions and motivation. Whereas the scientific mode strives to identify stable, reproducible patterns of actions that can be explained without reference to social intentions or purposes, the special subject matter of the narrative form is the 'vicissitudes of human intention'. Rather than social stability, the narrative is especially geared to the goals of the actors and the way changing goals and intentions causally contribute to social change. It seeks to comprehend and convey the direction and purpose of human affairs. Conceiving of behaviours—both their own and that of others—within the narrative framework, social actors employ

---

[3] To make the point Kaplan offers a comparison of a chronicle of welfare policy actions with a narrative story explaining the nature of the problem.

the framework to understand, discuss, and consider the effects that particular actions might have on the goals they pursue. In the phenomenological terminology of Chapter 3, it is the interpretive medium of communication in the social life-world.

THE NARRATIVE AS CONTEXTUAL EXPLANATION

It has been said that we virtually exist because we tell the story of our existence. To the historian, of course, this comes as no surprise: history is itself a rigorous form of storytelling. But for the social sciences it means that they have largely neglected or marginalized an essential aspect of their subject matter. Given this primacy of story-telling in our historical and cultural experience, the narrative form needs to have a central place in the explanatory forms of the human sciences. Because human experienced is 'storied', the meaning-making process of the researcher has also to be storied (Gudmundsdottir 1998: 1). In this sense, the narrative has to be understood as both phenomenon and the process.

The thing that distinguishes the characteristic 'epistemic fingerprint' of the narrative from that of the logical-analytic mode is its emphasis on the context of action. As we saw in Chapter 6, the written text of the logical–analytical mode seeks to present a closed self-referential world to the reader. Meaning and truth are in the accuracy of the observational statements and the logical soundness of the deductive conclusions that lead to the conclusion. Semantic meaning, in contrast, is to be found *inside* the text itself. For the narrative, on the other hand, the semantic content of a stories *resides* above the sentence (Schiffrin 1994; Schiffrin, Tannen, and Hamilton 2001). Where empiricism takes meaning to be fixed and determined, for the narrativist it is located in common-sense references to shared experience. The meaning of the story is, in short, determined by the context in which it is interpreted (Tannen 1985).

Storytelling expands epistemology beyond the narrow confines of observational statements and logical proof into the ways individuals are embedded in the wider social contexts of situation and society. Whereas empiricism bases causal explanation on the metaphors of either the mechanism or the organism, the narrative mode of knowing is geared to the metaphor of contextualism. An adequate account of social action requires the context of time and space (Sarbin 1986). Context 'presupposes an ongoing texture of elaborated events, with each being influenced by preceding episodes and influencing following ones and with each being affected by multiple agents who engage in actions' (Giovannoli 2000: 7). It is thus the historical event located in place and time that captures the constant change in the structure of situations and in the positions occupied by intentional actors oriented towards each other in the world. 'Often these actors have opposite positions, as if functioning on a stage as protagonists and antagonists, as they enter relations of love, hate, agreement or disagreement.' The protagonists' feelings, thoughts, and actions 'can only be understood as emerging from their relationships with antagonists, who are co-constructing reality in often unpredictable ways' (Giovannoli 2000: 7). This is especially evident in political understanding. To grasp this dialectic of thought and emotion one needs only to reflect on the Republican Party's merciless pursuit of former US President Bill Clinton, culminating in an impeachment trial to remove him from office for what normally would be considered private personal concerns, not matters of state.

The narrative form, as a basic process of interpretive *Verstehen*, permits us to consider the role of intentions and motivation which, as we saw, can themselves be a causal or quasi-causal force that needs to be taken into consideration in explanation. Contrary to empiricist efforts to dispel explanations that refer to subjective motivations, intentions and motives are in fact forces that make things happen in the real world of social action. They are inherent to the description and explanation of the causal mechanisms underlying political and social phenomena. A social science without them is an impoverished endeavour. While the fact that we can not directly observe motivations is problematic, they can often be made explicit in the form of texts and documents. Reference to such texts is perhaps best seen in the work of historians (as they, for example, seek to assess the motives of great political leaders). At other times, we can reconstruct intentions and motives by examining actions in particular social contexts. There is always room for reinterpretation, but this is the way it happens in social life.

There can be no surprise that the contextual orientation is the focus of both the novelist and the historian: for both the explanatory details are in the context. Offering *general* types, traits, or characteristics to portray events and actors, scientific explanations generally offer flat and lifeless portraits of human experience, as Kaplan (1993) nicely illustrates in his critique of welfare policy analysis. Lacking attention to social context, empiricism often presents oversimplified and unrealistic relationships of cause and effect that are insufficient to account for the multiplicity of events shaping the causal mechanism. They neglect, as such, the kinds of references to past, present, and future events, as well as the relationships with other actors, that work together to form an interconnected picture of 'reality'. In contrast, exploring such characteristics and traits in relationship to other characters and to the unfolding plot of experience, contextual explanations are sensitive to the particulars of time and space. Here the storyteller does not respond to external stimuli but rather is oriented to the construction of meanings relevant to the achievement of goals and purposes (as the work of any modern-day president's or prime minister's 'spin doctor' makes clear). While the contextual narrative acknowledges the developmental sequences of mechanistic and organic explanations, it also makes room for the unpredictable. The meaning that an individual gives to live events—for example, a job change, relocation to another city, an encounter with a significant other, the sudden loss of a friend, divorce of parents, or a life-threatening operation—can have unpredictable consequences that cannot be accounted for by empiricist metaphors. It is only through a contextual window that the thick realm of human experience can be adequately described and researched. To the degree that the narrative analyst is interested in generalizable statements, such propositions are determined by the extent that they can be located in the particulars of a social context.

But how do we know if a narrative analysis is good or bad? If the ability to enhance a body of knowledge through the application of a set of accepted theoretical approaches and techniques represents the essence of a scholarly discipline, what narrative techniques and representations merit acceptance, and how does one know if a particular narrative has satisfied them? Here we can identify two basic approaches, one concerned with the structure of the narrative and the other with the basic validity of its empirical and normative elements (Fisher 1989).

The structural approach to the quality of a narrative explores the rigour of the logical coherence running through the parts of the story. For instance, a good indication of narrative truth involves the internal connection among the basic elements of narrative—agent, act, scene, agency, and purpose. According to the basic rules of storytelling, some underlying consistency must be present among the holistic elements of a story. In Burke's (1945; 1950) classic statement, this means offering answers to five interrelated questions. What was done (act)? When or where was it done (scene)? Who did it (agent)? How he or she did it (agency)? And why (purpose)?[4]

Outside of the study of literature, the emphasis on context in storytelling is perhaps most rigorously developed in law. Courts ask defendants to tell their stories and a group of jurors, after listening to the lawyers challenge and defend the logic and credibility of the stories, are charged with deciding which one is the more believable. Given that everyday communication is constructed around this form of communications, both jurors and lawyers have their own ways of judging the logic of the story and neither takes the process to be 'irrational', as would the rigorous positivist social scientist. It is, in fact, simply the way information is given social meaning in the social world. When jurors retire to the jury room, they are asked to consider among themselves which of the two versions—that of the plaintiff and that of the defendant—makes the more sense. Basically, as in the process of *Verstehen*, they are asked to put themselves in the shoes of the other—that is, in the context—and decide if the story, based on their own shared social experiences, is credible. Organized by the kind of informal logic we discussed in Chapter 6, the process is not 'scientific', but it is also not irrational.

The second approach focuses on the substantive context of the narrative. Under what has been called the 'paradigmatic' approach, narratives can be analysed against criteria that would put them in one or another category. Case-study research in the conventional social sciences is often pursued in this fashion. Specific questions can also be organized as social-scientific hypotheses and tested empirically. Similarly, basic normative propositions can be probed for agreement or credibility through the methods of normative discourse, to which we return in the final discussion of the chapter.

In epistemological terms, narrative analysis, like interpretive and contextual analysis generally, also raises worries about relativism. Positivist social scientists, as we saw in Chapter 7, have long worried about an inability to empirically nail down valid, reliable explanations that can be demonstrated to be better that competing

---

[4] Similarly, for Labov (1972; 1982) an informed narrative analysis can be guided by identifying, isolating, and analysing the following features: (1) the most basic organizing statement of the narrative; (2) a statement of orientation (time, place, situation, participation); (3) the complication action (the sequence of events); and (4) an evaluation (significance and meaning of the action, and the attitude of the narrator).

explanations. Does not storytelling, they ask, lead inquiry into a hopeless quagmire of subjective relativity, a situation in which each interpretation is finally judged to be as valid as the others, as some postmodernists would have us believe?

This need not be as problematic as it seems. Much of the problem is with the extreme form of postmodernism. In such a radical constructionist perspective everything is a story. Events are seen to have no particular meaning; their meanings are imposed on them through the construction of narratives. Admitting to no possibility of firm truth, this position is thoroughly relativistic in nature. In the absence of truth, there are only stories. This view is as unrealistic as the rigorous positivist or realist approach, which limits the assessment of a story to its representation of empirical factors.

Following the epistemological position taken in Chapter 7, a postempiricist policy analysis needs to pave a path between these two positions. Towards this end, we can usefully turn to Fay's (1996: 194) approach of 'narrativism'. Outlining the deficiencies of both constructionist and realist approaches to the narrative analysis, narrativism seeks a 'a proper view of the relation of narrative to life [that captures] what is correct about realism (that narrative form is not accidental, nor a mere representational device; and that our identities as agents embody narratives) without including what is erroneous about it (that each person's life just *is* a single enacted narrative of which the agent is . . . a mere reporter)'. Narrativism, Fay (1996: 194) writes, tries to respect the insights of constructionism 'that the narrative account of any life is continually and infinitely revisable . . . without making its mistakes (that narrative and the form of narrative are mere creations imposed on material which is non-narratival)'. In short, narrativism seeks to establish a path between realism and constructionism. Narrativism, so defined, fits into the postempiricist approach pursued here. Rejecting the possibility of pure objectivity, it is nonetheless open to both empirical and normative inquiry.

The narrative paradigm, as Fisher (1989: xii) develops it, does not deny or neglect the fact that power, ideology, manipulatory distortions, or authoritarian forces are significant features of communicative practices. However, despite the distorting influences of such power, decisions and actions have to be taken and this always occurs in the context of ongoing stories about social and political phenomena, including the presence of the stories of the less powerful. If, as Fisher argues, power and ideology were the only important explanatory dimensions of communicative practices, decisions and action would only be a question of whose domination should we submit to. But, as he puts it, 'some stories are more truthful and humane than other', which can be sorted out through the discursive logic of good reasons. And in politics in a democratic society the struggle for power is in significant part played out over time through arguments about the 'best story'.

POLICY COMMUNICATION AS STORYTELLING

But what does all of this have to do with the practical issues of policymaking? Here again we find the centrality of stories. Given that stories are the language of human action generally, it comes as no great surprise to learn that policymakers (and other policy participants generally) also convey their interpretations through the telling of stories, whether for purposes of argument, claims-making, or expression of individual identity (Wagenaar 1997; 2001). They are the means—the only means—by which policymakers can negotiate the realities that confront them.

To translate the narrative structure into public policy, the beginning of the story is about a problem situation to be solved by a policymaker, the middle action or event introduces a policy intervention, and the end turns to the consequences of a policy outcome. Through the construction and interpretation of such narrative sequences, policymakers seek to weave their way through the uncertainty and unpredictability of politics and public administration. As Wagenaar (2001: 4) explains, through the narrative structuring of experiences policymakers learn about 'intentions, articulate vague goals and ambitions, we discover what is really important, what is marginal, realize the multiple constraints, often conflicting, that enable and limit our actions, and suggest courses of action by predicting consequences to . . . [themselves] and others.' As Neustadt and May (1986) counsel in their book on the uses of history in policymaking, when you want to know what the problem is, ask what the story is.

Recognizing the constitutive role of stories in politics and policymaking permits us to consider how such policy practices can themselves be understood as narratives. In so far as public policies are typically treated in terms of rules and regulations pertaining to efficient or effective performance, they often mask their own social meanings. As Schram and Neisser (1997: 2) put it, public policies also more fundamentally narrate 'our relations (between citizens, between citizens and the state, between states, etc.) in politically selective ways'. Regardless of whether 'stories are about foreign enemies . . . global environmental change, . . . welfare dependency, or the story of the state of race relations, the politics of public policy-making is played out in terms of stories that mediate how public problems are comprehended.'

An important issue in this regard is the site of narrative production. Czarniswska points to at least two important kinds of narrative production in public policy, 'narratives in the making' and 'ready narratives'.[5] Although the ways of approaching them might be similar, the distinctions for grasping the meanings of a policy can be important. The written policy narrative (made ready for the reader), as she explains, 'is the result of an intense narrative-making, which actually tries to remove the traces of work that went into it'. On the other hand, the study of 'a policy in the making shows the negotiations, the competition between narratives and counter-narratives'. Whereas the ready policy narrative seeks to obscure important social and political considerations behind the construction of the narrative, leaving the interpretations of their political meanings to the readers, the study of policy narrative-making permits us to see and better understand the way policies can comprise a sequence of

---

[5] Czarniawska' remarks are based on personal communication (17 July 2002). Whereas she sees conversational analysis as a fruitful way of analysing how the text of a policy is made, the way in which the researcher reads the text is best approached through discursive analysis. She also calls for an inclusion of the way other people read the text, which can be dealt with through literary approaches to reader–response theory.

ambiguous and conflicting claims that represent inconsistent responses to the interests of different groups.

In public policy analysis, the narrative mode of explanation has only begun to receive the attention it deserves. Most important have been the theoretical beginnings of Rein (1976), Stone (1988), Schoen and Rein (1994), Kaplan (1986; 1993), Roe (1994), and Hajer (1995*a*). Of particular significance is the work of Czarniawska (1997; 1998), although her work is more generally a contribution to public administration and organization theory. We devote the next sections of this chapter to an illustrative outline of the general concepts and research strategies advanced by Stone and Roe.

POLICY METAPHORS AND CAUSAL STORIES

No one has better illustrated the ways in which people understand policy problems through the medium of narratives than Stone (1988; 2002). Critical of the social sciences' efforts to avoid or downplay this dimension of policy analysis, Stone makes clear that the reliance on policy narrative is evident in even the most casual examination of policy discussions, whether in everyday or official form. Citizens, politicians—and yes, even policy analysts, as Forester's (1993; 1999) work demonstrates—tell causal stories to convey the nature, character, and origins of policy problems. Indeed, as we saw earlier, policy controversies often turn on the underlying storyline rather than the apparent facts typically presented by the policy analyst. It is not that the facts do not play a role; rather it is that they are embedded—explicitly or implicitly—in narrative accounts. What frequently seems to be a conflict over details, as Stone explains, is in actuality a disagreement about the basic story.

Stone's research on stories identifies two primary types of policy narratives. One focuses on decline or crisis, the other on human helplessness and the need for social control (Stone 1989). In the first type of story, things are seen to have got worse, with empirical data usually cited to make the case. Typical examples would be the loss of valuable forests or a level of human poverty that is taking on crisis proportions. In the second type of story, what had previously seemed to be a matter of fate or accident is now portrayed as an issue for change through political or policy action. An example would be the rise or spread of unemployment. Whereas it might have been believed that some people were simply destined to be members of the underclass, or that there were and always would be poor people, the story now portrays unemployment as a consequence of the failure of the political-economic system to provide a sufficient number of jobs and points to the ways in which it can be ameliorated.

Employing literary and rhetorical devices for symbolic representation, policy stories are tools of political strategy. As strategies for representing problems and interests, discursive devices such as synechdoches (which represent a whole by one of its parts) or metaphors (which make implied comparisons) are pervasive throughout policy language. Such linguistic constructions are designed and introduced to convince an audience of the necessity of a political or policy action; they help to identify both the responsible culprits and the virtuous saviours capable of leading us to high ground.

On the surface of the matter, such rhetorical devices would only appear to make comparisons between seemingly different things. But, as Stone (1988: 118) writes, they do more than just make comparisons; in more subtle ways they usually imply a whole story and prescription for action. She offers the example of describing something as 'fragmented'. Although the word appears at first only to offer a description, against the interpretive backdrop of a concern with order and efficiency, without anyone ever saying so, the word 'fragmentation' is usually also a call for reorganization.[6]

It is common in politics to portray our political opponents as engaging only in 'rhetoric'; that is, concealing the real story, they offer us a version of events constructed to promote their own interests and concerns. Missing from this view, however, is the recognition that all politics operates this way. Symbolic representation, in short, is basic to political argumentation. 'Symbolic devices', as Stone writes (1988: 122–3), can be 'especially persuasive and emotionally compelling because their story line is hidden and their sheer poetry is often stunning'. Frequently 'a metaphor is so much a part of our cultural way of saying things that it slips right by us'.

An important feature of symbols is their potential ambiguity. Symbols often typically mean two (or more) things at the same time: 'equal opportunity in education can mean giving everybody tuition vouchers for the same dollar amount', or it can mean 'providing extra resources for those with special needs' (Stone 1988: 123). Different people can thus understand symbols differently, especially when used in different social contexts.

For the empiricist conception of science, of course, this is problematic. The interpretation of events, social as well as physical, has to remain clear and constant for the work of the empiricist. To be replicable over time by different investigators, the objects of investigation require fixed categories. By contrast, symbolic ambiguity in art is generally taken to be a source of depth and richness. 'Symbols', as Stone (1988: 123) points out, 'call forth individual imagination, wish, and experience, and draw the observer into the work of art as an active participant'. In this sense, politics is more like art than science. For this reason, Stone (2002: 157) argues, 'a type of policy analysis that does not make room for the centrality of ambiguity in politics can be of little use in the real world'.

As we have already seen, nowhere is this relationship between language and the social construction of a problem more apparent in politics than in the process of problem definition. Always political in nature, problem definition generally involves an effort to portray a social situation in a way that favours one's own argument and course of action as being in the public interest. As Stattschneider (1960: 7) made clear, such strategic problem definition usually means 'manipulating the scope of conflict' by making some members of the public appear more affected by the conflict than others. Specific symbols such as freedom, free markets, decentralized government, or individual initiative are offered 'to restrict the scope of conflict, while others, such as equality, justice, and civil rights are calculated to expand it'

---

[6] For Schoen and Rein (1977: 235) this often subtle shift from problem description to policy description is based on what they call the 'normative leap'.

(Stone 1988: 122). Thus, problems 'are not given out there in the world waiting for smart analysts to come along and define them correctly'. Instead, 'they are created in the minds of citizens by other citizens, leaders, organizations, and government agencies, as an essential part of political maneuvering' (Stone 1988: 122).

The argument can be taken even deeper into the heart of empiricist territory. Emphasizing 'hard numbers', conventional social science, as we have seen, has ignored these rhetorical aspects of politics and policy. Typically, public policy problems are defined in significant part by the numbers assigned to them. But numbers, as Stone shows, are themselves symbols and, more than a little ironically, often function in ways similar to metaphors. To count something, as she (Stone 2002: 165) explains, is to categorize it, and, in doing so, we select a 'feature of something, assert a likeness on the basis of that characteristic, and ignore all the other features'. As with metaphors, counting requires categories that emphasize 'some feature instead of others and excluding things that might be similar in important ways but do not share that feature'.[7] Based on such selections counting, as such, can be a political act. Which items fit into a particular category? Which things are included in the category and which are left out? Categorization thus sets boundaries in the form of criteria and rules that determine whether or not something belongs (Stone 1988: 128). In this way, a deliberate decision to include or exclude particular items is or can be a political act, either explicitly or explicitly.

NUMBERS AS METAPHORS

By establishing recognizable boundaries, counting can normatively function like metaphors. In some cases, such boundaries create social or political communities. As Stone writes, 'any number is implicitly an assertion that things counted in it share a common feature and should be treated as a group, either natural or statistical communities.' Much of the counting made by government 'is an effort to identify a statistical community in order to demonstrate common interests or concerns and thereby stimulate creation of a natural community.' For this reason, counting is also used as a tool of political mobilization. To identify and select out common or shared problems or characteristics among individuals is to pull them into a group, however artificial the classification might be (Stone 1988: 136).

Numerical measurements can also normatively imply a need for action. In general, we tend to count things when we want to change them or change a behavioural orientation of others to them. 'Not only does measuring a problem create subtle pressure to do something about it', as Stone (1988: 131) puts it, 'but some level of the measure usually becomes established as a norm.' What is more, the norms established by measurements are sometimes ambiguous, particularly when they simultaneously tell explicit or implicit stories. Statistics are frequently used to tell a story, such as a story

---

[7] An interesting example is the contested Florida ballots in the 2000 US presidential election between Gore and Bush. The political struggle turned in significant part on what counted as counting a ballot. Was it the fact that the ballot went through the machine? Or was it that the machine couldn't detect the hole in the ballot?

in a policy debate about crisis or decline (1988: 134). But equally important as the explicit numerically based story can be an implicit story functioning independently of the would-be meaning of the numbers. For example, a hidden message is often conveyed in the very act of counting. The count itself serves as an implicit message signifying that an event occurs often enough to warrant getting counted, and thus should be taken seriously. Measurement, in this way, has to be recognized as a social process. As Stone (1988: 137) puts it, 'Numbers in politics are measures of human activities, made by human beings, and intended to influence human behavior.' They are, as such, 'subject to conscious and unconscious manipulation by the people being measured, the people making the measurements, and the people who interpret and use measurements made by others.'

Numbers in policy deliberations cannot be adequately comprehended without examining how they are assembled or produced. Why do people decide to count some things and not others? In what way is the link between the measurements and the things measured established? Are there strategic incentives to make some numbers high and other low? (Stone 1988). In trying to change activities, people try to influence those who make the measurements. Often the items 'being counted become bargaining chips in a strategic relationship between the measurers and the measured, so that at different points in the relationship, there are very different pressures to reveal or conceal.' For this reason, the selection of the measures is a strategic component of problem definition, especially as the outcomes of measures take on political character only when dressed up in a policy narration. As artefacts of political life, the numbers thus become symbols and metaphors themselves. Beyond describing the world, they are also real as artefacts, 'just as poems and paintings are artifacts that people, collect, recite, display and respond to'. However, the primacy of 'numbers as a mode of describing society in public policy discussion is only a relatively recent phenomenon; it is not the result of some underlying reality of numbers' (Stone 1988: 146).

POLICY METANARRATIVES

Roe (1994) asks how narrative policy analysis might be set out as a methodological procedure for examining competing narratives in policy controversies. Focusing on the coherence of narratives, Roe takes a structural approach to narrative analysis that in significant part can be understood as an approach to problem framing. Of particular importance is his emphasis on the role of 'metanarratives'. The process of identifying metanarratives, in Roe's view, offers the policy analyst a way of reframing controversies to identify potential resolutions.

For Roe, the analysis of narratives and metanarratives can be particularly useful in situations characterized by high degrees of problem uncertainty, socio-technical complexity, and political polarization. His focus is on policy problems that have so many unknowns—empirical, political, legal, and bureaucratic, among others—that there is little left to do but to examine the different stories policymakers and their critics use to articulate and make sense of such complexity and uncertainty. Methodologically, he develops the approach with the assistance of a literary theory designed to deal with ambiguity and uncertainty in written texts.

Although policy analysts have typically been ambivalent toward stories and story-telling, they are in fact surrounded by stories about policy problems (Roe 1994; Kaplan 1993; Krieger 1981). As Roe (1994: 1–4) explains, narrative stories are a basic reality in the everyday of practising policy analysts' and for this reason a rigorous approach to narrative analysis should be one of the tools available to them. His approach to narrative policy analysis is explicitly an effort to supply the field with such a method-ology. He sees it as a methodology to accompany the standard tools of microeconomic analysis, statistics, organization theory, and public management practice.

A basic premise underlying his narrative policy analysis is, in accordance with Stone, the need to accept and learn from ambiguity, a point much neglected by a dis-cipline that has emphasized the pursuit of certainty. Calling for analytical tolerance, Roe argues that analysts can choose sides but they need to reject the misconception that other ideas can be bridged, if not ignored. Most important, analysts must work to figure out and attend to the stories that are drowned out or marginalized by the dominant discourses. The analyst needs to identify the multitude of voices and hear their stories, as it is from such stories that a metanarrative or a counterstory can be found or constructed, should there be one to find. In this sense, Roe's metanarrative policy analysis is compatible with a strong, participatory democracy, although he generally seems to underplay this implication of his method.

The basic model proceeds through four steps. The analyst starts by identifying the conventional or accepted stories that dominate a policy controversy. After mapping out these narratives, he or she then tries to identify the existence of other narratives related to the issue (what he calls 'counterstories') that do not conform to or run counter to the controversy's dominant policy narratives. Through a process of com-paring these narratives, the analyst takes the third step and tries to see whether the comparison can be used to 'tell' a metanarrative. Here the work is adapted from the theory of literary narration developed by Riffaterre (1990). The metanarrative, as 'intertext', seeks to account for how two original policy narratives—each the polar opposite of the other—can both be the case at the same time. Showing ways that the same events can be retold from one or more different points of view, the metanarra-tive holds out the possibility of removing or easing the intractable elements of the controversy, thus enabling the discussion to move to new grounds. The analyst's last step is to determine if or how the metanarrative frames or recasts the problem in such a way as to make it more amenable to empirical policy-analytical tools.

Roe counsels analysts to look for asymmetries in narrative structure and content that signal the presence of deep-rooted uncertainties or power differentials, which may not otherwise be apparent. Power differentials, as Roe (1994: 72) explains, come into play as people argue and change their stories. The role of the policy analyst using these methods is to enable people to articulate their stories. In the process, differential access to information used in decision-making 'itself must become the focus of intervention and rectification' (1994: 73).

Van Eeten (1999), following Roe, links his use of Roe's approach to analyses of action in four environmental controversies in the Netherlands. In an analysis of a controversy over flooding dykes he shows how actors' stories about flooding and dyke improvement led to specific policy actions. In particular, he makes use of stories surrounding the events that are neither explicitly uttered or heard to uncover the underlying assumptions influencing the deliberative exchanges. His case study of the debate on the expansion of Amsterdam airport, for example, shows how three unrecognized policy narratives are submerged in the politically polarized narratives for and against further expansion (Van Eeten 2001). These three hidden narratives are seen to cut across the polarized coalitions of stakeholders, which provide alternatives that can define a new agenda that breaks the current deadlock in the policy debate. In addition, Van Eeten employs semiotic techniques to further develop these alternatives into an even richer set of options. In this and other cases, the analysis of hidden assumptions in policy narratives is seen to have direct implications for action-oriented decisions.

This line of work usefully elaborates the development of narrative policy analysis, especially in terms of Roe's emphasis on metanarratives. Many will find Roe's book difficult to read, in part because of an unfamiliarity with the terms and concepts of the approach, in part due to Roe's style. At times, moreover, the analysis seems perhaps be a bit too inventive or imaginative, especially when it comes to the construction of his metanarratives. Having said this, though, he has to be credited with having opened the door in policy analysis to the development of a new and important analytic approach.

Whereas the work of Stone is a contribution to a postempiricist perspective, Roe's efforts are geared more to serve or support mainstream empiricist approaches. Thus, from the perspective advanced here, there are several problems with his approach to narrative policy analysis that require attention. One is his reliance on the stories offered by the immediate participants in a particular controversy. Often the real problem to be dealt with in a public controversy is created by considerations outside the scope of everyday arguments. People may fail to see that their disagreements are lodged in the social systems or political beliefs that stand apart from more local considerations. These dimensions are not necessarily reflected in the narratives as Roe deals with them, although they can be—and often seem to be—lodged in the assumptions underlying the narratives he analyses. To get around this, the analyst has to reach beyond the stories being told in a particular place and time and include other available narrative discourses that bear on the analysis. It is a methodological problem that can be ameliorated with the assistance of the postempiricist logic of policy evaluation presented in Chapter 9.

Secondly, Roe's effort to construct a metanarrative does not directly involve the participation of the actors involved in the policy controversy, or at least need not. Construction of the metanarrative is the work of the policy analyst; he or she spells it out for the participants. As such, the approach fails to fully capture the dialectical and inventive sides of policy debates that often produce the kinds of creative insights that can facilitate the discovery or construction of a metanarratives. That is, the facilitation of discursive interaction in the search for a metanarrative or counterstory can uncover new ways of seeing. In the process, it can also serve as an educative function for the participants, as well as build the legitimization needed for an acceptable policy narrative. One example of this neglect of participation would seem to be illustrated by

Roe's (1994) development of a metanarrative for the policy debate over global warming. He is correct to argue that emphasis on the global dimension detracts from the fact that the problem can have different meanings in different social contexts, thus hindering the effort to come up with a common policy strategy, a critique which seems implicitly directed at the environmental narrative. Designed to redirect attention to local and regional contexts, his metanarrative has a point to make. But had it been developed as the product of conversations with actual participants—rather than his own construction—no serious environmentalist would have been much surprised or moved. The environmental movement, as reflected in the famous slogan of the German Green Party, 'think globally, act locally', has long recognized this policy orientation. And, one might add, it has scarcely served to shift the global warming debate.

It is also important to note that Roe fails to draw out the more constructionist implications of his approach. In particular, he resists turning narrative analysis on policy analysis itself. Rather than seeing policy analysis as a type of narrative with its own practices, he treats narrative analysis as only one of the tools of policy analysis, alongside the other methods such as cost-benefit analysis or forecasting. From a postempiricist perspective, all of these would be seen as part of the larger narrative of policy analysis. The fact that he acknowledges this point doesn't offset the problem, as he seems to suggest.

Indeed, for the postempiricist there is something of a troublesome technocratic orientation underlying Roe's approach. Although he tends to explain his method somewhat differently in different parts of the book, making it difficult to pin him down, more often than not he sees the technique primarily as a way to help policy analysts reshape issues in ways that will better lend them to the conventional tasks and tools of empirical analysis. This seems evident enough in the last of his four procedural steps, which appears to privilege empirical policy analysis methods. Indeed, the task is to support empirical analysis. Despite occasional references to participation, particularly as an appeal for a wider range of perspectives, the metanarrative is generally discussed as a way to help stabilize governmental decision-making assumptions in the face of complexity and uncertainty. That is, the model is envisioned to help managers with their decision problems, which is the conventional mission of policy analysis. Privileging the position of the manager, this uncritical instrumentalization of metanarrative analysis unfortunately neglects to adequately recognize or accommodate the politics underlying storytelling.

In his analysis of the California medfly controversy, for example, he faults the environmental critics for the incompleteness of their story, compared with the dominant policy story offered by State officials. Where the California officials wanted to spray the air with risky chemicals to eliminate the Mediterranean fruit flies that had infested the State's fruit farms, the environmentalists offered only a critique of the potential health risks associated with using the spray. Because the environmentalists offered no solution (that is, a completed story) in the face of the medfly crisis, Roe faults them for increasing uncertainty and the public sense of risk. This increased uncertainty, in his view, only made it more difficult for managers to deal with the medfly problem; and because the environmentalists presented no solution in the face of the need for action, they lost out to the dominant view. Because the State officials had a complete story—one with a beginning, end, and middle—they are judged to have had 'the better story', defined as the one that successfully underwrites and stabilizes decision-making in the face of controversy.

Environmentalists are thus seen, at least implicitly, as unable or unwilling to confront basic decision-making realities. But this is only a new way to state the techno-managerial critique of environmentalism. Missing from Roe's assessment is an appreciation of the fact that the environmentalists were most likely deliberately trying to *destabilize* the decision-making assumptions. They may have offered only a critique rather than a full story, but this is not because they could not supply one. More probable is that they chose for strategic political reasons to underplay or hide their story, as it was grounded in a call for a different kind of society with a different kind of decision-making system. Because their alternative system was not politically obtainable at the time of the medfly controversy—or any time soon—environmentalists may well have chosen to offer only a critique of the dominant system, with the hope of generating a dialogue that would lead to a discussion of alternative social arrangements, a point which is made clear if we look at the environmentalists' argument in terms of the levels of policy discourse outlined in Chapter 9. Within that framework we can easily see that the critique of spraying is indeed part of a larger ongoing dialogue about environment and industrial society. In this sense, Roe's approach functions to hide the actual politics underlying the issue by relegating them to matters related to the structural properties of stories. It is a point that would surely not be lost on the environmental movement's own policy analysts, assigned the job of generating counter-narratives.

These are disappointing aspects of Roe's approach, largely attributable to his adherence to a conventional understanding of policy analysis (a tradition to which he explicitly seeks to contribute). None of these points, however, necessarily obviates the usefulness of an emphasis on metanarratives or counterstories. These criticisms can easily be remedied with a postempiricist conception of narrative policy analysis. Fitting the empirical methods of policy analysis into the broader narrative discourse is well within the realm of methodological reconstruction, as we see in the next section. Furthermore, if we want to develop a metanarrative approach to policy controversy that builds in the participants, as well as addresses more systematically the relation of the empirical to the normative analysis, we can gain useful insights from both the communications approach to policy analysis taken up in Chapter 9 and the discussion of participatory policy analysis in Chapter 10.

In the remainder of the discussion here, we examine more specifically the relationship of empirical and normative inquiry to the narrative form, a concern much neglected in the literature on narrative analysis. Narratives contain assertions that can be isolated and examined with standard analytical methods. In fact, narrative theorists argue that most of what passes for empirical science has only been abstracted from narratives in the form of tables, charts, and equations. What does it mean for policy analysis? Whereas Roe seeks to structure narrative analysis to support empirical analysis, the postempiricist approach would emphasize empirical analysis to support narrative analysis. Towards this end, we conclude with an examination of how the logic of good reasons underlies the rationality of the narrative.

NARRATIVE RATIONALITY: THE ANALYTICS OF GOOD REASONS

Various theorists have examined the ways we can understand narratives on their own terms (Fisher 1989; McCloskey 1990): that is, how the various elements—such as facts, values, structural coherence, and metaphors—systematically come together in the logic of the narrative form, or what Fisher calls 'narrative rationality'. Whereas Roe's narrative analysis is trained on the structural component of stories, Fisher includes but moves beyond literary structures to show more systematically how empirical, normative, structural, and rhetorical components interact to supply narrative credibility, or 'good reasons'. To determine what constitutes good reasons for accepting a narrative account, he employs the same 'informal logic' introduced in Chapter 6. In his scheme, the informal logic of the narrative is constructed around three basic concerns, narrative probability, narrative fidelity, and characterological coherence. Narrative probability refers to the coherence of the story—whether it 'hangs together'. Not unlike the task of the literary scholar, this involves determining the probability that the components of the narrative structure are credibly linked together. Do they have material or substantive coherence with other stories told in related discourses? Are the kinds of behaviours exhibited by the characters in the story—both the narrators and the actors—relatively familiar, reliable, or predictable?

Here logical analysis is also brought to bear on the internal consistency of the plot and its sequences of action, including the story's metaphor. Often overlooked by social scientists, as McCloskey (1990: 63) points out, is the 'aptness or rightness' of the narrative's dominant metaphor, commonly understood in social science as a model (a model being a metaphor elaborated with details). Rather than examining a metaphor's prepositional truth, the analyst must ask whether the metaphor fits the story (R. Brown 1977). As a way of talking, does it stay on the subject or lead off into non-productive sidetracks? Can it reveal new insights that otherwise would not have been apparent?

Whereas narrative probability concerns the integrity of the story as a whole, narrative fidelity pertains to the individual components of the story: whether they constitute accurate assertions about social reality and thus are good reasons for belief and action. Facts, in this respect, serve as constraints on the story. As McCloskey (1990: 83) succinctly puts it, 'the fish in the fisherman's story was either a lake bass or a sunfish, and that's that'. Determining which, of course, is the task of empirical inquirer. But Fisher's concept of narrative fidelity is broader than just the truthfulness of the empirical facts. Governed by the informal logic of good reason, it involves applying criterial questions that can locate and weigh both the empirical information and the value judgements presented in—or engendered by—the story. In this sense, it includes formal logic, but also goes beyond it. Good reasons are conceived as those elements that 'provide warrants for accepting or adhering to the advice' fostered by any form of rhetorical communication (Fisher 1989: 107). A reason is considered good if it can meet the tests of fact, relevance, consequence, consistency, and transcendental values, criteria that we illustrate in more detail in Chapter 9. The ability of a narrative to meet the tests of these criteria supplies it with both its meaning and its persuasiveness.

Finally, but not least important, basic to all narratives is the question of character. 'Whether a story is believable', explains Fisher (1989: 47) 'depends on the reliability of characters, both as narrators and as actors.' Such determinations are made by interpretations of values reflected in the character's decisions and actions. Character, as such, can be understood as a repertoire of tendencies to act. If such 'tendencies contradict one another, change significantly, or alter in "strange ways", the result is a questioning of character.' In life, as in literature and history, we expect our fellow actors to conduct themselves characteristically. In the absence of 'this predictability, there is no trust, no community, no rational human orders.' Applying this criterion is an inquiry into motivation. As Fisher (1989: 47) puts it, 'its importance in deciding whether to accept a message cannot be overestimated.' Determining an actor's 'motives is prerequisite to trust, and trust is the foundation of belief.' For this reason, belief is not just a matter of what is said, but also of who is saying it. Some things may be empirically true, but certain people do not have the legitimacy to make the claims.[8]

Of particular interest to the policy inquirer, in this respect, is the role of the formal-analytic discourses in the assessment of narrative fidelity. One of the key tasks of an informal logic is to classify and clarify different types of discourses and the purposes to which they are put. Towards this end, it is also useful to more closely compare the interaction of informal or ordinary narrative discourse with scientific and normative discourses, which take the form of arguments. Indeed, for the postempiricist policy analyst this is a crucial epistemic task. It is important not only for understanding how the real-world narratives of politics and policy bring analytical methods into play, but also for establishing narrative discourse analysis in the policy curriculum. Without a clear statement of the narrative's relationship to what we normally identify as policy argumentation and analysis, narrative analysis will only struggle to gain something more than marginal status in the disciplines. We thus need to be able show both how these analytical perspectives relate to each other and, equally important, what difference it makes. Towards this end, we need to examine the relationship between the narrative and argumentation, to which we turn in Chapter 9.

CONCLUSION

This chapter extended the discussion of discourse and interpretive methods through an examination of the narrative form of discourse and its implications for policy analysis. Concerned with the stories that convey social and political experiences, the

---

[8] This consideration is also included among Habermas's (1987) criteria for ideal speech.

narrative mode is our basic form of human communication from early childhood on. Structured sequentially with a beginning, a middle, and an end, the narrative tells us about a state of affairs, an intervening event or action, and the resulting consequences. As a mode of thought, it furnishes communication with the particular details out of which social meaning is constructed. It is through storytelling that people assess social positions in their communities, understand the goals and values of different social groups, and internalize social conventions. Narrative stories do this by imposing a coherent interpretation on the whirl of events and actions that surround us. Threading these sequential components together through storylines, narratives place social phenomena in the larger patterns that attribute social and political meaning to them. In the process, the storyline is at the same time an invitation to moral reasoning.

Whereas the scientific mode of inquiry looks for stable empirically based causal connections between events, the narrative scheme includes the empirical but emphasizes social intentions and motivations. Shaped by the contexts of time and location that envelop actors and events, narrative inquiry is thus better suited than empirical analysis to render an understanding of social change. As storytelling, it is thus seen to expand our conception of knowledge beyond the narrow confines of observational statements and logical proof to include and understanding of the ways people are embedded in the wider social contexts of situation and society.

Besides introducing the narrative form, the chapter examined the role of policy narratives and storytelling through the contributions of Stone and Roe. From Stone we saw how literary representations and rhetorical devices are used in policy stories as tools of political strategy. Two basic types of causal stories were identified— stories of decline or crisis and stories about the need for social control. In contrast to standard policy analysis, we learned that disagreements over these basic stories—for example, the ways in which they frame events—are often more important to policy controversies than the specific empirical details embedded in them. Moreover, the numbers and statistics in the stories often are themselves political artefacts. Even the process of counting, by deliberately deciding what is in a particular category and what is not, plays a primary role in the allocation of political costs and benefits.

Roe, we saw, focused on the structural coherence of narratives to demonstrate the ways different stories frame policy problems. Of particular significance is his emphasis on the role of policy 'metanarratives', important for dealing with situations characterized by high degrees of problem uncertainty, socio-complexity, and political polarization. Despite some troublesome technocratic tendencies in his approach, Roe's narrative policy analysis is an important step along the way to a postempiricist policy analysis. Metanarrative analysis, especially from a more participatory perspective, offers the analyst a way of entering and reframing policy controversies that can lead to new ways of seeing capable of moving the disputants beyond policy impasses.

The chapter concluded with a brief methodological explication of the ways narratives can be assessed as good or bad. Following Fisher, we presented the informal logic of narrative rationality. Narrative rationality, as we saw, turns on two components: narrative probability (concerned with the structural coherence of the narrative) and narrative fidelity (concerned with the validity of its empirical and normative elements). A good narrative was seen to be one that can withstand the various criterial tests of the informal good-reasons logic advanced in Chapter 4.

Although they are often closely related, narratives are not the same thing as arguments per se. Formally, they have neither the same logical structure nor communicative purpose. In various kinds of communication, though, there is an interaction between narration and argumentation. For this reason, we turn in the next chapter to a closer examination at the logical structure of policy argumentation.

9

Policy Analysis as Discursive Practice: The Argumentative Turn

In this chapter we examine approaches to discursive policy analysis and policy argumentation with an emphasis on the integration of empirical and normative inquiry. Towards this end, we can gain useful insights from the communications or argumentative approach to policy deliberation, or what Fischer and Forester (1993) have called the 'argumentative turn'. Work in this direction has focused on clarifying the argumentative role of the analyst and developing interactive approaches that facilitate dialogue among analysts and participants.

In the previous discussion we identified a relationship between narratives and arguments, but noted that they are not the same thing. Although Roe (1994) conflates narrative and argument, as we saw, these two modes of thought have different purposes and logical structures. Whereas a narrative ties together a story with a beginning, a middle, and an end through the device of a plot, an argument is structured around premises designed to logically lead to conclusions. The narrative, moreover, is a mode of explanation designed to tell us what happened and what it means. While one can argue about 'what is', especially in empirical argumentation, argumentation is the form employed to persuade an audience that something 'ought' to be the case: that is, a particular action should—or should not—take place, that an event should be interpreted in one way rather than another, and so on. Put simply, narratives are primarily designed to deal with an 'is', although they can include a moral usually treated as a given. When it comes to making the case for an 'ought', we offer arguments.

This is not to overlook the fact that narratives are often constructed in ways that rest—implicitly or explicitly—on arguments. Frequently people construct stories in the hope that the storyline will itself facilitate or encourage the making—or acceptance—of a particular argument. Sometimes this occurs without the narrator fully recognizing the way he or she has actually designed the narrative. Such narratives can be intentionally or unintentionally structured to help or encourage a listener to arrive at a particular conclusion themselves. But this is a communicative strategy that should not be confused with the formal function of the narrative.

The job of the policy analyst, then, is not just to tell a narrative story. It is rather to translate a narrative into an argument, or to tease out the argument implicitly embedded in the story. This is important to recognize, as different people construct different arguments out of the same narrative, despite the fact that the author had something in particular in mind.

While political actors tell stories, it is the argument that constitutes the basic unit of real-world policy analysis. As Majone (1989: 7) has explained, most of the work of the policy analyst 'in a system of government by discussion . . . has less to do with the formal techniques of problem-solving than with the process of argument.' As he writes, 'the job of the analyst consists in large part of producing evidence and arguments to be used in the course of public debate.'[1] In view of this rhetorical and discursive nature of policy analysis, policy itself is thus best understood as 'crafted argument' (Stone 1988). In the effort to improve policy arguments, writes Hawkesworth (1988: 191), the goal of policy analysis is to illuminate 'the contentious dimensions of policy questions, to explain the intractability of policy debates, to identify the defects of supporting arguments, and to elucidate the political implications of contending prescriptions.' Such a task necessarily involves both empirical and normative analysis.

The growing interest in argumentation in policy analysis draws from both theoretical and practical perspectives. On the one side, as we have already seen, its diverse theoretical influences run through British ordinary-language analysis, French poststructuralism, the Frankfurt school of critical social theory, and a renewed appropriation of American pragmatism. On the other hand, it is based in practical terms on a range of experiments on the part of policy analysts and planners, from stakeholder analysis and participatory research to citizen juries and consensus conferences. These rich sources have helped postempiricists to recognize how language and modes of representation both enable and constrain their work. They have come to appreciate how their practical rhetoric depicts and selects, describes and characterizes, includes and excludes.

In this chapter we orient the discussion around a particular line of development in the argumentative turn, namely, a dialectical communications approach based on the informal or good-reasons logic of argumentation. In particular, we emphasize the productive capacities of the model, namely, its ability to generate ways of thinking and seeing that open new possibilities for problem-solving and action: or, in the language of Habermas's critical theory, its 'communicative power'.

→ DISCURSIVE POLICY PRACTICES: THE ARGUMENTATIVE TURN

The 'argumentative turn', heavily influenced by the work of Habermas, seeks to theoretically and practically integrate methodological and substantive policy issues with institutional and political practices. In the process, it illuminates the ways

[1] As he continues, 'it is this crucial argumentative aspect that distinguishes policy analysis from the academic social sciences on the one hand, and from problem-solving methodologies such as operations research on the other. The arguments analysts produce may be more or less technical, more or less sophisticated, but they must be persuasive if they are to be taken seriously in the forums of public deliberation. Thus analysts, like lawyers, politicians, and others who make a functional use of language, will always be involved in the technical problems of language, including rhetorical problems.'

policy analysts make practical arguments to diverse professional and political audiences. Employing concepts from rhetoric and communications theory, it examines how such arguments can be compelling in ways that can potentially generate new capacity-giving consenses.

In Chapter 6 we presented the epistemological basis for argumentation in policy analysis. There we saw that uncertainty, in both the physical and social worlds, requires analysts to make many interpretive judgements in the process of constructing and rendering their findings. As in the case of the physical sciences, the underdetermination of the empirical world means the policy analyst has to connect data and theories through arguments rather than prove them per se. Given the limits of both data and theory in the social sciences, it is even more essential in the case of policy analysis than in physics.

As policy decisions have to be politically legitimized, the tasks of explanation, justification, and persuasion play important roles in every stage of the policy cycle. Beginning with the problem-setting stage of analysis, well before plausible alternatives and recommendations can be delineated, the very determination of what 'the problem' is depends on deeply rhetorical and interpretive practices. Even after acceptable alternatives have been chosen and implemented, political justification has to receive continual attention. New arguments have to be constantly made to give 'the different policy components the greatest possible internal coherence and the closet fit to an ever-changing environment' (Majone 1989: 31). Policy development, as such, is guided by a discursive process of developing and refining ideas.

Despite the fact that these processes are not well understood, they are basic to the construction and reconstruction of policy problems. To better understand them the argumentative approach turns from the study of abstracted epistemological problems of analysis to the political and sociological significance of actual practices. Emphasizing the context-specific rhetorical character of analytical practices—the ways the symbolism of language matters, the ways the consideration of audiences needs to be taken into account, how solutions depend on problem construction, and so forth—the argumentative approach recognizes that policy arguments are intimately involved with relations of power and the exercise of power. Beyond merely emphasizing efficiency and effectiveness, it calls attention to the inclusion of some concerns and the exclusion of others, the distribution of responsibility as well as causality, the assigning of praise and blame, and the employment of particular political strategies of problem framing as opposed to others.

Sometimes the discursive role is quite explicit. This is especially the case when policy analysts are specifically asked to take on the role of advocate. In the advocacy role, the analyst is generally asked by the client to go beyond the issues of efficiency and offer advice about what the objectives themselves should be. Given the uncertainty of many policy problems, often including the very definition of the problem, the job also involves, as Majone (1989: 35) puts it, not only finding 'solutions within given constraints' but also taking the initiative and pushing 'out the boundaries of the possible in public policy'.

Given that policy problems can be represented in many languages, discourses, and frames, the link between the language of the analyst's arguments and the language of the political setting is always important. Moreover, the ways in which analysis has to be sensitive to the shifts in political power—from election to election, elite to elite, or coalition to coalition—are reflected not only in policy decisions but in the very language in which policy issues and choices are presented to the public. Given that decision-makers and the affected public alike can be baffled or mystified by technical languages of expertise, the argumentative approach is advanced to refine public understanding and ethical imagination.

Thanks to the careful examinations of writers like Forester (1999) and Hoch (1994), such discursive practices are documented in the everyday work of policy analysts and planners, a topic to which we return in Chapter 11. By examining policy argumentation in concrete institutional settings, this research calls attention to the kinds of organizational networking that analysts must do to build working policy relationships. A narrow focus on technical analysis of the content of the final document, as we have seen, misses the kinds of work that precede and follow the presentation of findings—including the scanning of the political environment for support and opposition to potential recommendations, anticipating the counter-reactions that policy measures might provoke, as well as being sensitive to the subtle negotiating that transpires among agency staff interested in maintaining their own strategic work relationships. The argumentative approach, in this respect, counsels the analyst to move beyond the separation of the political and the rational. Working in complex organizations structured by political processes, policy analysts are—or have to become—political actors, whether they wish to be or not. Confronting messy issues involving diverse populations with multiple and conflicting interests, they have to learn to balance the technical and the political components of the job.

And, not least important, the argumentative perspective draws attention to the democratic potential of policy analysis. Policy arguments cannot be presumed to be optimally clear, true, cogent, and free from institutional biases. Democratic deliberation, to be sure, is always precarious and vulnerable. But through thoughtful, passionate, and informed argumentative processes, what Barber (1984) calls 'democratic talk', citizens can learn. Policy analysis, moreover, can facilitate the process by promoting communicative competencies and social learning. To do this, however, it has to take into account the ways policy arguments can be skewed by inequalities of resources and the entrenched relations of power.

ARGUMENTATIVE POLICY ANALYSIS: THE COMMUNICATIONS MODEL

Various attempts have been made to develop procedures for an argumentative policy analysis. An important case in point is the 'forensic' or 'communications' approach to policy analysis that began to evolve in the late 1970s and early 1980s. This orientation has sought to turn the analytical problem on its head (Churchman 1971; Fischer 1980). Recognizing that the normative dimensions of policy questions can't be dealt with through the empirical mode of analysis—that is, by turning them into variables to be operationalized—these scholars have sought a viable alternative by turning the task around and beginning from the normative perspective and fit the empirical in. Indeed, as they show, this is how policy deliberation actually works. In politics, politicians and policy decision-makers advance proposals about what to do based on normative arguments. Empirical questions come into play where there are reasons to doubt factual aspects of the argument.

In this view, normative-based analysis can be facilitated by an organized dialogue among competing normative positions. Designed to identify or create potential areas of consensus, the model emphasizes the interactive and productive role of communication in cognitive processes. Unlike the process of pure or abstract thinking, the power of critical judgement depends on potential agreement with others. In fact, such judgement anticipates communication with others.

One influential approach to such a communications model has been to follow the example of law. In such a scheme, policy analysts and decision-makers each take on the assignment of preparing arguments for and against particular policy positions. As Rivlin (1973: 25) suggested, they would 'state their side of the argument, leaving to the brief writers of the other side the job of picking apart the case that has been presented and detailing the counter evidence.' Such policy argumentation starts with the recognition that the participants do not have solid answers to the questions under discussion, or even a solid method for getting the answers. With this understanding the policy analyst and decision maker attempt to develop a meaningful synthesis of perspectives. Churchman and his followers have suggested that the procedure take the form of a debate. They maintain that the problem posed by the absence of appropriate evaluative criteria can be mitigated by designing rational procedures to govern a formal communication between the various points of view that bear on the decision-making process.

In such a debate, each party would confront the other with counter-proposals based on varying perceptions of the facts. The participants in the exchange would organize the established data and fit them into the world views that underline their own arguments. The grounds or criteria for accepting or rejecting a proposal would be the same grounds as those for accepting or rejecting a counter-proposal and must be based on precisely the same data. Operating at the point where politics and science confront practice and ethics, both policy analysts and decision-makers would explore and compare the underlying assumptions being used.

Here we encounter a different approach to empirical and normative inquiry. Where conventional social science attempts to adapt qualitative data about norms and values to an empirical model through quantification, the communications model reverses the process by fitting the quantitative data into the normative world view. In the latter case, pragmatic validity is tested, criticized, and interpreted by qualitative arguments based on value perspectives or world views. The locus of the interpretation process shifts from the scientific community to the practical-world audience. In the transition, the final outcome of evaluative inquiry is determined by the giving of reasons and the assessment of practical arguments rather than scientific demonstration and verification. As in interpretive explanation generally, the valid interpretation is the one that survives the widest range of criticisms and objections. In the proposed debate model, each participant would cite not only causal relationships but also norms, values, and circumstances to support or justify a particular decision. As practical arguments, such interpretive evaluations connect policy options and situations by illuminating the features of those situations that provide grounds for policy decisions.

In this scheme, the formalized debate itself is seen as the most instructive part of the analytical process. The technique is designed to clarify the underlying goals and norms that give shape to competing world views, and enables qualitative judgement to be exercised in as unhampered a way as possible. The free exercise of normative judgement, released from the restrictions of the formal policy model, increases the chance of developing a synthesis of normative perspectives that can provide a legitimate and acceptable basis for decisions and actions based on the strongest possible argument. Even if analysts cannot agree, a communicative approach provides a procedure for probing the normative implications of recommendations and for indicating potentially consensual conclusions that offer productive ways to move forward. In the process, it also makes clear the basic points of dissensus that stand in the path of agreement.[2]

At a minimum, the technique goes a considerable distance towards removing the ideological mask that has often shrouded policy analysis. Such a communications approach, moreover, would not need to be confined to the interactions between organizational policymakers and policy analysts. Ideally, it could be extended to the full range of differing interests and political viewpoints drawn from the policy environment.

In addition to the numerous practical experiments Churchman and his associates have carried out with this model (Mitroff 1971; Mason 1969), a somewhat similar approach to organizing expert advice has been presented by George (1972) and Porter (1980) in policy areas such as national security and economic policymaking at the presidential level. For example, the basic assumption underlying what George (1972) calls 'multiple advocacy' is that a competition of ideas and viewpoints, rather than reliance on analyses and recommendations from advisers who share the perspectives of the policymakers, is the best method of developing policy. Multiple advocacy is described as a process of debate and persuasion designed to expose the policymaker systematically to competing arguments made by the advocates themselves. Through the efforts of an 'honest broker', the approach attempts to ensure that all interested parties are genuinely represented in the adversarial process, and that the debate is structured and balanced.

The communications approach is an important step towards the development of a dynamic methodology designed to facilitate complex dialectical exploration of facts and values throughout the policy research process. Like any step forward, however,

---

[2] In conflictual issues detailed knowledge about why people *dis*agree is often as important as information about why they agree. This has to do with the fact that decisions are never final and frequently reopened at a later time. Knowledge about the disagreements thus helps the parties to a dispute prepare themselves for a subsequent rounds of argumentation. Perhaps the best example is that of US Supreme Court decisions, where the dissenting justices also write up their views as guides to lawyers who will have a continuing interest in the issue.

it only brings us to the next set of hurdles. The inevitable question that arises is this: if both analysts and decision-makers are to employ the same grounds or criteria in their respective arguments, what are these criteria? Here the technique encounters the fundamental fact-value problem of normative criteria: are there criteria or grounds for mediating normative-based practical discourse? Practical debate brings the value dimensions of policy into sharper focus, but this is not to be confused with methodology per se. Given the long history of arguments about value judgements in philosophy and the social sciences, it is reasonable to surmise that the methodological success of a communications model ultimately rests on the elaboration of rules that govern the exchange of normative arguments. Rational inquiry—whether scientific or normative—depends on the availability of standards and rules that can serve as criteria for valid judgement (that is, operational rules permitting the formulation of more or less general propositions or conclusions that are not specifically included in the data but legitimately deduced, inferred, or extracted from them). In a normative exchange, it is often easy to agree that one argument is more persuasive than another, but it is not always clear how that is known. It is the absence of such normative judgements that has contributed to the epistemological demise of normative theorizing in the contemporary social sciences.

ARGUMENTATION: THE SEARCH FOR RATIONAL PROCEDURES

A number of writers have sought to deal with the problem or rational procedures by further extending the legal-oriented analogy of brief writing to include the concept of 'rules of evidence'. By studying the rules and procedures that govern legal arguments in the courtroom, the policy sciences might gain insight into rules of argumentation that can be adapted to the policy deliberation process. Such an approach would permit analysts to concede the limitations of empirical decision-making methods but, at the same time, salvage the contributions that they do offer. By combining empirical analysis, policy deliberation, and the development of rules of evidence, policy scientists can, in this view, move the policy evaluation process towards a judicious mix of pragmatism and rigour.

The Nobel Prize-winning economist Kenneth Arrow, noted for his empirical-analytic models, and Duncan MacRae, Jr are among those who have stressed the value of supplying policy analysis with a regulated discourse that commands the kind of rigour found in law.[3] The advantage of regulated communication, according to MacRae (1976: 85), is that it stands 'apart from the discourse of ordinary life in several attributes such as precise definitions, stress on written rather than oral communication, and limitation of meaning to what has been specified in advance'. In such a discourse, a statement or judgement can be given a precise definition and interpretation by a larger audience. A legal essay, for instance, written by trained

---

[3] Arrow's view was delivered in a presentation at a conference of the National Bureau of Economic Research, cited in Cain and Hollister (1972).

legal specialists, directs the attention of similarly trained readers to statements and conclusion that can be systematically re-examined by shared rules and methods.

The concept of rules of evidence in law suggests the development of logical rules for policy argumentation (Majone 1989: 49). Both MacRae and Anderson have urged policy analysts to explore the possibility of borrowing and adapting the rules of normative analysis employed in political philosophy. As Anderson (1978: 22) states, policy analysts fail to recognize that 'their concern with cost-benefit analysis is only an episode in a long Western tradition of defining principles appropriate to judge the legitimacy and propriety of political activity'. As a suggestive attempt to bridge this gap, MacRae (1976: 93) has introduced three logical tests that are employed in political philosophy: logical clarity, logical consistency, and generality.[4]

Another approach to the development of analytical rules in the policy literature refers more directly to the more practical tasks of policy methodology. Writers such as Hambrick (1974) and P. Brown (1976) have sought to offer checklists to assist analysts in judging the completeness of a policy argument. Hambrick, for example, approaches the task by studying the logical structure of arguments in policy controversies. He has laboured to explicate the propositional components that constitute a logically complete policy argument. With the assistance of such components, it becomes easier for analysts to determine the kinds of evidence needed to support, reject, or modify a policy proposal. His scheme, however, is limited by its emphasis on the empirical and technical questions that underlie policy arguments—questions about cause and effect, cost and benefits of alternative means, and unanticipated impacts. While the questions avoid the methodological abstractions of political philosophy, they fail to deal adequately with the tasks of normative analysis. Still missing is a statement of logical structure that relates factual evidence to normative deliberation.

More systematically, Dunn (1981) has elaborated a model for policy argumentation based on Toulmin's informal logical of practical argumentation. An important step beyond the mere checklist, this scheme offers a more dynamic picture of argumentation that moves from empirical data to the conclusions via a normative warrant and its backing. Of special importance is the model's incorporation of rebuttal arguments and qualifications to the concluding claims. Nonetheless, it too lacks a sufficiently detailed specification of the line of argument that supports the backing of the normative warrant. Without this line of argumentation, the scheme is unable to model the full integration of empirical and normative judgements. But this problem can be remedied, as we illustrate below.

The critical question, then, is how to develop a practical framework that integrates both empirical and normative discourses. Although the primary task of epistemology and methodology in philosophy and the social sciences is to analyse and clarify the basic concepts and rules that govern the logic of the discourse in which humans do

---

[4] MacRae is correct in stating that policy arguments are seldom proposed with the degree of clarity and consistency that his scheme provides. Unfortunately, his own logical procedures remain too abstract to serve as a basis for policy methodology. Moreover, it is unclear from MacRae's work how these logical rules interact with the factual dimensions of policy arguments.

their thinking, the realm of normative discourse, as we have seen, is far less developed than the logic of empirical discourse. Theorists have been unable to offer enough precision about these rules to make them useful. The work of ordinary-language philosophers has been an important exception. Focusing on practical discussion in everyday life, they have shown the study of practical reason to offer a useful avenue of methodological exploration for policy evaluation (Fischer 1980). From this tradition we gain insight into two basic questions: what does it mean to evaluate something? And how can such evaluations be justified?

⤳ THE LOGIC OF POLICY ARGUMENTS: PRACTICAL DISCOURSE

The logic of practical discourse, as we saw in Chapter 6, pertains to the systematic study of the rational processes related to human reason about action. It deals with cases in which decisions have to be made among various action alternatives. The concern is with the justification of real-world decisions, rather than with a formal system of logic applied to action, as in the case of formal decision models of systems analysis or operations research. Practical discourse, also called the 'theory of argumentation', holds that a decision depends on the person making it, and that such formal rules of decision-making cannot be abstracted from persons and their actions into a system of demonstration modelled on deductive logic. Here the word 'reasoning' refers to a method for convincing or dissuading adversaries, and for coming to an agreement with others about the legitimacy of a decision.

Practical reasoning operates between the logic of demonstration and theories of action and motivation. Not only does it include an empirical assessment of the situation, it also considers the actor's motives for an action. In practical reasoning, motives that have undergone the test of argumentation can count as good reasons. In contrast to positivist theories of behaviour, which deny or downplay the validity of reasons people give for their actions, practical reasoning takes seriously the arguments offered for a particular action. An argument as to whether theory A or theory B can be accepted and used as the basis for an action is judged on the merits of the evidence in the case, rather than as an acting out of the psychological or sociological forces that are behind the debate.

Practical arguments are, in this sense, propositions which seek to establish that particular acts are good and should have been performed. Practical reasoning takes into account, however, the conditions under which agents in real life accept these implied norms as meaningful and commit themselves to them personally. In seeking a decision on which action is to be taken, a practical argument begins with the norms to which the participants in the controversy are committed and then seeks, by means of argument, to ground the decision on them. Practical reasoning, in this sense, cannot originate in the absence of normative commitments. Such norms are never universal or eternal; all that is required in practical reasoning is that they be recognized by the audience—larger or smaller—to whom the discourse is addressed at the specific time of the argument. Practical reasoning, as such, always takes place among individuals or groups in a social context and in historical time. In contrast to the timelessness that is essential for deductive reasoning, the notion of temporality is basic to practical reasoning.

Practical reason, then, is basic to deciding among the interpretations of various subject matters and activities. This applies to empirical as well as normative inquiry. As a social practice, empirical science is itself related to the judicial–rhetorical mode of inquiry as much as or more than to formal demonstrative logic. Whereas a logical or mathematical proof is either true or false (and if it is true, purportedly accepted by those who understand it), practical arguments are only more or less plausible, more or less convincing to a particular audience. There is, moreover, no unique way to construct a practical argument: data and evidence can be selected in a wide variety of ways from the available information, and there are various methods of analysis and ways of ordering values.

Practical argumentation thus differs from formal demonstration in three important respects. Whereas formal demonstration is possible only within a formalized system of axioms and rules of inference, practical argumentation starts from opinions, values, or contestable viewpoints rather than axioms. It makes use of logical inferences but is not exhausted in deductive systems of formal statements. Second, a formal demonstration is intended to convince those who have the requisite technical knowledge, while informal argumentation always aims to elicit the adherence of the members of a particular audience to the claims presented for their consent. Finally, practical argumentation does not strive to achieve purely intellectual agreement but rather to provide acceptable reasons for choices relevant to action (such as a disposition to act at the appropriate moment).

Writers such as Toulmin (1958) and Perelman (1984) point to judicial or legal reasoning as the exemplifying case of practical reasoning. An analysis of legal reasoning, they show, provides important insights into the process of practical reasoning. Judicial procedures and proceedings, including the arguments of counsel and the decisions of judges and legislative decisions regarding the formation of laws, provide forms of practical reasoning that can clarify principles of argumentation. Drawing as well on traditional procedures of rhetoric, Perelman's theory of argumentation is offered as a 'new rhetoric' that avoids the negative image long associated with rhetoric by supplying it with a more complete theory of practical reasoning.[5]

Thanks to these theorists the long-neglected study of rhetoric has more recently returned to the social sciences. After having long been denigrated as a negative concept referring to verbal manipulation, even hypocrisy, writers such as

---

[5] The standard view of rhetoric has been problematic. Rhetorical styles of argumentation have generally been seen as a techniques for producing desired effects on an audience, regardless of the morality of the effect. Thus rhetoric has been understood as a form of moral relativism. Perelman (1984) redefined the rhetorical tradition by changing the audience, an orientation he called the 'the new rhetoric'. Rather than attempting to persuade a particular audience in a particular context, as was the aim of classical rhetoric, Perelman reconceptualized rhetoric to address a universal audience across time and space. An example would be human rights debates, universally applicable to all peoples through out history.

McClosky (1985; 1994), Klamer (1983), and Nelson, Megill, and McCloskey (1987) have laboured to restore rhetoric's traditional meaning and to employ it in fields such as economics and political science. In this perspective, as Battistelli and Ricotta (2001: 4) put it, rhetoric is characterized by a form of argumentation and practical reason 'that is not driven by apodictic syllogisms, but rather uses probable premises to develop relativized arguments, pragmatically oriented to obtain the consent of the receiver.' Respecting the rules of conversation, issues of fact and value in this 'new rhetoric' are assessed in the broader light of historical context, affective influences, and motivational factors. Most important, it recognizes the partiality of the premises in practical argumentation and their dependency on circumstance.

POLICY ARGUMENTATION AS PRACTICAL REASON

One of the first policy scholars to call for such a reorientation is Majone. The structure of a policy argument, Majone (1989: 63) writes, is typically a complex blend of factual statements, interpretations, opinion, and evaluation. The argument provides the links that connect the relevant data and information to the conclusions of an analysis. Majone's analysis of the features of a policy argument are an important contribution to the development of an argumentative policy analysis. But his work does not sufficiently account for or clarify the normative dimensions that intervene between findings and conclusions. From the preceding discussion, as well as the discussion in Chapter 6, we can formulate the task as a matter of establishing interconnections among the empirical data, normative assumptions that structure our understandings of the social world, the interpretive judgements involved in the data-collection process, the particular circumstances of a situational context (in which the findings are generated or the prescriptions applied), and the specific conclusions. The scientific acceptability of the conclusions depends ultimately on the full range of interconnections, not just the empirical findings. While neo-positivists see their approach as more rigorous and therefore superior to less empirical, less deductive methods, this model of policy argumentation actually makes the task more demanding and complex (McClosky 1994; Fischer 1995a). Not only does it encompass the logic of empirical falsification, it includes the equally sophisticated normative questions within which it operates. The researcher still collects the data, but now has to situate or include them in the interpretive framework that gives them meaning. No longer is it possible to contend that such normative investigations can be ignored, as if they somehow relate to another field of inquiry.

In *Evaluating Public Policy* (Fischer 1995b), I have outlined a multi-methodological framework for integrating these components. The framework takes its initial insight from Toulmin's informal logic of argumentation, introduced in Chapters 6 and 8. The framework begins by sketching out the logical connection between the empirical data collection process, the measurement of the data against a warrant, which leads to the statement of a concluding claim (see figure).

The defining feature of a postempiricist policy analysis is the elaboration of the normative line of argument involved in justifying the backing of the warrant.

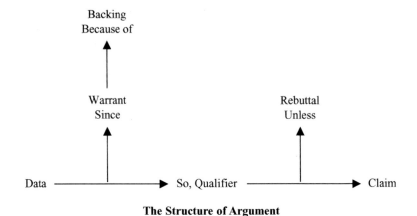

The Structure of Argument

Source: Fischer (1985).

Towards this end, the framework offers a logic of four interrelated discourses that outlines the concerns of a postempiricist policy evaluation. Extending from concrete questions concerning the efficiency of a programme up through its situational context and the societal system to the abstract normative questions concerning the impact of a policy on a particular way of life, the scheme illustrates how empirical concerns can be brought to bear on the full range of normative questions. Facilitating a dialectical communication between a policy analyst and the participants relevant to a deliberation, the discourses organize and illuminate the discursive components of a complete policy assessment.

As guidelines for deliberative inquiry, these four discourses are broken down into twelve more specific questions that probe a policy argument. The first two discursive phases of the logic of policy evaluation, constituting the level of first-order evaluation, are technical verification and situational validation. First-order evaluation focuses on the specific action setting of a policy initiative, probing both specific programme outcomes and the situational (or circumstantial) context in which they occur. The second two discursive phases of the logic, or the level of 'second-order evaluation', are societal vindication and ideological choice. Here evaluation shifts to the larger social system of which the action context is a part; it focuses on the instrumental impact of the policy goals on the societal system as a whole, and an evaluation of the normative principles and values underlying this societal order. Each of these discourses has specific requirements that must be addressed in making a complete justification of a practical judgement. For a reason to be considered a 'good reason', it must satisfy all four discursive phases of this methodological probe.

The logic of policy evaluation thus works on two fundamental levels, one concretely concerned with a programme, its participants, and the specific problem situation to which the programme is applied, and the other concerned with the more abstract level of the societal system within which the programmatic action takes place. A policy evaluation, in this sense, must always look in two directions, one micro, the other macro. For example, a policy to introduce a multicultural curriculum in a particular university should not only indicate specific course offerings, but also address the larger requirements of a pluralist society, such as the need for a set of common integrating values capable of holding the social system together.

It is important to emphasize that the logic of policy evaluation organizes four interrelated *discourses* rather than a single methodological calculus per se. The goal is not to 'plug in' answers to specific questions or to fulfil pre-specified methodological requirements. It is to engage in an open and flexible exploration of the kinds of concerns raised in the various discursive phases of the problem. In this regard, the questions do not constitute a complete set of rules or fixed requirements that must be dealt with in any formal way. Rather, they are designed to orient evaluation to a particular set of concerns. Within the framework of discourse, the deliberation may follow its own course in the pursuit of understanding and consensus. Policy evaluation, moreover, can commence at any one of the phases. Choosing the place to begin is dictated by the practical aspects of the policy to be resolved.

Towards this end, the questions serve as guidelines for deliberative inquiry. The methodological orientations accompanying each of the phases are tools capable of supporting the deliberative process, but need be brought into play only where deemed appropriate. For example, it is in no way mandatory to carry out a cost-benefit analysis in the verification of a programme outcome. Cost-benefit analysis is understood to be a methodological technique that addresses empirical concerns of verification, but need be used only when judged suitable to the specific concerns to hand. There are, in this sense, no hard and fast rules that must be followed. Rather, the objective is to initiate and pursue reasoned dialogue and consensus at each of the four discursive phases of deliberation. Short of consensus, the goal is clarification and mutual understanding among the parties engaged in deliberation.

Technical–Analytical Discourse: Programme Verification

In the policy sciences verification is the most familiar of the four discourse phases. In the informal logic of practical discourse it is addressed to the consideration of facts; in policy research it pertains to the basic technical–analytical or methodological questions that dominate empirical policy analysis. Concerned with the measurement of the efficiency of programme outcomes, the methodologies typically used to pursue questions of verification are the established tools of conventional policy analysis (Sylvia, Sylvia, and Gunn 1997). The basic questions of verification are:

- Does the programme fulfil its stated objective(s)?
- Does the empirical analysis uncover secondary or unanticipated effects that offset the programme objectives? and
- Does the programme fulfil the objectives more efficiently than alternative means available?

The goal is to produce a quantitative assessment of the degree to which a programme fulfils a particular objective (standard or rule) and a determination (in terms of a comparison of inputs and outputs) of how efficiently the objective is fulfilled (typically measured as a ratio of costs to benefits compared with other possible means).

Contextual Discourse: Situational Validation

From the empirical verification of outcomes, first-order policy evaluation leads to questions of validation. Validation focuses on whether or not the particular programme objectives are relevant to the situation: that is, in the language of informal logic it takes up the question of relevance. Instead of measuring programme objectives per se, validation examines the conceptualizations and assumptions underlying the problem situation that the programme is designed to influence. Validation centres around the following questions:

- Is the programme objective(s) relevant to the problem situation?
- Are there circumstances in the situation that require an exception to be made to the objectives?
- Are two or more criteria equally relevant to the problem situation?

Validation is an interpretive process of reasoning that takes place within the frameworks of the normative belief systems brought to bear on the problem situation. It draws in particular on qualitative methods, such as those developed for interpretive sociological and anthropological research, including situational analysis (Farr 1987).

Systemic Discourse: Societal Vindication

At this level, the logic of policy deliberation shifts from first-order to second-order evaluation, that is, from the concrete situational context to the societal context as a whole. Here the basic task is to show that a policy goal (from which the programme objectives were drawn) addresses a valuable function for the existing societal arrangements. As such, it engages the issue of instrumental or contributive consequences in the informal logic of practical discourse. Vindication is organized around the following questions:

- Does the policy goal have instrumental or contributive value for the society as a whole?
- Does the policy goal result in unanticipated problems with important societal consequences?
- Does a commitment to the policy goal lead to consequences (for example, benefits and costs) that are judged to be equitably distributed?

Here evaluation might ask if a focus on particular programmes designed to achieve particular outcomes tends to facilitate a particular type of social order. As such, second-order vindication steps outside of the situational action context in which programme criteria are applied and implemented in order to assess empirically the consequences of a policy goal in terms of the system as a whole. Coming to grips with unanticipated consequences often involves testing the policy's underlying assumptions about a systems functions and values.

Ideological Discourse: Social Choice

The fourth and final discursive phase of the logic of policy deliberation turns to ideological and values questions. Here the informal logic of criteria of consistency and transcendent values come into play. Social choice seeks to establish and examine the selection of a critical basis for making rationally informed choices about societal systems and their respective ways of life. Social choice raises the following types of questions:

- Do the fundamental ideals (or ideological principles) that organize the accepted social order provide a consistent basis for a legitimate resolution of conflicting judgements?
- If the social order is unable to resolve basic values conflicts, do other social orders equitably accommodate the relevant interests and needs that the conflicts reflect?
- Do normative reflection and empirical evidence support the justification and adoption of alternative principles and values?

Social choice involves the interpretive tasks of social and political criticism, particularly as practised in political theory and philosophy. Most fundamental are the concepts of a 'rational way of life' and the 'good society'. Based on the identification and organization of a specific configuration of values—such as equality, freedom, or community—models of the good society serve as a basis for the adoption of higher-level evaluative criteria. Although the function of such discourse is to tease out the value implications of policy arguments, it involves more than mere value clarification. It is concerned as well with the ways in which ideological discourse structures and restructures the world in which we live. This logic of questions is diagrammatically summarized in the figure on page 196.

A critical judgement is presented here as one that has been pursued progressively through the four phases of evaluation. The formal logic of an empirical assertion moves from data to conclusion, mediated by a warrant backed by normative and empirical assumptions. In normal discussion these assumptions generally serve as part of the background consensus and are called into question only during disputes. The task of a comprehensive-critical evaluation is to make explicit these assumptions through a progressive critique extending from validation to ideological choice (or from ideological choice to validation). It is here that we can understand Habermas's classical Aristotelian contention that in the last instance an empirical statement must be judged by its intentions for the good and life. As reflected through the logical link of an empirical assertion to the level of ideological choice, a full delineation of the logic of an evaluation discloses its meaning and implications for the pursuit of a particular conception of the ideal society.

An important methodological test of the four-level scheme is its ability to plug facts into normative policy deliberations. This can be demonstrated by relating it to

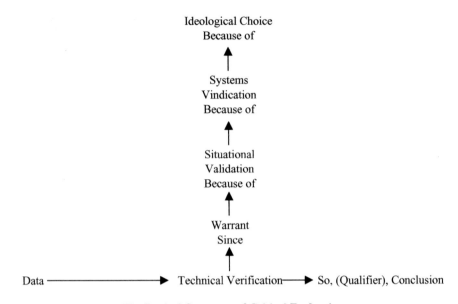

The Logical Structure of Critical Evaluation

Source: Fischer (1985).

the naturalist conception of ethical theory that emphasizes the contribution of empirical information to normative discourse (Fischer 1980: 211–12). Naturalists list six types of empirical knowledge that influence value judgements. All can be located across the twelve component questions of the four levels.[6]

The starting point for an evaluation generally depends on the particular policy at issue and the debates that it has generated. Typically, the issue of contention relates most specifically to one of the levels, potentially expanding to one or more of the others as an argument progresses. In policy issues that are highly contentious, however, there can be arguments emerging at all levels at the same time. The case of the Head Start compensatory educational programme for poor children in the US is a good illustration of point. An evaluation report commissioned by the federal government purported to show that the Head Start programme had failed to achieve its goals. There were, as I have shown elsewhere, people who concentrated on the question of whether the programme achieved a particular stated objective, namely, whether the children learned to read better as measured by test scores (Fischer 1995a). Others maintained that the programme was designed and tested for

[6] The basic types of empirical knowledge that naturalists advance as the basis for proving or improving normative judgments are: knowledge about the consequences that flow from alternative actions and knowledge about alternative means available (basic to technical verification); the particular facts of the situation and knowledge of the established norms that bear on the decision (situational validation); the general causal conditions and laws relevant to the problem (systems vindication); and knowledge about values that bear on the decision and about the fundamental needs of humankind (ideological social choice).

middle-class children and thus poorly suited for the circumstances that ghetto children found themselves in. Still others, arguing at the level of societal vindication, maintained that such a programme was essential for a society that emphasized equal opportunity for all citizens. And radical black organizations argued that they didn't want to prepare their children for achievement in middle-class American society. They called for a different kind of society based on egalitarian values.

The four-level discourse model has been applied to concrete policy issues in a number of ways. Most important has been the work of Hoppe (1993), who has shown how the four levels correspond to the types of argumentation that occur across the phases of the policy (Hoppe and Peterse 1993; Gabrielian 1998). Agenda-setting in significant part turns on ideological concerns; policy formulation concentrates heavily on issues of societal vindication; implementation is focused on issues pertinent to situational validation; and evaluation is a clear-cut case of technical verification. In this respect, Hoppe see the policy process as moving from the reflective to the practical orders of reason, which he interestingly illustrates by attaching his analysis to Lynn's (1987: 146–9) conceptualization of the policy process as a set of games: the high (ideological) game, the middle (systemic) game, and the low (technical) game.

Second, Hoppe (1990; Hoppe and Grin 2002) and associates use the four-level discourse model to map out the structural properties of policy belief systems (understood as clusters of normative and causal assumptions). Adapting Lakatos's theory of a scientific research programme as possessing a hard core surrounded by protective belts, in much the same way as Sabatier (1987: 667) and Majone (1989: 150) have, Hoppe, Pranger, and Besseling (1990: 124) conceptualize the level of ideological choice as the hard core of a policy belief system, the content of societal vindication as the near core, and the content of situation validation and technical verification as the secondary protective belts. Where the hard core of a policy belief system is stable and resistant to change, the secondary components are much more flexible. In this view, 'the hard core consists of strategies and methods for converting abstract ideas into action'. These 'strategies generate permissible and advisable courses of action, while excluding or discouraging others'. Like a scientific research strategy, 'a policy belief's systems' long-term destiny would be determined by the flexible periphery's capacity to generate a range of policy programs in a wide array of different policy areas'. Like a research programme's instructions for 'puzzle solving, a policy belief system's malleable periphery should generate (more so than rival belief systems) practical solutions and innovative ways of dealing with problems of everyday policy making', while 'degenerating tendencies in the periphery may become fatal to a policy belief system'. Hoppe, Pranger, and Besseling (1990: 139) argue that the four-level model assist in conceptualizing this by showing that 'first-order discourse may help explain why one rather than another course of action is in fact adopted', while 'second-order policy discourse analysis may help address the larger question of why others are quietly abandoned or simply forgotten'. In this view, policy discourse coalitions seek to deflect challenges away from the core assumptions and axioms and engage in argumentative combat at the level of secondary assumptions. The strategy is to protect core assumptions by attempting to redirect or redefine challenges to lower-level considerations (also see Lindquist 1997; Mathur 2003). Policy change thus mostly occurs at the levels below the core assumptions. Only when the protective belts cannot hold—that is, withstand rigorous criticism—will alternatives be made to the core, and even then not easily. This corresponds to Sabatier's view, with an important exception. Hoppe, Pranger, and Besseling (1990: 124) recognize the vulnerability of core assumptions to interpretive 'reality shifts'. As they put it, the 'capacity to reframe issues and harmonize interests from a new perspective may, in the end, be of the greatest importance'.

The ability to logically analyse policies—one's own or those of one's opponents—offers insights into the construction of acceptable alternative policies. After organizing a policy argument into its component parts, the analyst can turn his or her attention to political consensus formation. In much the same sense that Roe (1994) speaks of meta-narratives, the process involves an attempt to convert a static conception of a policy position into a dynamic argument with persuasive power. After identifying the possible areas of policy consensus and conflict, the analyst can design an alternative policy proposal that addresses the key issues of conflict. The test of the alternative argument is how well it stands up to the criticisms and objections of the political audiences it has to convince or persuade, the breadth of its appeal, the number of views it can synthesize, and so on. In many cases, this means the analyst must attempt dialectically to move the proposal beyond the narrow defence of a particular argument in order to present a more comprehensive picture of the political situation. Since a narrow argument can be defended only within a limited context of belief, as Hoppe argues, the policy analyst must at times try to offer a new or reformulated view to replace or revise a belief or value system that impedes the construction of consensus.

The development of such policy proposals must remain as much an art as a science. The process involves conjecture and speculation, analogy, and metaphor, and logical extrapolation from established causal relationships and facts. Unlike the scientist's analysis based on a closed, generalized model, the policy analyst's proposal has to be open and contextual. Where the former model follows the formal principles of inference, the latter is based on the rules and procedures of informal logic.

POLICY ARGUMENTATION AS COMMUNICATIVE INTERACTION: THE ROLE OF ANALYTICAL DISCOURSES

As we noted in Chapter 8, a key task of an informal logic is to classify and clarify different types of discourses and the purposes for which they are employed. Of special interest to the policy scholar, in this regard, is the role of formal-analytic discourses in the assessment of ordinary communication, in particular argumentation. If policy analysis is about improving real-world policy argumentation, what then is the epistemological relationship of its standard methodologies, such as cost-benefit or regression analysis, to the ordinary-language deliberations in the world of the political actors? Determining the relationship between argumentation, as an everyday discourse, and the formal empirical and normative analytical discourses is one of the crucial epistemic tasks for postempiricist policy analysis. This is important not only for understanding the nature of discursive practices, but also for establishing discourse analysis in the policy curriculum. Without a clear statement of an argument's relationship to what we normally identify as empirical analysis, discourse and narrative analysis will continue to struggle to gain something more than marginal status in the disciplines. We need to be able show both how the two analytical perspectives relate to each other and, equally important, what difference this makes. Towards this end, we can gain important insights on how to proceed with the investigation from Habermas's theory of communication action.

Borrowing from Habermas's (1987; 1973) work on communicative action and discourse, we can conceptualize the relationship between normal communicative interaction (as either argumentation or narrative discourse) and the formal discourses of scientific and normative theory. Basic to his theory is a distinction between the ordinary language communication of the everyday world and the theoretical discourses of both science and social philosophy. Whereas the phenomenological attitude of everyday life is oriented to belief, opinion, and common sense, the theoretical attitude emphasizes scientifically tested knowledge and critical normative reflection.

In the everyday context of communicative action, formal empirical and normative discourses can be called into play when the truth or correctness of background validity claims becomes subject to disputes by speakers. In normal discursive interaction, basic validity claims usually do not come into question. Indeed, everyday argumentation and storytelling are made possible by the fact that people share a wide range of commonly accepted assumptions that seldom have to be called into question. Most Americans, for example, do not question the values upon which a free enterprise economy is founded. Such consensus makes it possible to get on with talking about particular matters of business: who owns this, what is the price of that, and so on. Habermas (1973) identifies these underlying assumptions and interpretations as part of the 'background consensus' that is behind every narrative exchange. He refers here to underlying beliefs and norms that are more or less uncritically accepted by the speakers. It is nothing less than the existence of these *background* beliefs that makes the communication possible.

Discussions arise, of course, in which one or more of the background beliefs or assumptions becomes problematic in a fundamental way. Indeed, most political conflict concerned with social change pertains to controversies over such background assumptions (changes that discourse analysis is designed to detect). Arising within a framework of opinions and norms, these sorts of questions and controversies are generally difficult, if not impossible, to deal with in ways that simply yield to a request for more information, as if this might be enough to clear up a particular misunderstanding. To eliminate a disturbance in the background consensus, either by restoring the original consensus or by establishing a new one, a specific form of problem-solving appropriate to the validity claim in question must be called into play. That is, a 'truth' or 'legitimacy claim' has to be redeemed discursively through the logics of empirical or normative discourse. Only by entering into a normative discourse that has the sole purpose of judging the justification of a problematic norm, or an empirical discourse designed to get at the validity of a truth claim, can the disturbance or blockage be resolved.

As a break in ordinary communicative interaction, the speech situation of discourse requires that judgement about certain states of affairs or norms be treated as hypothetical and subjected to systematic argumentation motivated only by the desire to achieve a rationally grounded consensus that terminates in inter-subjective understanding, shared knowledge, and mutual trust. Such agreement is obtained only through the 'force of the better argument', governed by the logical properties of discourse. There are no absolutely fixed decision procedures or methodologies that differentiate a rational from a non-rational consensus. Nor is there any guarantee that such a process will end in consensus. What is important here is the adherence to the accepted criteria of rationality judgement. In absence of consensus, differences of opinion are always subject to further argumentation and reflection through extended empirical and normative discourses.

Citizens and politicians seldom themselves turn to formal discourses to solve their disagreements about arguments or stories, although this need not be ruled out. More typical is a turn to the existing bodies of knowledge in search of answers. In the absence of such knowledge, experts can be commissioned to get it, a relatively common practice on the part of politicians and government officials. If a question is pressing enough, it will emerge of its own accord as a scientific question in the relevant expert communities. Science, after all, takes its problems from the society of which it is itself a part. Broad policy controversies such as global warming can, in this respect, be understood as public narratives that continually await the latest findings of the scientific community. Similarly, local questions such as what is causing the children of a neighbourhood to suffer from leukaemia can at times lead dissatisfied citizens to seek out their own facts, as experiences with citizen-oriented participatory research such as popular epidemiology have illustrated, a topic we take up in Chapter 11 (Fischer 2000).

CRITICAL RATIONALITY AS UNDISTORTED COMMUNICATION

Many in policy analysis have simply understood the assignment as offering assistance to the decision-makers for whom they work, while some have argued for extending the process of argumentation to the relevant stakeholders (Innes 2003; 1998). Others argue for advancing arguments that more generally address issues related to the public interest. Much of the work pertaining to argumentation and the communications model is of this type. Such argumentation is clearly an advance over neo-positivist, top-down conceptions of policymaking, but it still leaves open the question of how to decide between arguments. It brings us again back to the issues of rationality and relativism.

One approach to the issue is to simply accept the relativity of argumentation and to understand the contribution of the argumentative process as enlightening its participants. Here the hope is to open up possibilities for agreement (Dunn 1993;

McAdams 1984: Paris and Reynolds 1983). Although an important contribution in any case, such argumentation remains bound to the policy frames from which they are forged. People can sometimes be persuaded to change their views, but there are no set criteria for judging between the basic argumentative frames.

Critical theory-oriented postempiricist policy analysts have sought to move beyond this position by turning to the procedural rationality spelled out in the Habermasian theory of communicative action, grounded in his concept of an 'emancipatory interest'. In this view, advanced in policy analysis by such theorists as Bobrow and Dryzek (1987: 161–82) and Forester (1985; 1993), the consensus-making process can be further judged and assessed in terms of the openness of the communicative process that shapes it. The goal is to identify what Habermas (1970*b*) calls 'systematically distorted communication' and to develop ways of increasing the awareness of individual actors by working to uncover and reveal the influences unknown to the participants that are shaping their beliefs, intentions, and actions. Some people, for example, could be assisted in seeing that their political socialization hinders their ability to fully understand their own best interests, or that the decision structures and institutions in which they participate are the products of an unequal social order and thus biased against the arguments advance by particular interests.

Such an approach calls for 'a continuous interchange of ideas, interpretations and criticism between social scientists and other political actors' (Bobrow and Dryzek 1987: 171). Emphasizing unrestrained discussion that imposes 'no restrictions on who may participate, what kinds of arguments can be advanced, and the duration of the discussion, the only resource actors have at their disposal is argumentation, and the only authority is that of the better argument'. Here consensus is seen as transcending submission to the arguments or frames of powerful actors or strategic political compromise among particular interests. Instead, such a consensus, grounded theoretically in the procedural rationality of ideal speech conditions, moves beyond the mere relativism of competing policy-analytical frames. Policy arguments based on different frames can be assessed and compared on the basis of an open, reflective acceptance by the full range of political participants. Moreover, theoretical knowledge for practical policy decisions would require the validation by non-expert laypersons affected by the decisions. We return to this topic in the discussion in Chapter 10 on the practices of participatory policy inquiry and the analyst as facilitator of citizen deliberation.

CONCLUSION

In this chapter we explored the 'argumentative turn' in policy analysis. Distinguishing the narrative from an argument, the discussion focused on the argumentative role of the analyst and the development of a discursive approach designed to facilitate dialogue among analysts and participants. In this view, policy analysis can be understood as 'crafted argument'. The goal is to improve policy argumentation by illuminating contentious questions, identifying the strengths and limitations of supporting evidence, and elucidating the political implications of contending positions. In the process, the task is to increase communicative competencies, deliberative capacities, and social learning. The discussion also examined the relationship of argumentative and institutional practices to methodological and substantive issues.

Drawing on a several related theoretical perspectives—in particular ordinary language philosophy, the informal logic of good reasons, and Habermas's critical theory of communication—the discussion presented a dialectical model of policy analysis that reverses the standard approach by fitting empirical findings into normative argumentation. Guided by the informal good-reasons logic of policy discourse, policy deliberation in this model is organized around four interrelated discourses. Extending from the concrete questions concerning efficiency up through the situational context and the societal system to the questions concerning the impact of a policy on a particular way of life, the levels constitute the discursive components of a comprehensive policy judgement. Working across two fundamental levels of evaluation, the four levels are concerned both with the level of the programme (its participants and the specific problem situation to which the programme is applied) and with the more abstract level of the societal order within which the programmatic action takes place. Each of the four discourses has specific requirements that must be addressed in making a complete justification of a practical judgement. For a reason to be considered a 'good' one, it must satisfy all four discursive phases of the methodological probe. Not only does the model help us to better understand the structure of the policy argument—as a complex blend of factual statements, norms, interpretations, opinions, and evaluations—than does the empirical approach to policy analysis, it is also more closely geared to the real-world, ordinary-language policy argumentation of real-world politicians and policymakers.

Drawing on Habermas's theory of communicative action, the latter part of the chapter demonstrated the interactive relationship of ordinary language communication to the formal-analytic discourses of the social sciences. It also pointed to the ways the logic of policy deliberation can facilitate a critical, policy analysis geared to the emancipatory goals of citizen empowerment. And finally it presented the procedural character of the logic of policy deliberation. Policy judgements are assessed in terms of the openness of the communicative processes that shape them. Towards this end, the goal of a critical policy analysis is to make political actors aware of the distorted or manipulated policy discourses that characterize inequitable or unjust political arrangements and the decision structures that produce them.

The logic of policy deliberation, emphasizing the force of 'the better argument', is thus a call for an ongoing deliberative interaction between policy analysts and political actors. This brings us in the final two chapters to a more detailed discussion of the discursive relationship of the policy analyst to those he or she seeks to advise, whether clients or citizens.

PART IV

DELIBERATIVE GOVERNANCE

10

Citizens and Experts:
Democratizing Policy Deliberation

Both democracy and science are defining values of Western society. Although many philosophers have tried to understand the two as mutually supportive, the tension between democracy and science has long been a critical theme in modern politics. Whereas democracy stands for open discussion on the part of all citizens, science has always been the domain of knowledge elites. Whereas democracy seeks to encourage a wide range of viewpoints and perspectives, science strives to limit the number of participants in pursuit of the one correct answer or assessment. Reconciling these differences has never proved easy. Instead of arguing that democracy can be grounded in the scientific pursuit of truth, perhaps the most prominent argument, the social constructionist perspective seeks to understand science in socio-political perspective. In this chapter we ask: to what degree can scientific practices be democratized? No easy or obvious question, Funtowicz has described it as the 'front battle line' of the debates over participation in the studies of science and society.[1] Towards this end, we begin with the question of democracy itself.

THE DEMOCRATIC CHALLENGE

Citizen participation is the cornerstone of the democratic political process. The case for democracy derives its basic normative rationale from the principle that government decisions should reflect the consent of the governed. Citizens in a democracy have the right—even obligation—to participate meaningfully in public decision-making and to be informed about the bases of government policies.

Beyond its essential contribution to democracy per se, citizen participation in the policy process can contribute to the legitimization of policy development and implementation. Participation, in this respect, can be understood as helping to build and preserve present and future decision-making capacities, or what we described earlier as communicative power (Diesing 1962: 169–234). Discursive participation offers, in particular, the possibility of getting around the debilitating effects of interest group competition that often plague liberal pluralism (Hiskes 1998). Taking aim at

Parts of this chapter have appeared in my *Citizens, Experts, and the Environment: The Politics of Expertise* (Fischer 2000).

[1] Silvio Funtowicz offered his remarks on 'Democratizing Expertise' at Workshop on Science and Democracy at Wissenschaftskolleg zu Berlin, 21–3 June 2002.

competitive interest group bargaining—at the root of many policy failures—the collaborative consensus-building inherent to participatory discourse makes possible the
identification and development of new shared ideas for coordinating the actions of
otherwise competing agents. By transforming ways of organizing and knowing, such
participatory deliberation has the possibility of building new political cultures that
increase the possibilities of communicative action (Healey 1997: 30).

Broad public participation, in this respect, makes an instrumental as well as a normative contribution to democratic policymaking. By decreasing conflict and increasing
acceptance of or trust in decisions by government agencies, it can provide citizens with
an opportunity to learn about policy problems. Such learning can improve the chances
they will support the resulting decisions. But even when it does not increase such
support, it offers the possibility of clearing up misunderstandings about the nature of a
controversy and the views of various participants. This can also contribute generally to
building trust in the process, with benefits for dealing with similar issues in the future.

Fiorino (1990) refers to a substantive rationale associated with citizen participation. As he explains, the relevant wisdom is not limited to scientific specialists and
public officials. Rather, participation by diverse groups and individuals will provide
important information and insights about policy problems. Non-specialists may
contribute substantially to problem characterization by identifying various aspects of
problems needing analysis, by raising important questions of fact that experts have
not addressed, and by offering knowledge about specific conditions that can
contribute more realistic assumptions for analyses. Lay participation can also play a
significant role in the examination and consideration of social, ethical, and political
values that cannot be addressed solely by analytical techniques.

Of particular interest from a postempiricist perspective are the ways participation can
contribute to formal inquiry itself. Participatory inquiry, in its various forms, has the
possibility of bringing to the fore both new knowledge—in particular local knowledge—
and normative interpretations that are unavailable to more abstract empirical methods
typically removed from the subjects of inquiry (Fischer 2000). Indeed, its ability to
deliver first-hand knowledge of the circumstances of a local context addresses a major
limitation of conventional methods, a central concern of postempirical analysis.

In addition to bringing to bear empirical local knowledge, attention to the multiple viewpoints of the citizenry plays an important interpretive role in the construction of social knowledge. Given the perspectival nature of dialectical knowledge,
citizen or participant interaction in the interpretive processes of knowledge
construction is an essential aspect of postempiricist research. Beyond the search for
a one-dimensional vantage point on the part of the positivist technocrat, participation is necessary to overcome the erroneous and excessively limited conception of
reason based on a dichotomous schism of the world into facts and values.

DELIBERATIVE POLICYMAKING AS CIVIC DISCOVERY

While a good part of the call for democratic renewal has come mainly from active
civic reform movements, one of the interesting calls for deliberative participation has

been advanced in public administration theory. Providing a bridge between democratic theory and concrete policy practices, the writings of Reich (1988; 1990) and Moore (1995) are especially useful in attaching the concerns of deliberation to more practical concerns of public administration and policymaking. They have sought to spell out a new theory of public management in the policy process grounded in the practices of public deliberation.

Reich and Moore take up a very old issue that has become especially chronic in the era of big government, namely, what to do about the fact that public agencies have become primary policymaking arenas. How are unelected public servants to justify their part in the policy process? For Reich (1988;1990) and Moore (1983; 1995) the prescription for this problem of policy discretion is *more* rather than less political engagement, at least understood in terms of public education and deliberation. In Moore's words, it is 'inevitable and desirable that public managers should assume responsibility for defining the purposes they seek to achieve, and therefore to participate in the political dialogue about their purposes and methods' (1983: 2). Reich seeks an approach that can 'inspire confidence among citizens that the decisions of public managers are genuinely in the public interest'. The solution, he argues, is to abjure a 'manipulative relationship ... with the public and its intermediaries' and to build instead 'a deliberative relationship' (Reich 1990: 7–8). Public managers must assume a more active role in fostering public deliberation. In this view, the goal of deliberation is to build legitimacy for policy decisions ultimately taken by public officials. 'Rather than making "decisions" and "implementing" them', as he puts it, the 'role is to manage an ongoing process of public deliberation and education', or what he calls 'civic discovery'.

Civic discovery as deliberation, according to Reich, refers to a 'process of social learning about public problems and possibilities' (Reich 1990: 8). The goal of deliberation is the 'creation of a setting in which people can learn from one another'. As an ongoing and iterative process requiring two-way communications, such deliberation focuses on 'how problems are defined and understood, what the range of possible solutions might be, and who should have the responsibility for solving them' (Reich 1990: 7).

To be sure, public executives in this model bring certain ideals and values to the process, even specific ideas about what they think should be done. But, most importantly, they look to the public and its intermediaries (for example, citizen groups, the press, and other government officials) as sources of guidance in setting direction. In addition to being straightforward about their own values and perspectives, they form their agenda only after listening carefully to the deliberations of others. In the process, these public servants do more than simply seek to discover what people want for themselves and then attempt to find the most effective means for satisfying these wants. Their task is also 'to provide the public with alternative visions of what is desirable and possible, to stimulate discussion about them, to provoke reexamination of premises and values, and thus to broaden the range of potential responses and deepen society's understanding of itself' (Reich 1990: 9).

Deliberation is time-consuming and uses scarce resources with 'no guarantee that the resulting social learning will yield a clear consensus at the end', concedes Reich (1990: 9). But over time, he argues, it can be far more effective in helping to define and sustain mandates than either the traditional emphasis on efficiency or the administrative advocacy orientation has proved to be.

Civic discovery provides a useful starting point for public sector reform. The approach, however, rests on a limited conception of democratic participation. As formulated, top-level public executives can still remain part of a relatively elitist policy community largely removed from the citizenry. While the approach would make available better information and arguments for ongoing processes of policy formulation, it remains unclear how it would bring citizens themselves closer to these processes. The model leaves us more or less dependent on the virtues of the new public manager to educate and guide us to a democratic consensus (Roberts 1995). Though commendable, there is little about education in a political world that is apolitical. Moral virtue alone has seldom proven to be a reliable form of protection in such a world. The alternative, as we argue in Chapter 11, would be found in a more participatory relationship between the public facilitator and the citizenry.

Others, though, approach the question from the other side of the issue; how realistic, they ask, is such a call for increased citizen participation? In practice, democratic participation and citizen engagement receive far more lip-service than they do serious consideration. Citizen participation remains, to be sure, an imperfect practice and it is important not to exaggerate the role of the citizens' capabilities in meaningfully participating in complex policymaking processes. Indeed, if we accept Barber's (1984) idea of a 'strong democracy' as government in which citizens participate at least some of the time in the decisions that affect their lives, we have a long way to go before we can speak of genuine democracy. Today the majority of the citizens in Western democratic polities feel themselves too far removed from the policymaking processes. Moreover, those who do participate tend to engage only in the act of voting, an activity in which the citizens of Western democracies increasingly neglect. In the United States only half of the citizens take the time to vote in national elections, with far fewer participating in state and local elections.

This has led many critical observers to explore more precisely why the levels of participation have fallen to such low levels. Although this is not a question to be answered here, one of the reasons certainly has to do with the complexity of modern society. It is simply not easy for people to participate in the complex decision processes that characterize the pressing issues of the day. Some writers go so far as to argue that it is impossible and rally support around other, weaker, forms of political representation.

Over the past three decades, however, there have been numerous participatory experiments that have shed a good deal of light on the possibilities of citizen inquiry. A more careful look at this work shows the situation not to be as bleak as many of the critics of greater involvement would have us believe.

CITIZEN INQUIRY: WHAT HAVE WE LEARNED?

One of the reasons that people do not participate is that most Western political institutions do not really give them a meaningful chance (King, Felty, and Susel 1998). Support for this is in part found in a number of unique experiences which show that people can in fact participate if the process is suitably structured and organized.

A classic example is found in the work of the Berger Commission in the 1970s in Canada. In this case, a judge appointed to assess the environmental impact of an oil pipeline intended to run through the traditional lands of native northern Americans innovated a series of deliberative fora that brought together members of the local indigenous communities, industry representatives, and government and political officials.[2] Heralded in many quarters as a major contribution to participatory policy inquiry and decision-making, the reports of the Commission were instrumental in halting a project widely viewed as portending social and environmental disaster for these distant native American communities of North-Western Canada (Berger 1977; Dryzek 1990).

Since the Berger Commission, many experiences from both social movements and institutionalized deliberative projects have shown citizens to be much more able to deal with complicated social and technical questions than the conventional wisdom generally assumes and that a range of strategies can be employed to assist them in doing that. No case better illustrates such capabilities of ordinary citizens than that of the gay movement's struggle against the spread of AIDS. As gay AIDS activists have shown, citizens can not only learn a great deal about science, they can take charge of their own experimentation when deemed necessary. Epstein (1996) documents the degree to which the boundaries between scientific 'insiders' and lay 'outsiders' have criss-crossed in the struggle to find a cure for AIDS, or what he calls 'credibility struggles'. In addition to revealing how scientific 'certainty is constructed or deconstructed', his investigations show non-scientists to have gained enough of a voice in the scientific world to have shaped to a remarkable extent National Health Institute – sponsored research.

Numerous other examples come from efforts to cite and operate nuclear power plants (Rabe 1994; Paehlke and Torgerson 1992). One study, for example, demonstrates the degree to which citizens were able to participate in sophisticated policy decisions concerning complex technical issues (Hill 1992). Once issues and questions are no longer posed in technical languages alien to the average citizens, comprehending and judging the basic elements of a policy argument about a complex technology is inherently no more complex than what the average citizen manages to accomplish in the successful running of a small business or a family. Similarly, an experimental project addressed to citizens' abilities to deal rationally with questions of risk found that most can learn and use enough science to judge questions of technological risk for themselves (Wildavsky 1997).

Basic to such cases is the emergence of cooperative relationships between citizens and experts. Rather than a matter of citizens merely going it alone, nearly all such cases reveal the involvement of a citizen expert of some sort. For example, citizen struggles against the siting of toxic wastes typically involves the presence a professional expert

---

[2] Rather than hiring experts to look into the pipeline questions, Berger and his associates went themselves to some 60 rural fishing villages and camps through the settlement area.

who assists the community in answering its own questions on its own terms (Levine 1982). Such experts emerge to help communities grasp the significance of evolving developments, think through strategies, and even directly confront a community's opponents (Edelstein 1988). Participatory consultation, in the process, serves to both broaden citizens' access to the information produced by scientists and to systematize their own 'local knowledge'. The most progressive example of such participatory consultation in the United States has taken the form of 'popular' or 'lay' epidemiology in political struggles about the impact of toxic chemicals on the health of local citizens.

Other scholars have experimented with deliberative strategies for bringing citizens and their preferences to bear more directly on policy decisions, such as Q-Methodology (Dryzek 1990; Durning 1999), deliberative polling and televoting (Lindeman 1997), national issue conventions (Fishkin 1996), scenario workshops (Andersen and Jaeger 1999), citizen juries (Crosby 1995), *Buergergutachten* (Dienel 1992), and consensus conferences (Joss and Durant 1995). Of particular importance have been a range of deliberative projects and experiments in Northern Europe. All of these approaches bring citizens together to assess complex policy issues. When experts are present, they only supply information and answer questions as the citizens find necessary. Although little-known among either academics or the general public, these experiences offer important insights into how to bring citizens closer to public decisions processes. Most importantly, they have shown that citizens are capable of much more involvement in technical questions than is conventionally presumed.

In the next section, we present two examples of citizen participation in policy inquiry, one concerned with institutional innovation, the other with the methodology of participatory policy analysis. We turn first to the Danish participatory model of the 'consensus conference', which offers perhaps the most sophisticated example of institutional innovation.

INSTITUTIONAL INNOVATION: THE CONSENSUS CONFERENCE

The consensus conference, developed by the Danish Board of Technology, has emerged as the most elaborate form of citizens' panel. Inspired in the 1980s by the now defunct US Office of Technology Assessment (OTA), the Board of Technology sought a new and innovative way to get around the divisive conflicts associated with environmentally risky technologies such as nuclear power. The idea was to find a way to make good on OTA's original mission of integrating expertise with a wide range of social, economic, and political perspectives (Joss and Durant 1995). Towards this end, the Board developed a model for a 'citizen's tribunal' designed to stimulate broad social debate on issues relevant to parliamentary level of policy-making. In an effort to bring lay voices into technological and environmental inquiries, the Board sought to move beyond the use of narrow expert advisory reports to parliament by taking issues directly to the public. In compliance with the long-standing Danish political tradition of 'people's enlightenment', which stresses the relationship between democracy and a well-educated citizenry, the Board developed a framework that bridges the gap between scientific experts, politicians, and the citizenry (Kluver 1995; Mayer 1997).

The formal goals of the consensus conference are twofold: to provide members of parliament and other decision-makers with the information resulting from the conference; and to stimulate public discussion through media coverage of both the conference and the follow-up debates. First implemented in 1987, conferences have dealt with issues such as energy policy, air pollution, sustainable agriculture, food irradiation, risky chemicals in the environment, the future of private transport, gene therapy, and the cloning of animals.

A consensus conference is organized and administered by a steering committee appointed by the Board of Technology. Typically, it involves bringing together from 10 to 25 citizens charged with the task of assessing a socially sensitive topic of science and technology. The lay participants are usually selected from written replies to advertisements announced in national newspapers and radio broadcasts. Interested citizens, *excluding* experts on the particular theme, apply by sending a short written statement explaining why they would like to participate in the inquiry process. The statements are evaluated by the steering committee to determine if a candidate is sufficiently dedicated to fully participate in the conference process. Citizens are asked to participate as unpaid volunteers, but the Board offers compensation for any loss of income that might result from the involvement. From around 200 to 300 written responses, an average of 15 citizens are recruited. Although the groups do not constitute a random sample of the population, they are selected on the basis of socio-demographic criteria such as education, gender, age, occupation, and area of residence. As such, a panel is generally a reasonable cross-section of ordinary citizens with no special interest or knowledge in the topic under investigation.[3]

From the choosing of a topic to the final public discussions after the formal conference proceedings, the process typically runs several months. Central to the inquiry process is a facilitator who works to assist the lay panel in the completion of its tasks. Professionally trained in communication skills and cooperative techniques, the facilitator is a non-expert on the topic of the conference. Working closely with the panel, he or she guides the process through an organized set of rules and procedures. In addition to organizing the preparatory informational and deliberative processes, he or she chairs the actual conference itself. Somewhat like a judge in a jury trial, the facilitator maintains the focus of the experts on the lay panel's questions during the conference and assists panellists in finding the most direct answers to their questions.

After the lay participants are selected, they are assembled for informal meetings on the topic. At the first meeting, the steering committee outlines the topic for the participants in general terms and informs them that they may define their approach to the topic in whatever way they see fit. Not only can they frame their own questions, they can seek the kinds of information they find necessary to answer them.

---

[3] In the Danish model, citizens reply to advertisements placed in newspapers, asking them to send a letter explaining why they would like to participate.

At the same time, panellists are supplied with extensive reading materials by the steering committee and given a substantial interval of time to study the materials at home.

After reading the materials, the panellists are asked to develop a list of questions pertinent to the inquiry. The steering committee uses the participants' lists of questions to assemble additional information for the panellists and to identify an interdisciplinary group of technological and environmental experts to make presentations to the citizen panel. During a subsequent informational meeting, the citizens review new materials and further refine their list of questions, dropping some as well as adding new ones. Evaluations of this phase show that, by the time of the actual conference, the participants are remarkably knowledgeable about the issues to hand. In some cases, a hearing is also organized for parties interested in the selected subject. Such groups—for example, individuals or companies with extensive knowledge, influence and/or dependence on the field, research institutions, research committees, traditional interests groups, and grass-roots organizations—are provided with an opportunity to contribute information to the deliberative process. These hearings may either be in writing or organized as meetings. The information culled is used to further both the organizational work of the steering committee and the thought and discussion of the lay panel.

The official conference begins at this point, typically lasting three or four days. On the first day the experts make presentations running from 20 to 30 minutes. After each presentation, the members of the lay group put questions to the experts and cross-examine them. In some cases, representatives from relevant interest groups are present and can also be questioned. Within the given time limits, citizens in the audience are also invited to make statements or ask questions. On the second day, the citizen panel more actively cross-examines the experts. Again, at specific points, the public and interested parties are themselves encouraged to ask questions. In some cases, representatives from relevant interest groups are also questioned.

At the end of this process, usually on the third day of the meeting, the citizen panel retires to deliberate on the exchanges. With the assistance of a secretary supplied by the steering committee, the group prepares a consensus report (from 15 to 30 pages in average length) that considers all of the issues that bear on the topic. Typically, the report reflects the range of interests and concerns of parties involved in the conference. Beyond scientific and technical considerations, it speaks to the spectrum of economic, legal, ethical, and social aspects associated with the topic.

Upon completion of the report, the citizen panel publicly presents its conclusions. Normally this takes place in a highly visible public setting in the presence of the media, a variety of experts, and the general public. Subsequently, copies of the report are sent to members of parliament, scientists, special interest groups, and members of the public. Consensus conference reports often complement expert assessments as part of larger technology assessment project.

Described as an exercise in 'counter-technocracy', the consensus conference has received favourable reviews from citizens, experts, the media, and politicians. Many Danish politicians have responded particularly favourably to the approach. Because they are themselves laypersons, they can easily identify with the inquiry process and its outcomes. They also find the conclusions to more clearly reflect the concerns of the population than do the more traditional expert assessments. An indication of this favourable evaluation is found in the positive impacts that consensus conferences have had on parliamentary decisions in a range of topics pertinent Danish environmental protection (Kluver 1995: 44). For example, panel recommendations have influenced the parliament to decide against the funding of animal gene technology research and development programmes, to restrict food irradiation, and accept a panel proposal for a tax on private vehicles, among others.

No less significant is the impact the consensus conference experience has had on the citizen participants themselves. Joss (1995: 3) reports that lay panellists report both an increased knowledge of the subject under discussion and a new confidence in their ability to deal with technical issues generally. Equally important, they tend to describe the conference experience as having supplied 'a stimulating and creative input to their personal life'. Joss quotes one participant as having said that the experience provided her with 'an increased interest in all sorts of subjects' that she previously thought were 'over my head', as well as the discovery that she 'could actually understand (and comment on) scientific issues'.

Since the outset of the Danish experience, consensus conferences have been sponsored by governments in Britain, Austria, Holland, New Zealand, Norway, and Switzerland (Joss 1998).[4] As a highly innovative contribution to the facilitation of democratic practices, the consensus conference provides a model for giving citizens a role in the environmental policy process. Not only has it been widely credited with invigorating contemporary democratic practices, it has built understanding and trust among citizens and experts as well.

METHODOLOGICAL INNOVATION: PARTICIPATORY POLICY ANALYSIS

In recent years a number of writers have called for introducing the practice of participatory policy analysis (Torgerson 1986; Fischer 1992; Laird 1993; Durning 1993; deLeon 1997). Torgerson (1986: 241) puts it this way: 'Just as positivism underlies the dominant technical orientation in policy analysis, so the postpositivism orientation now points to a participatory project.' Examining the case for such a project, deLeon (1997) finds that growing evidence that citizens are generally willing and able to engage in such activities and that participatory policy analysis holds out the possibility of renewing social capital and, in the process, revitalizing our commitment to democratic governance. Beyond technical rationality and hierarchical organization practices, he sees postpositivist policy analysis grounded in both democratic and epistemological commitments (deLeon 1997: 111–22). The practices

---

[4] In the US, a preliminary pilot project dealing with the topic of telecommunications was also conducted in Boston in 1997 by the Loka Institute and a subsequent effort was carried out at North Carolina State University under the direction of Patrick Hamlett in the summer of 2001.

of citizens juries and consensus conferences are, in his view, an important step toward the development of participatory policy analysis.

Laird (1993: 241–61) sees participatory analysis as 'a way of structuring the politics of policy-making' that opens up the discourse to questions fundamental to any democratic discourse: 'who we are, what we want, and how we might get it.' Rather than 'letting competing interests simply slug it out over the final details of a narrow problem, the concept of participatory analysis allows, indeed requires, a much broader scope to the activity, including problem definition and framing.' Towards this end, Laird offers a set of normative democratic criteria for assessing when and to what extent various modes of participatory analysis can contribute to improving both citizen learning and democratic policymaking.

Durning (1993:300) has identified four approaches to participatory policy analysis and finds that they all share a number of epistemological assumptions. In his words, 'all reject positivism, view phenomenology or a variation of it as a better way to interpret the nature of knowledge, and accept an interpretive or hermeneutic paradigm of inquiry.' In the view put forward here, a genuine postempiricist approach to participatory policy analysis should draw on the theory and practice of participatory research (Fischer 1995).

In significant part a product of the work of intellectuals, activists, and progressive professionals identified with Third World communities and the 'new social movements' of the more advanced industrial countries, participatory research is an important part of the contemporary struggle for participatory democracy. Grounded in efforts to empower ordinary citizens to make their own action-oriented decisions, participatory researchers have experimented with new ways to democratize the expert's relationship with the citizen or client (Tandon 1988; Fischer 2000).

Most fundamentally, participatory inquiry is part of the effort to translate the critique of positivist expertise into a practical methodological orientation. In particular, it addresses the argument that professional experts have—wittingly or unwittingly—aligned themselves with elite interests. In the name of democracy and social justice, alternative movements within the professions themselves have sought to develop new expert practices. Toward this end, participatory inquiry has emerged as an effort to bring citizens and their local knowledges directly into the policy process.

The classic tensions between expertise and participation are central to these experimental alternatives. Largely designed to counter the techno-bureaucratic and elitist tendencies that define contemporary political and organizational processes, such experimentation has in significant part been geared to social movements' emphasis on empowerment and self-help strategies. Emphasizing the development of a non-hierarchical culture, the theorists of these movements have asked the fundamental question: is it possible to restructure the largely undemocratic expert-client relationship? In particular, they have targeted the hierarchical relationship the professions maintain with their clients (Touraine 1981).

Participatory research is an effort to integrate 'scientific investigation with education and political action' (Cancian and Armstead 1992: 1427). Experts and researchers work cooperatively with community members to understand and solve local problems, to empower their residents, and to democratize the research process. It is seen to be a valuable alternative for social researchers who challenge 'the traditional values of being detached and value-free and who seek an approach that is less hierarchical and that serves the interests of those with little power'. As such, it is a valuable alternative for social researchers who challenge 'the traditional values of being detached and value-free and who seek an approach that is less hierarchical and that serves the interests of those with little power'.

A mode of inquiry designed as an enlightenment strategy for raising the consciousness of ordinary citizens with common interests and concerns, participatory research emphasizes the political dimensions of knowledge production and the role of knowledge as an instrument of power and control, as well as the politics of the citizen-expert relationship. Drawing its methodological foundations from a variety of sources common to the postempiricist orientation, it takes human beings to be co-creators of 'their own reality through participation: through their experience, their imagination and intuition, and their thinking and action' (Reason 1994: 324). At the heart of participatory inquiry's critique of conventional social scientific methods is 'the idea that its methods are neither adequate nor appropriate for the study of *persons*, for persons are to some significant degree self-determining' (Reason 1994: 325). As such, it seeks to overcome the conventional approach that excludes its human subjects from the thinking that goes into developing, designing, administering, and drawing inferences from the findings. Participatory research, as an inherently democratic practice, is fundamentally grounded in the idea that people can help choose how they live their lives.

Based on experiential knowing, the practice of cooperative inquiry seeks to understand individuals and their problems within their own socio-cultural context and the particular the 'logic of the situation' to which it gives rise (Heron 1981: 158). But participatory research seeks to do more. Beyond analysing the socio-cultural logic of action, it seeks to link the experiential situation to the larger social structure. It is an effort to interpret the situation in terms of the more fundamental structures of social domination that shape it. In the language of the logic of policy analysis presented in Chapter 9, it seeks to move the process from the situational validation to societal vindication and ideological choice. As such, participatory research casts its findings in the framework of a larger social critique, an epistemological step that links it to critical theory and an 'emancipatory interest'.

From a methodological perspective, the thing that differentiates participatory research from conventional social science is the attitudes and behaviour of the investigators (Chambers 1997: 212). On paper the basic methodological steps of a participatory research project don't look that different from those of a standard empirical research methodology. Eldon (1981: 257–8), for example, specifies four critical decisions confronting the participatory researcher: (1) problem definition: what is the research problem? (2) Choice of methods: which methodologies will best provide the required data? (3) Data analysis: how are the data to be interpreted? (4) Use of findings: how can the outcomes be used? Who learns what from the research findings? 'Research is participatory', Eldon explains (1981: 258), 'when the participants directly affected by it influence each of these four decisions and help to carry them out.'

These considerations make unique role demands on the professional, ranging from theoretician and expert to colleague and co-producer of knowledge (Callon 1996). In each case, the basic determinant of the expert's role choices must be his or her usefulness in 'facilitating' collaborative learning processes. The basic question is this: how can the expert's role facilitate the development of a learning process which, once set in motion, can proceed on its own?

The facilitation of participant learning is designed to enlarge the citizens'/clients' abilities to pose the problems and questions that are of particular interest and concern to them. Facilitation thus requires a focus on the social, emotional, and intellectual distance that separates the professional from the client's experiential life-world (Hirschhorn 1979). Indeed, distance has become the source of strident disagreements over the definition of the client's social situation, as well over who should have the responsibility for determining the issue. Such struggles invariably raise the question of social control, typically leading to acrimonious polemics about the professional's role in the delivery of services. The solution is found in the redesign of the professional-client relationship. The expert must learn how to be a 'facilitator' of client learning (Fischer 2000).

As a facilitator, the expert's task is to assist citizens and clients in their own efforts to examine their own interests and to plan appropriate courses of action. 'Professionals', in short, 'must become experts in how clients learn, clarify, and decide.' Emphasis is thus 'on establishing the institutional conditions within which clients can draw on their own individual and collective agencies to solve their problems.' The 'professional acts as a programmer, mobilizer of resources, and consultant to a self-exploration and learning process on the part of group members' (Hirschhorn 1979: 188).

Essential to the facilitation of empowerment, then, is the creation of institutional and intellectual conditions that help people pose questions in their own ordinary (or everyday) languages and to decide the issues important to themselves. Theorists interested in developing these concepts have most typically turned to models of social learning and discourse. The central focus of such models is how to innovate 'inquiring systems' that assist learners in the 'problematization' and exploration of their own concerns and interests.

Much of participatory research has been influenced by Freire's (1970; 1973) work on 'problematization' or 'problem-posing'. Problematizing is the direct antithesis of technocratic problem-solving. In the technocratic approach the expert establishes some distance from reality, analyses it into component parts, devises means for resolving difficulties in the most efficient way, and then dictates the strategy or policy. Such problem-solving distorts the totality of human experience by reducing it to those dimensions that are amenable to treatment as mere difficulties to be solved. To 'problematize', on the other hand, is to help people codify into symbols an integrated picture or story of reality that, in the course of its development, can generate a critical consciousness capable of empowering them to alter their relations to both the physical and social worlds.

In methodological terms, this can be understood as connecting first-order discourse, in particular the logic of the situation, with second-order discourse about the workings of the larger social system and basic ideological orientations, those of both the social system and its critics. The expert, as facilitator, attempts to help citizens and clients establish these basic connections and to determine what they might mean for them. In this sense, the taken-for-granted world of everyday life becomes reconnected to the social and political processes which have constructed it. For the citizen, in the process, biography becomes history and sociology.

EXAMPLES OF PARTICIPATORY POLICY ANALYSIS

Participatory research has in significant part emerged with issues such as indigenous farming, alternative technologies, and environmental risks. In North America and Western Europe the major examples concern struggles around environmental and technological risks. A typical case might be a group of town citizens resisting the citing of a power plant in their area. With the assistance of a local activist or local expert, meetings would be organized and a team of community members chosen to participate in the collaborative inquiry. After deliberations about the general nature of the problem confronting the town, as well as its goals and interests, a strategy would be established to create and discover the community's understanding, expression, and use of the data and information relevant to the situation, including that which they collect themselves. In the process, the community group would help other residents to learn more about their community and the pertinent governmental decision and planning processes, to gain the requisite participatory skills needed for pursuing an action strategy, and to compile and distribute such pertinent information in a report. The report becomes the basis for the deliberation on and selection of an alternative approach to the power plant and its relation to the town. Through discussions, formal and informal, with residents, community workshops, and public officials, the participatory team advances its alternative in the public sphere (Park *et al.* 1993; Fischer 2000).

In recent years participatory research has begun to play a role in policy analysis more formally understood. Participatory policy analysis has emerged in several government agencies in the United States. An important example is offered by Dan Durning (1993). Durning has carefully observed and reported on a 'stakeholder' approach to participatory policy analysis in the Georgia Division of Rehabilitation Service (DRS). In this case the Service assembled a team of the agency's employees to analyse its policy for selection of service recipients and to present advice to the agency's executive committee. His analysis shows that the team's analysis was not only well-received by top management, but also that the quality of the work was judged positively.

Compared with the professional approach to policy analysis, Durning judged the Georgia agency-stakeholder inquiry to illustrate important strengths of participatory policy analysis: 'Team members were a good source of opinions, data and information', especially as they 'thoroughly understood the context of the analysis'; 'Team members had the resources to construct a 'mental model' to predict the consequences of the propose alternatives'; the analytical process created significant positive spin-offs; and 'the analysis had credibility' within the agency (Durning 1993: 311–14). The effort, of course, was not without costs. It tended to be slow, used less sophisticated methods than technical policy analysis, and the costs of the analysis were not insignificant, especially as it removed employees from their regular jobs. But there was no doubt in the minds of the agency that the benefits outweighed the costs.

In Durning's (1993: 317) view, 'organization-stakeholder policy analysis is well suited for addressing...messy or ill-structured policy issues', defined as 'decision problems...for which decision makers, preferences or utilities, alternative, or outcomes, or states of nature are unknown or equivocal.' Moreover, such issues are often part 'of a complicated context in which ends may not be well defined, the def-inition of problems may not be settled, the meaning of data may be disputed, and the legitimacy of proposed policy instruments may be the subject of internal debates'. For such analysis, the standard technical methodologies of policy analysis are insuf-ficient, requiring the use of 'second-order' methods of analysis. Stakeholder policy analysis, which facilitates an understanding of the decision context, qualifies as a method of this second type.

Another important example is the World Bank's Participation Program. Having learned the relevance of local involvement and participation from many of its Third World investment failures, the World Bank in the 1990s took an interest in the advan-tages offered by direct local contact with the communities it sought to assist (World Bank 1994; 1995). Not only were senior Bank staff members directed to get to know their regions better through a week of total immersion in one of its villages or slums, the Bank developed a technique called 'participatory poverty assessment', designed 'to enable the poor people to express their realities themselves' (Chambers 1997: xvi). Adapted from other participatory research techniques, the Bank has now been involved in participatory poverty assessments in over 30 countries around the world, in particular in Africa (Norton and Stephens 1995).

Participatory poverty assessment represents an attempt to strengthen the Bank's analysis of the connections between its assistance strategies and the borrower coun-tries' own programmes to reduce poverty. Specially designed to inform its policy dia-logues with these governments, the Bank has sought ways to scale up participatory approaches from the project level to the country level. Towards this end, it has encouraged its operational managers to supplement their conventional poverty research with participatory poverty assessments. Such assessments have not been conducted as a discrete research process, but rather have been designed to produce results 'that can help to complement, inform and validate conclusions drawn from other kinds of more traditional Bank analysis' (Norton and Stephens 1995: 5).[5] Although the Bank's practices have been criticized as co-optive, which is not entirely

---

[5] Typically, these discussions among the Bank's analysts have focused on 'how best to integrate participatory and conventional methods, distinguished as "qualitative" and "quantitative" respectively in Bank discourse' (Holland 1998: 93).

untrue, the very fact that the Bank has felt compelled to acknowledge the role of participation is in itself something to take note of (Cooke and Kothari 2001).

Such participatory assessments scarcely originate with the World Bank; indeed, the Bank has got many—if not most—of its ideas from non-governmental organizations (NGOs) and other development institutions. NGOs have designed and conducted a growing number of participatory policy analysis projects, ranging, for example, from irrigation policy studies in India, wetland management policy investigation in Pakistan, food grains studied in Nepal, forestry issues in Scotland, educational policy matters in Gambia, and the relationship between poverty and violence in Jamaica to land tenure concerns in Madagascar, to name just a few.[6] These efforts have been judged to offer timely and useful policy experiences, especially when policy decision-makers are highly committed, the inquiry is of a high quality, and the results are tested against other sources. Offering a voice to the poor, such policy debates become grounded in local realities and citizen interpretations rather than would-be 'objective realities' designed by analysts sitting behind desks. The inquiry process offers an alternative mode of evaluation that not only provides local information, but has proved capable of uncovering insightful, often counter-intuitive surprises.

CONCLUSION

Taking up the tension between democracy and science, the discussion has sought to reformulate the relationship through the social constructionist perspective emphasizing science as a socio-political activity. Rather than taking scientific practices to be the ideal for politics, we asked to what degree scientific practices might be democratized. Towards this end, the discussion outlined the contributions of citizen participation to both policymaking and collaborative inquiry, from legitimization to local knowledge. By transforming citizens' ways of knowing and acting, participatory deliberation can build new political cultures capable of preserving and extending decision-making capabilities.

Against this background we turned to the more challenging question of the citizen's ability to collaboratively engage in the scientific inquiry process. We considered first the barriers that block such participation in the complex decision-processes of contemporary governance and then surveyed examples that show citizens to be more capable of engaging the pressing issues of the day than generally recognized. Examining participatory inquiry as a postempiricist methodology designed to facilitate citizen deliberation, the chapter looked at the ways citizens' local knowledge and normative interpretations can be brought to bear on the problem-solving processes, information generally unavailable to empirical methods more removed from the subjects of inquiry.

The discussion then turned to numerous participatory experiments that more specifically illustrate the possibilities and practices of citizen inquiry. In particular,

---

[6] For additional examples, see Park *et al.* (1993), Nelson and Wright (1995), Chambers (1997), van der Ploeg (1993), Brown and Mikkelsen (1990), and Liebenburg (1993).

it outlined the consensus conference and the methodology of participatory policy analysis. Basic to such cases, as we saw, is the emergence of cooperative relationships between citizens and experts. Such experts emerge to help communities grasp the significance of evolving developments, to think through strategies, to broaden citizens' access to information produced by scientists, to help systematize their own local knowledge. The basic question is: how can the expert facilitate the development of a learning process that, once set in motion, can proceed on its own?

Finally, it should clearly stated that citizen participation is not advanced here as a magic cure-all for economic and social problems. Nor is deliberation or argumentation meant to direct attention away from questions of interest and power. But it does hold out the possibility of bringing forth new knowledge and ideas capable of creating and legitimizing new interests, reshaping our understanding of existing interests, and, in the process, influencing the political pathways along which power and interest travel. Given the importance of such practices for postempiricist policy analysis, we turn in the next and final chapter to a more explicit examination of the conduct and practices of citizen-oriented deliberative policy analysis.

11

The Deliberative Policy Analyst: Theoretical Issues and Practical Challenges

In the preceding chapters we covered the theoretical and epistemological support for citizen participation in policymaking. In this final chapter, we take up more specifically its implications for the conduct of policy analysis, in particular the role of policy analysts as facilitators of deliberative practices. We turn, in short, to what Forester (1999) calls the 'deliberative practitioner'.

In the approach to participatory inquiry outlined in Chapter 10, the professional expert serves as facilitator of public learning and political empowerment. Rather than provide technical answers designed to bring political discussions to an end, the task of the analyst as facilitator is to assist citizens in their efforts to examine their own interests and in making their own decisions (Fischer 1992). Although this conception of the expert's role differs sharply from the standard understanding, it is not altogether new to the policy literature. Indeed, Harold Lasswell (1941: 89), the founder of the policy science movement, first envisioned the role of the scientific policy professional as that of 'clarifier' of issues for public deliberation. Following Dewey's (1927) call for improving the methods and conditions of public debate, Lasswell defined the professional role as that of educating a citizenry capable of participating intelligently in deliberations on public affairs. Policy science was thus initially seen as a method for improving citizen understanding and deliberation. Towards this end, Lasswell spelled out a 'contextual orientation' for professional analytic practices that would extend policy science beyond the professional realm to include the insights and judgements of the citizenry, or what he called the policy science of democracy (Torgerson 1985).

If this contextual orientation was lost to the subsequent development of a technocratic policy science, it has more recently returned in the policy-oriented literatures of public administration and planning, especially in the postempiricist and postmodern literatures of the fields. In postmodern public administration theory, the administrator seeks to facilitate and clarify communication rather than decide which group is right (Rosenau 1992: 86–7). By the 1990s, such ideas had moved to the forefront of theoretical discussions in many circles of public administration and planning. Most of the advocates of this view are quick to argue that the approach is neither nihilistic nor hostile to reason. Rather, it is a search for new forms of knowledge and reason that carry us forward without the pretence of an immutable universal 'Truth.' Basic to the effort is an emphasis on local knowledge (Fischer 2000).

Resting on a postempiricist epistemology, this 'argumentative' or 'communicative' turn in planning and policy analysis takes social meaning as central and understands social reality to be constituted by shared beliefs. While not denying the physical dimensions of experience, as we saw in Chapter 10, such a postempiricist analysis emphasizes a critical assessment of the assumptions that organize and interpret our ways of knowing and the knowledge that results from them. Such an interpretive approach is thus 'distinctive in saying that knowledge is not the exclusive province of experts, and in accepting a subjective element in all knowledges' (Innes 1990: 32). Instead of hiding behind the guise of value neutrality, the expert must actively employ his or her own subjectivity to under actors' views—citizens, politicians, and decision-makers, among others. More than just an alternative epistemological orientation, it provides a more useful and realistic description of the actual relationships between citizens and experts (Fischer and Forester 1993; Forester 1999; Healey 1997).

Grounded in particular contexts, interpretive knowledge requires the professional to involve himself or herself in the modes of thought and learning of everyday life, that is, the local knowledge of the ordinary citizen. Knowledge is in this way recognized to be more than a set of relationships among selected data or variables isolated or abstracted from their social context (Innes 1998). To be meaningful for the world of decision and action, such variables have to be interpreted in the situational as well as the larger social contexts to which they are to be applied. In this view, as we saw earlier, what we call 'knowledge' of the social world is a product of negotiations between those with technical expert knowledge and the participants in the everyday world, including the experts as 'citizen experts'. Moreover, as Innes (1990: 232) puts it, such 'knowledge is about whole phenomenon rather than simply about relationships among selected variables or facts in isolation from their contexts'. As such, knowledge and reasoning are recognized as taking many forms, from empirical analysis to expressive statements in words, sounds, and picture (Healey 1997: 29). Of particular importance, as we have seen, is the narrative form of the story; in everyday life, it is the primary means of giving meaning to complex social phenomena. The narrative is the device that situates the empirical data in the phenomenon as a whole.

Bringing together professional knowledge and lived experience, citizens and experts form an interpretive community. Through mutual discourse this community seeks a persuasive understanding of the issues under investigation. This occurs through changes—sometimes even transformations—of individual beliefs, including social values. In the process, the inquirer, as part of a community, is an agent in the social context rather than an isolated, passive observer. Means and ends are inseparably linked in such a discursive process, and, importantly, those who participate need to accept the practical and moral responsibilities for their decisions and their consequences.

This postempiricist facilitator also accepts the tasks of working to embed such an inquiry in actual organizational and policy processes. This involves developing arenas and forums in which knowledge can be debated and interpreted in relation to the relevant policy issues. One example of such inquiry is the consensus conference;

another is participatory research. Ideally the goal is to establish institutional mechanisms for using the resulting knowledge. The task is to incorporate the findings in the regular work of an implementing agency through face-to-face communication among experts, citizens, and decision-makers, as was the case in the Georgia State agency.

Such interactions between social scientists as facilitators and the citizens-clients can be likened to a conversation in which the horizons of both are extended through mutual dialogue. Building on such a conversation, Jennings (1987: 127) suggests, requires the analysts 'to grasp the meaning or significance of contemporary problems as they are experienced, adapted to, and struggled against by the reasonable, purposive agents who are members of the political community.' He or she must then work to clarify the meaning of those problems in such a way 'that strategically located political agents (public officials or policy makers) will be able to devise a set of efficacious and just solutions to them.' Emphasizing a procedural route to policy choice, the analyst strives to interpret the public interest in a way that can survive an open and non-distorted process of deliberation and assessment. In the process, interpreting the world and changing it are complementary endeavours. The analyst as counsellor seeks to 'construct an interpretation of present political and social reality that serves not only the intellectual goals of explaining or comprehending that reality, but also the practical goal of enabling constructive action to move the community from a flawed present toward an improved future' (Jennings 1987: 127). This is not dissimilar to the process Roe (1994) describes as developing a 'metanarrative'.

COMMUNICATIVE POLICY ANALYSIS IN CRITICAL PLANNING THEORY

While these ideas are relatively unfamiliar to many policy analysts with formal backgrounds in political science, public administration, or economics, this is not the case in the discipline of planning. There the communication model or argumentative turn has over the past ten or 15 years become a dominant theoretical orientation in the field, some say *the* dominant understanding of planning practices. Indeed, the policy analysis community more generally can learn much from the theoretical debates that have engaged this close disciplinary relative.[1] Led by theorists such as Forester, Healey, Innes, Hoch, and Throgmorton, the objective of a critical communicative approach is to examine the way the planner, including the planner as policy analyst, engages in political and professional practices. Focusing on the relationships between knowledge and power, as Ploger (2001: 221) puts it, they examine the 'acts of power such as words in use, argumentation in action, as well as gestures, emotions, passions, and morals representing institutional politics and ways of thinking'. At the same time, it means analysing the forms of participatory or collaborative planning (Healey 1997).

These scholars assume that the primary activity of the planner is to facilitate processes of deliberations. Towards this end, they propose an argumentative or

---

[1] Policy analysis is formally considered one of the specialties of planning. During the past 15 years numerous writers have defined it as a major task of the planner.

discursive analysis of planning practices (Forester 1999). From this perspective, a primary source of knowledge about planning is the discursive activities of planners at work: their written and spoken words in their deliberations, plans, and other relevant documents. In Forester's view, no aspect of public planning is more important than communication. Focusing on public disputes and contested information in the face of power, his focus is on 'words in practice'. Recognizing that the institutions in which planners work are a basic source of distorted communication, critical analysis must focus on 'the politics (status, strategies, effects, and implications) of who says what, when and how in planning-related organizations' (1999: 53).

For theorists such as Forester, the investigation of such discursive practices emphasizes the individual professional in local settings, whether the town meeting or the office of the department of planning. They want to know what actually happens when planners speak and listen in the course of their practical activities (Forester 1999: 49), in particular how these communicative actions are interpreted through basic systems of meaning (Healey 1997: 49). The goal is to help planners to learn to critically reflect on their own discursive practices, in particular their ways of arguing. They need to discover the messages that are latently conveyed through the language they use, as these are often the critical meanings of what otherwise appear to be clear statements of intent. As Ploger (2001: 221) explains it, the objective is to make policy planners and analysts 'more conscious of the hidden forms of communicative power they practise (often unconsciously) in order to develop a democratic, yet rational, public communication.'

Underlying this perspective, especially for Forester and Healey, is a Habermasian perspective on 'distorted communication'. Through descriptions of concrete cases, the goal is to make the practising planner aware of the often manipulated or distorted nature of communications in the planning process. Such work reflects an interest 'in the relationship between knowledge and power, in the potential for oppression inherent in instrumental rationality, and including a more emancipatory way of knowing' (Sandercock 1997: 96). Only when planners themselves become aware and self-critical of these often subtle power mechanisms, it is argued, is it possible to develop a communicative solidarity. Towards this end, the planner's task is to equalize communicative forces of power by establishing rational communicative counteractions. The planner should see himself or herself not only as an agent of political-institutional power, but also as part of the effort to reform society (Yiftachel 1998). Forester and others therefore interweave advocate planning, social learning, and radical planning as a mode of self-critical communicative practice.

In the process, such planners seek to create spaces and opportunities for more consensual modes of planning and policymaking. As Sandercock (1997: 96) puts it, the task is to assure 'representations of all major points of view, equalizing information among group members, and creating conditions within group processes so that the force of argument can be the deciding factor rather than an individual's power or status in some pre-existing hierarchy.' In political terms, the goal is to understand how public deliberation among the social actors affected by the consequences of implementation facilitates less technocratic, more democratic planning and policy processes. Epistemologically, following Dewey as well as Habermas, the challenge is to understand how deliberative processes are basic to reason itself. Such planners conceive of reason and rationality as residing in discursively negotiated and communicated understandings and intentions within communities bound together by traditions, conventions, and agreements forged through democratic deliberation (Hoch 1996: 31).

For those who adhere closely to Habermas's theory of communicative action, communicative planning and policy analysis can be analysed in terms of the normative requirements of ideal speech. From this perspective a critical policy analysis is grounded in a 'universal pragmatic' that is understood to be inherent to speech. If deliberative dialogue is based on the sincerity, comprehensibility, truthfulness, and normative legitimacy of arguments, then the universal principles of ideal speech can be employed to evaluate speech claims as they unfold through inter-subjective communication (Hoch 1996). These universal criteria can serve as 'practical moral guidelines to a democratic, intersubjective communication and as premises to uncoerced reason as the outcome of discussion' (Ploger 2001: 221).

COMMUNICATIVE THEORY: REPLYING TO THE CRITICS

The communications approach to planning and policy analysis is scarcely without its critics. Indeed, it has set off a thoroughgoing debate in the field. Given the distance between communicative theory and traditional theory in planning, especially the rational-empirical model, this comes as no surprise. As Mazza (1995) argues, the professional planner is typically engaged in a wide range of activities not well accounted for by the communications approach. For one thing, it would seem to neglect the empirical activities of the planner as researcher. For another, it would seem to ignore the traditional focus of such research, namely, the cities and urban areas (Fainstein 2000). To be sure, the communicative planner is typically working in a city planning department. But the stress is more on his or her efforts to understand communicative interactions and to facilitate deliberations among the relevant groups, citizens, administrators, and politicians.

Moreover, the critics argue that an emphasis on the communicative activities of the working planner scarcely constitutes a critical approach to theory and practice. Given that most practitioners work for city agencies of one type or another, the conversations to be recorded in a government agency are by their nature a form of communication distorted by administrative and political interests embedded in the organizational structures and processes. One can learn how successful planners strategically use language to persuade, but it scarcely constitutes an ideal communicative setting capable of generating an authentic consensus.

The critics of communicative planning ask how policy analysts and planners working in the 'belly of the beast' can actually employ such principles. Are not their practices constrained by the ideas and discursive practices embedded in the institutions for which they work? Indeed, it would not even be wrong to argue that many of their professional practices are a product of the needs and interests of planning agencies. The discipline itself emerged to serve this function. In this light, no one can reasonably dispute the fact that most conventional planners and policy analysts, as public servants working for the state apparatus, mainly reproduce the existing power relations embedded in the institutions in which they work. For this reason, asks Flyvbjerg (1996: 388), can policy planners change the rationality of policy and planning practices by employing the good manners of 'the noble planner'?

The formal answer, of course, is 'no'. After conceding this point, though, the issue becomes more complicated. First, communicative theorists make no such claim. Writers such as Forester, Healey, and Hoch understand the limitations of bureaucratic communication; the argument is something of a simplification of the theoretical orientation. Moreover, Forester often argues that his own particular interest is in this type of communication and that somebody should study it. While the point is valid, however, it can be problematic for a theory that has emerged as a dominant theory of planning per se. In fact, in reading these works it is at times quite easy to neglect or ignore the other aspects of planning. Like any theory, communicative planning is a distribution of emphasis. And the literature of communicative planning does tend to divert attention away from the substantive questions pertinent to our understandings of urban processes (for instance, what sort of housing should be built?)

Part of the problem can be resolved by more clearly understanding that the communicative approach relates to—or should relate to—the conduct of the professional planner at work, not planning as a whole. Viewed in this way, it is on solid ground, as traditional planners have almost altogether ignored this important topic, one of special importance to an applied discipline such as planning. Planning research may not be about advice per se, but a major expectation of those who hire planners is that they will be able to offer and apply advice based on planning knowledge and research. Indeed, the communications approach is a response to this task. Whereas planners have traditionally adopted—explicitly or implicitly—a technocratic approach to advice giving (that is, technical information speaks for itself and the practitioner simply informs the client in the language of planning), the communications model has sought to understand the epistemological gaps between these various communities of inquirers—citizens, politicians, administrators, and so on—and to seek ways to communicate across these barriers.

With regard to the substantive content of planning, the communications approach is a response to another, related dimension of this epistemological gap. Some of the critics speak as if this orientation hinders or diverts attention away from the task of generating empirical knowledge needed to contribute to solutions to pressing social and economic problems. What they neglect to acknowledge is that the profession has yet to develop such knowledge. There is no such body of knowledge, as we made clear in earlier chapters. And it is not for lack of empirical analysis of pressing problems. Rather, it has to do with the nature of the social world and our ability to understand the complex phenomena that define it. While this is not to say that we don't have expert knowledge about social and economic problems, it is to recognize that what we do have is only partial and can be applied only through a discursive examination of the uncertainties of this knowledge in terms of a range of other empirical and normative considerations basic to the context to which it is to be applied. The communicative planner thus seeks a way out of a dilemma. It is an action-oriented attempt to find, to understand, and to interpret the partial knowledge that we have in the practical context to which is to be used. This might not be planning theory per se, but it has to be a very important part of a planning discipline that hopes to be able to usefully apply its knowledge.

Other critics such as Fainstein criticize the model as being too narrowly focused on the bureaucratic tasks of the planner, but take a different turn. They suggest that the profession return to its original normative ideas. For Fainstein that means an emphasis on 'the just city'. Among the just-city theorists one finds two categories: those who call for a revitalization of political economy, emphasizing social equity and justice in the distribution of benefits and burdens; and radical democrats who see progressive urban change happening only through the exercise of power by citizens generally excluded from the decision-making processes. Both approaches seek to get beyond the stakeholder approaches seen to characterize much of the work of communications theorists. Moreover, both variants understand the goal of planning and policy analysis as 'the analysis of the possibilities for attaining a better quality of human life within the context of a global capitalist political economy'. An approach to such analysis is to frame a model of the good city and then to examine how it might be realized. Such a model can be a theoretical utopia or extracted from other places that provide a unusually good quality of life (Fainstein 2000: 470).

Such a view clearly lifts the planner up out of the institutional confines of planning agency, and positively so. But the point that does not receive enough recognition here is that such a normative framework itself remains by its nature the stuff of political deliberation and discourse. There is no firm agreement to be found on what constitutes a superior quality of life, or which means might be acceptable in pursuing it. Paris, for instance, is a beautiful city, but large parts of it were built through means that most of these theorists scarcely accept. Thus, the just city model does not resolve the question of planning theory; it only moves it to a higher level of theoretical/normative discourse. And it is in this respect that we can return to the discursive model presented in Chapter 9 and understand the task of a discourse perspective as connecting the various levels of planning or policy discourse. That is, the communication theorists, in their concentration on the discourses of working planners, have largely focused on deliberations at the levels of technical verification and situational validation and in the process have largely neglected the higher-level discourses of societal vindication and ideological critique. Although such concerns might indeed be in the minds of some of the participants, they are seldom heard in the meeting rooms of the planning office.

But, of course, the opposite point can be made against the critics. They have largely ignored the practical tasks of communication at the level of the workplace and the community, mainly assuming them away as either uninteresting or unimportant in the larger political scheme of things. For their part, they have directed attention to second-order issues of justice and equality at the expense of first-order concerns.

Viewed in terms of the levels of discourse, the task of the communicative approach is to develop a more comprehensive perspective across all four levels of practical deliberation, one that connects the first-order discursive practices in the institutions with the second-order critique of the societal institutions themselves.

Among contemporary communicative planning theorists, the work of Healey is in this respect perhaps the most sensitive to these political contextual concerns.[2] Healey acknowledges that government planners are forced to represent and defend agency political decisions and seldom have the possibility of functioning as facilitators of debate. But it is nonetheless important, she argues, to recognize that power relations 'are part of us, and they exist through us, and citizens should therefore be aware of the sources of power they can seek and develop' (1997: 66). If the planner or policy analyst is aware of how to challenge the dominant power system, it is possible to struggle to change the existing forces rather than merely reproducing them. Collaboration, in her view, is seen as a way of connecting community members across disparate networks, and in the process can change their ways of seeing, knowing, and acting. In this way, collaborative planning, as communicative power, has the potential to alter power relationships.

For Healey (1997: 244–5), then, 'a process of deliberate paradigm change' refers to the need to engage 'the consciousness of the political and organization culture of a place'. Envisioned as an enlightenment strategy, it involves 'embedding new cultural conceptions, systems of understanding and systems of meaning' in the world views of social actors. As an approach that seeks to reveal exploitative structures, communicative structures in this case, it can help citizens become better aware of their own interests and how to pursue them (Ploger 2001: 225).

Collaborative planning also means identifying or creating political spaces for democratic participation and representative governance that can supply a place for reason in both goal-setting and conflict management.[3] By asking who is privileged and who is marginalized by existing forms of governance, inclusionary planning and policy analysis challenges the formal institutions to be democratic and collaborative (Healy 1997: 201). The task is to both make clear the sorts of power that oppress and to obtain the kinds of knowledge that lead to empowerment.

Often lurking beneath these debates is a more fundamental question about the nature of social change and how to bring it about. Whereas the just-city critics typically call for political struggle on material considerations (usually involving people protesting around city hall to put direct pressure on decision-makers), communicative theorists more typically rely on a theory of social change that understands the need for a critical dialectic between the objective structures of existing institutional arrangements and the subjective understandings of the actors working in them, especially those who seek

---

[2] Focusing less on the working role or words of the planner, Healey's work emphasizes the need to bring in the voices of all those involved in the construction and uses of planning discourses. But she sees the planner as more than a facilitator. As she puts it, the task is 'to be able to mobilize enough attention to be able to address difficult policy issues'. In the process, the planner seeks to supply *different kinds* of knowledge to those involved in the process (personal communication, 15 August 2002).

[3] For Healy (personal communication, 15 August 2002), 'a place for reason' includes 'being prepared to argue, bring values, gut reactions, etc. out into the open, to inspect what "reasons" they give us for deciding something and to examine alternative reasons and ways of reasoning'.

change. Change, in this view, is a subtle process that, to be sure, occurs slowly and mainly incrementally. But it does occur and for communicative theorists an important precondition for change—indeed, at times the motor of such change—is a tension between a critical understanding of existing practices and the institutions themselves. Even radical change, mainly the product of forces external to the institutions, requires people—change agents—inside the agencies who can do the communicative work of, first, representing the views of people in the streets in the course of the struggle and, secondly, later translating the issues and demands into new organizational practices (Needleman and Needleman 1974). A critical communicative planner or policy analysis is thus part of the struggle for change, even a necessary part, seeking to move institutions in directions of greater democracy and social equity.

In many ways the question here is not so much whether one can work inside the bureaucracy but rather how to change the bureaucracy. Too often one still confronts the age-old question of piecemeal versus revolutionary change, an either/or debate that largely goes nowhere. A more sophisticated view understands an interaction between the larger forces of social change and the more gradual struggles that take place in and through the institutions.[4]

It is also a question that takes us back to the Habermas–Foucault debate in the postempiricist camp. Whereas the Foucauldians emphasize the large historical questions, they have neglected the normative questions of agency in the social life-world. On the other hand, it is just these micro communicative struggles that the Habermasians take on, but too often at the expense of the larger socio-historical contexts in which they take place. The task ahead for critical planners and policy analysts is to develop a theory of agency that is appropriately situated in the larger macro political contexts in which micro struggles take place. In the language of the levels of discourse, we need a theory that includes both the local dimensions of first-order discourse and the larger societal and ideological concerns of second-order discourse.

From the perspective of the everyday practical tasks of planning and policy analysis these discourses can be better conceptualized in the model of participatory research than in the stakeholder model. First, as we saw in Chapter 10, it lifts the tasks of the policy analysts out of the narrower context of the agency analyst; secondly, it is explicitly geared to the processes of public enlightenment and citizen empowerment. In this respect, the kind of listening that Forester suggests should also be carried out in participatory research engaged in civil society, whether a community group trying to develop an alternative action plan or a social movement deliberating about alternative futures. In these settings, while still not ideal, the bureaucratic pressures of the agency are removed and the barriers of equality can be considerably reduced. It is here that we can better experiment with and test alternative approaches to participatory democracy.

---

[4] The Soviet Union, for example, didn't disband simply because of powerful historical economic and political forces, but also because an inside cadre of reformers recognized and began to lay plans for such a transition long before others knew anything about it. The result of their efforts was Michel Gorbachev and perestroika.

The task of the policy analyst and planner, of course, is not limited to the citizen empowerment and community oppositional strategies. Although the postempiricist policy analysts try to extend the range of interests in the deliberative process, most of them will still work for government, in one way or another. One way to bridge these competing tasks is to understand the deliberative dimension of participatory inquiry in the way that Throgmorton (1991) has suggested. For Throgmorton the postpositivist analyst has to mediate between three separate interpretive or epistemic communities—those of the scientific community, the political or policy decision-makers, and the public citizenry.

Each of these groups speaks a different language that does not necessarily communicate to the members of the other communities. As we have already seen, the scientific language of the policy analyst does not resonate well with the kinds of normative, goal-oriented deliberations of the decision-maker, nor with the public citizens who need a jargon-free discourse concerned as much with the social meanings of the recommendations as with the empirical findings seen to support them. For Throgmorton this means that the task of the postempiricial policy analyst has to be that of a translator across these differing interpretive communities. Situated between the scientific community, the political world of government, and the ordinary language world of the citizen, the policy analyst or planner has to learn the languages of each. Throgmorton (1991) illustrates the point with an example of such expert translation on the part of a biologist who assisted community members at the toxic waste site in Love Canal, New York, to organize and engage in 'popular epidemiology', a form of participatory research.

POLICY EPISTEMICS

Given the central role of these socio-epistemological issues, coupled with their sophistication, there is a need in policy inquiry for a new underlying specialization that might be suitably be called 'policy epistemics'.[5] Borrowing from Willard (1996: 5), epistemics addresses predicaments of modern decision-makers, namely, their dependence on the interrelationship of knowledge and authority, 'their inability to assess the states of consensus in disciplines, their incompetence in the face of burgeoning literatures, and their proneness to mistaken agreements.' Towards this end, policy epistemics would focus on the ways people communicate across differences, the flow and transformation of ideas across borders of different fields, how different professional groups and local communities see and inquire differently, and the ways in which differences become disputes. Of particular importance in this respect is the interaction between expert inquiry and the processes of political and policy argumentation.

Willard proposes the 'field of argument' as a unit of analysis. By 'argument' he means polemical conversation, disagreement, or dispute, which is the principal

---

[5] For a more extensive discussion of policy epistemics, see Fischer (2000). Following Sheila Jasanoff, one could also think in terms of 'civic epistemics'. Remarks at Workshop in Science and Democracy, Wissenschaftskolleg zu Berlin, 21–3 June 2002.

making a case: an argument

medium by which people—both citizens and scientists—maintain, relate, adapt, transform, and disregard ideas. Focusing on how people construct their policy arguments, policy epistemics would examine the interplay between specific statements or contentions and background consenses upon which they are constructed—traditions, practices, ideas, and methods of particular groups—of the groups that understand and communicate with them.

By 'field of argument' Willard means fields of inquiry organized around particular judgemental systems for deciding what counts as knowledge as well as the adjudication of competing claims. Such communities of inquiry, as vertically structured social entities, are defined as much by their disputes as their agreements. Although fields vary in the degree to which they inspire confidence, most policy-oriented fields are sufficiently public and open to criticism that people have enough confidence in them to consider them justifiable. One reason for that confidence, according to Willard, is the belief that the field itself can be held accountable in terms of its 'grasp and reach'. One can hope or expect to identify movement towards the achievement of the field's ideal, hopes, and ambitions.

For *policy* epistemics, this means focusing on arguments and debates that constitute and shape the various policy networks or 'policy communities' (the network of social scientists, policy experts, journalists, politicians, administrative practitioners, and involved citizens that engage in an ongoing discourse about policy matters in a particular substantive areas, such as health, poverty, and the environment). The goal would be to study the ways in which their members share background assumptions about the particular problem areas, their ideas about the relations of particular science to decision-making, the role—if any—for citizen involvement, and how they respond to outside opposition.

Another way to approach a field of argument is by studying the ways in which it gets organized or distributed across a particular policy agency. Policy organizations, those entities in which policy analysts typically serve, can be understood as arenas of policy argumentation. As structures designed to fit intentions to practices, such organizations are animated by practices harnessed to mundane realities. Their rationalities lie in the concrete cases in which knowledge is created, used, and changed. They differ because they are functionally fitted to different aims, methods, and contexts. As such, each field has its own sociology of knowledge. And for this reason we need to study these organizational bases of knowledge. This would include an ethnographic examination of how such organizational actors go about their discursive interactions, such as Forester (1999) has carried out in planning agencies.

Basic to policy epistemics would be the interrelationships between the empirical and the normative, the quantitative and qualitative inquiry. Whereas traditional policy analysis has focused on advancing and assessing technical solutions, policy epistemics would investigate the way interpretive judgements work in the production and distribution of knowledge. In particular, it would focus on the movements and uses of information, the social assumptions embedded in research designs, the specific relationships of different types of information to decision-making, the different ways arguments move across different disciplines and discourses, the translation of knowledges from one community to another, and the interrelation-ships between discourses and institutions. Most important, it would involve innova-tive methods needed for coordinating multiple discourses in and across institutions.

Grappling with the reliability of knowledge claims and the credibility of advocates is common to all policy fields, as we have seen in these pages. That failures in policy-making can often be attributable to simplistic technocratic understandings of these relationships is clearly seen in a wide range of cases, ranging from Nimby in envi-ronmental policy to development policy in the Third World. It is to these kinds of socio-cultural rationalities underlying citizens understandings and responses to expert advice that policy epistemics would turn our attention. It would it help to make clear not only why citizens are hesitant to accept the authority of the experts, but how that knowledge gets translated and processed in the citizens' interpretive community. Such knowledge would help us better understand the ways in which the various players react to the scientific uncertainties that plague such policy areas. It holds out the possibility of finding ways around the political stand-offs characteristic of 'intractable' policy problems. While policy epistemics might not offer us policy solutions per se, at least it could show us the ways to 'keep the conversation going' (Rorty 1979).

Policy studies has almost totally neglected this epistemic translation involved in policymaking. And it has done so at considerable cost. Many of the most important failures that the discipline has confronted can, as we have seen, be directly attribut-able to this neglect. Most significant for present purposes is the centrality of the issue to the relation of citizens to experts. Policy epistemics, for this reason, can be posed as a—perhaps the—major challenge involved in developing a more relevant mode of professional practice. Participatory democrats within the professions should place the working-through of these epistemic interconnections among citizens and experts and their institutional implications at the top of the research agenda. Whether we are talking about large or small numbers of citizens (for instance, a political party or an advisory group), the prospects of democracy in a complex society would seem to depend on it.

THE CURRICULUM: PARTICIPATORY TRAINING AND QUALITATIVE INQUIRY

Nowhere are the implications of such policy epistemics more important than in the contemporary policy curriculum. Still largely dominated by an outmoded conception of scientific epistemology, the social and policy sciences ill-equip their students (especially doctoral students) for the world they are sent out to confront. Armed mainly with empirical research designs and statistical methods, many of them have little or no training to understand the normative and interpretive foundations of the tools they have learned to rely upon, or the social setting to which these techniques are to be applied. Some, to be sure, recognize these interpretive dimensions of the practices, but for reasons of examination and employment are compelled to con-centrate on empirical methods. As students come to see the limits of these methods, the disciplinary neglect of these issues and concerns can breed more than a little cynicism. Some simply are turned off; others go through the academic ritual but turn away from—if not against—these methods after jumping over the requisite set of hurdles.

For a long time, a major argument—sometimes more tacitly understood than articulated—against changing the curricular focus has turned on the problem of alternatives. Give the absence of credible alternatives, so the argument goes, it is better to hang on to the traditional—albeit problematic—methods than to step into a methodological void. But this no longer need be the case. Postempiricism, as we have shown here, sufficiently outlines the beginnings of a new orientation. Not only does it offer a theory of the social sciences that is readily identifiable in our existing practices, it also constitutes an incorporation of new methods and approaches rather than a simple rejection of old ones. By giving new life to our methods and practices, it opens the way to a richer and more productive approach to social and policy inquiry.

To be sure, the issues of curriculum reform raise some daunting questions. In the remaining discussion we outline two of them. At issue here is the need to eliminate the dominant professional commitment to—and trust in—the superiority of technical rationalities and the hierarchical superior-subordinate practices that accompany them. In the case of participatory inquiry, for example, once we recognize that it is as much a creative undertaking (resembling an art form as much as a science), we venture into complicated pedagogical territories. Unlike formal scientific methodology, the craft of participatory inquiry can have no set formulas, making it difficult to teach. How, for example, do we educate students of the professions to appreciate the emancipatory potentials of a situation or, say, the boundaries of human virtue? This no doubt requires greater exposure to the humanities—history, novels, and poetry—than regression analysis.

Basically, what we are talking about is developing and introducing the postempiricist curriculum (based on theory and methods of the type introduced in Part III). For this reason, we need only note here that we know a fair amount about what such a methodology looks like; the problem is that it remains at the margins, if not altogether outside, of the standard curriculum. Social constructionism shows that socio-cultural judgements are already part of the process (they are just embedded in ways that largely obscure them). From a constructionist perspective, moreover, we can see that a postempiricist epistemology offers a better understanding of what professionals are already doing than does neopositivist empiricism. The task is then is as much political and practical as epistemological. Adopting postempiricism involves countering ideological arguments and the interests that support empiricism more than it does introducing a new and speculative epistemological formula.

The second point is in many ways much more difficult: it involves the problem of socializing professionals into a more egalitarian, democratic relationship with nonprofessionals. This places unique social-psychological demands on the professional. Given that one of the major reasons why people become experts is to enjoy greater socio-economic status and authority, we confront here the problem of career ambition—often coupled with ego problems—and the continual temptations offered by more attractive, upwardly mobile career opportunities. This is to say that, if such cooperative research is to work, it requires experts with high levels of social commitment and personal self-development.

This means confronting the social, emotional, and intellectual distance that separates the professional from the client's experiential life-world. Such training has to bring professionals into closer contact with the clients' natural settings—their everyday experiences, culture, and interests. The practitioner has to also appreciate that a commitment to participatory dialogue, although clearly political in its import, is not to be confused with political proselytizing. The facilitator may passionately advance ideas about how people should think and act, but his or her views must be presented to the learners for the same kind of critical scrutiny to which the educator subjects other views (of which he or she is personally critical). Theoretically, this point is obvious, but in practice it is much more difficult than we normally recognize or acknowledge. Participatory research, as well as participatory inquiry in general, thus poses sophisticated challenges for professional training. This is especially the case as it raises issues of professional conduct—in particular behaviour and attitudes towards client groups—more than it does matters of research methodology per se. One major issue concerns the role of leadership. Because it is egalitarian—even radically egalitarian—participatory research places unique demands on those who seek to initiate it. As Rahman (1991: 84) argues, in so far as 'movements for social change are normally led by intellectuals who are in a position to provide leadership not because of any particular aptitude but because they are privileged by their economic and social status', there are 'many dangers of relying on an elite leadership for social transformation: the dangers of inflated egos, the fragility of the commitment in the face of attractive temptations; the problems of the growth in size of the elite class as a movement grows and the danger of attracting new adherents holding altogether different commitments', as well as the self-perpetuating nature of institutions established to supply such leadership.

These changes underscore a central tension in participatory inquiry. Unless someone with the skills, commitment, and time is willing to initiate such a research project, it will almost never come into existence. Almost inevitably, such persons are members of a privileged, educated group with elite status in the society, especially in the developing world. For such research to work, however, it also has to be conducted by people with high levels of personal self-development. One of the most important but often overlooked psychological dimensions is the ability or skill of finding 'ways of sidestepping one's own and others' defensive responses to the painful process of self-reflection' (Reason 1994: 332). The training to reach such interpersonal skills, or what Torbert (1976) describes as 'transformational leadership', has to be rigorous and formidable. In response to the challenge, numerous researchers have developed and established training programmes for the teaching of such interpersonal, participatory inquiry.

Basic to such training must be the tension between participation and the practical demands of competence and leadership. The tension, as a 'living paradox', is something the professional has to learn to live with; it requires finding a 'creative resolution moment to moment'. It can be worked out only through an 'emergent process that participants are first led through' which they can then 'amend and develop in the light of their experience, and finally embrace as their own' (Reason 1994: 335). Heron (1989) sees the management of this tension to involve a never-ending balance among hierarchical structure and the legitimate exercise of authority, group recognition of peers and shared power, and a respect for each group member's right to exercise his or her judgement.

Once we recognize that participatory research is as much a creative art as a science, we venture into complicated pedagogical territories. Scientific methodology texts, perhaps unfortunately, can be organized like cookbooks. An art form is a different matter. Not only are there no set formulas, little is known about the creative impulse itself. How, for example, do we educate an analyst to appreciate the range of human folly or the boundaries of human virtue? How do we train the investigator to intuitively sense openings and opportunities in human affairs? If there is an answer, it no doubt includes greater exposure to the creative arts, novels, poetry, culture, and so on. But these are only generalities; the question remains open.

Beyond the creative dimension, however, one requirement is relatively straightforward. In more immediate terms, the professional-client collaboration requires the expert to have special knowledge of the client's needs, interests, and values. Towards this end, there have been numerous projects designed to re-socialize professionals to the client's 'natural setting'. Gottlieb and Farquharson (1985: 31), for example, have spelled out the elements of a pedagogical strategy designed to accommodate the student-practitioner 'to the ways that citizens handle their own health and welfare needs'. Most important is 'the need first to undermine the professional's trust and beliefs in the ascendancy of technology, and force a reexamination of a professional enterprise that casts nonprofessionals into the subservient role of client or patient'. Specifically, professionals must gain first-hand knowledge of encounters with self-help groups and other collective projects. They must 'get acquainted with local residents who have animated and enabled others to take into their own hands the responsibility for effecting change'; and they must learn at first hand 'the empowering impact of a mutual-aid group'.

In addition to teaching the standard analytical methods, then, an alternative approach to professional training means building into the curriculum educational experiences that bring the student into closer contact with clients' everyday experiences, language, local knowledge, and culture. Such experiences must be designed to wean professionals away from their faith in technique, their adherence to hierarchy, and their reliance on the ideologies of expertise.

The training must also pay special attention to the political dimensions of facilitation in the expert-client relationship. Facilitation and its problem-posing orientation are founded on the long-established but largely ignored assumption that teaching and education, including the creation and change of beliefs and values, and actions are ways through which we manifest and affirm our humanity (Brookfield 1986). Although clearly political in its import, a commitment to such dialogue is not in and of itself to be confused with a commitment to a specific doctrine or ideology. For participatory researchers firmly committed to democratic values, educational facilitation and political proselytizing are geared to fundamentally different objectives. Political ideologues, accepting their beliefs as the one true way of thinking about the world, proselytize with a predetermined definition of the successful outcome; diverging views are simply dismissed as wrong thinking, bad faith, or false consciousness. By contrast, the facilitator may passionately advance ideas about how people should learn and act, but such views must themselves be presented to learners for the same kind of critical scrutiny to which the educator has subjected other views of which he or she is personally critical. The end of the encounter, in other words, is not the acceptance by participants of the facilitator's preordained values and beliefs. Rather, it is to pose problems and questions for critical dialogue and group consensus-formation.

CONCLUSION

In this final chapter we took up more specifically the conduct of policy analysis, in particular the role of the policy analyst as facilitator of deliberative practices, or the 'deliberative practitioner', in Forester's conceptualization. The professional expert, as a practitioner of a policy science of democracy, serves as facilitator of public learning and political empowerment. By examining communicative interactions in policy argumentation and institutional politics, deliberative practitioners seeks to advance discursive interaction through collaborative methods of inquiry. Drawing on Habermas's theory of communicative action in an effort to foster democratic forms of deliberation, they work to uncover the hidden or distorted dimensions of communicative power. Towards this end, they have theoretically formulated a self-critical mode of communicative practices that weaves together advocacy planning, social learning, and practical reason.

The discussion then answered a number of criticisms that have been directed at the communicative model, especially its neglect of important empirical and normative issues inherent to the practice of planning. In an effort to lift the communicative perspective up from a narrow focus on the deliberative activities in planning agencies to include both the larger empirical dynamics of urban processes and the pressing questions of social justice, the chapter recast the arguments in the framework of the four-level model of policy deliberation put forward in Chapter 9. Viewed this way, the goal of the communications approach would be a more comprehensive model of discourse that connects the first-order communicative practices in the institutions with the second-order discourses concerning the larger societal institutions and world views of which they are a part.

In addition to bringing in the missing discourses, such a model helps to remind us that discourse always takes place within a configuration of power and that the task of the critical planner or policy analyst is to dialectically engage the existing political forces rather than merely reproduce them. Towards this end, the objective of collaborative planning is to create political spaces for democratic participation that offer a place for reason in both goal-setting and conflict management. Asking who is privileged and who is marginalized by the established forms of governance, such policy analysis challenges the formal policy institutions to be democratic and collaborative. Basic to this task are forms of participatory policy analysis.

The chapter then sought to promote a 'policy epistemics' for discursive policy analysis, focused on the ways people communicate across differences, how ideas flow and are transformed across boundaries of different fields, how different professional groups and local communities see and inquire differently, and what turns differences into disputes. Whereas traditional policy analysis has emphasized technical solutions, policy epistemics would underscore the role of interpretive judgements in the production and distribution of knowledge. Finally, the chapter examined some of the implications of a discursive, participatory approach for the policy analysis curriculum.

References

Adams, G. B. and Richardson, L. (2002). 'Deliberative Governance: Building a New Public Service'. Paper presented at the Annual Meeting of the American Political Science Association, Boston, 29 August.

Agger, B. (1990). *The Decline of Discourse: Reading, Writing, and Resistance in Postmodern Capitalism*. New York: Falmer.

Allison, G. T. (1971). *Essence of Decision: Explaining the Cuban Missile Crisis*. Boston: Little, Brown.

Althusser, L. (1971). 'Ideology and Ideological State Apparatuses', in L. Althusser (ed.), *Lenin and Philosophy and Other Essays*. London: New Left Books.

American Talk Issues Foundation (1994). 'Steps for Democracy: The Many versus the Few', 24 (January): 9–19.

Amy, D. (1987). 'Can Policy Analysis be Ethical?', in F. Fischer and J. Forester (eds.), *Confronting Values in Policy Analysis*. Newbury Park, CA: Sage.

Andersen, I. and Jaeger, B. (1999). 'Scenario Workshops and Consensus Conferences: Towards More Democratic Decision-Making'. *Science and Public Policy*, 26: 331–40.

Anderson, C. W. (1978). 'The Logic of Public Problems: Evaluation in Comparative Policy Research', in D. Ashford (ed.), *Comparing Public Policies: New Concepts and Methods*. Beverly Hills, CA: Sage.

Anderson, M. S. and Liefferin, D. (eds.) (1997). *European Environmental Policy*. Manchester: University of Manchester Press.

Austin, J. L. (1962). *How to Do Things with Words*. Cambridge, MA: Harvard University Press.

Baker, R. (1985). 'The Queen Gambit', *New York Times*, 19 June: A23.

Ball, T. (1987). 'Deadly Hermeneutics; or, Sinn and the Social Scientist', in T. Ball (ed.), *Idioms of Inquiry: Critique and Renewal in Political Science*. Albany, NY: SUNY Press.

Banfield, E. (1970). *The Unheavenly City*. Boston: Little, Brown.

Barber, B. R. (1984). *Strong Democracy*. Berkeley: University of California Press.

Battistelli, F. and Ricotta, G. (2001). 'Management Rhetoric and Citizen Participation in Three Italian Cities: The Politics of Administrative Reform'. Paper presented at the Annual Meeting of the American Political Science Association, San Francisco, 31 August.

Baudrillard, J. (1989). *America*. New York: Verso Books.

Baumgartner, F. and Jones, B. (1983). *Agendas and Instability in American Politics*. Chicago: University of Chicago Press.

Baumol, W. J. (1991). 'Toward a Newer Economics: The Future Lies Ahead!'. *Economic Journal*, 101: 1–8.

Beck, J. (1986). *Communication and Domination*. New York: Ablex.

Beck, U. (1995). *Ecological Politics in the Age of Risk*. London: Polity Press.

Bell, D. (1973). *The Coming of Post-Industrial Society*. New York: Basic Books.

Bennett, C. J. and Howlett, M. (1992). 'The Lessons of Learning: Reconciling Theories of Policy Learning and Policy Change'. *Policy Sciences*, 2: 275–94.

Berger, P. and Luckmann, T. (1966). *The Social Construction of Reality: A Sociology of Knowledge*. London: Penguin Books.

Berger, T. (1977). *Northern Frontier, Northern Homeland: The Report of the Mackenzie Valley Pipeline Inquiry*, Vols 1–2. Ottawa: Supply and Services Canada.

——(1985). *Village Journey. The Report of the Alaska Native Review Commission*. New York: Wang and Hill.

Bernstein, R. J. (1976). *The Restructuring of Social and Political Theory*. New York: Harcourt Brace Jovanovich.

——(1983). *Between Objectivism and Relativism: Science, Hermeneutics, and Praxis*. Philadelphia: University of Pennsylvania.

Best, J. (1989). *Images of Issues: Typifying Contemporary Social Problems*. New York: Aldine De Gruyter.

Bobrow, D. and Dryzek, J. (1987). *Policy Analysis by Design*. Pittsburgh: University of Pittsburgh Press.

Bogason, P. (2000). *Public Policy and Local Governance: Institutions in Postmodern Society*. Cheltenham: Edgar Elgar.

Bohman, J. (1991). *New Philosophy of Social Science: Problems of Indeterminacy*. Cambridge, MA: MIT Press.

——(1996). *Public Deliberation: Pluralism, Complexity, and Democracy*. Cambridge, MA: MIT Press.

——and Rehg (eds.) (1997). *Deliberative Democracy*. Cambridge, MA: MIT Press.

Borel, A. (1983). 'Mathematics: Art and Science'. *Mathematical Intelligencer*, 5/4: 9–17.

Boyte, H. (2000). 'The Struggle Against Positivism'. *Academe*, 86/4: 46–51.

Bozeman, B. (1986). 'The Credibility of Policy Analysis: Between Method and Use'. *Policy Studies Journal*, 14: 519–39.

Braun, K. and Herrmann, S. L. (2001). 'If Discourse is the Solution—What is the Problem? The Politics of Discourse on Biomedicine in Germany'. European Consortium for Political Research, 29th Joint Sessions of Workshops, 6–11 April, Grenoble, France.

Brookfield, S. D. (1986). *Understanding and Facilitating Adult Learning*. San Francisco: Jossey-Bass.

Brooks, S. and Gagnon, A. (eds.) (1994). *The Political Influence of Ideas: Policy Communities and the Social Sciences*. Westport, CT: Praeger.

Brown, N. (1977). *Perception, Theory and Commitment: The New Philosophy of Science*. Chicago: Precedent Publishing.

Brown, P. G. (1976). 'Ethics and Policy Research'. *Policy Analysis*, 2: 325–40.

Brown, P. and Mikkelsen, E. (1990). *No Safe Place: Toxic Waste, Leukemia, and Community Action*. Berkeley: University of California Press.

Brown, R. H. (1977). *A Poetic for Sociology: Toward a Logic of Discovery for the Human Sciences*. New York: Cambridge University Press.

Bruner, J. (1986). *Actual Minds, Possible Worlds*. Cambridge: Harvard University Press.

Buergergutachten Uestra (1996). *Attraktiver Oeffentlicher Personennahverkehr in Hannover*. Bonn: Stiftung Mitarbeit.

Burke, K. (1945). *A Grammar of Motives*. New York: Prentice-Hall.

——(1950). *A Rhetoric of Motives*. New York: Prentice-Hall.

Buethe, T. (2002). 'Taking Temporality Seriously: Modeling History and the Use of Narratives as Evidence'. *American Political Science Review*, 96: 481–93.

Cain, G. G. and Holister, R. G. (1972). 'The Methodology of Evaluating Social Programs', in P. Rossi and W. Williams (eds.), *Evaluating Social Programs*. New York: Seminar Press.

Caldwell, L. K. (1975). 'Managing the Transition to Post-Modern Society'. *Public Administration Review*, 35: 567–72.

Callon, M. (1996). 'Four Models for the Dynamics of Science', in S. Jasanoff *et al.* (eds.), *Handbook of Science and Technology*. Newbury Park, CA: Sage.

Cancian, F. and Armstead, C. (1992). 'Participatory Research', in E. F. Borgatta and M. Borgatta (eds.), *Encyclopedia of Sociology*. New York: Macmillan.

Caplan, N. (1979). 'The Two Communities Theory and Knowledge Utilization'. *American Behavioral Scientist*, 22: 459–70.

Chambers, R. (1997). *Who Reality Counts? Putting the First Last*. London: Intermediate Technology Publications.

Churchman, C. W. (1971). *The Design of Inquiring Systems*. New York: Basic Books.

Clemons, R. S. and McBeth, M. K. (2001). *Public Policy Praxis*. Englewood Cliffs, NJ: Prentice Hall.

Cobb, R. W. and Elder, C. D. (1972). *Participation in American Politics: The Dynamics of Agenda-Building*. Boston: Allyn and Bacon.

—— —— (1983). *The Political Uses of Symbols*. New York: Longman.

Cohn, J. (1999). 'Irrational Exuberance: When Did Political Science Forget About Politics?' *The New Republic Online*, 25 October: 1–14.

Collingsridge, D. and Reeves, C. (1986). *Science Speaks to Power: The Role of Experts in Policymaking*. New York: St Martin's Press.

Collins, H. (1992). *Changing Order: Replication and Induction in Scientific Practice*. Chicago: University of Chicago Press.

Cooke, B. and Kothari, U. (eds.) (2001). *Participation: The New Tyranny?* London: Zed Books.

Cox, R. (1994). 'The Crisis in World Order and the Challenge to International Organization'. *Cooperation and Conflict*, 29: 99–113.

Crosby, N. (1995). 'Citizens Juries: One Solution for Difficult Environmental Problems', in O. Renn, T. Webler, and P. Wiedermann, P. (eds.), *Fairness and Competence in Citizen Participation: Evaluating Models for Environmental Discourse*. Dordrecht, Netherlands: Kluwer.

——, Kelly, J., and Shaeffer, P. (1986). 'Citizens Panels: A New Approach to Citizen Participation'. *Public Administration Review*, 46: 170–8.

Czarniawska, B. (1997). *Narrating the Organization: Dramas of Institutional Identity*. Chicago: University of Chicago Press.

—— (1998). *A Narrative Approach to Organizational Studies*. Thousand Oaks: Sage.

Danziger, M. (1995). 'Policy Analysis Postmodernized: Some Political and Pedagogical Ramifications'. *Policy Studies Journal*, 23: 435–50.

deLeon, P. (1988). *Advice and Consent: The Development the Policy Sciences*. New York: Russell Sage Foundation.

—— (1992). 'The Democratization of the Policy Sciences'. *Public Administration Review*, 52: 125–9.

—— (1997). *Democracy and the Policy Sciences*. Albany, NY: New York: SUNY Press.

—— (1999). 'The Stages Approach to the Policy Process: What Has It Done? Where Is It Going?', in P. A. Sabatier (ed.), *Theories of the Policy Process*. Boulder, CO: Westview Press.

DeLeuze, G. and Guatani, F. (1987). *A Thousand Plateaus*. London: Athlone Press.

Denzin, N. (1989). *Interpretive Interactionism*. Newbury Park, CA: Sage.

—— (1997). *Interpretive Ethnography*. Thousand Oaks, CA: Sage.

—— and Lincoln, Y. S. (eds.) (2000). *Handbook of Qualitative Research*. London: Sage, 324–39.

Dewey, J. (1927). *The Public and its Problems*. New York: Swallow.

Diesing, P. (1962). *Reason in Society. Five Types of Decisions in Their Social Contexts*. Urbana: University of Illinois Press.

Dienel, P. C. (1992). *Die Plannungszelle: Eine Alternative zur Establisment-Demokratie*. Opladen: Westdeutscher Verlag.

Douglas, M. (1988). *Purity and Danger—An Analysis of the Concepts of Pollution and Taboo*. London: Routledge.

Dowie, M. (1995). *Losing Ground: American Environmentalism at the Close of the Twentieth Century*. Cambridge, MA: MIT Press.

Dray, W. (1957). *Laws and Explanation in History*. Oxford: Oxford University Press.

Dryzek, J. S. (1982). 'Policy Analysis as a Hermeneutic Activity'. *Policy Sciences*, 14: 309–29.

——(1990). *Discursive Democracy*. Cambridge: Cambridge University Press.

Dunn, W. N. (1981). *Public Policy Analysis*. Englewood Cliffs, NJ: Prentice-Hall.

——(1988). 'Methods of the Second Type: Coping with the Wilderness of Conventional Policy Analysis'. *Policy Studies Review*, 9: 720–37.

——(1993). 'Policy Reforms as Arguments', in F. Fischer and J. Forester (eds.), *The Argumentative Turn in Policy Analysis and Planning*. Durham, NC: Duke University Press, 254–90.

Durning, D. (1993). 'Participatory Policy Analysis in a Georgia State Agency'. *Journal of Policy Analysis and Management*, 12: 297–322.

——(1999). 'The Transition from Traditional to Postpositivist Policy Analysis: A Role for Q-Methodology'. *Journal of Policy Analysis and Management*, 18: 389–410.

Dye, T. R. (1984). *Understanding Public Policy*. Englewood Cliffs, NJ: Prentice-Hall.

Eakin, E. (2000). 'Political Scientists Leading a Revolt, Not Studying One'. *New York Times*, 4 November: B11.

Edelman, M. (1971). *Politics as Symbolic Action: Mass Arousal and Quiescence*. New York: Academic Press.

——(1971). *Politics as Symbolic Action: Mass Arousal and Quiescence*. New York: Academic Press.

——(1977). *Political Language: Words that Succeed and Policies That Fail*. New York: Academic Press.

——(1988). *Constructing the Political Spectacle*. Chicago: Chicago University Press.

——(2001). *The Politics of Misinformation*. Cambridge: Cambridge University Press.

Edelstein, M. R. (1988). *Contaminated Communities*. Boulder, CO: Westview Press.

Eldon, M. (1981). 'Sharing the Research Work: Participative Research and its Role Demands', in P. Reason and J. Rowan (eds.), *Human Inquiry: A Sourcebook of New Paradigm Research*. New York: John Wiley.

Entman, R. M. (1993). 'Framing: Toward a Clarification of a Fractured Paradigm'. *Journal of Communication*, 43/4: 51–8.

Epstein, S. (1996). *Impure Science: AIDS, Activism, and the Politics of Knowledge*. Berkeley: University of California Press.

Erlandson, D. A., Harris, E. L., Skipper, B. L., and Allen, S. D. (1993). *Doing Naturalistic Inquiry: A Guide to Methods*. Newbury Park, CA: Sage.

Fainstein, S. (2000). 'New Directions in Planning Theory'. *Urban Affairs Review*, 35: 451–78.

Fairclough, N. (1992). *Discourse and Social Change*. Cambridge: Polity Press.

Fairhead, J. and Leach, M. (1998). *Reframing Deforestation: Global Analysis and Local Realities*. London: Routledge.

Farr, J. (1987). 'Resituating Explanation', in T. Ball (ed.), *Idioms of Inquiry: Critique and Renewal in Political Science*. Albany, NY: SUNY Press.

Fay, B. (1975). *Social Theory and Political Practice*. New York: Holmes and Meyers.

——(1996). *Contemporary Philosophy of Social Science*. Oxford: Blackwell.

Fiorina, M. P. (2000). 'When the States Are High, Rationality Kicks In'. *New York Times*, 26 February: B11.

Fiorino, D. J. (1990). 'Citizen Participation and Environmental Risk: A Survey of Institutional Mechanisms'. *Science, Technology, and Human Values*, 15: 226–43.

Fischer, F. (1980). *Politics, Values, and Public Policy: The Problem of Methodology*. Boulder, CO: Westview Press.

——(1985). 'Critical Evaluation of Public Policy: A Methodological Case Study', in J. Forester (ed.), *Critical Theory and Public Life*. Cambridge, MA: MIT Press.

——(1987). 'Policy Expertise and the "New Class": A Critique of the Neoconservative Thesis', in F. Fischer and J. Forester (eds.), *Confronting Values in Policy Analysis: The Politics of Criteria*. Newbury Park, CA: Sage.

——(1990). *Technocracy and the Politics of Expertise*. Newbury Park, CA: Sage.

——(1991a). 'Risk Assessment and Environmental Crisis: Toward an Integration of Science and Participation'. *Industrial Crisis Quarterly*, 5: 113–32.

——(1991b). 'American Think Tanks: Policy Elites and the Politicization of Expertise'. *Governance*, 4: 332–53.

——(1992). 'Participatory Expertise: Toward the Democratization of Policy Science', in W. Dunn and R. Kelly (eds.), *Advances in Policy Studies since 1950*. New Brunswick: Transaction Press.

——(1993). 'Policy Discourse and the Politics of Washington Think Tanks', in F. Fischer and J. Forester (eds.), *The Argumentative Turn in Policy Analysis and Planning*. Durham, NC: Duke University Press.

——(1995a). *Evaluating Public Policy*. Belmont, CA: Wadsworth.

——(1995b). 'From Technocracy to Participatory Research: First World Practices and Third World Alternatives', in B. Galjart and P. Silva (eds.), *Designers of Development: Intellectuals and Technocrats in the Third World*. Leiden, Holland: CNWS Publications.

——(1998). 'Beyond Empiricism: Policy Inquiry in Postpositivist Perspective'. *Policy Studies Journal*, 26: 129–47.

——(2000). *Citizens, Experts, and the Environment: The Politics of Local Knowledge*. Durham, NC: Duke University Press.

——and Forester, J. (eds.) (1987). *Confronting Values in Policy Analysis: The Politics of Criteria*. Newbury Park, CA: Sage.

————(1993). *The Argumentative Turn in Policy Analysis and Planning*. Durham, NC: Duke University Press.

——and Hajer, M. (eds.) (1999). *Living with Nature: Environmental Politics as Cultural Discourse*. Oxford: Oxford University Press.

Fisher, W. R. (1989). *Human Communication as Narration: Toward a Philosophy of Reason, Value, and Action*. Columbia: University of South Carolina Press.

Fishkin, J. S. (1996). *The Voice of the People: Public Opinion and Democracy*. New Haven, CT: Yale University Press.

Flyvbjerg, B. (1996). 'The Dark Side of Planning: Rationality and Realrationalitaet', in S. J. Mandelbaum, L. Mazza, and R. W. Burchell (eds.), *Explorations in Planning Theory*. New Brunswick, NJ: Rutgers University Press.

——(2000). *Making Social Science Matter*. Cambridge: Cambridge University Press.

Forester, J. (1985). *Critical Theory and Public Life*. Cambridge, MA: MIT Press.

—— (1993). *Critical Theory, Public Policy, and Planning Practices*. Albany, NY: SUNY Press.

—— (1999). *The Deliberative Practitioner: Encouraging Participatory Planning Processes*. Cambridge: Cambridge University Press.

Foucault, M. (1972). *The Archeology of Knowledge*. New York: Pantheon.

—— (1973). *The Order of Things*. New York: Vintage Books.

—— (1977). *Discipline and Punish*. New York: Pantheon.

—— (1980). *Power/Knowledge: Selected Interviews and Other Writings 1972–77* (ed. C. Gordeon). Brighton: Harvester Press.

—— (1984). *The Foucault Reader*. New York: Pantheon.

Fox, C. J. (1995). 'Reinventing Government as Postmodern Symbolic Politics'. Paper presented at the Annual Meeting of the American Society of Public Administration, San Antonio, Texas, 22–6 July.

—— and Miller, H. T. (1996). *Postmodern Public Administration: Toward Discourse*. Thousand Oaks, CA: Sage.

Fraser, N. (1989). *Unruly Practices: Power, Discourse, and Gender in Contemporary Social Theory*. Minneapolis: University of Minnesota Press.

—— (1997). 'Sex, Lies, and the Public Sphere: Reflections on the Confirmation of Clarence Thomas', in N. Fraser (ed.), *Justice Interruptus: Critical Reflections on the 'Postsocialist' Condition*. New York/London: Routledge.

Freire, P. (1970). *Pedagogy of the Oppressed*. New York: Seabury Press.

—— (1973). *Education for Critical Consciousness*. New York: Seabury Press.

Friedmann, J. (1973). *Retracking America*. New York: Doubleday.

—— (1987). *Planning in the Public Domain*. Princeton: Princeton University Press.

Gabrielian, V. (1998). 'Toward a Discursive Comparative Public Management: Study of Privatization in the U.S., U.K. and Russia'. Ph.D thesis, Department of Public Administration, Rutgers University.

Gadamer, G. (1976). *Philosophical Hermeneutics*. Berkeley: University of California Press.

Gaddis, J. L. (2002). *The Landscape of History*. New York: Oxford University Press.

Galison, P. (1997). *Image and Logic: A Material Culture of Microphysics*. Chicago: University of Chicago.

Gamson, W. A. (1995). 'Constructing Social Protest', in H. Johnson and B. Klandermans (eds.), *Social Movements and Culture*. London: UCL Press.

Geertz, C. (1973). *Interpretations of Cultures*. New York: Basic Books.

—— (1983). *Local Knowledge: Further Essays in Interpretive Knowledge*. New York: Basic Books.

George, A. (1972). 'The Case of Multiple Advocacy in Making Foreign Policy'. *American Political Science Review*, 66: 761–85.

Gergen, K. J. (1999). *An Invitation to Social Construction*. Thousand Oaks, CA: Sage.

Gibbons, M. (1987*a*). 'Interpretation, Genealogy and Human Agency', in T. Ball (ed.), *Idioms of Inquiry: Critique and Renewal in Political Science*. Albany, NY: SUNY Press.

—— (1987*b*). 'Introduction: The Politics of Interpretation', in M. Gibbons (ed.), *Interpreting Politics*. New York: New York University Press.

Giddens, A. (1995). 'In Defence of Sociology'. *New Statesman and Society*, 7 April.

Gill, S. (ed.) (1993). *Gramsci: Historical Materialism and International Relations*. Cambridge: Cambridge University Press.

Giovannoli, R. (2000). 'The Narrative Method of Inquiry.' www.somic.net/~rgiovan/essay.2.ht

Gleick, J. (1987). *Chaos Theory: Making a New Science*. New York: Viking.

Goffman, E. (1974). *Frame Analysis: An Essay on the Organization of Experience*. Cambridge, MA: Harvard University Press.

Goldstein, J. and Keohane, R. (eds.) (1993). *Ideas and Foreign Policy: Beliefs, Institutions and Political Change*. Ithaca, NY: Cornell University Press.

Goodman, N. (1978). *Ways of Worldmaking*. Indianapolis: Hackett.

Gottlieb, B. and Farquharson, A. (1985). 'Blueprint for a Curriculum on Social Support'. *Social Policy*, Winter: 31–4.

Gottweis, H. (1995). 'Genetic Engineering, Democracy, and the Politics of Identity'. *Social Text*, 42: 127–52.

——(1998). *Governing Molecules: The Discursive Politics of Genetic Engineering in Europe and the United States*. Cambridge, MA: MIT Press.

——(2000). 'Theoretical Strategies of Post-Structural Policy Analysis: Towards an Analytics of Government'. Paper presented at the Conference on Theory, Policy and Society, University of Leiden, 22 June.

Gramsci, A. (1971). *Selections from the Prison Notebooks*. New York: International Publishers.

Guba, E. G. (1990). *The Paradigm Dialog*. Newbury Park, CA: Sage.

——and Lincoln, Y. (1989). *Fourth Generation Evaluation*. Newbury Park, CA: Sage.

Gudmundsdottir, S. (1998). 'How to Turn Interpretive Research into a Narrative?' Lecture at Oulu University, Finland, February. www.sv.ntnu..no/ped/sigrun/publikasjoner/narroulu.ht

Gulbenkian Commission (1996). *Open the Social Sciences: Report of the Gulbenkian Commission on the Restructuring of the Social Sciences*. Stanford, CA: Stanford University Press.

Gusfield, J. (1981). *The Culture of Public Problems*. Chicago: University of Chicago Press.

Haas, P. (1989). 'Do Regimes Matter/Epistemic Communities and Mediterranean Pollution Control'. *International Organization*, 43: 377–404.

——(1992). 'Epistemic Communities and International Policy Coordination'. *International Organization*, 46/1: 1–35.

Habermas, J. (1970*a*). *Toward a Rational Society*. Boston: Beacon Press.

——(1970*b*).'On Systematically Distorted Communication'. *Inquiry*, 13: 205–18.

——(1971). *Knowledge and Human Interests*. Boston: Beacon Press.

——(1973). *Legitimation Crisis*. Boston: Beacon Press.

——(1987). *The Theory of Communicative Action*, 2 Cambridge, Mass: Polity.

Hajer, M. (1993). 'Discourse Coalitions and the Institutionalization of Practice: The Case of Acid Rain in Great Britain', in F. Fischer and J. Forester (eds.), *The Argumentative Turn in Policy Analysis and Planning*. Durham, NC: Duke University Press.

——(1995*a*). *The Politics of Environmental Discourse*. Oxford: Oxford University Press.

——(1995*b*). 'Interpreting Policy Change: Discourse Coalitions versus Advocacy Coalitions'. Paper presented at Annual Meeting of the American Political Science Association, Chicago, 31 August.

——(2003). 'A Frame in the Fields: Policy Making and the Reinvention of Politics', in M. Hajer and H. Wagenaar (eds.), *Deliberative Policy Analysis: Understanding Governance in the Network Society*. Cambridge: Cambridge University Press.

——and Wagenaar, H. (eds.) (2003). *Deliberative Policy Analysis: Understanding Governance in the Network Society*. Cambridge: Cambridge University Press.

Hall, P. (1986). *Governing the Economy: The Politics of State Intervention in Britain and France*. New York: Oxford University Press.

—— (1992). 'The Movement from Keynesianism to Monetarism: Institutional Analysis and British Economic Policy in the 1970s', in S. Stemino, K. Thelen, and F. Longstreth (eds.), *Structuring Politics: Historical Institutionalism in Comparative Analysis*. New York: Cambridge University Press.

—— (1993). 'Policy Paradigms, Social Learning and the State'. *Comparative Politics*, 25: 275–96.

—— and Taylor, R. C. A. (1996). 'Political Science and the Three Institutionalisms'. *Political Studies*, 44: 936–57.

Hambrick, R. (1974). 'A Guide for the Analysis of Policy Argument'. *Policy Sciences*, 5: 469–78.

Hannigan, J. A. (1995). *Environmental* Sociology: *A Social Constructivist Perspective*. London: Routledge.

Hanninen, S. and Palonen, K. (eds.) (1990). *Texts, Contexts, and Concepts: Studies on Politics and Power in Language*. Helsinki: Finnish Political Science Association.

Haraway, D. (1991). *Simians, Cyborgs, and Women*. London: Free Press.

Hawkesworth, M. E. (1988). *Theoretical Issues in Policy Analysis*. Albany, NY: SUNY Press.

Healey, P. (1997). *Collaborative Planning*. London: Macmillan.

Heclo, H. (1972). 'Review Article: Policy Analysis'. *British Journal of Political Science*, 2: 83–108.

—— (1974). *Modern Social Politics in Britain and Sweden*. New Haven, CT: Yale University Press.

—— (1978). 'Issue Networks and the Executive Establishment', in A. King (ed.), *American Political System*. Washington, DC: American Enterprise Institute for Public Policy Research.

Heineman, R., Bluhm, W., Peterson, S. A., and Kearney, E. N. (1990). *The World of Policy Analysis: Rationality, Values, and Politics*. Chatham, NJ: Chatham House.

Heron, J. (1981). 'Philosophical Basic for a New Paradigm', in P. Reason and J. Rowan (eds.), *Human Inquiry: A Sourcebook of New Paradigm Research*. Chichester, UK: John Wiley.

—— (1989). *The Facilitator's Handbook*. London: Kogan Page.

Hilgartner, S. and Bosk, C. L. (1981). 'The Rise and Fall of Social Problems: A Public Arenas Model'. *American Journal of Sociology*, 94: 53–78.

Hill, S. (1992). *Democratic Values and Technological Choices*. Stanford, CA: Stanford University Press.

Hirschhorn, L. (1979). 'Alternative Service and the Crisis of the Professions', in J. Case and R. C. Taylor (eds.), *Co-ops, Communes and Collectives: Experiments in Social Change in the 1960s and 1970s*. New York: Pantheon.

Hiskes, A. L. and Hiskes, R. P. (1986). *Science, Technology, and Policy Decisions*. Boulder, CO: Westview Press.

Hiskes, R. P. (1998). *Democracy, Risk and Community: Technological Hazards and the Evolution of Liberalism*. New York: Oxford.

Hoch, C. (1994). *What Planners Do*. Chicago: APA Planners Press.

Hofferbert, R. I. (1990). *The Reach and Grasp of Policy Analysis*. Tuscaloosa: University of Alabama Press.

Hofmann, J. (1995). 'Implicit Theories in Policy Discourse: Interpretations of Reality in German Technology Policy'. *Policy Sciences*, 18: 127–48.

Holland, J. (ed.) with Blackburn, J. (1998). *Whose Voice? Participatory Research and Policy Change*. London: Intermediate Technology Publications.

Hoppe, R. (1993). 'Political Judgment and the Policy Cycle: The Case of Ethnicity Policy Arguments in the Netherlands', in F. Fischer and J. Forester (eds.), *The Argumentative Turn in Policy Analysis and Planning*. Durham, NC: Duke University Press.

—— and Grin, J. (2002). 'Traffic Problems Go Through the Technology Assessment Machine: A Culturalist Comparison', in N. Vig and H. Paschen (eds.), *Parliaments and Technology: The Development of Technology Assessment in Europe*. Albany, NY: SUNY Press.

—— and Peterse, A. (1993). *Handling Frozen Fire: Political Culture and Risk Management*. Boulder, CO: Westview Press.

——, Pranger, R., and Besseling, E. (1990). 'Policy Belief Systems and Risky Technologies: The Dutch Debate on Regulating LPG-Related Activities'. *Industrial Crisis Quarterly*, 4: 121–40.

Houck, D. W. (2001). *Rhetoric as Currency: Hoover, Roosevelt, and the Great Depression*. College Station: Texas A & M.

Howarth, D. (2000). *Discourse*. Buckingham: Open University Press.

Howlett, M. and Ramesh, R. (1995). *Studying Public Policy: Policy Cycles and Policy Subsystems*. Oxford: Oxford University Press.

Immerwahr, J. and Johnson, J. (1994). *Second Opinions: Americans' Changing Views on Healthcare Reform*. New York: Public Agenda Foundation.

Ingram, H. M. and Smith, S. R. (eds.) (1993). *Public Policy for Democracy*. Washington, DC: Brookings Institution.

Innes, J. J. (1990). *Knowledge and Public Policy* (2nd edn). New Brunswick, NJ: Transaction Books.

—— (1998). 'Information in Communicative Planning'. *Journal of the American Planning Association*, 64/1: 52–63.

—— (2003). 'Collaborative Policy Making: Governance Through Dialogue', in M. Hajer and H. Wagenaar (eds.), *Deliberative Policy Analysis: Understanding Governance in the Network Society*. Cambridge: Cambridge University Press.

Irwin, A. (1995). *Citizen Science: A Study of People, Expertise, and Sustainable Development*. London: Routledge.

Jameson, F. (1992). *Postmodernism, Or the Cultural Logic of Late Capitalism*. Durham, NC: Duke University Press.

Jasanoff, S. (1990). *The Fifth Branch: Science Advisors as Policymakers*. Cambridge, MA: Harvard University Press.

—— (1995). *Science at the Bar: Law, Science, and Technology in America*. Cambridge, MA: Harvard University Press.

——, Markle, G., Pinch, T., and Petersen, J. (eds.) (1995). *Handbook of Science and Technology*. Newbury Park, CA: Sage.

Jennings, B. (1987). 'Policy Analysis: Science, Advocacy, or Counsel?', in S. Nagel (ed.), *Research in Public Policy Analysis and Management*. Greenwich, CT: JAI Press.

Jenson, J. (1991). 'All the World's a Stage: Ideas About Political Space and Time'. *Studies in Political Economy*, 36: 43–72.

John, P. (1998). *Analyzing Public Policy*. London: Pinter.

Johnstone, B. (2001). *Discourse Analysis*. Oxford: Blackwell.

Joss, S. (1995). 'Evaluating Consensus Conferences: Necessity or Luxury?', in S. Joss and J. Durant (eds.), *Public Participation in Science: The Role of Consensus Conferences in Europe*. London: Science Museum.

—— (2000). 'Participation in Parliamentary Technology Assessment', in N. J. Vig and H. Paschen (eds.), *Parliaments in and Technology: The Development of Technology Assessment in Europe*. Albany, NY: SUNY Press.

——and Durant, J. (eds.) (1995). *Public Participation in Science: The Role of Consensus Conferences in Europe*. London: Science Museum.

Kaplan, T. J. (1986). 'The Narrative Structure of Policy Analysis'. *Journal of Policy Analysis and Management*, 5: 761–78.

——(1993). 'Reading Policy Narratives: Beginnings, Middles, and Ends', in F. Fischer and J. Forester (eds.), *The Argumentative Turn in Policy Analysis and Planning*. Durham, NC: Duke University Press.

Kathlene, L. and Martin, J. (1991). 'Enhancing Citizen Participation: Panel Designs, Perspectives, and Policy Formation'. *Journal of Policy Analysis and Management*, 10: 46–63.

Kellert, S. H. (1993). *In the Wake of Chaos: Unpredictable Order in Dynamic Systems*. Chicago: University of Chicago Press.

Kelly, R. M. (1987). 'The Politics of Meaning and Policy Inquiry', in D. J. Palumbo (ed.), *The Politics of Evaluation*. Newbury Park, CA: Sage.

Kennedy, J. F. (1962). 'Commencement Address at Yale University', in *Public Papers of the President of the United States: John F. Kennedy*. Washington, DC: Government Printing Office.

Kinder, D. R. (1998). 'Opinion and Action in the Realm of Politics', in D. T. Gilbert, S. T. Fiske, and G. Lindzey (eds.), *The Handbook of Social Psychology*, Vol. 2 (4th edn). New York: McGraw-Hill.

——and Sears, D. (1985). 'Public Opinion and Political Action', in G. Lindzey and E. Aronson (eds.), *The Handbook of Social Psychology* (3rd edn). New York: Harper and Row.

King, A. (1973; 1974). 'Ideas, Institutions and the Politics of Governments: A Comparative Analysis, I and II'. *British Journal of Political Science*, 3: 291–313; 409–23.

King, C. S., Feltey, K. M., and Susel, B. O. (1998). 'The Question of Participation: Toward Authentic Public Participation in Public Administration'. *Public Administration Review*, 58: 317–26.

King, G., Koehane, R. O., and Verba, S. (1994). *Designing Social Inquiry: Scientific Inference in Qualitative Research*. Princeton: Princeton University Press.

Kinneavy, J. (1971). *A Theory of Discourse*. New York: W. W. Norton.

Kiser, L. L. and Ostrom, E. (1982). 'The Three Worlds of Action: A Metatheoretical Synthesis of Institutional Approaches', in E. Ostrom (ed.), *Strategies of Political Inquiry*. Beverly Hills: Sage.

Klamer, A. (1983). *Conversations with Economists*. Totowa, NJ: Rowman and Allenheld.

Kluver, L. (1995). 'Consensus Conferences at the Danish Board of Technology', in S. Joss and J. Durant (eds.), *Public Participation in Science*. London: Science Museum.

Knorr-Cetina, K. and Mulkay, M. (eds.) (1983). *Science Observed: Perspectives on the Social Study of Science*. London: Sage.

Kolakowski, L. (1968). *The Alienation of Reason: A History of Positivist Thought*. Garden City, NY: Doubleday.

Kramer, R. (1969). *Participation of the Poor*. Englewood Cliffs, NJ: Prentice-Hall.

Krieger, M. (1981). *Advice and Planning*. Philadelphia: Temple University Press.

Kristof, N. D. (1986). 'Professor Takes a New Course, Again'. *New York Times*, 2 February: 7.

Kritzer, H. M. (1996). 'The Data Puzzle: The Nature of Interpretation in Qualitative Research'. *American Journal of Political Science*, 40: 1–32.

Kuhn, T. (1962). *The Structure of Scientific Revolutions*. Chicago: University of Chicago Press.

Labov, W. (1972). 'The Transformation of Experience in Narrative Syntax', in W. Labov (ed.), *Language in the Inner City*. Philadelphia: University of Pennsylvania Press.

Labov, W. (1982). 'Speech Actions and Reactions in Personal Narrative', in D. Tannen (ed.), *Analyzing Discourse: Text and Talk*. Washington, DC: Georgetown University Press.

Laclau, E. and Mouffe, C. (1985). *Hegemony and Socialist Strategy: Towards a Radical Democratic Politics*. London: Verso.

Laird, F. (1993). 'Participatory Policy Analysis, Democracy, and Technological Decision Making'. *Science, Technology, and Human Values*, 18: 341–61.

Lakatos, I. (1971). 'History of Science and its Rational Reconstruction'. *Boston Studies in the Philosophy of Science*, 8: 42–134.

Lasswell, H. D. (1941). *Democracy through Public Opinion*. Menasha, WI: George Banta Publishing Company.

——(1951). 'The Policy Orientation', in H. Lasswell and D. Lerner (eds.), *The Policy Sciences*. Stanford: CA: Stanford University Press.

Latour, B. (1987). *Science in Action*. Cambridge, MA: Harvard University Press.

——and Woolgar, S. (1979). *Laboratory Life*. Newbury Park, CA: Sage.

Lau, R. R., Brown, T. A., and Sears, D. O. (1978). 'Self-Interest and Civilians' Attitudes Toward the Vietnam War'. *Public Opinion Quarterly*, 42: 464–83.

Laudan, L. (1977). *Progress and its Problems*. Berkeley: University of California Press.

Lawlor, E. F. (1996). Book review in *Journal of Policy Analysis and Management*, 15/1: 110–21.

Lemert, C. (1995). *Sociology after the Crisis*. Boulder, CO: Westview Press.

Levine, A. (1982). *Love Canal: Science, Politics, and People*. Boston: Lexington.

Liebenburg, L. (1993). 'Give Trackers Jobs: Conservation Can Ensure the Survival of Traditional Skills'. *New Ground*, Spring: 24–6.

Liefferin, D. and Andersen, M. S. (eds.) (1997). *The Innovation of EU Environmental Policy*. Copenhagen: Scandinavian University Press.

Lin, A. C. (1998). 'Bridging Positivist and Interpretive Approaches to Qualitative Methods'. *Policy Studies Journal*, 26/1: 162–84.

Lincoln, Y. S. and Guba, E. G. (1985). *Naturalistic Inquiry*. Newbury Park: CA: Sage.

Lindblom, C. E. (1990). *Inquiry and Change: The Troubled Attempt to Understand and Shape Society*. New Haven, CT: Yale University Press.

——and Cohen, D. (1979). *Usable Knowledge: Social Science and Social Problem Solving*. New Haven, CT: Yale University Press.

Lindeman, M. (1997). 'Building Diversified Deliberative Institutions: Lessons from Recent Research'. Paper prepared for presentation at the Annual Meeting of the American Political Science Association, Washington, DC, 28 August.

Linder, S. (1995). 'Contending Discourses in the Electric and Magnetic Fields Controversy: The Social Construction of EMF Risk as a Public Problem'. *Policy Sciences*, 28: 209–30.

Lindquist, P. (1997). 'The Cleavable Matter: Discursive Orders in Swedish Nuclear Power Policy 1972–1980'. Ph.D. thesis, Lund University, Department of Sociology, Sweden.

Litfin, K. (1994). *Ozone Discourses*. New York: Columbia University Press.

Lovins, A. (1977). *Soft Energy Paths*. Cambridge, MA: Ballinger.

Lowi, T. (1972). 'Four Systems of Policy, Politics and Choice'. *Public Administration Review*, 32: 298–310.

——and Ginsburg. B. (1996). *American Government*. New York: W.W. Norton.

Luke, T. (1987). 'Policy Science and Rational Choice Theory: A Methodological Critique', in F. Fischer and J. Forester (eds.), *Confronting Values in Policy Analysis*. Newbury Park, CA: Sage.

Lynn, L. E. Jr. (1987). *Managing Public Policy*. Boston: Little, Brown.

——(1999). 'A Place at the Table: Policy Analysis, its Postpositive Critics, and the Future of Practice'. *Journal of Policy Analysis and Management*, 18: 411–24.

McAdams, J. (1984). 'The Anti-Policy Analysts'. *Policy Studies Journal*, 13: 91–101.

McCarthy, T. (1978). *The Critical Theory of Juergen Habermas*. Cambridge, MA: MIT Press.

McCloskey, D. N. (1985). *The Rhetoric of Economics*. Madison: University of Wisconsin Press.

——(1990). *If You're So Smart: The Narrative of Economic Expertise*. Chicago: University of Chicago Press.

——(1994). *Knowledge and Persuasion in Economics*. Cambridge: Cambridge University Press.

MacDonell, D. (1986). *Theories of Discourse: An Introduction*. Oxford: Blackwell.

MacRae, D. Jr. (1971). 'Scientific Communication, Ethical Argument and Public Policy'. *American Political Science Review*, 65: 38–50.

——(1976). *The Social Function of Social Science*. New Haven, CT: Yale University Press.

Majone, G. (1989). *Evidence, Argument, and Persuasion in the Policy Process*. New Haven: Yale University Press.

——and Wildavsky, A. (1979). 'Implementation as Evolution', in J. Pressman and A. Wildavsky, *Implementation*. Berkeley: University of California Press.

Mandela, N. (1994). *Long Walk to Freedom*, Boston: Little, Brown.

Mannheim, K. (1936). *Ideology and Utopia*. New York: Harcourt, Brace and World.

Mansbridge, J. J. (1980). *Beyond Adversarial Democracy*. New York: Basic Books.

March, J. and Olsen, J. P. (1984). 'The New Institutionalism: Organizational Factors in Political Life', *American Political Science Review*, 78: 732–49.

Marsh, D. and Rhodes, D. (eds.) (1992). *Policy Networks in British Government*. Oxford: Clarendon.

Mason, R. O. (1969). 'A Dialectical Approach to Strategic Planning'. *Management Science*, 15/April: B403–B414.

Mathur, N. (2003). 'Urban Revitalization as Participatory Planning: A Discursive Analysis of Policy Deliberation in Newark'. Ph.D. thesis, Department of Public Administration, Rutgers University, Newark, NJ.

Maxwell, J. (1992). 'Understanding and Validity in Qualitative Research'. *Harvard Educational Review*, 62: 279–300.

Mayer, I. (1997). *Debated Technologies*. Tilburg, Netherlands: Tilburg Press.

Maynard-Moody, S. and Kelly, M. (1993). 'Stories Public Managers Tell About Elected Officials: Making Sense of the Politics-Administration Dichotomy', in B. Bozeman (ed.), *Public Management: The State of the Art*. San Francisco: Jossey-Bass.

Mayntz, R. and Scharpf, F. W. (1973). *Plannungsorganisation*. Munich: Piper.

Mazza, L. (1995). 'Technical Knowledge, Practical Reason and the Planner's Responsibility'. *Town Planning Review*, 66: 389–409.

Meadows, D. H., Meadows, D. L., Randers, J., and Behrens, W. W. (1972). *The Limits to Growth*. New York: Universe Books.

Meinhof, U. (1993). 'Discourse', in W. Outhwaite and T. Bottomore (eds.), *The Blackwell Dictionary of Twentieth Century Social Thought*. Oxford: Blackwell.

Miller, D. C. (1991). *Handbook of Research Design and Social Measurement*. Newbury Park, CA: Sage.

Miller, H. (2002). *Postmodern Public Policy*. Albany, NY: SUNY Press.

Mishler, E. G. (1990). 'Validation in Inquiry-Guided Research: The Role of Exemplars in ·Narrative Studies'. *Harvard Educational Review*, 60: 415–42.

Mitroff, I. I. (1971). 'A Communications Model of Dialectical Inquiring Systems–A Strategy for Strategic Planning'. *Management Science*, 17/June: B634–B648.

——and Pondy, L. (1974). 'On the Organization of Inquiry: A Comparison of Some Radically Different Approaches to Policy Analysis'. *Public Administration Review*, 34: 513–20.

Milward, B. H. and Wamsley, G. L. (1984). 'Policy Subsystems, Networks and the Tools of Public Management', in R. Eyestone (ed.), *Public Policy Formation*. Greenwich: JAI Press.

Moffat, M. (1989). *Coming of Age in New Jersey*. New Brunswick, NJ: Rutgers University Press.

Moore, M. (1983). 'A Conception of Public Management' (Working Paper). Cambridge, MA: Kennedy School of Government, Harvard University.

——(1995). *Creating Public Value: Strategic Management in Government*. Cambridge, MA: Harvard University Press.

Morcol, G. (2001). 'Positivist Beliefs Among Policy Professionals: An Empirical Investigation'. *Policy Sciences*, 34: 381–401.

——(2002). *A New Mind for Policy Analysis: Toward a Post-Newtonian and Postpositivist Epistemology and Methodology*. Westport, CT: Praeger.

——and Dennard, L. F. (eds.) (2002). *New Sciences for Public Administration and Policy*. Burke, VA: Chatelaine Press.

Morehouse, T. A. (1972). 'Program Evaluation: Social Research Versus Public Policy'. *Public Administration Review*, 32: 873–85.

Morrow, R. A. and Brown, D. (1994). *Critical Theory and Methodology*. Thousand Oaks, CA: Sage.

Mottier, V. (1999). 'Narratives of National Identity: Sexuality, Race and the Swiss "Dream of Order" '. Paper presented at the European Consortium for Political Research Workshop on 'The Political Uses of Narrative', Mannheim, 26–31 March.

Moynihan, D. P. (1965). 'The Professionalization of Reform'. *The Public Interest*, Fall: 6–16.

Mueller, J. E. (1973). *War, Presidents, and Public Opinion*. New York: John Wiley.

National Research Council. (1996). *Understanding Risk: Informing Decisions in a Democratic Society*. Washington, DC: National Academy Press.

Natter, W., Schatzku, T., and Jones, J. P. III (eds.) (1995). *Objectivity and its Other*. New York: Guilford.

Needleman, C. and Needleman, M. (1974). *Guerrillas in the Bureaucracy*. New York: Wiley.

Nelson, J. S., Megill, A., and McCloskey, D. N. (1987). *Rhetoric of the Human Sciences: Language and Argument in Scholarship and Public Affairs*. Madison: University of Wisconsin Press.

Nelson, N. and Wright, S. (1997). *Power and Participatory Development: Theory and Practice*. London: Intermediate Technology Publications.

Nelson, R. N. (1977). *The Moon and the Ghetto*. New York: Norton.

Neustadt, R. and May, E. (1986). *Thinking in Time*. New York: Free Press.

Noble, C. (1987). 'Economic Theory in Practice: White House Oversight of OSHA Standards', in F. Fischer and J. Forester (eds.), *Confronting Values in Policy Analysis*. Newbury Park, Sage.

Norton, A. and Thomas, S. (1995). *Participation in Poverty Assessment*. Environmental Department Papers Participation series, Social Policy and Resettlement Division, World Bank, Washington DC, June.

Novak, G. (1968). *Empiricism and its Evolution*. New York: Merit Publishers.

Oakeshott, M. (1959). *Rationalism in Politics and Other Essays*. Indianapolis: Library Press.

References 251

Orren, G. R. (1988). 'Beyond Self-Interest', in R. B. Reich (ed.), *The Power of Public Ideas*. Cambridge: Harvard University Press.

Paehlke, R. and Torgerson, D. (1992). 'Toxic Waste as Public Business'. *Canadian Public Administration*, 35: 339–62.

Pal, L. (1992). *Public Policy Analysis*. Toronto: Nelson Canada.

Paris, D. C. and Reynolds, J. F. (1983). *The Logic of Policy Inquiry*. New York: Longman.

Park, P., Brydon-Miller, M., Hall, B., and Jackson, T. (eds.) (1993). *Voices of Change: Participatory Research in the United States and Canada*. Toronto: OISE Press.

Parsons, W. (1995). *Public Policy; An Introduction to the Theory and Practice of Policy Analysis*. Cheltenham: Edward Elgar.

Pecheux, M. (1982). *Language, Semantics and Ideology*. London: Macmillan.

Perelman, C. (1984). 'Rhetoric and Politics'. *Philosophy and Rhetoric*, 17/3: 129–34.

Peters, G. B. (1998). *Comparative Politics: Theory and Methods*. New York: New York University Press.

Philpott, D. (1996). 'The Possibility of Ideas'. *Security Studies*, 5: 183–96.

Piven, F. F. and Cloward, R. (1971). *Regulating the Poor*. New York: Vintage.

Ploger, J. (2001). 'Public Participation and the Art of Governance'. *Environment and Planning B. Planning and Design*, 28: 219–41.

Polkinghorne, D. (1984). *The Methodology for the Human Sciences: Systems of Inquiry*. Albany, NY: SUNY Press.

——(1988). *Narrative Knowing and the Human Sciences*. Albany, NY: SUNY Press.

Polsby, N. (1984). *Political Innovation in America*. New Haven, CT: Yale University Press.

Popper, K. (1959). *The Logic of Scientific Discovery*. London: Heinemann.

Porter, R. B. (1980). *Presidential Decision Making: The Economic Policy Board*. Cambridge: Cambridge University Press.

Pressman, J. and Wildavsky, A. (1973). *Implementation*. Berkeley: University of California Press.

Proctor, R. N. (1991). *Value-Free Science? Purity or Power in Modern Knowledge*. Cambridge, MA: Harvard University Press.

Putt, A. D. and Springer, J. F. (1989). *Policy Research: Concepts, Methods, and Application*. New York: Prentice Hall.

Rabe, B. G. (1994). *Beyond Nimby: Hazardous Waste Siting in Canada and the United States*. Washington, DC: Brookings Institution.

Radin, B. A. (2000). *Beyond Machiavelli: Policy Analysis Comes of Age*. Washington, DC: Georgetown University Press.

Rahman, M. D. A. (1991). 'Glimpses of the "Other Africa"', in O. Fals-Borda (ed.), *Action and Knowledge*. New York: Apex Press.

Rampton, S. and Stauber, J. (2001). *Trust Us, We're Experts*. New York: Penguin Putnam.

Rappaport, J., Seidman, E., Toro, P. A., McFadden, L. S., Reischl, T. M., Roberts, L. J., Salem, D. A., Stein, C. H., and Zimmerman, M. A. (1985). 'Collaborative Research with a Mutual Help Organization'. *Social Policy*, 15/Winter: 12–17.

Reason, P. (1994). 'Three Approaches to Participatory Inquiry', in N. K. Denzin and Y. S. Lincoln (eds.), *Handbook of Qualitative Research*. London: Sage.

——and Rowan, J. (eds.) (1981). *Human Inquiry: A Sourcebook of New Paradigm Research*. New York: John Wiley.

Reich, R. B. (1988). *The Power of Public Ideas*. Cambridge, MA: Harvard University Press.

——(1990). *Public Management in a Democratic Society*. Engelwood Cliff, NJ: Prentice-Hall.

Rein, M. (1976). *Social Science and Public Policy*. New York: Penguin Books.

—— and Laws, D. (1999). 'Controversy, Reframing and Reflection'. Paper presented at a Conference on Theory, Policy and Society, University of Leiden, 22 June.

—— and Schoen, D. A. (1977). 'Problem Setting in Policy Research', in C. H. Weiss (ed.), *Using Social Research in Public Policy Making*. Lexington, MA: Lexington Books.

—— —— (1993). 'Reframing Policy Discourse', in F. Fischer and J. Forester (eds.), *The Argumentative Turn in Policy Analysis and Planning*. Durham, NC: Duke University Press.

Ricci, D. (1984). *The Tragedy of Political Science: Politics, Scholarship, and Democracy*. New Haven, CT: Yale University Press.

Rich, R. F. (1979). *Translating Evaluation into Policy*. Beverly Hills, CA: Sage.

Riessman, C. K. (1993). *Narrative Analysis*. Thousand Oaks, CA: Sage.

Riffaterre, M. (1990). *Fictional Truth*. Baltimore, MD: Johns Hopkins University Press.

Rivlin, A. (1973). 'Forensic Social Science: Perspectives on Inequality'. *Harvard Educational Review* (Reprint Series, No. 8). Cambridge, MA: Harvard University Press.

Roberts, A. (1995). 'Civic Discovery as a Rhetorical Strategy'. *Journal of Policy Analysis and Management*, 14: 291–307.

Rochefort, D. A. and Cobb, R. W. (1993). 'Problem Definition, Agenda Access, and Policy Change'. *Policy Studies Journal*, 21: 56–71.

Roe, E. (1994). *Narrative Policy Analysis*. Durham, NC: Duke University Press.

Rorty, R. (1979). *Philosophy and the Mirror of Nature*. Princeton, NJ: Princeton University Press.

Rose, R. (1993). *Lesson-Drawing in Public Policy: A Guide to Learning Across Time and Space*. Chatham, NJ: Chatham House.

Rosenau, P. M. (1992). *Post-Modernism and the Social Sciences: Insights, Inroads and Intrusions*. Princeton: Princeton University Press.

Rosenberg, A. (1988). *Philosophy of Social Science*. Boulder, CO: Westview Press.

Rouse, J. (1988). *Knowledge and Power: A Political Philosophy of Science*. Ithaca, NY: Cornell University Press.

Russett, B. M. and Hanson, Elizabeth C. H. (1975). *Ideology and Interest: The Foreign Policy Beliefs of American Businessmen*. San Francisco: Freedman.

Sabatier, P. A. (1987). 'Knowledge, Policy-Oriented Learning, and Policy Change'. *Knowledge: Creation, Diffusion, Utilization*, 8: 649–92.

—— (1988). 'An Advocacy Coalition Framework of Policy Change and the Role of Policy-Oriented Learning Therein'. *Policy Sciences*, 21: 129–68.

—— (1993). 'Policy Change over a Decade or More', in P. A. Sabatier and H. Jenkins-Smith (eds.), *Policy Change and Learning: An Advocacy Coalition Approach*. Boulder, CO: Westview Press.

—— (1999). 'The Need for Better Theories', in P. Sabatier (ed.), *Theories of the Policy Process*. Boulder, CO: Westview Press.

—— and Jenkins-Smith, H. (eds.) (1993). *Policy Change and Learning: An Advocacy Coalition Approach*. Boulder CO: Westview.

Sabia, D. R. Jr and Wallulis, G. (1983). 'The Idea of a Critical Social Science', in D. R. Sabia and G. Wallulis (eds.), *Changing Social Science: Critical Theory and Other Critical Perspectives*. Albany, NY: SUNY Press.

Sandercock, L. (1997). *Towards Cosmopolis: Planning for Multicultural Cities*. New York: Wiley.

Sarbin, T. R. (ed.) (1986). *Narrative Psychology: The Storied Nature of Human Conduct*. New York: Praeger.

Saretzki, T. (1998). 'Post-postivistische Policy-Analyse und Deliberative Demokratie', in M. T. Greven, H. Muenkler, and R. Schmalz-Bruns (eds.), *Buergersinn und Kritik*. Baden-Baden: Noos Verlagsgesellschaft.

——(2003). 'Aufklaerung, Beteiligung und Kritik: Die "Argumentative Wende" in der Policy-Analyze', in K. Schubert and N. C. Bandelow (eds.), *Lehrbuch der Politikfeldanalyse*. Munich: R. Oldenburg Verlag.

Schiffrin, D. (1994). *Approaches to Discourse*. Oxford: Blackwell.

——, Tannen, D., and Hamilton, H. (eds.) (2001). *The Handbook of Discourse Analysis*. Oxford: Blackwell.

Scharpf, F. W. (1973). *Plannung als politischer Prozess*. Neuwied: Luchterhand.

Schiller, H. I. and Smythe, D. W. (1992). *Mass Communications and American Empire*. Boulder, CO: Westview Press.

Schloming, G. C. (1991). *Power and Principles in International Affairs*. San Diego: Harcourt Brace.

Schmidt, V. A. (2001). 'The Impact of Europeanization on National Governance Practices, Ideas, and Discourse'. Paper presented at European Consortium for Political Research Workshop on Policy, Discourse and Institutional Reform, Grenoble, France, 6–11 April.

——(2002). *The Futures of European Capitalism*. Oxford: Oxford University Press.

Schneider, A. L. and Ingram, H. (1993*a*). 'Social Constructions of Target Populations'. *American Political Science Review*, 87: 334–7.

————(1993*b*). 'How Social Construction of Target Populations Contributes to Problem in Policy Design'. *Policy Currents*, 3/1: 1–4.

————(1997). *Policy Design for Democracy*. Lawrence: University of Kansas Press.

————(eds.) (2003). *Deserving and Entitled: Social Constructions and Public Policy*. Albany, NY: SUNY Press.

Schoen, D. (1983). *The Reflective Practitioner*. New York: Basic Books.

——and Rein, M. (1994). *Frame Reflection*. New York: Basic Books.

Schram, S. F. (1993). 'Postmodern Policy Analysis: Discourse and Identity in Welfare Policy'. *Policy Sciences*, 26: 249–70.

——and Neisser, P. T. (eds.) (1997). *Tales of State: Narrative in Contemporary U.S. Politics and Public Policy*. New York: Rowman and Littlefield.

Schuman, D. (1982). *Policy Analysis, Education, and Everyday Life*. Lexington, MA: D. C. Health.

Schutz, A. (1962). *Collected Papers*, Vol. 1. (ed. M. Natanson). The Hague: Martinus Nijhoff.

——(1967). *The Phenomenology of the Social World*. Evanston, IL: Northwestern University Press.

Scriven, M. (1987). 'Probative Logic', in F. H. van Eemeren *et al.* (eds.), *Argumentation: Across the Lines of Discipline*. Amsterdam: Foris.

Sears, D. O., Hensler, C. P., and Speer, L. K. (1979). ' "Whites" Opposition to Busing: Self-Interest of Symbolic Racism'. *American Political Science Review*, 73: 369–84.

——, Lau, R. R., Tyler, T. R., and Allen, H. M. Jr. (1980). 'Self-Interest Versus Symbolic Politics in Policy Attitudes and Presidential Voting'. *American Political Science Review*, 74: 670–84.

Sederberg, P. C. (1984). *The Politics of Meaning: Power and Explanation in the Social Construction of Reality*. Tucson, AZ: University of Arizona Press.

Shapiro, I. (2000). 'A Model That Pretends to Explain Everything'. *New York Times*, 26 February: B11.

Shapiro, M. (1981). *Language and Political Understanding: The Politics of Discursive Practice*. New Haven, CT: Yale University Press.

Sheridan, A. (1980). *Michel Foucault: The Will to Power*. London: Tavistock Publications.

Simon, H. (1957). *Models of Man*. New York: Wiley.

Sinclair, T. J. (2000). 'Reinventing Authority: Embedded Knowledge Networks and the New Global Finance'. *Environment and Planning C: Government and Policy*, 18: 487–502.

Sirianni, C. and Friedland, L. (2001). *Civic Innovation in American*. Berkeley: University of California Press.

Skocpol, T. (1985). 'Bringing the State Back In: Strategies of Analysis in Current Research', in P. Rueschemeyer and T. Skocpol (eds.), *Bringing the State Back In*. New York: Cambridge University Press.

Smith, M. (1993). *Pressure, Power and Policy*. Hemel Hempstead: Harvester Wheatsheaf.

Smith, S. (1988). 'Belief Systems and the Study of International Relations', in R. Little and S. Smith (eds.), *Belief Systems and International Relations*. Oxford: Basil Blackwell.

Stattschneider, E. E. (1960). *The Semisovereign People*. Hindsdale, IL: Dryden Press.

Steinberger, P. (1980). 'Typologies of Public Policy: Meaning Construction and their Policy Process'. *Social Science Quarterly*, 61/September: 185–97.

Steinmo, S. (1993). *Taxation and Democracy*. New Haven, CT: Yale University Press.

Steward, J. (1992). 'Corporatism, Pluralism, and Political Learning: A Systems Approach'. *Journal of Public Policy*, 2: 243–55.

Stockman, N. (1983). *Anti-Positivist Theorists of the Sciences: Critical Rationalism, and Scientific Realism*. Dordrecht: D. Reidel.

Stone, D. (1996). *Capturing the Political Imagination: Think Tanks and the Policy Process*. London: Frank Cass.

Stone, D. A. (1988). *Policy Paradox and Political Reason*. Glenview, IL: Scott, Foresman and Company.

——(1989). 'Causal Stories and the Formation of Policy Agendas'. *Political Science Quarterly*, 104: 281–300.

——(2002). *Policy Paradox: The Art of Political Decision-Making* (2nd edn). New York: W.W. Norton.

Sylvia, R. D., Sylvia, K., and Gunn, E. (1997). *Program Planning and Evaluation for the Public Manager*. Prospect Heights, IL: Waveland.

Tandon, R. (1988). 'Social Transformation and Participatory Research'. *Convergence*, 21: 5–18.

Tannen, D. (1985). *Analyzing Discourse: Text and Talk*. Washington, DC: Georgetown University Press.

——(1989). *Talking Voices: Repetition, Dialogue and Imagery in Conversational Discourse*. Cambridge: Cambridge University Press.

Thompson, M. (1984). 'Among the Energy Tribes: A Cultural Framework for the Analysis and Design of Energy Policy'. *Policy Sciences*, 17: 321–39.

Thompson, W. B. (2001). 'Policy Making Through Thick and Thin: Thick Description as a Methodology for Communication and Democracy'. *Policy Sciences*, 3: 63–77.

Throgmorton, J. A. (1991). 'The Rhetorics of Policy Analysis'. *Policy Sciences*, 24: 153–79.

Torbert, W. (1976). *Creating a Community of Inquiry: Conflict, Collaboration, Transformation*. New York: John Wiley.

——(1991). *The Power of Balance: Transforming Self, Society, and Scientific Inquiry*. Newbury Park, CA: Sage.

Torgerson, D. (1985). 'Contextual Orientation in Policy Analysis: The Contribution of Harold D. Lasswell'. *Policy Sciences*, 18: 241–61.

—— (1986). 'Between Knowledge and Politics: The Three Faces of Policy Analysis'. *Policy Sciences*, 19: 33–59.

—— (2002). 'What is Policy Discourse?'. Unpublished manuscript.

Toulmin, S. (1958). *The Uses of Argument*, Cambridge; Cambridge University Press.

—— (1983). 'The Construal of Reality: Criticism in Modern and Postmodern Science', in W. J. T. Mitchell (ed.), *The Politics of Interpretation*. Chicago: University of Chicago Press.

—— (1990). *Cosmopolis: The Hidden Agenda of Modernity*. Chicago: University of Chicago Press.

Touraine, A. (1981). *The Voice and the Eye*. Cambridge: Cambridge University Press.

Traweek, S. (1996). 'Unity, Dyads, Triads, Quads, and Complexity: Cultural Choreographies of Science'. *Social Text*, 46/47: 129–39. All rights reserved. Used by permission of Duke University Press.

Uchitelle, L. (1999). 'A Challenge to Scientific Economics'. *New York Times*, 23 January: B7.

Van de Graaf, H. and Hoppe, R. (1996). *Beleid en politiek. Een inleiding tot de beleidsweten-schap en de beleidskunde*. Bussum: Coutinho.

van der Ploeg, J. D. (1993). 'Potatoes and Knowledge', in M. Hobart (ed.), *An Anthropological Critique of Development: The Growth of Ignorance*. London: Routledge.

Van Dijk, T. (ed.) (1985). *Handbook of Discourse Analysis*, 4 vols. London: Academic Press.

Van Eeten, M. J. G. (1999). *Dialogues of the Deaf: Defining New Agendas for Environmental Deadlocks*. Delft: Eburon Publishers.

—— (2001). 'Recasting Intractable Policy Issues: The Wider Implications of the Netherlands Civil Aviation Controversy'. *Journal of Policy Analysis and Management*, 20: 391–414.

Van Gorp, B. (2001). 'The Implementation of Asylum Policy: Which Frame Dominates the Debate?'. Paper presented at the European Consortium for Political Research, 29th Joint Sessions, Grenoble, France, 6–11 April.

Verba, S. and Orren, G. (1985). *Equality in America*. Cambridge, MA: Harvard University Press.

Wagenaar, H. (1997). 'Policy as Fiction: Narrative and its Place in Policy Practice'. *Beleid and Maatschappij*, 1: 55.

—— (2001). 'Bureaucratic Order and Personal Order: Negotiating Administrative Work Through Narrative'. Paper presented at the European Consortium for Political Research, 29th Joint Sessions, Grenoble, France, 6–11 April.

Wagner, P. (1995). 'Sociology and Contingency: Historicizing Epistemology'. *Social Science Information*, 34/2: 179–204.

—— (2001). *A History and Theory of the Social Sciences*. London: Sage.

Weber, M. (1948). *The Social Psychology of the World Religions*, reprinted in H. H. Gerth and C. Wright Mills (eds.), *From Max Weber*. London: Routledge.

Weick, K. (1969). *The Social Psychology of Organizing*. Reading: Addison-Wesley.

Weiss, C. (1990). 'Policy Research: Data, Ideas or Arguments?', in P. Wagner *et al.* (eds.), *Social Sciences and Modern States*. Cambridge: Cambridge University Press.

White, H. (1981). 'The Value of Narrativity in the Representation of Reality', in W. J. T. Mitchell (ed.), *On Narrative*. Chicago: University of Chicago Press.

White, T. H. (1967). 'The Action Intellectuals'. *Life*, 9 June, 16 June, 23 June.

Whyte, W. H. (1956). *The Organization Man*. New York: Simon Schuster.

Wildavsky, A. (1997). *But is it True? A Citizen Guide to Environmental Health and Safety Issues*. Berkeley: University of California Press.

Willard, C. A. (1996). *Liberalism and the Problem of Knowledge: A New Rhetoric for Modern Democracy*. Chicago: University of Chicago Press.

Williams, B. (1985). *Ethics and the Limits of Philosophy*. Cambridge, MA: Harvard University Press.

Williams, W. (1998). *Honest Numbers and Democracy: Social Policy Analysis in the White House, Congress, and the Federal Agencies*. Washington, DC: Georgetown University Press.

Windhoff-Heritier, A. (1987). *Policy-Analyse: Eine Einfuehrung*. Frankfurt: Campus Verlag.

Wood, R. C. (1993). *Whatever Possessed the President?: Academic Experts and Presidential Policy, 1960–1988*. Amherst: University of Massachusetts Press.

Woolgar, S. (1988). *Science–The Very Idea*. London: Tavistock.

World Bank (1994). *The World Bank and Participation*. Washington, DC: Operations Policy Department, World Bank, September.

——(1995). *World Bank Participation Sourcebook*. Washington, DC: Environmental Department Papers, World Bank, June.

World Commission on Environment and Development (1987). *Our Common Future*. New York: Oxford University Press.

Wynne, B. (1982). *Rationality and Ritual: The Windscale Inquiry and Nuclear Decision in Britain*. Chalfont St Giles: The British Society for the History of Science.

Yanow, D. (1993). 'The Communication of Policy Meanings: Implementation as Interpretation and Text'. *Policy Sciences*, 26: 41–61.

——(1996). *How Does a Policy Mean? Interpreting Policy and Organizational Actions*. Washington, DC: Georgetown University Press.

——(2000). *Conducting Interpretive Policy Analysis*. Newbury Park, CA: Sage.

Yee, A. (1996). 'The Causal Effects of Ideas on Policies'. *International Organization*, 50/1: 69–108.

Yiftachel, O. (1998). 'Planning and Social Control: Exploring the Dark Side'. *Journal of Planning Literature*, 12: 395–406.

Index